ESSAYS ON SOCIOLOGY AND SOCIAL PSYCHOLOGY

INTERNATIONAL LIBRARY OF SOCIOLOGY
AND SOCIAL RECONSTRUCTION

Founded by Karl Mannheim
Editor: W. J. H. Sprott

A catalogue of the books available in the INTERNATIONAL LIBRARY OF SOCIOLOGY AND SOCIAL RECONSTRUCTION, and new books in preparation for the Library, will be found at the end of this volume

ESSAYS ON
SOCIOLOGY AND SOCIAL
PSYCHOLOGY

by

KARL MANNHEIM

EDITED BY PAUL KECSKEMETI

ROUTLEDGE & KEGAN PAUL LTD
Broadway House, 68–74 Carter Lane
London

First published in 1953
by Routledge & Kegan Paul Ltd
Broadway House, 68–74 Carter Lane
London, E.C.4
Second impression 1959
Third impression 1966
Fourth impression 1969
Printed in Great Britain by
Lowe & Brydone (Printers) Ltd., London, N.W.10

SBN 7100 3318 4

Editorial Note

THE present second volume of 'Essays' completes the edition or re-edition of the shorter scientific papers, which Karl Mannheim wrote during the last twenty-five years of his life. Publication of the 'Essays' has been preceded by the treatise on *Freedom Power and Democratic Planning*, issued in 1950. They are to be followed by a final volume, the posthumous publication of another systematic work drafted by the author during the early thirties.

Whereas the first volume of the 'Essays' was composed exclusively of material previously published in German scientific magazines, most of the contributions to the present volume were originally written in English. This is not true of the first two essays, one being a revised version of Mannheim's doctoral dissertation, the other his famous empirical test of the sociology of knowledge on the data of German Conservatism. These papers supplement and round off the material presented in the first volume.

Of the English writings only the studies printed in Sections 2 and 3 have been published before. The essays on 'The History of the Concept of the State as an Organism' and the four lectures on 'Planned Society and the Problem of Human Personality' appear here for the first time.

The editorial work has again been in the experienced hands of Dr. Paul Kecskemeti, Research Associate of the Rand Corporation, Santa Monica, California. He made the final selection of the papers to be included in this volume, taking into account the wide range of Mannheim's scientific interests and the lasting significance of the contributions chosen. He reproduced the hitherto unpublished essays from the manuscripts left by the author with a minimum of editorial changes.

The first draft of the English translation of 'Structural Analysis of Epistemology' was prepared by Edith Schwarzschild, London, England; the English version of 'Conservative Thought' was drafted by the author himself. Dr. Kecskemeti, who checked and partly revised both translations, takes the responsibility for the text as it now stands. He has again contributed an introduction, which should greatly aid the reader in comprehending the context, personal and general, in which these writings were conceived by the author.

The Rockefeller Foundation awarded a grant to the Institute of World Affairs of the New School for Social Research towards the cost of preparing this manuscript for publication.

ADOLPH LOWE

Institute of World Affairs
New School for Social Research
New York, N.Y.

July 1952

Contents

PART ONE
STRUCTURAL ANALYSIS IN SOCIOLOGY

PART TWO
GERMAN AND WESTERN SOCIOLOGY

PART THREE
SOCIOLOGICAL PSYCHOLOGY

CONTENTS

PART FOUR

PLANNED SOCIETY AND THE PROBLEM OF HUMAN PERSONALITY: A SOCIOLOGICAL ANALYSIS

Introduction

DURING his German academic career, which was cut short by Nazism, Mannheim's approach to sociology—and to social and historical reality—was dominated by the idea of 'structure'. It was the 'structure' of social reality, and the position of individuals and groups within this 'structure', which determined thinking and action and guided it into intelligible channels.

Structure, as conceived by Mannheim, exhibited the following characteristics:

1. It was the most *comprehensive* feature of reality. No component part of society as such could be said to have structure. On the contrary, the structural idea meant that one could comprehend the patterning of any *partial* phenomenon only in terms of the comprehensive structure of the *whole*.

2. It was a *dynamic* entity. The 'structure' of social reality did not consist of static relationships that persisted as such, and to which any social conflict was, so to speak, extraneous. Antagonism and conflict was of the very essence of structure; the structure of social reality *was* the configuration of antagonistic forces which contended for supremacy and mutually shaped and influenced one another while locked in combat. 'Structure' always implied 'polarity'.

3. It was an *intelligible* principle. The clash of forces exhibited not a blind dynamism but goal-directedness. Structure had a discoverable meaning; and although this meaning was fully visible and interpretable only for the past, the greatest challenge for the present consisted precisely in *divining* it for our own period. The highest goal and greatest happiness of the individual consisted in being in tune with the creative process which was going on in the depths of the structure.

Underlying this concept of structure was, then, a metaphysical, quasi-religious belief in the creative function of history. Not that man was to be looked upon merely as a passive participant in the process, as a tool or product; man's activity, his striving, was precisely the stuff of which the structural process was made. But still, that active striving had to be based upon a faith, and the core of this faith was the idea of history as a positive, creative, and in a sense all-powerful ultimate force.

It is easily seen that such an attitude toward history could be maintained intact only as long as the history of our days was something one could say 'yes' to. Mannheim never could say 'no' to history, not even at the darkest moments—that would have meant to say 'no' to life, to man, to God. But his exuberant and hopeful 'yes' had to be qualified as the historical horizon darkened over Germany. It had to become, not 'no', to be sure, but 'yes, all the same', or 'still yes, if at all possible'. Not all historic reality was acceptable. Nazism, Fascism, and totalitarian Communism certainly were not; but then, nothing could be won by just rejecting them. This would have meant for Mannheim a sterile withdrawal from reality by which no problem could be solved. The task was rather to comprehend these frightening phenomena, to see how the 'structure of reality' could account for them, and to overcome them in this fashion.

In his earlier writings, Mannheim had already reached the position that the 'structural meaning' of historical reality was never exhausted by one dominant current. One class, and the style of thinking congenial to it, may have been triumphant at a certain time; but still, counter-currents harking back to the past or invoking a visionary, 'utopian' future co-existed with it. Once this was realized, an all-embracing, tolerant position towards *all* currents and tendencies represented in the 'structure' became possible. But such a serene 'synthetic' point of view could not be adopted towards the totalitarian trend embodied by Nazism and Stalinism. For it had been implied in the earlier 'synthetic' viewpoint that the antagonistic forces making up the 'structure' were tending towards adjustment and harmony; and this was obviously not true of the new totalitarian forces. These were not simply counter-currents asserting themselves against a dominant trend and introducing an element of strife and variety into a picture which otherwise would have been too monotonous and one-sided. The totalitarian currents themselves denied synthesis and harmony; the earlier theory, based upon the idea of gradual adjustment and an emergent synthesis, could not cope with them.

Hence, the problem of interpreting historic reality and adopting the historically 'right' position assumed a new form for Mannheim when totalitarianism emerged as a dominant trend. The first thing was still to understand for what 'structural' reasons totalitarianism could gain the upper hand in Germany, Italy and Russia. But the answer to this question could no longer be given in terms of the old structural theory. For that theory presupposed a 'wholeness' of social reality in which no part could be missed, and none was illegitimate. The social process was 'intelligible' because its 'dynamism' could be analysed and explained with reference to a 'comprehensive' totality. With the emergence of totalitarianism, however, the spell of history was broken; one had to recognize that the historically dominant trend was a destructive aberration rather than a legitimate component of an intelligible, dynamic, comprehensive process. This trend had to be counteracted and overcome in order to restore the wholeness and meaningfulness of human reality.

For this, it was no longer sufficient to seek inspiration and guidance *within* the historic process as such. One needed extra-historical principles to resist and correct the aberrant forces which history brought to the fore. It became particularly important to explore the conditions on which freedom of individual action and choice depended. Not that the individual could *disregard* the 'comprehensive' nature of the historic-social process; but reference to the comprehensive whole was no longer *sufficient* for orientation toward the self and society. This was the position toward which Mannheim was moving when, driven from his chair in Frankfurt by the Nazis in 1933, he settled in London.

II

The Nazi experience, I think, was the most important factor in the change Mannheim's thinking underwent at that time. But the new environment also contributed to this change. Academic life was far less Olympian and less inbred in England than in Germany. And within academic life, sociology also was far less self-contained and self-assured. To Mannheim, transplantation into such a more fluid, more humane and less status-bound world was by no means a loss; he was, even in Germany, and in spite of the rather formidable and rarefied abstractness of his early writings, the antithesis of the Olympian 'Geheimrat' type. It was the 'human dialogue' that he sought in his teaching as well as in his theorizing: he was not content until he broke through to the inmost layer in man which hid the naked impulse. It is surprising that he succeeded in this to a remarkable degree among the proverbially reserved English—far more than among the supposedly spiritually and subjectively oriented Germans. The English responded to him in spite of the language barrier which he overcame only with difficulty. But he in turn was also profoundly influenced by the Anglo-Saxon mind. The historically oriented, structural analysis of the whole of social reality could no longer occupy a central place in his thinking, not only because faith in history called for reservations, but also because he saw the merits of a more concrete, more peripheral, less systematic and more pragmatic approach. Since history could no longer be relied on to reveal all ultimate meaning in answer to searching faith, the important thing became to make a good choice among the alternatives it still left open. Faith had to be tempered by prudence, and the empirical and pragmatic English method answered this need.

Not that Mannheim ceased to think structurally. For him, no other way of thinking was possible. But he gradually incorporated new elements in his basic idea of 'structure'. One of these was the *psychological* aspect of the social process. Mannheim turned to Freudian psychoanalysis in order to clarify some of the decisive factors responsible for social change, and for the *pathological* phenomena associated with that change in particular. It is significant that in his contribution to a symposium about 'Peaceful Change' in 1937 Mannheim elected to deal with the 'Psychological Aspect'.[1] The main problem which he discusses in this paper is that of the drive constellation underlying war : a 'pathological' phenomenon. How does it happen that basic human drives, as shaped by a social and cultural *milieu*, sometimes seek outlet in organized violence? It was clear to Mannheim that this question could not be answered merely in terms of individual conflicts and frustrations endured in early childhood within the family—the primary focus of psychoanalytical research. In order to understand a large-scale, social phenomenon, one had to consider cultural and institutional factors. The psychoanalytic approach could be applied successfully to the problem of war only if we did not stress exclusively 'the fixation which occurs in early childhood', but devoted 'at least as much attention to the capacity of institutions for influencing the psychic life of adults' (p. 103). The main problem emerging here is 'collective insecurity'—a situation which arises when institutions established to allay deep-seated anxieties are no longer able to exercise this function under changed conditions. When available outlets for individual aspirations and strivings are suddenly blocked, man must look for substitute satisfactions and may find these in pathological, mechanized and aggressive groupings manipulated by irrational megalomaniacs. The problem of totalitarianism thus becomes one of psychopathology: an approach which has played a considerable role in American social psychology since Harold D. Lasswell's *Psychopathology and Politics* (1930).

Mannheim expressly acknowledged the stimulus he received from Lasswell's book; eventually, in developing this psychological

[1] C. A. W. Manning (ed.) *Peaceful Change*, London, 1937, pp. 101–32.

approach, he reached conclusions substantially parallel to those which have emerged in more recent American research. Status insecurity, substitute satisfactions and 'rigid', 'mechanized' personality structures, for instance, have been isolated as some of the key factors underlying totalitarian personality formation (cf. *The Authoritarian Personality*, New York, 1950, by T. W. Adorno, E. Frenkel-Brunswik, D. J. Levinson and R. N. Sanford). In this and related research work, the fusion of psychological and sociological categories, postulated by Mannheim in the thirties, was one of the guiding principles of methodology.

Sociology, then, had to emerge from isolation and achieve integration with other social sciences (cf. the paper 'The Place of Sociology', pp. 195–208 in this volume). In particular, 'sociological psychology' had to be developed. This 'sociological psychology', Mannheim held, had to utilize the results, insights and methods of various psychological schools, not only psychoanalysis. Above all, it had to maintain a *social perspective*; it had to differentiate itself from *all* individual psychology as such. 'We cannot jump straight from the general observation of individuals and their psychic mechanisms to the analysis of society. The psychology of society is not a million times that of an individual. . . . What for our purpose is needed is an historically-differentiated psychology by which the change in attitudes, motivations and symbol-transformations in different periods among different classes and under different social situations will be made plain' (p. 129).

The problem of a 'sociological psychology' is taken up again in another discussion paper (1940) 'On War-Conditioned Changes in Our Psychic Economy' (in this volume, pp. 243–51). Here Mannheim takes issue with the idea (advanced by the psychoanalyst Glover) that in order to understand the psychological impact of the war, one should subject concrete groups to psychoanalytic observation and study. This, Mannheim says, would still give us only individual rather than properly 'sociological' psychology. 'When, as in our case, the task consists in collecting observations relevant to a psychological and social history of the war, what one has to observe is not the rigid and limited group units as such, nor the life of individuals in its relation to these groups, but rather the changing behaviour of individuals in correlation with the comprehensive mechanisms operating in the society' (p. 246).

The question then is this: How does the overall situation in society and the institutional environment influence and shape individual behaviour? This is not merely a theoretical problem; it has practical and pragmatic implications. The reason why we seek a psychological understanding of institutionally shaped behaviour is that this behaviour may become utterly irrational and destructive under certain conditions. Far from serving a purely theoretical interest, our study must deal with the eminently practical question of how one can inhibit the destructive, aberrant behavioural effects inherent in a given social constellation, and promote the rational and beneficial ones.

In other words: we must adopt a value-position, as it were, outside the stream of history, in order to direct that stream into safe channels. In doing this, we cannot and must not abandon the 'structural' perspective, for we can influence history only if we find out all we can about its inherent law of 'structural' process. But communion with history will no longer be sufficient to make us discover what should be done. For this purpose, we must apply standards such as 'health' v. 'pathology', 'reason' v. 'unreason', 'peacefulness' v. 'aggressiveness', which to a large extent remain constant throughout the flux of history. Mannheim's new position, a position beyond historicism, was based upon an increasing application of these standards.

III

This programme found its most pregnant expression in the motto of 'planning' which came to dominate Mannheim's thinking increasingly until his untimely death in February 1947.

It is easy to misunderstand Mannheim's preoccupation with planning. 'Planned society' is, of course, a collectivist slogan, and planning is generally understood to be the crowning triumph of the collectivist trend in history, to be hailed or deplored, depending on whether one is for or against collectivism. The curious thing in Mannheim's case was, however, that adoption of the principle of social planning coincided with loss of faith in the 'comprehensive' structural forces of history and with increased interest in the role and the problems of the individual. The original idea of 'structure' *excludes* conscious planning: it is History and Life itself which 'plan' mankind's course. In order to act rationally and to realize his potentialities to the full extent, the individual then must above all be sensitive to the promptings of history and of the vital forces of which the fabric of social reality is woven. Conscious planning emerges as something both possible and necessary only when this original idea of 'structure' is qualified in the sense that the 'vital forces' are capable of producing pathological aberrations against which the individual and society must be protected.

In the four Oxford lectures on 'Planned Society and the Problem of Human Personality' which Mannheim delivered in 1940 (published here for the first time, pp. 255–310), the central problem is the freedom, spontaneity and self-realization of the individual. The argument he presents may be summarized under three points:

1. It is a mistake to believe with the extreme liberals that human freedom consists in the individual's being independent of and unaffected by environmental and collective factors. 'Freedom' in this sense is an illusion. The individual is always moulded to some extent by his social environment, even when he thinks he is only following his own bent.

2. The social environment may be left to itself, so that tensions arising within it are resolved by spontaneous mutual adaptation of groups and individuals; or a central agency of 'planners' acting on behalf of society may devise certain patterns of adjustment and impose it by using its controlling power. When spontaneous adjustment does not 'work', i.e. when social forces left to themselves can produce only extremely undesirable or even intolerable results, 'planning' becomes inevitable.

3. This planning may be of the totalitarian type, i.e. the planners may resort predominantly to command and coercion to make individuals adjust to and co-operate with one another and promote social goals. The self-realization and freedom of the individual is then necessarily stunted, since he can never decide for himself and adjust in an intelligent manner. But planning may also be of a different kind: the planners may rearrange and manipulate the social environment without resorting to much outright dictation and coercion, and relying rather on their knowledge of human motivations and strivings which enables them to predict what arrangement of the environment will call forth the most desirable, co-operative and productive responses. Under such a system, the individual's position need not be radically different from his uncoerced, 'free' and responsible status under liberalism. As under liberalism, the individual will respond as a free and intelligent agent; the main difference is that he will not be frustrated by the destructive conflicts and the paralysis of productive co-operation which are unavoidable under present-day conditions in the absence of 'planning'.

As we see, Mannheim argues here on two fronts—both against liberalism and against totalitarianism. As against liberalism, he stresses, on the one hand, the erroneousness of the extravagant liberal conception of freedom understood as the individual's absolute independence of the social environment; on the other hand, he points to the necessarily disastrous *factual* consequences of *laissez-faire*. But when all this is said, he still sees a valid core in liberalism as a value position—this is the freedom and self-realization of the individual understood not in an extravagant but in a legitimate sense. Planning can be a socially beneficial and constructive principle only if it preserves this freedom and indeed if fostering freedom of the individual is the planner's central objective. Planning indifferent or hostile to individual freedom may avoid the unfavourable *factual* results of *laissez-faire*, but it will lead to other results equally or even more undesirable. Western society, Mannheim pleads, must adopt planning of the 'free' type in order not to be caught in a crisis which will leave the door open only to planning of the 'totalitarian' type.

The 'planner for freedom' does not seek conformity. His aim is not 'the suppression of individuality but rather . . . differentiation providing the space where it may grow and the social stimuli which regularly foster it' (p. 260). In order to attain his objective, he must know, above all, what kind of social environment is most conducive to a healthy growth of personality. In other words, he must be a psychologically oriented sociologist, or a sociologically oriented psychologist—the problem of a 'sociological psychology' thus reappears as that of the necessary foundation of 'planning for freedom'. Unless we have a good working 'sociological psychology', we cannot even begin to plan. In the second lecture, Mannheim gives an outline of the basic psychological knowledge needed by the planner, largely along psychoanalytical lines. But he does not assume that the psychological knowledge available at present fully answers the requirements of 'sociological psychology'. Psychoanalysis provides a framework of the study of personality in individual and biographical terms; the role of the *institutional* environment and of large-scale social influences still remains to be explored. A behaviouristic stimulus-response psychology, on the other hand, uses 'mechanical patterns' which may have a limited applicability and validity but cannot do justice to the *whole* of personality and of society (p. 306). The necessary equipment of the 'psychologically oriented sociologist' being so incomplete, one is left with the impression that the *immediate* prospects for 'planning for freedom' are not very promising.

Mannheim did not draw such a discouraging conclusion from his analysis. Since he considered—perhaps somewhat hastily— *laissez-faire* (or whatever is left of it in a world of imperfect competition and pressure-group legislation) as completely hopeless, 'planning for freedom' remained for him the only practical approach to achieve 'freedom and individualization' in the near future (p. 308). He thought, perhaps, that our psychological knowledge, even though fragmentary, provided at least a provisional basis for a rational, factual discussion of social problems (cf. the conclusion of the fourth lecture, p. 309). In any case, he forcefully draws attention to the 'limitations of the sociological concept of the self' (p. 303) and of the possible pitfalls of planning. 'The possibilities of planning are great, but the dangers are greater' (p. 309). The main danger for him was that the planner, baffled by the difficulty of the right approach, might take the short cut of bureaucratic regulation and of totalitarian suppression of the individual.

At any rate, 'planning' was for Mannheim a *corrective* to the blind and unregulated workings of the collective dynamic forces of society, rather than a *culmination* of the trend towards collective dynamism. Its function was a hygienic and prophylactic rather than creative one. Mannheim's concept of planning has nothing to do with the idea (usually associated with 'planned society') of developing a 'blue-print' of a new social order and reshaping society according to its specifications, after one has made a *tabula rasa* of the old unplanned system. Far from proposing to start from scratch, Mannheim envisages planning as proceeding within the institutional framework of mature democracies. His later work on the problem of planned society was mainly devoted to an investigation of the potentialities which present institutions afford for the development of planning (see the posthumously published volume *Freedom, Power and Democratic Planning*, London and New York, 1950). In this, too, he was profoundly influenced by British gradualism.

IV

Karl Mannheim always maintained that science does not develop in a vacuum but is part and parcel of the social process, with its concrete content of clash and strife of real group interests. From the point of view of his own methodology, it was only to be expected that his conception of social science would change when his own social 'location' underwent a radical shift. In Germany, his 'location' was that of a progressive intellectual, 'detached' from contending interest groups but seeking 'attachment' to the creative social forces of the future. In England, he became a 'refugee' who had some dreadful tales to tell, and for whom that was vividly remembered past which for the host society was merely a potential future, viewed with apprehension. Neither the 'detachment' he had practised nor the 'attachment' he had sought in Germany were possible in the new situation. Instead, he had to be 'useful' as a newcomer—he had to put his experience at the disposal of the society in which he lived. In accordance with this change of role, his concept of sociology also became less systematic and more pragmatic. Not that he had ever considered sociology as 'pure' theory—in his German period, too, scientific work to him was the expression of a vital urge, ultimately founded in collective strivings. In this sense, his concept of science was always 'pragmatic'. But in Germany, the systematic exploration of 'structural' relationships was itself a complete and sufficient realization of the basic urge behind scientific endeavour. In England, this was no longer the case; 'structural' findings—as we have seen—had to be combined with psychological ones in order to produce 'applicable' results.

This transformation of the concept of sociology took place only gradually; Mannheim seems to have thought at first that the best contribution he could make would be the cultivation of his own 'structural' type of sociology. England, as he says in his article on 'German Sociology' (published in *Politica*, February 1934, and reprinted in this volume, pp. 209–28), was also moving towards a more critical social situation in which awareness of 'structural' facts would be indispensable. The Germans, with their longer experience of social crisis, had developed the conceptual tools to deal with such situations. 'German sociology anticipated its sister-sociologies in that it was forced by the social crisis to pay attention to problems which sooner or later were destined to shake the rest of the world too; and since it was the first to concern itself with these problems, German sociology devised methods for the observation and interpretation of complex general situations. . . . Thus the rapidly growing similarity of the basic social problems with which different countries have to grapple finds its reflection not least in the *rapprochement* between the trends of sociological thought pursued in those countries' (pp. 227–8). (American sociology, we read in the same paper, has not come to grips with such 'structural' problems as the class problem, because vertical social mobility and the possibility of finding new fields of activity have 'veiled' the class structure of society (p. 225).

The contrast between 'German' and 'American' sociology is also discussed in a review of Stuart A. Rice's 'Methods in Social Science' from the *American Journal of Sociology* (September 1932), reprinted here (pp. 185–94). American sociology is commended here for its practical, concrete orientation; sociologists, Mannheim notes, are doing 'field work' and seek remedies for immediately felt practical difficulties. But, on the other hand, Mannheim takes exception to the timidity of American sociologists in evolving 'broad theories', to their shrinking 'from inquiring into the structural aspects of social life as a whole at a given stage' (p. 191), and to their fascination with natural science. 'Although it is admitted that all social phenomena are not measurable, still numerical proportions are the ideal of exactness toward which most scholars are striving' (p. 190). And Mannheim deplores the tendency, displayed in some sociological work in America, to 'aim in the first place at being exact, and only in the second place at conveying a knowledge of things' (p. 189). German sociologists, given to *a priori* speculation, may have been guilty on occasion of a 'certain arrogance' in attempting 'to solve the Gordian knot of big problems at one stroke', but there is also 'a certain false modesty of the empirical scholar whom his "exactitude complex" prompts to ignore the genuine basis of his own questioning' (pp. 191–2). Mannheim concludes that 'there were hardly ever two different styles of study so fit to supplement each other's shortcomings as are the German and American types of sociology' (p. 193).

In his later work, Mannheim himself tried to fuse the two styles of thought; he dealt with 'immediate' problems, viewed empirically and experimentally, without 'ignoring the genuine basis of his questioning'. The present publication of his essays illustrates a subtle intellectual drama of our time: the struggle of a first-rate mind to salvage an intellectual tradition, buried under the debris of historic debacle, which once had carried the high spiritual hopes of a generation, and to infuse new life into it by grafting it on to another tradition of an altogether different nature. It may be hoped that both streams of tradition will be enriched and strengthened by this experiment in cross-fertilization.

v

The present volume contains two essays which in fact belong to the series of the 'Essays on the Sociology of Knowledge'; the doctoral dissertation 'Structural Analysis of Epistemology', and the essay on 'Conservative Thought'. All other papers contained in this volume, with the exception of the book review mentioned above, were written in England. One, an unpublished paper on the 'History of the Concept of the State as an Organism', remains within the framework of the original 'structural' method developed by Mannheim. The others represent the new trend I have tried to characterize above—pointing beyond the 'structural' position towards a concept of planning based upon 'sociological psychology'.

PAUL KECSKEMETI

PART ONE

★

STRUCTURAL
ANALYSIS IN SOCIOLOGY

CHAPTER I

Structural Analysis of Epistemology[1]

SECTION 1
Of the Logic of Philosophical Systematization

I. CONCEPT OF A LOGIC OF SYSTEMATIZATIONS

T HE object of this inquiry is to analyse the structure of a branch of philosophy, i.e. epistemology, with a view to contributing towards a logic of philosophy and so towards an all-embracing theory of systematizations in general.

Since the questions with which we are going to deal can only be understood properly in relation to this wider field, it seems advisable to preface the analysis of our specific topic, epistemology, with a few remarks about these more comprehensive subjects.

Ever since Lask[2] first postulated the need for a logic of philosophy and sketched it in broad outlines, interest in contemporary philosophical circles has centred on this problem, but nobody has ever attempted to provide a solution *in concreto*. The inevitability of this demand from quite a different aspect has also been pointed out with much force by Croce in the opening paragraphs of his book on Hegel. 'Strange is the aversion', he says, 'to this conception of a logic of philosophy (for it is really very simple and should be accepted as irresistibly evident). It is the idea, in other words, that philosophy proceeds by a method peculiar to itself, the theory of which should be sought and formulated. No one doubts that mathematics has a method of its own, which is studied in the logic of mathematics; that the natural sciences have their method, from which arises the logic of observation, of experiment, of abstraction; that historiography has its method, and that therefore there is a logic of the historical method; that poetry and art in general give us the logic of poetry and art, i.e. aesthetic; that in economic activity is inherent a method, which is afterwards reflected in economic science; and that finally the moral activity has its

---

[1] First published in *Kantstudien*, supplementary vol. 57, Berlin, 1922.
[2] E. Lask, *Die Logik der Philosophie und die Kategorienlehre*, a study on the domain of logical form, Tübingen, 1911.

method, which is reflected in ethic (or logic of the will, as it has sometimes been called). But when we come to philosophy, very many recoil from this conclusion: that it, too, from the moment of its inception, must have a method of its own, which must be determined. Conversely, very few are surprised at the fact that treatises on logic, while giving much space to the consideration of the disciplines of the mathematical and natural sciences, as a rule give no special attention to the discipline of philosophy, and often pass it over altogether in silence.'[1]

Whether or not ethics should be conceived as nothing but a 'logic of the will' (as the passage quoted above would have it), economics as simply a logic of economic activities, and so on, may be left undecided; but we unreservedly accept the fundamental idea expressed by Croce, namely, that every mental intellectual or cultural field has a structure of its own, so that it will always be legitimate to ask for a thorough-going structural analysis from which we may deduce the structural peculiarities of the various individual fields—whether they belong to the sphere of theory, of practice, or of *poiesis*.

Actual inquiries into the logic of philosophy have not been forthcoming, although the problem is there for all to see, and this omission may be due, for the greater part, to the present-day schism in logic, which has so far prevented any agreement on how to set about such an undertaking, or where to bring the weight of logical analysis to bear for the purpose.

Croce, judging by the above remarks, looks on the logic of philosophy as a problem of methodology. Lask takes its proper sphere to be in the main the development of a theory of philosophical categories, while others again would confine themselves to an exploration of the nature of philosophical concept-formation.

This should be enough to show that we cannot so much as begin with the logical analysis of any particular field until we have made up our minds about what we are to think of the systematic connection among the different branches of logic itself; whether we are to say, for example, that the method of a discipline determines the formation of its concepts, or whether, on the contrary, the conceptualization explains the method; in short, which of the relevant logical forms is to be regarded as central to the logical examination.

To state our main contention right away: in our view, primacy among logical forms belongs to systematization. The simpler forms can be understood, in our opinion, only in terms of this 'highest', 'all-embracing' form.

[1] B. Croce, *What is Living and what is Dead in the Philosophy of Hegel*, transl. Douglas Ainslie; Macmillan & Co., 1915.

That is not to say, however, that this form is to be examined in isolation from the others; quite the reverse: it is in fact essential to a comprehensive structural analysis of any field that it should if possible cover all the different logical elements; but the inquiry should be guided throughout by the systematization of the field in question. The specific concepts, problems and methods characterizing a field can be understood only from its peculiar 'impulse to systematization' (if we may use this subjectivist term for the time being).

If it is already odd that no positive logic of philosophy has ever been worked out, it is even more surprising that the common textbooks on logic have nothing at all, or nothing of real significance, to say about the most fundamental logical form, i.e., systematization.[1] All the same, our attempt to treat systematization as the central concept of logic does not seem to be out of tune with contemporary trends in philosophy.

There can in fact be no mistaking that the trend which is becoming predominant today, at least in the cultural sciences, runs counter to the precept once given by Descartes to proceed, as it were, in atomizing fashion and explain more complex structures in terms of simpler ones; the present trend is, on the contrary, to explain simpler structures in terms of more complex ones.

It may already be a sign of this new spirit in research that Sigwart, Windelband, Rickert and a host of others place the emphasis in logic no longer upon the theory of concepts, as was customary before them, but upon the theory of judgment; i.e. that they seek to understand the simpler forms in terms of the more comprehensive ones. Admittedly, this greater emphasis upon judgment in many contemporary scholars largely stems from a psychologistic bias which inevitably seeks to stress the genetic factor; nevertheless, the fact cannot be overlooked that they place the more complex, the 'higher' forms above the simpler ones.

Systematization must above all receive pride of place in a logic which puts $\phi\acute{u}\sigma\epsilon\iota$ $\pi\rho\acute{o}\tau\epsilon\rho o\nu$, rather than $\pi\rho\acute{o}\tau\epsilon\rho o\nu$ $\pi\rho\grave{o}s$ $\mathring{\eta}\mu\hat{a}s$, at the head. Some further explanation is in order, however, if we go all

---

[1] The problem of order or systematization is given prominence in the following works:

H. Driesch, *Ordnungslehre*, Jena, 1912.

J. Royce, "Prinzipien der Logik' in the *Enzyklopädie der phil. Wissenschaften*, vol. 1: *Logik*, ed. A. Ruge, Tübingen, 1912.

A particularly outstanding contribution towards an all-round theory of systems was made before his untimely death by the Hungarian Béla Zalay, who devoted his researches to this very field. Cf. in particular his 'A filozófiai rendszerezés problémája' ('The Problem of Philosophic Systematization'), publ. in the journal *Szellem*, Budapest, 1911.

Also worthy of mention is A. Liebert's work, *Das Problem der Philosophie*, in the 2nd edition of 1920. It contains much that is illuminating on the fundamental significance of the systematic principle.

E.S.—2

the way in this direction, and confer priority upon that sector of logic which appears as its final culmination rather than as its starting point. To maintain the priority of systematization over the concept and the judgment is not to say, quite obviously, that the thinker as an existent person must be in possession of a clear-cut philosophical system to begin with, in order to be able to form a concept at all; that, of course, would be sheer nonsense. What it does mean is this: each concept implies, as its tacit presuppositions which for the most part do not become the object of conscious reflection, certain connections, certain configurations reaching beyond the seemingly isolated concept. Conscious reflection turns towards these presuppositions as a rule only if, for reasons into which we need not go here, a doubt arises as to the content comprised by a concept, when it becomes necessary to elucidate its signification with the help of other concepts, by bringing the whole context to bear on the problem. The meaning of an individual concept is rooted in its whole context, and this can further be demonstrated from quite a different approach.

Take the formation of a new concept in science—or, for that matter, in everyday life. This can be shown always to involve three things. What is pertinent in the first place is the—as yet in-determinate—matter concerned, which is always before us as a matrix differentiating a new meaning. In the second place we pay attention to the concepts we already have and which have a bearing on the concept to be formed. And finally we somehow take into account the systematization as a whole which, quite un-reflectedly as a rule, is constantly with us whenever we form a new concept, as the general pattern of the entire context. The outcome of this process (considered, for the time being, from a genetic point of view) is that all concepts are more or less closely correlated with others, that any one concept implies others as having already been posited. This correlatedness is most clearly evidenced by what we know as complementary concepts like form and content, or mountain and valley, where it is perfectly obvious that the one has meaning only in respect of the other. And something of this complementariness inheres in concepts of every kind. The mutual interdependence of concepts in this sense constitutes a continuum, but not the one represented by the Aristotelian scale of forms (where concepts are ordered according to the different degrees of universality, and where the locus in the pyramid of concepts is adequately determined by giving the *genus proximum* together with its *differentia specifica*). It is to be understood, rather, as a chain-sequence which (as we have seen in the case of complementary terms) leads on from one link to the next, and which seems to suggest an infinite progression.

However isolated it may seem, a concept still has systematic presuppositions. Let us assume for argument's sake what is never in fact the case, that concepts are simply proper names of concrete things; it can be shown of even such completely a-systematic concepts that they involve a systematization. If a concept were nothing but a proper name of a 'This here'—something like pointing at the thing with a finger—and if it contained nothing beyond this ostensive reference, then it would be a concept in a truly minimal sense. But it will be shown that even this rudiment of a concept involves an implicit systematization. It would be possible, under certain circumstances, to develop a sign language corresponding to concepts reduced to the mere pointing out of things 'here and now'— for instance, by assigning a particular letter of the alphabet as a proper name to an individual object we meet. This table in front of me would be called a, this chair b, and so on. No letter could be used twice over in this game—another table, for instance, could not be called a—or else we should be going beyond the hypothetical minimal conceptualization. If we applied a symbol to several objects, it would no longer be a mere proper name; by proceeding in this way, we should introduce into our concept formation the tacit assumption that there are real objects of the same kind which can occur more than once. Furthermore, if our conceptual scheme is to be devoid of any systematizing presuppositions, it must under no circumstances be thought of as ordered in a series like numbers or the letters of the alphabet, because this would mean adding a systematizing element to mere naming as such—that is, in the case of numbers, the law governing the series of the natural numbers, and in that of the alphabet, the notion that every letter (and consequently the object denoted by it) has its proper place in a series in which, despite the absence of a law underlying the series, the position of each term is fixed with reference to its neighbours. Supposing, then, that we eliminate all these factors of systematization, and merely retain isolated, and therefore isolating, proper names, which could thus cover the infinite number of things by infinitely many symbols—symbols which show no order like the alphabet; even if our conceptual system is thus reduced to a minimum, some systematizing presupposition will still have crept in unawares; that is, naming itself in fact proceeds on the assumption that the initially indefinite variety of the things which can be named can be transformed, by the act of naming, into a collection of discretely identifiable individualities.

This example goes to show that even a minimal conceptual system, the 'system of proper names', presupposes some kind of systematization, that even a rudimentary concept cannot come into being without implying some systematizing presuppositions, however unreflected. The same example also serves to lay down what is to be understood by a tacit assumption, an implicit presupposition. It is not an antecedent line of thought which the individual must have gone through before he can understand or form a concept; it is a set of implications he has to accept, acknowledge, take for granted, whenever he uses a theoretical concept significantly or turns his attention to it.

That the concepts with which we actually have to do in the sphere of theoretical thought are not 'minimal concepts' in this sense, i.e. that they are more than such 'proper names', hardly needs detailed proof. If, however, even such rudiments of concepts already involve systematic presuppositions, we shall expect these to be present to an even higher degree in the concepts of common sense, let alone of science. We must begin, therefore, by working out some of the systematic presuppositions which are involved by any theoretical concept whatever.

The 'minimum of theoretical systematization' which must already be assumed for the genesis of conceptual proper names might be formulated as the principle of 'delimiting the individual elements as isolatable from one another'. This is in sharp contrast to the systematic presupposition underlying our nonrudimentary, fully developed concepts, which holds that they form a *continuum* of closely interrelated elements. And if, as modern logic would have it, judgments are nothing but the locus where concepts originate, concepts in turn being condensed and stored judgments, then our principle, applied to the theory of judgments, will assume the following form: in the theoretical sphere, one has to presuppose a closed chain of continuously connected propositions. Something of this nature was Bolzano's view when he taught that every truth is correlated with all other truths in the sphere of validity. Yet this 'principle of continuity', the systematizing assumption in the theoretical sphere, does not apply to the aesthetic sphere, where indeed a contrary principle appears to hold (as G. Lukács maintains among others). In primary experience a work of art is taken to be an isolated monad. One truth always implies another truth, and for that reason a new insight can do away with former knowledge, show it up as a mistake and cancel it; but none of this holds good for art, since one work of art never follows in any way from another—consequently, a new work in this sphere can never prove another wrong. The Ptolemaic and the Copernican systems cannot both be true, but no painting will ever contradict a picture by Giotto.

This fundamental dissimilarity in the guiding principles of these two 'systematizations' (of the theoretical as against the artistic sphere) is also responsible for the difference in the structure of their respective histories. The historical pattern of science can only be adequately represented as a unilinear series of approximations towards the one and only possible form of truth, where the last assumption simply discounts as error all previous hypotheses about the same facts; whereas the history of art shows the most varied works of art existing side by side without contradiction. The history of philosophy on the other hand—as will be seen in more detail later—is presented most adequately as a history of problems where the permanence of the problems does constitute a kind of supratemporal unity, yet—in spite of the fact that here, too, only one truth is possible in principle—the individual answers do not obliterate one another in quite the same sense as they do in the history of science ; whereas, on the other hand, they also do not tolerate one another in the same way as they do in the history of art. As a matter of fact, philosophy alone is really amenable to the method of the history of problems; this method is not altogether inapplicable to the history of art (as witness, for example, Riegl's history of problems), but when it is actually applied, this is always due to the importation of alien theoretical categories. These are quite suitable to the description of the evolution of certain elements and phases of the works of art, but cannot do justice to the history of the works as such, as viewed in a congenial artistic contemplation.[1]

This digression about the historical structure of different spheres was needed to show from another angle that the various mental spheres differ in structure; their different histories are due to their different systematizations, since these determine the structure of the individual elements which together make up the history.

Coming back to the general structure of the theoretical sphere as such, we can now state its systematizing principle to be such as to ensure a certain continuity for the various elements which occur within it. It might almost seem as if it were enough to assume a single chain of propositions, a closed circle as it were; but even a cursory inspection, let alone a deliberate following-up of the relevant matters of fact, will convince us that the structure of conceptual and judgmental connections is not comparable to a circle. We need only select and attempt to fit together a few random members of the body of concepts at present known to us—let us say the categorical imperative, the force of attraction, sensation, form, content, etc.—and it will be clear immediately that this aggregate of concepts can far better be ordered in terms of *several* self-contained circles. Every one of the concepts listed points to a

---

[1] Cf. Ernst Heidrich, *Beiträge zur Geschichte und Methode der Kunstgeschichte*, Basel, 1917. See especially the review of Jantzen, pp. 82 ff.

different context in which it is originally at home. These various contexts could be called the different levels of theoretical systematization—levels or strata advisedly, not simply planes, since a thorough examination will show that they form a hierarchy rather than a mere juxtaposition of regions having the same 'rank'. Some of these levels, in fact, are capable of comprising in a way all 'elements', and these will be called the *primary systematizations*. Ontology, for instance, is one of them, inasmuch as each concept —no matter where it is originally at home—is also constituted within the ontological system. It is impossible to form a concept without at the same time determining the *modus existendi* of its content. In such a case, of course, being cannot be understood to mean real existence exclusively, which in current philosophical usage denotes the existence of things in physical space. A complete ontology distinguishes various modes of being; at present we are familiar with the spatio-temporal physical, the temporal-psychic, and the supra-temporal 'spheres of being', and as soon as a thought element is fixed in form of a concept, one of these modes of existence is posited together with it.

In addition to these universal primary systematizations, which will be discussed in detail below (pp. 48 ff.), there are a number of distinct and sharply defined levels, in one of which the τόπος νοηός of a novel concept is always to be located. On this showing, thinking in general can be regarded as an endeavour to find the logical place of a concept in the total framework of the mental spheres; in other words, a thing is taken to be explained, comprehended, in so far as we have discovered its place in the currently accepted orders, series and levels.

That we have to assume several different systematization *series* is shown, above all, by the existence of a number of different sciences, most of which have their own separate series of interrelated concepts—although we would like to stress that the sciences are not identical with the systematization series as defined by us. The unity of many a science derives from quite superficial considerations; whether a science owes its existence to the crudest practical considerations, or to a far subtler unifying principle rooted in methodology, its unity as a science is always partly determined by methodologico-practical considerations, as against which the pure levels must be reconstructed by digging down to their constitutive principles, to their ultimate presuppositions. We shall see in the case of epistemology that, although from an heuristic point of view it does at first appear as a well-grounded unity, from the point of view of a pure axiomatic theory, i.e. of structural analysis, it turns out to represent a mixed systematization. Let it be said straight away that the reconstruction of the pure levels is altogether an internal affair for logic, and in no way intends to reform the existing sciences. There are good reasons why scientific thought usually works with mixed systematizations. Still there is every justification for a logical examination to distinguish between the underlying pure series concerned—it is in fact a vital enterprise for logic.

It should already now be clear that the pure systematizations only comprise those series of related concepts which—if their internal connectedness is steadily traced back—will eventually lead to fundamental concepts or correlations of concepts in which the series in question originates. Wherever we shall have occasion to lay bare the final postulates of certain series, we shall find them to be based on patently complementary conceptual couples rather than upon unitary concepts. It may be assumed, then, that systematizations obey the principle which H. Rickert introduced under the name of 'heterothesis'[1]: the ultimate elements of the series seem to be somehow rooted in each other. The unity of logic (as we shall see in the sequel) is constituted by the correlation of form and content, the unity of epistemology by the subject-object correlation. Correlations of the constitutive concepts of a series can be regarded as quasi-axiomatic postulates of the sphere concerned. But obviously one must not jump to conclusions; even if the unity of a sphere is guaranteed by 'axioms' of this kind, and even if the propositions belonging to it are somehow interconnected, it would be going too far to assume that all disciplines proceed in the same way as exact mathematical sciences do, where a limited number of axioms is enough to deduce all further theorems and secondary concepts. It certainly will not do to assume beforehand that all the diverse series must necessarily exhibit the same principle of construction. Methodical pluralism is called for at this stage of the inquiry, and it should be enough to note that the basic concepts of the less exact disciplines also constitute a systematic unity, even if we are not yet in a position to characterize their respective principles of construction. It is problematic whether a deductive procedure is practicable in every field without doing violence to it. It cannot be doubted, however, that concepts only occur in series, and that consequently there is no such thing as an isolated concept; this is demonstrated beyond doubt by the fact that even the most 'inexact' concept has a place where it properly belongs, and that it will show at once if it is 'transferred' into an alien sphere, where it can only be applied 'metaphorically'.

Language, however, is not an infallible guide: one and the same word frequently names various concepts. And it is of paramount importance to clear up these systematic ambiguities; we

---

[1] H. Rickert, *System der Philosophie*, Pt. 1, pp. 56 ff., 1921.

shall discover further on, for example, that the term 'subject' covers several different concepts. We must above all differentiate between these concepts, even though it is quite likely that no ambiguity would have arisen, had they not had something in common in spite of their differences. The same applies also to the term 'time' and the various concepts named by it—the cosmological, the psychological, the historical,[1] and the philosophico-historical conceptions of time are all vastly different and can only be properly understood within the frame of reference, the context of meaning to which they belong. Even a seemingly simple, straightforward concept like 'man', for example, has various meanings according as it is used as an anthropological, ethical, or philosophico-historical term. No matter how loosely we use language, we can convey only *one* of these meanings at a time. It is quite evident, therefore, that even within the theoretical sphere itself we have to assume several serial systematizations, and that every single concept, simply by being conceived, presupposes the existence of at least that serial systematization within which it is constituted.

Before going any further, however, it seems advisable to differentiate between three fundamental terms which always occur in a discussion of the logic of systematization, i.e. *systematization*, *system* and *architectonic*. Up to now we have only talked about systematizations—individual systems have not been mentioned so far—and by these we always meant an entire set of serially connected, mutually defining elements.

Systematization is distinguished from *system* in that the former is a *constitutive* form, while the latter is a *reflected, methodological* form. With regard to the genesis of these forms in a subject, we may say that a 'systematization' is created by the transcendental-logical subject, and a 'system' by the empirical subject.

Systematization is constitutive to such an extent that anything 'given' (this term still understood in a subjective and genetic sense)—any 'fact of experience' (in the broadest sense)—must already belong within one of the existing systematizations, in so far as it is theoretically grasped at all. The simplest, most primitive way of 'objectifying' an element is to range it, fit it in, with one of these inevitably presupposed orders. There is more to it than that, since the phrases 'range with', 'fit in with', still fail to convey what is really happening. 'Ranging' an element with a series, 'fitting it in', is apt to sound as if this element already had its true identity, as if it were a 'something itself', before it is ever put into the appropriate series; as if in the constitutive sphere a

[1] Cf. M. Heidegger, 'Der Zeitbegriff in der Geschichtswissenschaft', *Zeitschrift für Philosophie und phil. Kritik*, vol. 160, pp. 173 ff., Leipzig, 1916.

series and an element were two mutually independent, self-subsisting entities and only had somehow to be brought together. Nothing could be further from the truth than such a conception. An 'element', in fact, only gets its proper identity by adopting the structure of the series to which it belongs, and this series in turn consists in nothing but the identity of structure shared by certain elements that belong together.

We must consider systematization as a constitutive form, since a theoretical object that is not systematized is altogether inconceivable. Even those who are 'on principle' adverse to systems of any kind, who would deliberately think 'unsystematically', even they have to rely on systematization. It is of course quite another matter whether a *system* (as opposed to systematization) is also a necessary form of thought; that is for the individual disciplines alone to decide from case to case. Thus it is one of the most vital problems for philosophy, among others, whether its own systematizations do not, in virtue of their innermost structure and tendency, irresistibly demand to culminate in some system or other—whether philosophical concepts as such do not merely involve a systematization but also the necessity of a system.

If so, there would have to be some internal connection between the various systematizations and the systems which they make possible. If systematization is nothing but the first ordering of the 'elements of experience' (in the most general sense), as performed by the transcendental-logical subject, then these elements which are thus placed on the same level should already contain the germ of the possible solutions to the problems with which the reflecting subject is going to be confronted. The more so, since the reflective thinking of an empirical self is for the most part simply the analytic exposition of what has already been systematized by the transcendental-logical subject. Accordingly, an individual reflecting subject, who orders his thoughts into a complete system in strict accordance with a principle, is really doing no more than push to its logical conclusion a tendency already prescribed in the very systematization. On this account we must think of systematization within any sphere as ever open—it is a still to be completed chain of interdependent concepts belonging to the same level; whereas a system is always closed—one of the possible solutions predetermined by the logical structure of the prior systematization. According to this view the reflective subject is merely finishing off the work of logic begun by the transcendental-logical subject. (By introducing the concepts of a reflective and of a transcendental-logical subject and by raising the issue of the empirical and transcendental-philosophical genesis of knowledge, we gave the discussion an epistemological turn. This was done for the sake of conciseness—communication in genetic terms is easier. Needless to say, it is possible to do without the epistemological considerations brought to the above exposition; the distinction can be formulated purely in terms of logic, as the difference between constitutive and reflective forms.)

Architectonic must be distinguished from systems as being an entirely secondary matter, a mere mode of presentation. As a rule its construction is quite different from that of the system to be presented, and it is commonly imported from alien spheres, usually with a disruptive effect on the original sequence of thought. The architectonic 'order' is governed by principles quite heterogeneous with the original context (such as symmetry, dichotomy, trichotomy or any other formal arrangement). Adickes[1] has shown, for example, how largely Kant depended for the exposition of his system on an architectonic borrowed elsewhere (from the construction of logic), how time and again he was led to rearrange his thoughts in deference to his architectonic fetish, and how he even modified the positive content of some of his ideas for the sake of trichotomies and similar principles.

The analysis of a system turns on its pure form, purged of architectonic; it acts on the assumption, of course, that the 'natural' order, the logical hierarchy of the fundamental ideas of system can always be reconstructed. If an account of the ideas of a thinker is to be more than a servile copy of the original way of presentation, it will have to be an effort at a systematic reconstruction of this kind. That the job can be done well or badly is irrelevant to the issue that it is not, in principle, a futile undertaking. Even though it may be justified in individual cases, e.g. owing to pedagogical considerations, to adopt a way of presentation which closely follows the arrangement of the original, this form of presentation must be discarded and treated as a mere architectonic whenever it is the inner meaning, the pure logical structure, of the system we have to communicate.

One of the assumptions involved in any theoretical proposition —to take up this question again—is that, although we are at no time in possession of these series, orders, connections, levels (or whatever name you may choose to designate the 'systematic' forms underlying theoretical propositions) in their complete and true, their only possible, final form—although 'systematizations', as they are formulated in actual fact, always contain erroneous and tentative elements—nevertheless we have to take it for granted that an ultimate, true and complete form of any systematization exists objectively, independently of our own contributions. This is not to be interpreted in the sense of a moral or aesthetic norm,

---

[1] E. Adickes, *Kants Systematik als systembildender Faktor*, Berlin, 1887.

but as a stringent logical postulate implied in every concept, in every theoretical construct. No doubt in the actual process of thinking we shall always have the 'feeling', the 'impression', that we ourselves form the concepts, judgments, theories and sequences, that we create them and that the whole series then seems to confront us as something of our own making; yet the notion of a subjective creativity (a concept of 'psychological systematization') is quite useless in the logical sphere, since it always falls short of the meaning of a theoretical construct.

A theorem, a judgment, a concept, a solution to a problem, all these have meaning only on the assumption that there is a correct solution, however wrong or tentative the present one may be, that independently of us and our doings there is a valid truth (no matter whether it has the form of many closed circles or one), and that this does not originate with our thinking but is, on the contrary, sought by it, intended and, if we are lucky, attained. If we are to have concepts at all, if we are to state any judgment, we have to take the systematizations in their postulated forms as completely self-contained and valid in themselves.

Any single statement—even the proposition that there is no truth, no validity *in se*—can by virtue of the structure of theoretical systematization only be either true or false. It follows that the *content* of this proposition contradicts those presuppositions that are inescapably implied by its *form*; after all, this, like any other statement, only has theoretical meaning if its content can be said to be either true or false. If the content expressed—that there is no truth valid *in se*—is true, then this at least must be thought valid, or it would be meaningless to assert it; if it, too, is false, then it still must be recognized that falsity is meaningful only if we assume the possibility of truth, of self-sustaining validity. And the validity of a single proposition at the same time implies the entire context, from which alone, whether it is explicitly known or not, the sentence derives its full meaning; the concepts contained in the statement involve all other concepts, and in its logical form all other logical forms are involved. It is thus implied in the very structure of the theoretical sphere that it must itself be assumed as a-temporally valid, and this in the form of one or more continuous, chain-like sequences. Just because it is a fact that actual thinking is open to error (that we can distinguish between true and false statements), it is imperative to postulate a self-sustaining sphere of validity beyond the factual; otherwise that fact itself would lack that background which alone can give it meaning. Just because it is a fact that actual thinking proceeds in terms of correlations, i.e. of fragments of series (which again can only be either true or false), it follows that we must assume one or several series to exist independently of our own doing, and such that our ordering activity can merely seek to attain them. Positing such a sphere of ideal validity does not mean that we indulge in dreams of an idealistic Beyond, spun by a metaphysics of validity; on the contrary, certain constant features of actual thinking (the notion of possible error, continual ordering) demand to be complemented by this sphere if they are to have any meaning at all. Now arguments like these—which re-formulate the old principle of the self-certifying nature of truth in the language of a theory of logical levels—have been attacked as involving a fallacy. Although this is certainly wrong, it must nevertheless be admitted that there is something unsatisfactory about these arguments—they deliver no proof that truth is valid in itself, but only show that the concept of this validity is necessarily implied in the meaning of theory as such. It is, however, inherently impossible to prove such a proposition, because any such proof would again have to presuppose it; it is incapable of proof simply because it is itself the necessary condition for the possibility of all proof. That is why we must consider it neither as a *fiction*, nor as an *idea*, but as an inevitable postulate involved in the existence of a theoretical sphere as such.

It is characteristic of this sphere of pure validity that it may be conceived independently of any kind of genetic approach, as belonging to a stratum removed from all subjectivity—transcendental as well as psychological. Translated into the language of the theory of levels, this means that it is not only possible but even necessary to 'order' the logical facts without positing the subject-object relation, i.e. without attending to the problems raised by the latter. It has ever been the legitimate aim of 'logical objectivism' to develop this stratum in complete purity.

If we draw a distinction between pure and applied logic, the one to examine the forms and characteristics of valid truths as such, the other to characterize the process of attaining these verities, then the concept of a subject will only be found in the latter, in applied logic. Going on to the further question which of these two logics has priority (not genetically but, as always in this essay, in a purely logical sense), we shall discover that one can develop a pure logic without recourse to the concept of a subject, while applied logic, the methodology of thinking, already presumes the existence of a pure logic; for, if the science of thinking is not content to be simply a psychology of thought, and merely to describe the flux of ideas as determined by the laws of association, but rather wants to characterize logically correct thinking as such, then it must presuppose the laws of logical correctness as set forth in an antecedent discipline of pure logic. Genetically it is the actual process of thinking, the topic of applied logic, that has priority; hence it is easier to speak the language of applied logic. Hierarchically, however, i.e. in the sense of a hierarchy of constitution levels, priority belongs to pure logic as the doctrine of a self-sustaining validity.

The concepts of pure logic, moreover, are independent, not only of those of the science of thinking, but also of those of epistemology. Pure logic may go beyond the mere characterization of the sphere of validity as such, and inquire into the peculiar nature of the various logical forms (the categories) upon which validity is based. This inquiry into forms, however, needs as an axiomatic basis only the correlation between form as such and content as such; it remains wholly unconcerned with the role of the subject which explores the forms as well as with the reality to which the truths constituted by means of the forms are to be applied. The question whether such a reality located beyond the realm of logic should be assumed, and whether valid truth is applicable to it, is one which must come up sooner or later in the total framework of the sciences—in fact, this is the problem with which epistemology actually deals ; it certainly does not, for all that, belong to pure logic which could have no means of answering it in terms of its basic concepts.

That there can be a pure logic which need not concern itself with questions of empirical or transcendental genesis is the only explanation for the serene history of formal logic which went its way relatively undisturbed by metaphysical and epistemological controversies.

Pure logic need not even be 'formal' in the manner described. It may examine any content as a meaning-differentiating factor; and still epistemology does not enter into it, because logic need not inquire into the origin of the given content which is responsible for the differential meaning of forms. Epistemological questions arise only in connection with this problem of origin; these will then have to be put separately. But the fact that pure logic can be established independently of the theories of thinking and knowledge, independently of the concepts which constitute epistemology—this fact has its negative side too: pure logic is altogether incapable of settling any epistemological issue one way or the other. The notion of validity refers to the possibility of ordering a certain content, no matter what its source is, in a unique way determined by a norm of correctness. But whether anything is 'apprehended' by this ordering, in the sense that a reality to be posited beyond it is thereby 'attained', this sort of problem would introduce entirely new postulates, characteristic of epistemology which is the topic of our study. At this point, I merely want to stress that I assume a structural independence of pure logic as against epistemology. As regards the controversy of principle as to whether epistemology or logic is prior,[1] my position is the following: the two are always interdependent in the total framework of cognition, of actual thinking; but if they are distinguished according to their ultimate presuppositions, and the question is raised which of them can get along without the premises of the other, our answer will have to be that a pure logic is feasible whereas a pure theory of knowledge (i.e. epistemology without auxiliary sciences) is not.

The postulate common to all theoretical spheres now stands in clear outline; it could be formulated for our purposes as follows: any systematization whatever can in the end permit but a single correct ordering of its elements. All concrete acts of thinking are searching for this sequence, and even if it cannot be found in this way until the end of time, it is still the indispensable presupposition of meaning for any and every act of thinking.

2. DIFFICULTIES PERTAINING TO A LOGIC OF SYSTEMATIZATIONS

At this stage of the inquiry—once this common postulate has been revealed—we are ready for the structural analysis of a particular discipline, i.e. epistemology. But how are we to set about it?—that is the immediate difficulty. History offers an abundance of material: a rich variety of successive or co-existing theories of knowledge. But to choose the one correct epistemology among them—assuming it has already been realized in history— that is more than the logician is able to do with the means at his disposal. If he tried, he would be falling into the typical error of the philosophers of the Enlightenment who, having satisfied themselves that there can be only one correct solution, went on to identify the position reached by their own time—an altogether transitory affair—with eternal truth as such.

Fortunately enough, a logic of epistemology need not wait upcn the solution of this problem; it is not immediately concerned with the structure of the only true system of epistemology, but would merely determine the structure of epistemological systematization as such. Now is there as much as a single concept which could be regarded as a timeless constituent of all epistemology? Is there to

[1] On this controversy cf. the works, among others, of the following two groups of authors: On the one hand, Kant (*Logik*, ed. Jäsche); Drobisch (*Neue Darstellung der Logik*, 5th edition; 1887); Riehl ('Logik und Erkenntnistheorie', publ. in *Kultur der Gegenwart*, pt. I, sect. VI, p. 73 ff.); Husserl (*Logische Untersuchungen*, vol. I, Halle, 1913); on the other: F. A. Lange ('Logische Studien', I. *Formale Logik und Erkenntnistheorie*, Leipzig, 1894); Ueberweg (*System der Logik*, 5th edition, 1882); Schuppe (*Erkenntnistheoretische Logik*, Bonn, 1878); Koppelmann ('Untersuchungen zur Logik der Gegenwart', pt. I: *Lehre vom Denken und Erkennen*, Berlin, 1913). This last with a detailed bibliography.

be found in the historical process of epistemological thinking even one element which can claim to stand above history?

Let us, to begin with, briefly consider a few relevant facts. However much the various epistemologies may differ in their historical development, they all the same belong to a continuity of one idea (which is the reason why all are called 'epistemologies', 'theories of knowledge'). There must accordingly be some concepts at any rate, some perennial problems, some constellations which always recur and thereby make this continuity possible. The attempted solutions may be widely divergent—and still there must be something to these problems, some factor in the set of postulates concerned, in virtue of which these systems, much as their historical expressions differ, are somehow commensurable and can thus be designated as epistemologies, one and all.

These common factors and ultimate premises observable in every theory of knowledge might then be collected empirically. That would be one way of doing it, and quite instructive at that —the trouble is, of course, that it would not be a method *a priori*. That is, it could not be taken as proof that these concepts already belong to the body of supra-historical systematization. As it happens, however, some of the elements which empirical comparison first shows to be shared by all historical systems, can also be apprehended as endowed with logical necessity. There are some concepts—though their number is small—which are so much part and parcel of epistemology that (over and above their actual empirical ubiquity) they present much the same *a priori* character as absolutely necessary mathematical correlations do; there are concepts, postulates and categories which belong to the frame of epistemology to such an extent that the historical development of theory of knowledge is only possible because of them.

The further investigation revolves mainly on throwing these factors into relief,[1] and it is claimed that, purely typological issues aside, I have succeeded in establishing such an *a priori* framework of epistemology as such. The *a priori* character of the discussion (it need hardly be emphasized) cannot be denied on the ground that we must acquire empirical knowledge of existing epistemologies before we can attempt to isolate the underlying *a priori* form of epistemology as such. Even *a priori* propositions cannot be known without being learned somehow; but although all knowledge is acquired in the course of experience, not all knowledge is empirical as regards the source of its validity, and it is not impossible to gather from experience something of *a priori* character, provided its inherent necessity can be demonstrated.

---

[1] How this part of the inquiry would compare with an 'Eidetic' in Husserl's sense is an interesting question but cannot be dealt with here.

If, however, we had an empirical collection of a few elements absolutely integral to the a-temporal standard of epistemology, this would not give us more than a few fixed points in the total framework we call epistemological systematization. (By the way, the existence of such a standard does not in itself prove that the epistemological problem can be solved by us, but only that any epistemological question that is raised must of necessity contain such and such elements.) But since we are interested in the interdependence of the elements, in the way they are rooted in the totality of a system, rather than in the isolated elements as such, we must look further for clues which will help us proceed from the elements to the systematization. If we seek to make our structural analysis as comprehensive as possible, we shall be faced, after the structural elements are ascertained, with the alternative between—the former difficulty crops up anew—selecting as basis some definite theory of knowledge which seems representative, or else—and this is the line we are going to take—regarding the historical realizations as various possible solutions of a perennial problem, from the *synoptical* study of which the character of epistemological systematization may be discoverable.

If one were to choose the former method of determining the structure of epistemology from a picked theory of knowledge, one would first have to prove this to represent the only correct solution of the epistemological problem, to demonstrate, in short, a point-to-point correspondence between epistemological systematization and that particular system. That would mean getting tied up with epistemological questions, and the problem of analysing the structure of epistemology would have to be put off indefinitely. We are not concerned with an epistemology of epistemology but, avowedly, with a logic of the theory of knowledge; and this has no means of its own to arrive at a decision in such disputes. For this reason it seems to be the right procedure simply to consider all the different epistemologies as in a way 'equally possible', no matter how much we should like to take sides as independent thinkers.

The sole remaining assumption, then, would be that the successive words forming the historical body of 'epistemology' are commensurable up to a point and may be taken to be attempts to solve one and the same theoretical problem. This, if admissible at all, will ensure that the possible ways of putting a problem, and also the attempted solutions arising from them, will not be infinite in number, and that there will be a certain point in respect of which they are commensurable. What we have to do is precisely to track down this point of comparison. As long as it is not mere chance that the individual theories of knowledge have a common name it ought to be possible, however divergent they may be in detail, to consider their divergencies as the ramifications of a common path they all take at the start.

Since epistemology is a theoretical discipline proceeding by way of construction, and as a discipline of this character possesses a continuity logically following from the nature of the problems with which it deals, the quest for such a typology should not, in principle, be a hopeless enterprise.

Now if the various epistemologies were monadic wholes consisting of individual *motifs*, no typology could be developed—even if a perfectly close, organic union of the various *motifs* were achieved within any one individual theory. It would be quite impossible, for instance, to work out a typology in this sense for all the lyrical poems, or plays, that are possible. Their constituent elements are *motifs* which, though their individual histories can be traced, do not lend themselves to an adequate historical presentation in terms of a series of partial solutions to a persistent historical problem, and on this count a typology must be doomed to failure. Even in the province of epistemology the plan to work out a typology does not involve a presumption to compute every detail of all theories of knowledge realized so far and those still to be realized. That would be a sheer absurdity—seeing that epistemology, like any other work realized in the course of history, is contingent upon a multitude of factors (motives and points of view originating with the age and with the individual thinker) which can never be amenable to a systematic analysis. What should be possible—as long as it is agreed that, in spite of all discrepancies, there is an underlying unity of approach and systematization to all these attempts—is to throw into relief those moments in respect of which the solutions are still commensurable and on this showing to group the possible attempts, to order them and so to lay the foundations for a typology which conceives of the various solutions within the same field as referring to a unitary problem. If the various possible ways are here—quite deliberately—put on the same footing, that does not amount to an acceptance of relativism but is merely a consequence of the task the analyst of structure has set himself. He must—on peril of becoming an epistemologist—keep aloof from the internal differences between these theories and focus on the formal conditions, and their locus, in which these various conceivable ways become possible.

In the last passages we used expressions like 'possible ways', 'possible (attempted) solutions'; this needs to be elaborated.

The terms are quite familiar in a philosophical discussion. Once a problem has been put and we believe we have found the correct answer, we go over the previous attempts at a solution, considering some to be meaningless and impossible, others as indeed possible though 'this or that would be against it'. What is the logical reason for hesitating to decide between true and false—in philosophy above all—without first passing in review those solutions which are 'possible'? This, evidently: that the logical structure of the problem concerned is such that its fundamental concepts permit of a number of different alternative solutions. In principle, no doubt, only one answer can be correct, but this will have to present itself initially as one 'possibility' among others, and it can assert itself over the others but gradually by adducing arguments in its own favour. That a system is 'possible', then, is no guarantee that its procedure and its solutions are absolutely right; 'possibility' means only that no absurdity is involved. Structural analysis, then, is concerned merely with exploring these 'possible' solutions and the way they are founded in the logical structure of systematization. Our aim must be to demonstrate from the logical structure of the epistemological systematization the point at least where a solution becomes a possible one.

All this seems to suggest that the philosophical disciplines in general—and epistemology in particular—differ in structure from the special sciences. The fact that a philosophical typology is meaningful at least to a certain extent, that types of possible solutions can be anticipated, this alone goes to show what has long been suspected, that truth-seeking in philosophy proceeds in a different way from that followed in the special sciences. Let us consider the import of the idea of *possible* solutions from another angle.

The historical structures of science and of art have already been appealed to once before, and it was then shown that the history of exact science can only be described fittingly as the quest for one possible truth; the postulation of such a unique possible truth shapes the history of science in such a way that, whenever a new solution is found, the old one is simply cast aside as erroneous and thereafter belongs to 'mere' history.

In art, on the other hand, there is nothing like this kind of becoming obsolete. When a work or art has once achieved aesthetic validity, that is, once it has become part of the artistic realm, it can only be judged by its own intrinsic 'idea'—it 'refutes' nothing and is not made obsolete by anything. (In this context, obsolescence can only have a sociological significance.)

Viewed from these contrasting positions, the history of philosophy cannot be brought under the same heading with either of these types—though it is decidedly closer to science than to art. Philosophy has in common with science, first of all, the character of being a theoretical pursuit, and secondly, the fact that its dominant concept is that of truth; that is, philosophy can admit on principle only one correct solution of its problems. On the other hand, one trait common to philosophy and art is that a philosophical solution, even though it may be a failure, is never discarded into 'mere' history to the same extent as obsolete scientific solutions are. Something of the timeless glory accruing to a work of art clings also to abandoned philosophical solutions, provided that they can be recognized as 'possible' solutions in the sense described above.

There is still another feature of the historical development of philosophy which cannot be overlooked—that is, the role played in it by the logical category of 'problem'. It is quite striking what stock we always take in the correct formulation of a problem, irrespective of the truth or falsity of the subsequent solution. Problems, in fact, have their proper home in philosophy. If in the history of art we speak of the 'solution' of an artistic 'problem', this way of talking, though it may be justified and instructive in isolated cases, is always artificial and fictitious. Art in its concrete reality simply does not develop as a solution to various problems of representation—although from a theoretical point of view it may be considered as such. In contrast, the problems which come up in an historical survey of philosophy are the very stuff of philosophy itself.

It might perhaps be shown that the special sciences, as long as they deal with their own topics and do not transcend their proper fields, are always concerned only with answerable 'questions' (no matter how complicated the answers might be), rather than with 'problems' properly so called. If a real 'problem' does come up in a special science, it always has to do with marginal methodological aspects of that science—with a difficulty of procedure which makes the investigator stop and reflect. And that already amounts to philosophy: the philosophy of the science concerned.

One of the most fascinating logical inquiries would be the examination of the logical structure of problems, and of the difference between problems and questions. Ultimately the structure of a problem can only be understood from the structure of the entire systematization—and it may well be that the present discussion will incidentally provide a few clues to this topic as well.

It has now been shown that the structures of the historical development of the various disciplines differ among themselves, and that especially that of philosophy differs from the rest. These differences of structure stem from the different relations the various disciplines bear to their object. Because there is no denying that there can be but a single truth, that accordingly for any question in any field only one solution can be correct and that the history of thought is only the road, through error and confusion, to truth, from this indisputable postulate it does not follow that the shape of this path must always be the same. And so there is a constant need not only to investigate into the structure of the timeless sphere of validity as such, but also to get somehow to understand the particular shape of the historical process which leads up to that sphere.

3. THE MAKE-UP OF HISTORY AND THE IDEA OF A SYSTEM

This discussion is designed to serve the logical purpose (for its own sake) which was set out at the very beginning: to lay bare the logical structure, conceived unhistorically, of a selected discipline; but for all that it may be admissible at least to indicate, as a sort of by-product, the applicability of such a typology (which, however, will only be touched upon in outline, not developed in detail). Typologies of all kinds[1] have been attempted of late ; as a rule they are conceived in a-temporal terms, but are nevertheless valuable for the understanding of the historical development of the discipline for which they are designed. It is not necessary here to decide whether an *a priori* typology is always possible, or whether there are certain fields where only empirical typologies would seem practicable. We shall also pass over the question whether a typology, however empirical, may not inevitably include elements *a priori*; in any case, we are aware of the fact that typology means something different in theoretical and in non-theoretical fields. We shall inquire into just one question: What does typology contribute to history? What can a typology of epistemology in particular do towards our understanding of epistemological problems in their historical aspect? For one thing it can separate the non-historical elements from the purely historical ones. Every individual work in its actual historical form, e.g. any particular epistemology, contains elements which can be explained only with reference to the individual personality of the philosopher concerned, and others which can be interpreted only in terms of the structure of the mentality of the age in question. Now the more completely we succeed in identifying those features

---

[1] Cf. Wilhelm Dilthey, 'Die Typen der Weltanschauung und ihre Ausbildung in den metaphysischen Systemen', Publ. in the collection *Weltanschauung*, ed. Max. Frischeisen-Köhler; Berlin, 1911. Further *Kultur der Gegenwart*, pt. 1, sect. VI, pp. 1–72. (An excellent recent account in English of this typological enterprise is H. A. Hodges' *Wilhelm Dilthey: An Introduction*, Kegan Paul, 1944—Ed.)

Max Weber, *Gesammelte Aufsätze zur Religionssoziologie*, vol. 1, Tübingen, 1920. In particular pp. 536–73, containing a typology of asceticism and mysticism.

Karl Jaspers, *Psychologie der Weltanschauungen*, Berlin, 1919.

of the epistemological systems which stem from the nature of the problem, from the persistent, timeless task itself, the easier it will be to distinguish those features which, if present, have to be explained differently. Where the principle of sufficient reason is at a loss, we have to rely on merely causal, and at bottom real factors in order to explain the actual historic form of a given work. The more stringent, the more rational the structure of the systematization to which the work belongs, the less effectively will real causes enter into the explanation of its genesis, and conversely: the more possibilities appear compatible with the structure, the greater the scope of historical causation.

Yet even in domains of supreme precision, where every step is rationally determined and the type of merely 'possible' solution does not occur at all, there still remains one question which calls for an historical explanation: the question why this task, this particular problem, has been set at all. Supposing it could be shown for the province of epistemology that so and so many ways of putting the problem are possible, that such and such solutions would make sense, we should still need an historical explanation for the fact that the epistemology of one particular age is more metaphysical in nature, while that of another is more logical or psychological; that a subjectivist tendency prevails at one time and an objectivist trend at another (cf. below, p. 49). This circumstance will always afford the grounds for a causal explanation of the actual ascendancy at a given time of just this *a priori* possible type. Why and when exactly solutions of a certain kind will predominate can only be explained historically. Yet the possibility *a priori*, still less the positive or negative truth-value, of the type in question can never be demonstrated by an historical causal explanation—and that is its limitation. The former can only be decided by an immanent analysis of structure (i.e. one devoid of explanations from historical causes), the latter by an immediate investigation of the content as such (in the case of epistemology, for example, only by an epistemological examination, not by a logical analysis of structure).

The historical interpretation of a meaningful whole is a possible and necessary task, but all too often the mistake is made of trying to explain the meaning itself with reference to the temporal features of the works in question—with reference to empirical, real factors. If we seek to validate or invalidate meanings by means of such factors, we shall inescapably fall into relativism. The temporal as such contains only the conditions for the realization of the meanings, but not the meanings themselves; they can only be represented by means of a structural analysis. The analytic of structure in combination with the philosophy of history can significantly ask how the timeless can become temporal: the ancient problem of contingency.

One might in fact put the questions: if it is essential to presuppose for the theoretical disciplines a non-temporal form *a priori*, what function must then be ascribed to the temporally conditioned factors in the process by which this external verity becomes actual? What is the significance of the temporal for the non-temporal? That is roughly the way in which Hegel would have put the problem; his approach is grounded in metaphysics and the philosophy of history. We, however, shall confine ourselves to the logical aspect of the problem, as it presents itself to the structural analyst; and what we have to say from this point of view is this:

Not every idea which is 'possible' *in se* is 'possible', that is, capable of being realized, at no matter what time; so much is certain already because it is of the essence of the theoretical that no question can be asked if it has not been reached by a definite route. (This is true even of emotional experiences, even though, in their case, the various hierarchical stages are not rationally determined: for instance, an emotional feeling tone of 'decadent' character is impossible in a primitive civilization.) It should be determinable in principle (though in practice only with a higher or lower degree of approximation) what ideas are possible in a certain epoch (much as the history of art ascertains that only such and such a treatment of the medium, this or that conception of space, etc., was possible in a given period).

An inquiry on this basis could be expected to reveal a certain connection obtaining between different branches of philosophy, as well as between different theoretical sciences and also between different non-theoretical fields of creative activity. This connection may be designated as 'historico-philosophical contemporaneity'; we mean by this term a certain structural affinity between various cultural manifestations of an epoch.

Thus, it seems plausible to assume a definite affinity between a type of ontology (metaphysics) and a type of epistemology, and we shall try to indicate the point in the structure of epistemology where such a contact with other disciplines may be achieved (cf. below, p. 49, footnote). It need hardly be stressed, on the other hand, that the metaphysics of an age is intimately related to its general attitude. Thus, it is possible to show, at least for the principal branches of philosophy, that the 'historico-philosophically contemporaneous' works of various disciplines show structural parallelism and that, in addition, the various contemporaneous fields of culture could be somehow co-ordinated. Admittedly, the more the a-temporal systematizations of the various fields differ, the more difficult it will be to establish a clear-cut temporal parallelism.

The main point in all this is that it is perfectly possible to view cultural manifestations historically without plunging into historical relativism. To say that a certain creation of the mind can be explained with reference to its period is far from involving a relativistic stand as to its validity. Historical factors determine only the materialization of the mental content in question. The mere fact that history brings to light various types of systems of thought (and among them theories of knowledge) by no means entails an historicist, relativist philosophy of truth. The process can still be conceived as a quest, as a necessary, roundabout way to the only correct solution, where history and the individual thinkers will appear as the concrete vehicles for the various viewpoints 'possible' for timeless Reason as such. In such a conception the temporally contingent factors (whose historically determined interconnections can always be studied anew) are no more than the occasion for an *a priori* possible view to become realized. History, then, is not a lawless process where everything depends entirely on temporally determined factors; on the contrary, the various creations of the mind are grounded in timeless rules which admit only a limited number of possible solutions among which a comparison is feasible, if not right away, then at least on principle. Thus it seems that history is not just a flux, but a directed flow towards some ultimate goal.

It follows from this that if we want to give a comprehensive explanation of any creative work, we have to specify, on the one hand, its *genetic* cause, i.e. its historical connections and affinities, and on the other, its *systematic* origin, i.e. its basis in the timeless systematization of the field to which it belongs.

But that is by the way; the historical application of structural analysis has only been touched upon in order to round out the picture. Our main interest, however, must remain focused on our logical theme—the idea of a logic of philosophy, restricted in the present case to the structural analysis of epistemology.

The reason why our age is so deeply engrossed in the historical aspects of every issue is that the philosophical task of the present time is to work out the solution of the problem of historicity and timeless validity. In solving this task, however, we must never lose sight of the enormous tension that prevails between the doctrine of a timeless validity and the simultaneous awareness that every creative work is fast rooted in its age.

Contemporary thought is determined by two fundamental currents which are *prima facie* mutually contradictory. On the one hand, there is the gradual and laborious ascent from relativism to the doctrine of absolute truth, finding its most sophisticated expression in the present-day philosophy of validity (*Geltungsphilosophie*); on the other hand, our historical perspective becomes ever wider, and, what is still more important, we have a wholly unprecedented faculty of transporting ourselves into every historical epoch, and of understanding and justifying its achievements from its own viewpoint. On the one hand, there is the insight that the very meaning of theory implies that there can only be a single truth; on the other, there is the recognition that anything subject to the process of becoming demands to be comprehended in terms of time, and that we ourselves are ultimately part of the historical process and shall have to look upon ourselves as historical beings.[1] Here the knowledge of a supra-historical sphere; and there, historical consciousness; here the Bolzano-Kantian doctrine, recognized as justified; there—to mention two representative 'ideal types'—the dynamic experience of Hegel and Dilthey. There is a threatening rift between the realm of validity and the temporal process. The doctrine of pure validity, admitting nothing save eternal truth, is forced to look on the entire historical process, in so far as it has not hit on the sole correct solution, as a string of errors: historicism, on the other hand, flounders helplessly as soon as it treats all historical solutions as equivalent, and

[1] This latter conception would finally lead to the postulation of a 'dynamic' logic according to which not only the matter of history but also the categories by which it is grasped are subject to change and evolution. From which it would follow—in concrete application—that the present analysis of structure would also have turned out differently, had it been attempted at a different time. That may in fact be true, except for the few postulates which provide the logical backbone for the evolution of any theory; and we are altogether receptive to a doctrine that tries hard to do justice—maybe even more than justice—to the meaning of history. Yet, we believe that such a doctrine is bound to become entangled in difficulties which are roughly the same as beset straight historicism owing to the relativism to which it necessarily leads. The indubitable fact that everything in history is subject to change must not be carried over into the realm of meaning and validity; by doing so, we should unwittingly controvert our own assertions. It may be the case that at a given time certain truths were not yet or no longer recognized; yet, the truths as such have neither beginning nor end. It may be the case that men will not always seek the truth, and that they have not always cultivated and will not always cultivate epistemology (and also that much of what we today regard as epistemology was something quite different at one time)—but as long as we do engage in epistemology, we are necessarily committed to certain *a priori* principles. In every sphere of creative activity, theoretical as well as non-theoretical, the elements are connected according to a law peculiar to the sphere. We may not change these laws; the only freedom we have is to enter the sphere or remain outside. Nobody compels us to think or to engage in artistic activity; but if we elect to do so, it must be in strict conformity with the structure of the field in question.

This essay of mine is an attempt to do justice to the historical process on the basis of static logic; such an effort must eventually, owing to its structure, culminate in a typology. Even though a structural analysis should turn out differently if it were carried out by a better thinker or at another age, it is true for this, as for all theoretical works, that one solution alone can be the right one. But even if the present study should fail to lay bare the ultimately valid categories, the discovery of its erroneousness would imply the possibility of a correct solution.

allows the notion of validity to lapse. If we are to avoid equally the dangers of rigidity, of an abstract philosophy of value, and the dangers of wayward flexibility, of historicism, the problem of contingency will need to be restated in terms appropriate to the present stage of thinking.

All this, however, is merely mentioned in passing, so as to indicate the wider problems linked up with these questions.

In conclusion, the limitations of such a structural analysis of epistemology should be indicated. It does not purport to be an epistemology of epistemology, but simply a logic thereof. As such it is in no position to take up arms for or against a specific epistemology, or even for epistemology in general. For such a purpose it would have to employ epistemological postulates in its own inquiries, and would consequently itself become epistemology rather than logic.[1] As compared with a pure logic of epistemology —which we intend our analysis to be—a study of the kind mentioned would be a particular type of epistemology which our typology would have to classify as a possible case.

SECTION 2

The Structural Analysis of Epistemology

1. WHAT IS REQUIRED OF A STRUCTURAL ANALYSIS OF EPISTEMOLOGY

We now propose to summarize briefly those results of the foregoing analysis which can be turned to profit in the following concrete typological survey.

As hitherto, we shall mean by structural analysis of a theoretical discipline a logical investigation, primarily dealing with the systematization of the discipline in question and seeking to interpret all other components of the discipline in terms of the systematization. In other words, the individual logical entities will not be torn from the organic whole of the total framework and examined in isolation, but will be preserved in the context from which their meaning derives, and understood with reference to this. Thus, the highest logical form will serve to make subordinate forms comprehensible; the meaning of the highest form, in turn, will be made clear by concentrating on the omnipresence of the systematization, as shown by the fact that all elementary logical entities involve a reference to the whole.

We shall attempt to review all important types of epistemo-

[1] An epistemology of this type—which has not even emerged in history so far—will be discussed in the course of our structural analysis (cf. below, p. 70, footnote 3). It would be an epistemology that takes for its ancillary discipline the analytic of structure as a special kind of logic.

logical thought from this point of view; for this, however, we have to discover the inner motor, the dynamic principle of epistemology, i.e. the force which in this discipline drives the mind on from one question to the next. This principle would give the clearest indication of what our discipline is about, and also of the reason why it is just this or that science which epistemology uses as an ancillary discipline. Once the ancillaries and the original stock of the discipline are sharply distinguished, we shall be able to point out the specific nature and correlatedness of the concepts proper to the field, as distinct from the concepts borrowed from other sciences. We shall then go on to examine the possible ways of formulating the problem of epistemology and note the logical correlation between a certain formulation of the problem and the solution it makes possible. Finally we must apply the analytic of structure to the problem of valuation; and at this stage we shall inquire whether we meet again in valuation the same principles of construction we had previously observed. Once we have brought all these particular questions under the common denominator of one and the same systematization, the particular nature of epistemology will confront us with a still greater task. All solutions of the epistemological problem have the form of a system; hence, the structural analysis in this field will only be complete if it succeeds in deducing the *a priori* possibility of the diverse epistemological systems from the epistemological systematization as such.

In detail this requires an investigation of how the individual systems, even though they are so very different, can still belong to a continuity of thought; and on the other hand, an explanation how it is possible that a more or less uniform way of setting out the problem can yet allow of different answers, of a determinable number of possible solutions. Where—we must ask—is the point at which, no matter how rigorously and uniformly we define the problem, ways to the solution fan out in different directions, and what is the principle which determines in advance the number and kind of possible answers?

Thus, the structural analysis of epistemology involves a wider problem, pertaining to the analytic of systems as such, and bearing a dual aspect: how is it possible, on the one hand, that a single question, concerning a single topic—the problem of knowledge— can be solved in different ways, all equally justifiable in a certain sense? and on the other hand, that, although in the course of history there have been so many different ways of approach, such infinitely variable premises, the various types of solution are yet finite in number and display certain similarities, so that a typology of epistemological solutions can be set up?

Both the unity which underlies epistemological thinking, and the distinguishing principle which is the condition for the variety of individual systems, result from the logical structure of epistemological thought. As we shall see, the nature of epistemological concept formation explains a great deal in itself; every formulation of the epistemological problem entails certain indissoluble concept correlations, the possible resolutions of which are logically limited and prejudge the lines along which a solution can be sought. So much for concept formation; in addition to it the whole logical structure of epistemological thinking must be brought to light if we want to understand the reasons for the uniformity of the systematization of epistemology as well as the *a priori* grounds for the differences among the various epistemological systems.

That a variety of epistemological systems is possible can be deduced *a priori* from the characteristic structure of epistemological systematization which commits us in a certain way but does not determine our conclusions in a unique fashion.

Evidently a structural analysis thus defined must ultimately (as hinted before) aim at a typology to show up the affinities and interrelations among the individual systems of epistemology (not in their historical interplay but as consequent upon their structure), and to demonstrate at the same time that every historically realized type can be described as one of the *a priori* possible solutions to one perennial problem.

On this account the analysis of the systematic structure of the sciences is a task of logic. While general logic explores the most general forms of thought and accordingly seeks to evolve a general axiomatic system, the analytic of structure keeps closer to actual thinking and seeks to explore the special axioms underlying one particular discipline.

Thus it is not only the most general logical laws which are not further deducible, but the various sciences, too, have their own constitutive logical principles, which are incapable of further logical analysis.

In this paper, we propose only to outline the procedure to be followed by the structural analysis of epistemology so defined; many details will not be elaborated, so as to avoid obscuring the main problem.

2. THE NATURE OF THE EPISTEMOLOGICAL PROBLEM, AND THE POSSIBLE WAYS TO A SOLUTION

The nature of epistemological systematization will only stand fully revealed if our efforts can discover in the epistemological process of thought a tendency not found anywhere else, and characterizing epistemology in a more profound fashion than the epistemological problem as such does. If we tried to define epistemology—as we well might—in terms of the problems it is dealing with, such as: what is knowledge? is it valuable? does it reach its goal?—then we should undoubtedly have reduced all theories of knowledge to a common problem; but the essence of epistemology would be determined only in terms of content. Structural analysis, however, cannot limit itself to a discussion of the content of scientific statements, and the essence of epistemology is not exhausted by an identity of content; on the contrary, epistemology achieves the status of a theory entirely *sui generis* only because it answers a primitive question in a peculiar way not met with in any other science.

All other sciences reply to the question: what is this? by fitting the designated element into a context, into an 'order', without bothering to make a special study of this context as a whole. In contrast, epistemology would determine the nature and value of its object, i.e. knowledge, by looking into the connections that are presupposed in every cognition without being explicitly discussed. What is common to all theories of knowledge, in a word, is that they transform the question about the nature of knowledge into a question about the presuppositions of knowledge—and they are by no means all agreed, it must be stated at once, that these are logical presuppositions.

Questions about the nature of these ultimate presuppositions, and their actual solution from case to case, already fall within the province of individual epistemologies, but the characteristic that they search for ultimate presuppositions as such is common to all. Nor is it the only common trait: each epistemology would itself like to be without any presupposition while inquiring into the presuppositions of all and every kind of knowledge.

Epistemological thinking unfailingly reaches a point in the course of its inner development where its task of exploring the ultimate presuppositions confronts it with the necessity of doing entirely without presuppositions. This aspiration may be explained from the paradoxical situation into which epistemology is forced by its particular task; while epistemology seeks to explore and assess the presuppositions of any possible kind of knowledge, it represents itself a type of knowledge, and as such it makes use of precisely those very presuppositions whose nature and value it is striving to ascertain.

It will quite understandably make every effort to get round such a *petitio principii*, and to avoid prejudging in the course of its inquiries that very point which is under discussion, i.e. what cognition is and what value it has. This explains why every epistemology seeks to achieve the ideal of presupposition-free knowledge. Whether it is indeed possible to think without pre-supposing anything, and how epistemology can get over this self-imposed difficulty, does not concern us here. But this much is certain: it is typical of all theories of knowledge that their search for ultimate pre-conditions is inseparably linked up with a pre-tension to be without presuppositions—a fact which engenders a peculiar dialectical movement in the history of epistemology, often resulting in an infinite regress and a stalemate.

But this peculiar disposition is not the only moment which singles out epistemology from all other spheres of thought; the very task it sets itself, the quest for ultimate presuppositions, appears out of tune with the usual object-oriented procedure of everyday as well as scientific thinking. Hence, a short discussion of the possi-bility of such an unusual orientation of thinking may be in order.

The quest for the ultimate presuppositions of knowledge de-pends upon a peculiar quality of mind which might be called the power of 'choice of reference'.

What this power is may be understood by imagining a type of mind which is able to ascend to higher and higher levels of knowledge, passing through whole chains of logical connections, but which differs from the human mind in that it cannot get away from the 'natural' approach, directed entirely at the objects as such. To such a mind the universe would present itself as a uniquely determined context where everything has its proper place—it would then be literally inconceivable that anything might perhaps be different. The trend of thought can only lead from one thing to another; and in such a petrified world there would be nothing to show that knowing is an activity of a special kind. With knowledge concentrated in this way on things, the very possibility of a theory of knowledge would be unthinkable.

Epistemology only becomes possible because we are able now and again to get away from thinking about things and can, if we like, turn our attention reflectively upon the act of knowing itself.

Because of this free choice of reference, we can see not only that things stand in interconnection, but that this their connected-ness can itself be objectified as something apart from the things themselves, thus becoming an object of cognition in its own right. In fact if we want to define the 'choice of reference' in purely logical terms, free from any psychological flavour, we may formu-late it as follows: *the presuppositions of knowledge are always capable of becoming objects of knowledge in their turn.*

The most significant types of this free choice of reference are Cartesian doubt (*de omnibus dubitandum*) and the Kantian trans-cendental question (how is experience possible?).

Both Cartesian doubt and Kantian transcendentalism display a common feature, an ἐποχή, i.e. a type of suspension of the validity of a judgment which cannot be classified under the familiar headings of affirmation, negation or interrogation. Cartesian doubt is not tantamount to the negation of a thesis, since it involves no affirmation of a counter-thesis,[1] any more than a limitation of the thesis itself. It cannot be identified with the interrogative form either, because recent research has shown that a question expresses ignorance merely of the final decision within the frame of an already apprehended context; Cartesian doubt, on the other hand, knows and maintains both the question asked and the decision passed; it does not seek to modify either; all it tries to do is to introduce a novel kind of evidence in validating the judgment. Up to this point the Kantian approach is wholly in line with Cartesian doubt; the correspondence lies above all in the refusal to deny the findings of science; their validity is merely suspended by the raising of a new kind of question: may not the states of things as apprehended within science point to something else as their grounds, something that science as such cannot examine or explain? Let us take a physical sentence, such as '*a* is caused by *b*'. Here, the transcendental question is not concerned with this correlation between *a* and *b*, but merely with something tacitly implied in the sentence, something without which the sentence could not be valid, that is, with the principle of causality. The Kantian type of epistemology restricts its own problems of validation to implications of this kind, artificially isolated from any other type of question. Here, in fact, cognition, by virtue of a novel choice of reference, has its own presuppositions rather than a mere state of things as its object.

If cognition of things is *immanent* knowledge, then the other type of cognition, which is aimed not so much at the content of propositions as at their implicit presuppositions, should be termed *transcendental*. Transcendental presuppositions can never be discovered by seeking mere immanent knowledge.

The investigation of ultimate presuppositions in the manner described constitutes a method exclusive to epistemology. This kind of approach is inevitably barred to every other science, since, after all, sciences are concerned with their objects alone rather than with the principles by virtue of which they attain cognition.

As we are not concerned with Kantian epistemology as such but propose to characterize the method of epistemology in general, we must beware of defining the transcendental method in too narrowly Kantian terms. It would amount to a too narrowly

[1] Cf. E. Husserl, *Ideas: General Introduction to Pure Phenomenology*, vol. 1, p. 108, transl. W. R. Boyce Gibson; George Allen & Unwin, 1931.

Kantian definition of the transcendental method if we insisted that the transcendental validation of any finding of science not only has to transcend the field of the objects of that science but also to invoke an underlying principle of transcendental *subjectivity*. From the point of view of structural analysis, the fact that Kant solved the transcendental problem in terms of subjectivity—that his answer to the question, 'how are synthetic *a priori* judgments possible', involved the spontaneity of a transcendental consciousness—this fact is mere chance, just one man's way of solving the problem of epistemology. What is inextricably bound up with the nature and destiny of epistemology as such is merely general principle, namely, that the immanence of knowledge must be transcended somehow; Kant merely provided the most pointed formulation of this principle.

We have to differentiate between epistemological method in general, and the specific form given it by Kant, in yet another respect. In addition to the thesis of transcendental subjectivity, there is another specifically Kantian thesis which epistemology in general need not adopt, namely, that the ultimate presuppositions of knowledge are logical in nature. One glance at the history of epistemology is sufficient to realize that one may assume —no matter with how much justification—that the ultimate presuppositions of knowledge are psychological or ontological, and still remain within the field of epistemology. The method as such remains the same, even if conclusions as such differ; and considered from this angle, the strictest Kantian method has much in common with a genetic (e.g. psychologistic) method, inasmuch as they both seek to transcend—each in its own way—the immanent framework in its entirety. Accordingly we shall find that the principle of epistemological method can best be stated by taking the widest formulation of the transcendental approach as follows: epistemology is looking for all ultimate presuppositions by virtue of which cognition as such is possible; and in addition, by a separate effort, it also strives to determine the value of these ultimate presuppositions.

It follows that epistemology has two formally distinguishable objectives: (1) to ascertain the ultimate presuppositions of any possible knowledge, and (2) to evaluate the cognitive achievement as such, on the basis of the evaluation of the presuppositions underlying it. The theory of knowledge thus presents itself as having both an analytical and an evaluative tendency.

Now at last it is manifest why epistemology can indeed determine the direction in which its task points, but is incapable of accomplishing this task on its own without calling in some ancillary discipline. There is no such thing as pure and independent epistemological analysis; epistemology always makes use of the concrete analyses of logic, psychology or ontology, and adapts them to its own purposes. And according to whether an epistemology defines the ultimate presuppositions of knowledge as logical, psychological or ontological—thus opting for one of these sciences as its ancillary—we shall say that it belongs to one or the other of the three principal types of epistemology.

3. THE FUNDAMENTAL DISCIPLINES FOR THE THEORY OF KNOWLEDGE

(*The Priority Contest*)

What the ancillaries contribute towards solving the problem of knowledge is therefore no accidental matter but a decisive element in the development of the epistemological system concerned. Although the theory of knowledge represents an entirely new point of view, a novel approach, within the range of scientific research, it cannot solve its problem or furnish the analysis required for a solution without relying on one of the ancillaries; and on that count these disciplines ought to be called fundamental rather than ancillary.

The first step must obviously be to discover some criterion by which a discipline may be judged as able to fulfil such a function. Since epistemology calls upon its fundamental sciences in order to find an answer to the question: 'What are the ultimate requirements for all possible knowledge?', these disciplines must at any rate possess a certain degree of universality.

If this need of epistemology can in fact be supplied, it is thanks to the existence of some systematizations which may be described from a certain viewpoint as universal, and which therefore may be considered as the primary systematizations. These are the systematizations we have indicated before: those of logic, of psychology, and of ontology.

Their universality consists in that they are capable of encompassing 'anything that exists' by creating a certain abstract framework. Under the aspect of psychology everything is 'experience', in the light of logic all is 'meaning', and for ontology everything appears as 'being' in the same fashion. (In how far this specific homogeneity of reference is justified in the respective universal systematizations must here be deliberately left open.[1]) As soon

---

[1] That, of course, is the precise point where the critique of a particular theory of knowledge would have to enter, if the object in view is absolute truth-value. We, on the other hand, have to limit ourselves to a discussion of the 'possibility' of these viewpoints, and of its grounds. They cannot all be true at a time, but nevertheless all three may be 'possible' as significant points of view. The grounds of these possibilities are to be found in the universal scope of every one of these systematizations.

as an object is subsumed under one of these systematizations, it distinctive features disappear; everything is brought to a common denominator, as it were, and it is this which monopolizes attention. Which one of the three fundamental disciplines is selected as the one whose material provides a specific epistemology with its basic presuppositions, that varies in accordance with the varying philosophical 'slant' of the different epochs.[1]

There are three ways of putting the unitary problem of epistemology (that of the ultimate presuppositions of knowledge). We can ask: how does knowledge come about? (1. the genetic approach); or again: the validity of what principles is the basis upon which all knowledge is founded and which is presupposed by all scientific propositions, implicitly if not explicitly? in other words, what principles are implied as valid whenever we make a theoretical statement? (2. the validity approach).

Either approach can be called a *direct* one, because both deal directly with knowledge as such, seeking to explore its genetic or logical foundations. As distinct from these, the third approach would have to be designated as *indirect* because, impelled by the inner dialectic of the priority contest (which will be dealt with right away), it would seek to ascertain the ultimate presuppositions by first developing a comprehensive theory of primary systematizations as a means to determine the region where knowledge has to be grounded (3. the approach through primary systematizations). Which approach is chosen determines in advance which of the above systematizations is to serve as fundamental discipline for the ensuing theory of knowledge.

The genetic approach leads to solutions of the kind known as 'psychologism', but it can also end up with a naïve ontological type of epistemology. In contrast, the validity approach must unfailingly lead to epistemologies of a logical character.

The question through what approach the genuine 'ultimate presuppositions of knowledge' can be reached must be settled before one embarks upon working out a definite epistemology. At the stage where we argue about the question whether the ultimate presuppositions of knowledge are psychological, logical or ontological, we are engaged in a discussion which may be called the 'priority contest' among these disciplines. This dispute reveals most clearly the hopeless and yet unremitting aspirations of all epistemology to do without presuppositions. The problem of priority simply cannot arise within the various sciences which

---

[1] This would be the place for a philosophico-historical 'explanation' of the kind referred to in pt. 1 (cf. above, pp. 41 ff.), why a definite theory of knowledge selects precisely this or that one of the possible fundamental sciences. This is also the point where epistemology can be 'infiltrated', to a certain extent, by the various world views, and by other philosophical disciplines (cf. above, p. 38).

may serve as fundamental disciplines; since, being an 'intersyste-matic' problem, it overlaps the primary systematizations of these sciences, it must be recognized as a specifically epistemological problem.[1]

Priority for psychology is assured, according to the psychologistic theory of knowledge, on the argument that everything the sciences can talk about is originally given in the form of experience. From which it would follow that the fountain-head of all knowledge can be reached (genetic approach!) by going back a stage beyond the matters of fact we know to that mode in which knowledge initially arises for us, and on which alone we can draw, namely to experience. And because psychology is the science of experi-ence, we must admit it to be the fundamental, universal science.

Priority for logic is pleaded on the following counterclaim: granted that everything the sciences can talk about is first en-countered at the level of experience, it still is by no means proved that all we can *know* about this original experience is also given in experiential immediacy. And even assuming that all we know about experience belongs in the domain of psychology, surely the fact remains that psychology itself is a science and must as such 'work out' these ultimate pre-scientific data with logical means in order to make them intelligible. From which it would follow, rather, that the alleged 'ultimate origin', the irrational itself, is only to be reached by means of logic and, once it is reached, becomes transformed into something entirely logical. In a word, psychology is, like any other science, of logical structure.

Priority for ontology, in turn, is urged on the ground that every-thing to be met with at all is an instance of 'being' in the most general sense. From this point of view, both experience and logical validity[2] also appear as modes of being. Whatever we are talking about, the reference is to some interrelated existents; hence, we should seek to determine, before everything else, the possible kinds of being and their possible interconnections. The knowing subject is here itself taken for a component of Being; the general laws of Being as such contain and validate the special laws of Knowing. The logical connections are reinterpreted as ontological ones. A metaphysical system is presupposed, and epistemology is worked out on its pattern.

Epistemology based on ontology can again be of two types. There are those epistemologies which remain this side of episte-mological doubt, failing or refusing to recognize that the only

[1] The intersystematic character of epistemology will be discussed further in the sequel (cf. below, p. 71).
[2] An example of such an ontological conception of validity would be Lask's doctrine.

way in which Being can be given to us is as a *known* Being (naïve metaphysics). And on the other hand, there are those epistemologies which, although they have passed through epistemological doubt, nevertheless admit that the ultimate elements of all knowledge can only be grasped in ontological terms. Although it is possible to get along for a time without identifying the ultimate elements as Being, any theory of knowledge that is carried to its logical conclusion will have to reintroduce Being at some stage or other, because we cannot, in the last analysis, grasp these ultimates as 'not Being' or 'beyond Being'. The difference between the two types is that the naïve ontological theory posits the objects of knowledge as Being in the unmodified form as they are empirically given, whereas the latter theory of knowledge holds that the ontological constitution of the object is a matter of the ultimate elements.

This type of epistemology can be contrasted with the former, naïve theory as '*ex-post ontological* theory of knowledge' because it can reach its conclusion only by way of refuting the arguments of 'logicist' epistemology; its doctrine is that the very nature of thinking entails the necessity of the ontological hypostasis, of the acceptance of the primary systematization of ontology.

Ex-post ontological theory of knowledge is unmistakably the outcome of the third approach we mentioned above, the indirect one (cf. above, p. 49). It is, as we know, characteristic of this method that it does not aim directly at the ultimate presuppositions but prefers the indirect approach, i.e. it begins by exploring which one of all the possible postulates will finally stand revealed as an indispensable assumption.

If we analyse this approach further, and ask in what sense the ontological postulate is indispensable, then it will at once become manifest that this postulate is indispensable in building up any epistemological system. Logic can be developed without making any ontological assumptions, but not epistemology grounded in logic; the reason for this is that the epistemological question at some point implies a reference to Being, and that as soon as this reference is eliminated the epistemological problem itself will vanish.

This non-eliminability of the ontological postulate in epistemology is intimately bound up—as we shall show from another angle and in greater detail—with the correlation of the knower and the known, specific to epistemology. This correlation cannot be eliminated from epistemology without suppressing epistemology itself. And the correlation of the knower and the known cannot be maintained if they are not recognized as 'being' in a certain sense.

So we see there is nothing accidental about the type of epistemology that starts with logic and ends up with an onto-logical postulate. Its indirect approach enables such a theory to become aware of the ultimate basic axioms of every possible epistemology in general; it also compels the theory, on the other hand, to see in these axioms the ultimate presuppositions of all knowledge. For epistemology of this type, the ultimate presuppositions of knowledge itself would be none other than the in-dispensable postulates of epistemology.[1]

The principal arguments advanced by the three, or rather four, types of epistemology in the priority contest can now be given in a progression of brief mottoes as follows:—all that is given is (exists)—however, everything is given, in the final analysis, as experience; but then, every experience, inasmuch as we are aware of it, is an experience known; and again, the whole of it, experience as well as validity, is nothing but various types of Being. That these theses can all be asserted at the same time and in a way with the same justification is only possible because every one of the universal systematizations (psychology, logic, and ontology) makes visible in a recognizable, if modified and inadequate, form the basic fact underlying the other two to which it accords a new function within its own context; experience can be looked upon as a kind of meaning, meaning as a mode of being, and both being and meaning can again be regarded as different experiences (the experience of logical convincingness or evidence, for instance, which is so important for judging, reappears in the logical systematization again as validity). All these systema-tizations are formally universal precisely because they can absorb no matter what object. And as soon as an element is incorporated in an alien system, the new function it assumes there will appear, from the viewpoint of the original systematization, as an arbitrary hypostasis (in the example just cited, timeless logical validity will appear, from the point of view of psychology, as an unjusti-fiable hypostasis of the psychic feeling tone of evidence).

Hypostasis will in fact have to be redefined in a wider sense than usual. Most writers only deal with ontological hypostasis,

[1] There can be no doubt but that this type of epistemology (whose historical realization has not yet emerged) would employ as its fundamental science just this analytic of structure *qua* logical doctrine of systematizations, and that it would recognize, as its ultimate presupposition, the primary systematization laid bare by such an analysis. The possibility of such a theory of knowledge is supported by the fact that, as we have seen, logic is eminently fit to be a fundamental science for epistemology. Is there any reason why a logic that is oriented on philosophical know-ledge no less than on knowledge of natural science should not become the fundamental discipline for epistemology? Whether such an epistemology—which would have its own logic as basis—would in fact amount to a *meta-critique* of all epistemology in general presents an exceedingly knotty problem. This is not the place to follow it up since my object is deliberately confined to a logic of epistemology (cf. above, p. 41).

which is taken to mean that some element, organically belonging in some other systematization, is arbitrarily transplanted into the ontological sphere. It is, however, possible to hypostatize on other planes the ontological one as well; thus, validity, the basic fact of logic, appears from the psychological level, as shown, as the hypostasis of an experience. The term ought therefore to be defined in the context of a comprehensive doctrine of systems, as the way in which a basic fact appears when viewed from the perspective of a systematization other than its own.

If the discussion in this chapter has made clear the contributions of logic, psychology and ontology to the corresponding type of epistemological system, if it has succeeded in showing at the same time that the basic difference between the three possible types of epistemology consists in their relying on different fundamental sciences, then the further question will now have to be raised whether the disciplines that affect epistemology so decisively will not carry with them their own conceptual systems. In order to elucidate the role of the fundamental sciences in the working out of the conceptual system of epistemology, however, we must first clearly delimit the concepts which can be considered as 'specifically epistemological'.

4. SPECIFICALLY EPISTEMOLOGICAL CONCEPTS ANALYSED

(Subject-object Correlation)

So far we have tried, wholly on the basis of an analysis of the task of epistemology, to mark off its limits and its relation to any of the fundamental sciences with which it may be associated. The same approach should further disclose the specific concepts which are always involved in the raising of the epistemological question. What is it—we shall have to ask—that we posit of necessity just as soon as we raise the epistemological problem? Or we might put it in this form: what happens to a discipline, or to science in general, when it is made the object of an epistemological inquiry? Science as such consists in consolidating certain images into facts.[1] Epistemology, in its turn, adopts these same 'facts' as its material, without the least modification of their matter or form, merely by labelling them 'cognitions'. From the status of directly apprehended facts they are transferred to the status of facts *qua* known. What is implied in the statement that something is removed from the status of a fact to the status of a cognition? It means that the concept of knowledge involves that of the subject-object correlation.[2] By stamping the facts of science

[1] Cf. W. Windelband, *Einleitung in die Philosophie*, pp. 194 ff., Tübingen, 1919.
[2] Where 'object' denotes the object to be known or cognized.

with the hall-mark of knowledge, epistemology places them in between the two terms of the subject-object correlation. Only in so far as there is an object, cognitively apprehended by a subject, can anything be knowledge.

Yet this point already calls for some reservations. Subject and object are by no means such unambiguous and clear-cut concepts —at any rate in respect of their content—that we could make use of them as if they were exactly defined. The concept of subject, for instance, has a different content in logic, psychology, and ontology; it means something quite different in aesthetics[1] and ethics. Besides, the empirical Ego is far too vague to serve as a starting-point, especially since a thorough analysis of the pragmatic use of this term will disclose considerable variations in its denotation[2]: it may mean a kind of pale derivation of the concept of ontological substance, and again of the logical or psychological Ego.[3]

Which Ego-concept, then, is the one employed by the theory of knowledge? There is no peculiarly epistemological concept of the Ego, and a comparison among the diverse theories of knowledge will show it to vary from case to case; all, however, have one thing in common—they are directly borrowed from that discipline which the epistemology in question uses as its fundamental science. If the ultimate presuppositions are taken to be logical, we shall be confronted with the logical subject; if they are regarded as psychological or ontological, we encounter the psychological or ontological subjects respectively.

In accordance with this, we must modify the previous dictum that the subject-object concepts are the specifically epistemological concepts. Epistemology, in fact, has to borrow its concepts of subject and object from other sciences, varying from case to case. Nevertheless, there is something constant in epistemology—the logical tension obtaining between these two terms, their correlation which can be inspected as a logical entity in its own right. The structure of any correlation implies, of course, that the correlation as such is not affected by any modification of the terms. The correlative nexus can be inspected in its own right, it may become the object of an act of thinking directed to it *qua* relation, without any definite idea being entertained concerning the specific nature of the terms; the correlation is a functional logical unit as contrasted with the various possible sets of its terms.

[1] Cf. G. Lukács, 'Die Subjekt-Objektbeziehung in der Aesthetik', *Logos*, vol. 7, 1917–18.

[2] Cf. Rickert's analyses in *Der Gegenstand der Erkenntnis*, ch. 2, Tübingen, 1915.

[3] What Rickert chooses to call the epistemological Ego would in our terminology be defined as the logical Ego. The two are synonymous for him since, following Kant, he grounds epistemology in the fundamental discipline of logic.

This subject-object correlation as such, unaffected by any idea of the nature of the terms, is the proper contribution of epistemology to the elements borrowed from the fundamental sciences; here we have tracked down those concepts which are specific to epistemology. 'Knowledge' in the expression 'theory of knowledge' essentially involves this correlation as a variable function. By calling the findings of science 'cognitions', epistemology inserts them, so to speak, between the two poles of the indeterminate subject-object correlation.

Confronting, however, this conclusion derived from the mere analysis of the concept of 'knowledge' with the various epistemologies that have actually materialized in the course of history, we shall be disappointed to find a good many discrepancies. Thus we are led to review our previous conclusions; careful analysis, then, will show that they also suffer from an internal contradiction. Our next task is, accordingly, to elucidate and, if possible, eliminate this two-fold difficulty.

The inherent contradiction in our final result is principally this: We said at one point that the sciences consolidate subjective images in the form of facts. This means that it is of their very nature to de-subjectify to the limit; inasmuch as they transform what was first and foremost a subjective state into an objective scientific finding, they eliminate all that could possibly smack of a subject. And the reason why all science is objectification, utmost de-subjectification, is that every science is of logical structure.[1] Yet if it is true that science is maximal de-subjectification, how could we ever claim that epistemology needs a subject to 'fill out' its indeterminate subject-object correlation, and that it will borrow this subject from one or another fundamental science? If, being sciences, they are predicated upon de-subjectivization, they could not possibly provide epistemology with a subject-concept.

The second difficulty—also pointing the need for revising our previous line of thought—is raised by the evidence of actual historic theories of knowledge, as follows: Although it is true that the subject-concept crops up repeatedly in individual epistemological systems, these latter hardly ever, for all that, put the problem as one might expect, i.e. 'how is the subject related to the object?' Instead, they prefer some other formulation, such as the relation between consciousness and being; and in logistic theory the same question reappears as one concerning the relation of truth and reality, or, more pointedly, that of objectivity and reality.

[1] On the characteristic of the logical as, essentially, de-subjectification, cf. among others, R. Hermann Lotze, *Logik*, pp. 15 ff., Meiner, Leipzig, 1912.

Once the two difficulties are compared, it becomes manifest that the immanent contradiction involved by the analysis of the cognitive concept and its discrepancies with historical facts both boil down to the same thing. The same reason which prevents the various sciences from making use of the concept of Ego also impels the actual, historically developed theories of knowledge to substitute such terms as consciousness, truth, or objectivity for the term 'Ego' in developing the idea of the subject-object correlation.*

And this reason is, quite simply, that whenever epistemology presses the findings of logic or psychology into service, it cannot there discover an Ego but only its different objectifications: data that already owe their being to scientific de-subjectification and are thus of an objective import. Even in psychology, which would appear to be the discipline most intimately tied to a subject, concrete 'experience' fails to appear; we only have to do with 'experience' as de-subjectivized and transformed into an objective 'phenomenon' through the intervention of certain general categories of thought. The aggregate of all objectified appearances is defined in psychology as 'consciousness', and as 'objectivity' (the totality of all valid propositions) in logic. That is why we meet in the theories of knowledge with either 'consciousness' or 'objectivity', rather than with an 'Ego'.

The essence of the objective disciplines is that they desubjectivize the actual experiences, and produce neutral 'meanings'. Thus, when the theory of knowledge makes use of these, it can only confront meanings with meanings. The subject itself is never 'cognizable', because it is not a unitary something that a theory could objectify. It is the 'vehicle' of every 'experience', but never an element among all given elements.

All this, however, accentuates our difficulty still further: what is it, then, that we call the Ego in logic and in psychology? —for of course we have no intention of denying that the term has a legitimate use there. The solution is this: although the sciences never have room for a subject as an object to be known, it is always possible to construct a subject as a complement to the objectivized logical or psychological subjects—and it is this we are in the habit of designating briefly as the logical or psychological subject.[1] Subjects of this kind are not 'really' (in this sense of the word) 'directly known' or 'intuited'; they are constructs. And the further puzzle now is: how can they differ from one another in this case? how is it possible that the logical subject should be different from the psychological one, seeing that both

[1] As far as the ontological subject is concerned, the position seems to be rather more complicated, so that the above account will not necessarily do just as it stands.

are reconstructed *via* an objectified subject? If all sciences are alike made up of objectfications, one would expect the reconstructed subject always to be the same. However, even if it is true that all sciences objectify, they do so to a different extent. The degree of objectification possible is dependent upon the particular meta-logical and primitive 'given' we wish to pick out from the 'flow of experience' for the purpose of objectification. Every meaning refers to something—and the farther this something is from being completely objectifiable, the more intimately it is bound up with the stream of experience from which it is raised to the object-status, the more subjective, also, will be the corresponding meanings. Meanings always clearly show a greater or lesser degree of objectivity in that they are more or less intimately bound up with the 'flow of experience', and it is always possible to ascertain this degree of objectivity by inspecting them.[1]

The primary 'given' of psychology, ineffable in itself and indicated but vaguely by the 'experience', is open to a far lower degree of de-subjectivization than the basic fact of logic; the basic facts of aesthetics and ethics, in their turn, can be graded in between these two extremes with regard to their degree of objectivity.

To be sure, all the various disciplines alike operate with meanings; these meanings, however, invariably show the measure of this rootedness in the flow of experience—they refer back to the 'primary stratum' from which they have been objectified. This degree of closeness to the concrete experience differs from one science to another, and the concepts of the 'reconstructed' subjects, evolved alongside the 'objectivized' subject concepts of the various sciences, vary accordingly. Epistemology then proceeds to use these 'constructs'—based upon the objectivized concepts provided by the various fundamental sciences—to give substance to the subject-object correlation which is its own specific contribution. These subject concepts are 'constructs' (which is not to say they are without truth-value), because they are not obtained by the objectification of something initially given; subjects of this kind do not appear *within* the series of successive objectifications but are reconstructed as *counterparts* to the various objectifications, corresponding to their degree of definiteness and de-subjectivization.

In this complicated way alone is it possible to explain such a complex idea of subject as Kant's 'consciousness as such'. By its structure and by its content, it unmistakably reveals itself as something reconstructed; it is nothing but the vehicle of

[1] Cf. E. Lask, 'Gibt es einen Primat der praktischen Vernunft in der Logik?', in the *Proceedings of the Third International Congress on Philosophy*, p. 674, Heidelberg, 1908.

universally valid forms—a concept that has not arisen in the normal course of cognition as a result of objectification, but reconstructed as a subjective correlate to universal validity.

5. ELEMENTS OF A TYPOLOGY OF THE THEORIES OF KNOWLEDGE

The exposition and analysis of the subject-object correlation have provided us with the most important factors of epistemological concept-formation. This correlation is so specific to epistemology that we may go so far as to declare that any train of argument will tend to become an epistemological one as soon as this correlation enters into it, even though it be only implicitly; and, conversely, even the most characteristically epistemological theory will cease to be epistemological in nature the moment it is driven by its inner dialectic to make either of the terms of the correlation absolute, thus destroying the correlation as such.

In order to avoid any ambiguity, we shall replace the term 'subject-object correlation' by the terms 'knower' and 'to-be-known', and accordingly re-formulate our thesis as follows: the epistemological position is the outcome of characterizing the 'facts' given in science as 'knowledge', i.e. of inserting them as a third term between the two terms in the correlation of the knower and the to-be-known. This is how the triadic relation of epistemology comes about, i.e. the *knower*—the *known* (the cognition or knowledge)—the *to-be-known*.

Every epistemological systematization is based upon this triad, and every conceivable formulation of the problem of knowledge is given by these three terms in some combination (provided it is logically meaningful).

What a typology of epistemology would have to do, then, is this: to prove that the number of possible approaches hinges on this logical structure, and to examine how this simple state of affairs is complicated by concepts and correlations imported from the fundamental sciences. This will make it clear how even the most complex systems grow out of the most general schema of epistemological systematization, and show up the simple, formal-logical framework that constrains every kind of epistemological *motif*, however varied in content, into a single edifice of thought.

Nor is this logical typology of the possible ways of putting the problem all we can do; since the number of possible solutions we may attempt is equally limited, it is also possible to set up a typology of possible solutions. Finally, once the typology of formulations and solutions of the problem is completed, the most important question remains to be dealt with, namely: how does the formulation of the problem predetermine what solutions will be possible? It would, in short, be necessary to determine certain close connections that exist between the formulation of our problem and its subsequent solution.

To fill in the details of this general outline is beyond the scope of the present study; all that will be said here is in the nature of contributions towards such a prospective typology, not going beyond setting the course for such a further elaboration.

Insertion of the foregoing analytic results into the above-mentioned triadic relation will yield the following diagram of epistemology in general:

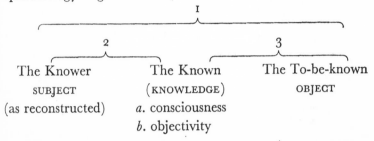

As we are already aware, the three basic concepts—the knower, the knowledge, the to-be-known—vary in content along with the fundamental science employed by a particular theory of knowledge. Of the three, it is the middle term that changes most conspicuously; in logistic epistemology it is called objectivity (the totality of valid propositions), in a psychologistic theory consciousness (the totality of possible experiences). The place of the knower, too, was found to be occupied by various subjects alike only in that they are all reconstructions. The nature of the third term, however, is ontological from the beginning; none but the monist system would blur this characteristic in their concept-formations, they alone seek to resolve it in one of the other two.

The three terms of the relation can be coupled in three different combinations (indicated by numbered braces on the diagram), and every one of these can serve as the starting-point for approaching the epistemological problem; the remaining two relations will then adapt themselves to the one chosen as starting-point.

Ontologically grounded theories of knowledge consider as primary above all the relation between the knower and the to-be-known (no. 1). It is tacitly taken for granted, even before the epistemological problem is raised, that this connection is onto-logical. Even before the problem of epistemology is raised, we know, implicitly or explicitly, that the knowing subject as well as the object to be known are of the same 'stuff of Being' (cf. a solution like Leibniz': both the knower and the world to be known are monads). Since on this showing the ontological relation must be taken as unproblematical, the only question to be dealt with is how the relation between the knower and the known (2), and that of the known and the to-be-known (3) are to be conceived.

In contrast with this, the logistic theory of knowledge starts from the relation between objectivity and reality (no. 3), and the others, (1) and (2), take shape accordingly. (Kant's epistemology exemplifies this type, though not in complete purity; the logical tendency inherent in it is developed most consistently by the Marburg School.)

Even at this stage of the proceedings we are able to recognize a special problem for logistic epistemology, a problem that can only be seen in sharp focus from the viewpoint of structural analysis. On a logistic theory of knowledge, namely, the knowing subject can appear as the first term in two distinct correlations—as paired with objectivity (2), or again with a reality to be known (1). Now 'objectivity' belongs to the realm of logical validity, and 'reality to be known', to that of ontology; by being paired with the former and the latter successively, the subject term itself alternately assumes a 'validity' or 'reality' character: the first term is, so to speak, affected by the character of its correlate. 'Consciousness as such', for instance, as the subject in the Kantian system is called, is originally a reconstructed subject of a purely logical character without any ontological overtones whatsoever; yet as soon as it is brought into correlation with the 'thing-in-itself' it immediately partakes of this latter's 'manner of being' which is essentially ontological.

Needless to say, epistemology of a purely logistic type will go to any length in order to avoid even this minimal ontological hypostasis, and will therefore do its best to get rid of the thing-in-itself altogether. The trouble is that that can only be done at the level of pure logic. No sooner does the subject of epistemology come up again, than it will be necessary to assume a thing to be known and its content, if only as an ideal limit; and though it would be possible to cut down the content of this limiting concept to zero, even that would not dispose of the concept itself as an ontological postulate.

After this somewhat longer discussion of logistic epistemology, we must go on to inquire more closely into the relational tie which in the theory of knowledge links the terms chosen as the starting-point. It would be far too vague to say that the epistemological starting-point is simply a bringing into relation of the three basic terms; in fact, the category of relation is much too general to do justice to the differences among individual systems in this respect. In any given case we meet with connections calling for a more specific characterization than that afforded by the indiscriminate use of the term 'relation'. Consciousness and being, for example, are not just related in the various systems, but a specific theory will always contain a clúe as to whether this relation is as whole to its parts, or as ground and consequence, etc.

How many forms this correlation can take is determinable *a priori* on the following principle: there can be as many concrete relations as there are categories of dyadic relations in logic which can be applied reasonably, without material contradiction. Consciousness and being, the self and reality, can stand in the categoreal relations of correspondence and causality, or of inherence and identity.

The point has at any rate been raised, thanks to Windelband,[1] that the relational categories already to some extent predetermine the solutions that will be possible. In a way the very setting of the problem of knowledge already prescribes the possible theories of knowledge, such as the dogmatic, the sceptic, the agnostic, the problematic, the phenomenological, the solipsist and the conceptualist; and according to Windelband the various solutions are primarily determined by the categoreal relation which connects the terms chosen as the starting-point.

This categoreal relation is already specified by the way of formulating the problem, and it determines at the same time the distance between the correlate terms. Strictly speaking, the attempt to solve the epistemological problem only begins at the point where we try actually to bridge the distance in this fashion.

The essence of epistemological systematization may, then, be seen as consisting—in so far as its logical structure is concerned —in the resolution of the correlations involved in formulating the problem. That is the central task on which turns every effort of epistemological thinking, down to the smallest detail: to resolve a self-made correlation, or to span a self-made gap.

It is exceedingly difficult, for instance, to bridge over the gaps between objectivity on the one hand, and the subject and reality respectively on the other—or, in other words, to appraise the proper share of both the subject and reality in the attainment of objectivity.

To the performance of this task, epistemology can rally surprisingly few types of mediating solutions, considering the complexity of the problem. Kant[2] already recognized the three

[1] *Op. cit.*, pp. 213 ff.
[2] Immanuel Kant, *Critique of Pure Reason* (B 166 ff.), pp. 174 ff., transl. Norman Kemp Smith; Macmillan & Co., 1933.

possibilities, and Leibniz, too, advanced a typology of the conceivable ways to bridge the gap in his analogy of the two clocks. The three types of mediation are: (1) the knower achieves knowledge by reproducing that which is to be known—the representational or copy-theory; (2) the object world, the known, is evolved by the unaided effort of the knowing subject—the spontaneity-theory; (3) knowledge arises on the basis of an order pervading the knower and the to-be-known alike—the theory of preformation or pre-established harmony.

In what way a given epistemology bridges its gap depends, firstly, on the categoreal relation that determines the distance between, for example, consciousness and reality; secondly, on the fundamental science employed; and finally, on whether the mediating operation starts from the subjective or from the objective end. Rickert[1] laid special emphasis on this last circumstance. A comprehensive typology would at this point have to follow up certain phenomena which always occur together, in order to find out which of these types of mediation correspond to what point of departure. Here it need only be mentioned in passing that starting from the object is *prima facie* likely to lead to some kind of copy-theory, while starting from the subject would be apt to issue in a spontaneity theory. And it is no less plausible that a theory of knowledge, having started from the subject and then, in the course of developing its thesis, drawing closer to the stand of realism or objectivism, will eventually be forced to abandon its characteristic concept of spontaneity, and will have to adopt a copy-theory or else some principle of pre-established harmony. A case in point is Kant who, in his polemic against Eberhard, reached a position where he was ready to assume a Leibnizian type of pre-established harmony[2]; another would be Lask[3] who set out with the intention of building upon Kant, but, in the course of working out his ideas, found himself compelled to introduce the concept of copy.

All in all, it is surprising how few ways of mediating between the terms of its correlations are available for epistemology, and one can hardly help believing that future developments might bring about an increase in their number.

That alone goes to prove that the various ways of mediating are a less specific and clear-cut criterion of epistemological thinking than the subject-object correlation is. No *a priori* survey could cover them, since their number may always increase, whereas the

[1] Rickert, 'Zwei Wege der Erkenntnistheorie. Transzendentalpsychologie und Transzendentallogik', *Kantstudien* XIV, pp. 169 ff., 1909.
[2] Cf. A. Brunswig, *Das Grundproblem Kants*, pp. 41 ff., Leipzig-Berlin, 1914.
[3] E. Lask, *Die Lehre vom Urteil*, Tübingen, 1912.

subject-object correlation is amenable to an *a priori* typology, independent of historical developments. That the types of mediation are more or less derivative, that they are imported from alien spheres, is apparent from their historical contingency and can be confirmed further by a simple analysis of their meaning along the following lines: A closer look at the concept of spontaneity, say, will soon convince us that this concept properly belongs with psychology, or conceivably with ontology; such spontaneous activity can, after all, be attributed only either to a consciousness or to a substance. Yet Kant attributed spontaneity to an unreal, a merely reconstructed subject, i.e. 'consciousness as such'; and the paradox involved in this will only be explicable if we recall the hybrid character peculiar to epistemological systematization. To be sure, the imported concepts, spontaneity and the like, serving as logical mediators, all undergo a metamorphosis in the employ of an epistemological system, in the course of which they gradually shed the last traces of their foreign derivation; and in virtue of this they qualify, though not as 'basic' concepts, yet at least as 'stock' concepts of epistemology—the more so as they occur in all three types of epistemology.

Taking, then, the subject-object correlation together with these stock concepts as the specific elements of epistemology, the question arises whether a typological survey based upon such a small number of classificatory concepts can in fact do justice to the profusion of historically realized systems. A detailed typology would, furthermore, also have to pay attention to those concepts which have been taken over from one or the other fundamental science.

Our main concern is with the determination and analysis of elements specific to the theory of knowledge, so that there is no obligation to go beyond what has been said already. All the same I propose to add a brief discussion of the concepts which a logistic theory of knowledge takes over from logic—not more than is needed to give us an idea of how the originally simple typological situation is complicated by the intervention of elements from alien systems, and what lines a thorough typology would have to pursue on this account.

Logistic theory of knowledge proceeds, as stated above, from the relation between objectivity (cognition) and reality (the to-be-known); to be quite accurate, it really begins by analysing the middle term of the triadic relation, i.e. with an analysis of 'knowledge'. To this end, epistemology, according to our previous conclusions, has no means of its own, and utilizes on occasion the findings of logic, which thereby becomes its fundamental science. The analysis which logic performs on knowledge splits up this latter into moments of form and of content; that is how the form-content correlation comes into logistic epistemology. All logistic theories of knowledge are at one in that they comprise this correlation—where they differ is in the ways of resolving it.[1]

In this correlation, then, which cannot be derived from extra-logical premises, logic has a characteristic, quasi-axiomatic foundation, and the various possibilities of resolving the fundamental correlation afford the distinguishing principle for the systems erected on a logical basis; the form-content correlation is, so to speak, the source of all further ramifications.

The possibilities of resolving it are of three kinds: the reduction of content to form (Marburg School), or the reduction of form to content (logical realism, and in a certain sense Lask as well), or the assumption of some principle of a higher order in which the two coincide—but the last as a rule leads into metaphysics. Then, of course, there is also the way of strictly preserving this dualism, never allowing it to be resolved—the way of Kant.

It is on this fundamental logical correlation of form and content that logically oriented epistemology builds on a higher plane the essential epistemological correlation of subject and object. Sometimes the form falls to the part of the subject while the content is somehow to be derived from the object, and sometimes the form falls to the part of the object, the content being subjective—thus, thinking and systematizing are more fluid, in so far as this point is concerned; it is here that the different schools and currents which all started out with the same initial premises clash with one another.

Here at last we also can offer a more concrete formulation of the problem we described as the ultimate question with which every structural analysis has to deal: how far is it possible to deduce from the structure of epistemological systematization both the uniformity of epistemological thinking and the principle of differentiation which makes for the sundry individual systems? (Cf. above, pp. 42 ff.).

On the evidence available so far we can already state: the uniformity is guaranteed by the correlations that are posited with quasi-axiomatic necessity; the differences, on the other hand, can be accounted for by the fact that the correlation, owing to the peculiar nature of its givenness, allows for various logically possible resolutions. The logical structure of epistemological systematization—which commits us to a certain course but does

---

[1] That various ways of resolving this correlation are possible without contradiction is only explicable in view of the peculiar way in which the correlation of form and content is given to us. This point should be analysed separately; for some remarks on this problem see p. 69, below.

not exactly determine the path to be followed— must be recognized as the pivot of any typology, as well as the guarantor of its very possibility.

For epistemology as such, the specific subject-object correlation is constitutive, and any epistemological theory is concerned with the determination and resolution of this correlation. In so far as one variant of epistemological theory, the logistic one, is concerned, however, this overall task is supplemented by the introduction of another correlation: that between form and content. This involves further possibilities of resolution, thus rendering the task more complex.

In a logistic theory of knowledge the fundamental correlations are partly indigenous to epistemology, partly taken over from logic; every such correlation in turn allows for several possible solutions. Each logistic theory of knowledge, then, represents a combination of two of these *a priori* possible solutions. The same applies to either of the other types of epistemology, i.e. the psycho-logistic and the ontological theory of knowledge, with the only difference that the basic correlation of the respective fundamental science takes the place of the form-content correlation. An ontological theory, for instance, will substitute the correlation of substance and accident for that of form and content.[1]

6. STRUCTURAL ANALYSIS OF EPISTEMOLOGICAL VALUATION

We have mentioned above (p. 47) the dual task of all epistemology: firstly, to analyse all possible knowledge with a view to laying bare its ultimate presuppositions, and secondly, to ascertain whether these ultimate presuppositions can guarantee the cognitions grounded in them to be true knowledge—in other words, to evaluate those ultimate presuppositions. Epistemology involves both a task of analysis and one of evaluation. Up to this point, our study has been concerned only with the former task; we asked merely how epistemology manages to succeed in its quest for the ultimate presuppositions of knowledge. We spoke of epistemology as if it were merely a theory of knowledge and not an evaluation of knowledge as well. And it now remains for us to investigate this aspect of it—the evaluative one.

The outcome of the preceding discussion—which we must still bear in mind—was that epistemology cannot uncover the ultimate presuppositions that constitute its topic by a method and instrumentalities of its own, by an analysis *sui generis*—that it must, on the contrary, rely on other sciences if it is to acquit

[1] Cf. A. Pauler, 'A Korrelativitás elve' ('The Principle of Correlativity'), pp. 46, 48, publ. in the journal *Athenaeum*, Budapest, 1915.

itself of this self-appointed task, and that it is precisely in connection with this fundamental problem that those alien sciences
intervene and invade its domain as its fundamental sciences. It
further emerged that the analysis as such is by no means all that
is borrowed from alien spheres, but that epistemological concept-
formation also is influenced by the respective fundamental
science. Uniquely specific to the theory of knowledge, as we have
come to see, is alone the correlation of subject and object, and
even that only as an undetermined function. Its actual content
is in every case supplied by the discipline that operates as the
fundamental science for the analysis.

At this point the question arises whether the theory of knowledge also borrows elsewhere the standard of value it needs
to evaluate the ultimate presuppositions discovered; more precisely, what is the relation between a particular appraisal of
ultimate presuppositions and the value involved by it, on the one
hand, and the specific discipline from which the analysis derived,
on the other.

The most direct way to an answer seems to consist in subjecting
the current criteria of (cognitive) truth to a structural analysis;
it is in them, in fact, that epistemological valuation culminates.
There are three distinct types:

I. The transcendent, ontological criterion of truth: every proposition must be accepted as truth if it corresponds to reality,
to being.

II. The formal or logical criterion of truth: every proposition
must be accepted as truth if its thought is fraught with logical
necessity (conforms to logical forms).

III. The psychological criterion of truth: every proposition
accompanied by a feeling of evidence must be accepted as
truth.

A critique of these criteria of knowledge would be out of place;
we shall limit ourselves to structural analysis and merely ask
which value factor is stressed by the various criteria.

Every one of these criteria of knowledge comprises three important factors: (1) that which valuated; (2) the value in respect of
which the former has to be considered valuable; (3) a third
term which serves as the standard for the prospective valuation.
The first two terms are the same for all three criteria—the
valuated is always the proposition, the value in terms of which it
is judged is truth; it is only the standard that varies from case to
case.

The first criterion of knowledge applies the yardstick of being,
the second that of logic, and the third the feeling of evidence. It
becomes immediately apparent that the number of the criteria

of knowledge is the same as that of the types of epistemology we have distinguished on the basis of the possible choices of fundamental sciences, every criterion being correlated with a specific type of epistemology. Ontological theory of knowledge elects for its epistemological standard the ontological criterion of knowledge, logical epistemology employs the logical criterion, and psychological theory of knowledge the psychological criterion.

Contrary to what one might expect, a theory of knowledge does not measure the ultimate presuppositions laid bare by its fundamental science against one of these alien yardsticks; what it does do is, rather, to set up this ultimate presupposition, implicit in its concept of knowledge and underlying its analysis, as itself the standard of value, the criterion of knowledge. In other words: the truth criteria occurring within an epistemology are closely related to the particular science that supplied the analytic means for the quest after ultimate presuppositions. The locus of the ultimate cognitive presuppositions is also taken to be that of the cognitive value standards. If knowledge is claimed to be experience at bottom, then experience will be the bearer of value and its guarantee; if it is asserted to be ultimately logical, then it is logic that will provide the criterion of truth; and the same applies to the ontological theory of knowledge.[1] The case for the criterion to be chosen is already settled in accordance with the outcome of the priority contest that precedes the adoption of a specific epistemology. The way in which the problem is formulated also determines the *distance* between that which is to be valuated and the standard by which it will be judged.

In case I, for instance, the relation that is to hold between being and the known (the proposition) is determined as soon as the criterion is set up, that is, before the solution. For if I assert that propositions corresponding to being can alone be true, then even before adopting this criterion (which points to the realm of Being) I must already hold some preliminary metaphysical and ontological theory warranting that my two terms are homogeneous and commensurable. The theory of knowledge hinging on this criterion recognizes no obligation, on this showing, to adduce evidence that the ultimate principle—in this case, being—is a value; that is always somehow taken for granted. The aim of such a theory is rather to make clear (usually by recourse to a hypothesis of pre-established harmony), the value character of Being understood once and for all, how these two kinds of Being

---

[1] The most consistent in this respect is the logical theory of knowledge. Epistemology, being a theoretical discipline, cannot be valid without postulating the validity of the entire sphere in which it belongs.

(the known and the to-be-known), can enter into a relation one to the other, or how the former can manage somehow to embrace the latter.

The position is precisely the same in case II. Here too the relation between thought-current and being is fully determined before any discussion on this point; but being now appears as a kind of thought-content (just as thought-content was before taken as a kind of being). Being occurs only in the form of being thought, and we have merely the criteria of logic to determine which of the *a priori thinkable* contents are 'real'. The concept of objectivity, as expounded by Kant and his followers, is the inevitable consequence of adopting a starting-point exclusively from logic. To be real is to be the product of certain logical forms— it is impossible to adduce another concept of reality from other spheres for purposes of comparison. There is no need to prove that the objectivity engendered by logical principles is veridical, i.e. that its constitutive forms are valuable; what has to be done is merely to make clear—the value character of the logical forms serving as basic presuppositions being understood—how this objectivity with which we are confronted comes by its privileged character (in Kant's philosophy, this task is performed by the assumption of spontaneity).

The epistemological paradox can now be described as follows: Epistemology sets itself the task of solving on its own the problem of the cognitive efficacy of all factual knowledge and of appraising its value; in the course of its inquiry, it pushes this question of value further and further back, until it appears as the problem of the value of the ultimate presuppositions of all knowledge; and finally, it is compelled—after analysis has laid these ultimate presuppositions bare—simply to proclaim them as value (in the case of a sceptical theory, as negative value). Once this is done, the task of epistemology—supposing that its aetiological verdict is positive—assumes the following form: since the knowledge we have is known to be valuable by virtue of its presuppositions, *all we have to do is to construct a system to show after the event how we have managed to acquire such valuable knowledge;* or, in Zalay's formulation[1] of this dual demand: 'What must the knower be like if he is to be capable of actually getting to know that which is to be known, and what must knowledge be like if it is to be valid knowledge for a knower?'

Because of this internal reorientation, this rearrangement of the problem, the epistemological critique does not succeed in being, as it would have us believe, the critique of knowledge,

[1] *Op. cit.*, p. 173.

but only a new kind of systematization of it. Structural analysis discloses that epistemology actually solves a problem which is entirely different from the one it has set itself. *Instead of a critique of value, it turns into a theory about how a particular value can be attained and realized.*

Any theory of knowledge is hard put to it when it comes to the point of proving the ultimate presuppositions to be true values. That is the explanation for the well-known paradox in the Kantian system, whereby Kant grounds the necessity of *synthetic a priori* judgments in the concept cf spontaneity, justifying the latter in turn by means of the *a priori*. The circularity is anything but accidental, as we are now in a position to realize: it is the necessary consequence of the paradox involved in any epistemology.

Now we have to ask more specifically whether epistemological value is as such an alien element, an importation from the fundamental sciences, or whether these only determine in each case whether it is the one or the other thing—i.e. the ontological, the psychical or the logical—that is value-creating and valuable. We have previously recognized a phenomenological distinction between the value on the basis of which we evaluate, and the standard by which we judge. Is it, then, the value itself that the theory of knowledge borrows from some alien discipline, or is it only the standard that varies with the choice of the fundamental discipline?

The second hypothesis alone is borne out by the preceding analysis of epistemology. The truth-value remained a constant in every one of the criteria—the only variable being the standard. The value of being-known, the fact of being-true, is specific to the epistemological approach, and has come into being together with it. And this could not be otherwise, since it is quite impossible to borrow any value whatever (in this case that of epistemological truth) from any of the fundamental disciplines, these being no sciences of value at all—at least not psychology and ontology.

With regard to logic the situation is rather more complex. Here, it seems, the value of correctness is already involved—which is not to be identified, however, with epistemological truth. But even this value does not yet occur in pure logic which can be construed devoid of all reference to a subject. The domain of pure *logos* is as such—to quote Lask—'the plain interlocking of form and content' ("*das schlichte Ineinander von Form und Inhalt*"), a self-contained realm of meaning, also termed 'validity''. Not until we come to it from a 'science of thinking' or from epistemology, both of them taking the initiative of introducing the striving subject and thereby turning this self-contained sphere of univocally ordered elements of whatever nature into something to be attained, does this realm become a normative one, a realm of values and standards. Only in this way is the 'plain interlocking' of that which is valid *in se* transformed into something valuable.[1]

From the perspective of the 'science of thinking', of applied logic, the value is that of 'correctness'. It states no more than that only one kind of ordering of thought-contents is desirable for a thinking subject.

Correctness, which is the 'validity' of pure logic seen in the light of the science of thinking, is still far from mediating the knowledge of anything, from reaching or grasping a real or ideal object beyond the content of meaning. It is nothing save the putting of previously given contents into the right theoretical order pattern. In this respect, the procedure is still completely analogous to the order obtained—though by different formal laws—in the aesthetic sphere; there too it would make no sense to say that the aesthetically valuable (corresponding to the logically correct), the individual work of art, somehow reaches (let alone recognizes) some object beyond itself. Just as the aesthetically valuable ('lovely') melody[2] can be normative without representing anything external, so a logic devoid of epistemological premises (a science of thinking) need only be concerned with organized theoretical contents, not even raising the question whether anything can be at all known in this way.

What in pure logic appears as a valuation-free, 'plain arrangement', with its constitutive forms which only assume the character of 'correctness' in applied logic, is endowed by logistic epistemology with the value of 'truth' as well, so that in such a theory the value of correctness coincides with epistemological truth.[3] This, incidentally, is a reason why the difference between the two values is so elusive. (Even here there was talk of truth and validity when as yet no more than correctness was involved. It is only at the level at present reached by our inquiry that a firm distinction between the two becomes possible.)

If we now leave applied logic aside, it is clear that the facts of the logical sphere as such can be formulated without using normative language, no less than those of the psychological and ontological spheres; the realm of validity pure and simple is

[1] Cf. a hint in this direction on p. 126 of Lask's *Lehre vom Urteil*.

[2] I have deliberately chosen music, rather than any of the other arts, to illustrate my point since the problem of representation or reproduction would only complicate matters to no useful purpose. But even in the case of representational art, it should not be difficult to prove that the attainment of a model ("*sujet*") is (*a*) a problem of secondary importance, and (*b*) something entirely unrelated to the attainment of an object in the sense of "knowing" or "cognition".

[3] We have already noticed a similar congruence between the logical and the epistemological subject for such a theory (cf. above, p. 41, footnote 1).

as far from involving any specifically epistemological value as any of the other fundamental sciences.

Nothing can appear as valuable or normative as long as we remain within the context of psychological, ontological, or logical systematizations. A state of things which merely 'obtains' may become valuable and normative only if we look at it from another, alien systematization. Any purely descriptive state of things can be transformed into a normative, value-laden one by relating it to a value from a different viewpoint, by labelling it as 'something-which-is-to-be-attained'. There is nothing normative about the laws of mechanics as such; for the technician, however, who is engaged in building a machine, they will become norms, standards of that which is to be attained. This drastic example is only intended to drive home the point that, from the point of view of structural analysis, a value judgment always implies that we are looking at a state of things from an alien systematization which provides a value standard. This alone can explain the fact that there is a 'relatedness' involved in every valuation. (This, however, should not be taken as meaning that any descriptive field can be referred to any value whatever.) Epistemology is a systematization *sui generis* precisely because it alone enables us to place ourselves outside of the various universal systematizations, whereby it becomes possible to relate the purely descriptive states of things of the latter to the epistemological value of 'truth', to transform them into matters of value, into standards.[1]

The value of epistemology, the determination of its possibility, is not our concern. What we have been interested in throughout was only to lay bare its structure, with special reference to the question what is specific to the theory of knowledge as against all other systematizations, and whether it is to be regarded as a pure or a mixed systematization.

The result can be summed up to the effect that epistemology is far from pure in the sense in which the primary systematizations of ontology, logic, and psychology are pure systematizations. There is no serious obstacle in the way of conceiving a pure logic, or a pure ontology, free of all epistemological premises; but it is impossible in principle to construct a pure theory of knowledge. The latter does not belong to the primary systematizations. Moving among the primary systematizations, its essential contribution is to provide a foothold from where it becomes possible to observe these regions in their full extent. But although epistemology is an intersystematic pursuit, it is nevertheless not

[1] This intersystematic character of the theory of knowledge was already mentioned in the discussion on the priority contest (cf. above, pp. 48 ff). It is also related to the faculty of 'free choice of reference' (see pp. 45 f. above).

extrasystematic, for, after all, no pursuit of reason could be that. There is no such thing as a completely and finally isolated, self-sufficient mental creation. Even an action, let alone a concept, displays the structure of a systematization; it is this structure which gives it meaning and constancy, which in fact makes it what it is. A concept thus always presupposes a systematization, but that is by no means to say that within the realm of reason as a whole various systematizations, differing in the structure and coherence of their respective elements, could not co-exist. In fact, by contrasting the homogeneous 'primary' systematizations with the 'mixed', intersystematic ones, we have already indicated the co-existence of two radically different types of systematization; epistemology, of course, belongs to the latter. Now epistemology—notwithstanding its dependence on essentially alien fundamental sciences—still has a coherent field of its own, because it (1) deals with a question specific to it, (2) is concerned with a value *sui generis*, and (3) possesses a fundamental correlation particular to it, the subject-object correlation, which has to be posited quasi-axiomatically and is needed for the integration of the theoretical sphere.[1]

As a further characteristic of epistemological systematization, we must mention the 'constructive' nature of epistemology which became especially apparent while we examined the constitution of the various Ego-concepts. Epistemology constructs, instead of directly 'describing', an object. Although it must be recognized that so-called 'direct' description is not nearly as direct as the naïve view would have it—in that it, too, operates with concepts having a theoretical structure and a systematic locus—there is still a difference between a description and a construction. Only what is somehow presented to us can be described; but where the question points insistently beyond what is presented we have to infer and to construct. A descriptive science always answers questions of the form: 'How is it?' while the questions answered by a constructive discipline have the form: 'How must it be?' The epistemological question leads so far beyond what is presented—that being its proper meaning—that in its case any attempt to describe would be futile, and a construction alone is in order.

The preconceived notion that only 'direct sensual experience' accompanied by 'description' can lead to truth is, however, quite unjustifiable. The full value of truth attaches to a 'construction' as well, provided that its starting-point is *cum fundamento in re*

[1] As soon as the subject-object correlation is posited (i.e. once we decide to regard theoretical propositions as knowledge), there is no escaping any of a number of cognate problems. Hence, even the sceptic who doubts the solubility of the task of epistemology will have an epistemology in the sense of acknowledging a set of inescapable problems,

and its conclusions are free from contradiction; and that is the case with regard to epistemology.

Any attempt to vindicate epistemology from this point of view should begin by ascertaining how far the initial material of epistemology, presented in immanence, reaches and where the construction based on that material begins; it should then proceed by determining to what extent the immanent material not only permits, but requires a constructive complement by virtue of the very way in which it is given. The analytic of structure which is essentially interested in no other aspect of epistemology than the logical make-up of its constructive part would have to be supplemented by an inquiry into the mode of presentation of its ultimate presuppositions. *Nothing but an analysis of the mode of presentation of ultimate presuppositions could suggest a reason why divergent solutions of the epistemological problem are possible.* For it is characteristic of the constructive—as opposed to immanently descriptive—disciplines that, although in both only one of several suggested solutions can be true, the wrong solutions in the descriptive sciences are always impossible as well, whereas in a constructive discipline a wrong answer can be, not true, to be sure, but nevertheless possible. And this simply because the true thesis cannot triumph by recourse to a given but on the whole only by argument. Problems of this kind, however, go far beyond a logic and structural analysis of epistemology, and require a separate investigation and solution.

CHAPTER II

Conservative Thought

INTRODUCTION

1. *Styles of thought*

THERE are two main ways of writing the history of thought. On the one hand there is what might be called the 'narrative' way, which simply sets out to show the passage of ideas from one thinker to another, and to tell in epic fashion the story of their development. On the other hand there is the way with which we want to experiment here, which is based on the recently developed sociology of knowledge.[1]

At the heart of this method is the concept of a *style of thought*. The history of thought from this point of view is no mere history of ideas, but an analysis of different *styles of thought* as they grow and develop, fuse and disappear; and the key to the understanding of changes in ideas is to be found in the changing social background, mainly in the fate of the social groups or classes which are the 'carriers' of these styles of thought.

Anglo-Saxon sociology has developed a concept very similar to the German 'style of thought' in the term '*habit of thought*', and although there are considerable similarities there are also very great differences which we cannot ignore. The term 'habit of thought' simply expresses the fact that people automatically use established patterns not merely in their overt behaviour but in their thought too. In most of our intellectual responses we are not creative but repeat certain statements the content and form of which we have taken over from our cultural surroundings either in early childhood or in later stages of our development, and which we apply automatically in appropriate situations. Thus they are the products of conditioning just as are our other habits. The term is unsatisfactory, however, because it only covers

[1] Cf. Max Scheler, *Probleme einer Soziologie des Wissens*, Munich and Leipzig, 1924; K. Mannheim, 'Das Problem einer Soziologie des Wissens', in *Arch. f. Soz.-wiss. und Soz.-pol.*, vol. 53, pp. 577–652, 1925; 'Ideologische und soziologische Betrachtung der geistigen Gebilde', in *Jahrb. f. Soziologie II*, Karlsruhe, 1926; R. K. Merton.

one aspect of the phenomenon in question. Our concept of a 'style of thought' is similar to it in so far as it also starts with the assumption that individuals do not *create* the patterns of thought in terms of which they conceive the world, but take them over from their groups. But our concept is meant to imply a less mechanical attitude to the history of thought. If thought developed simply through a process of habit-making, the same pattern would be perpetuated for ever, and changes and new habits would necessarily be rare. A more careful observation of the history of thought makes it clear, however, that in a differentiated, and especially in a dynamic, society the patterns of human thought are continually changing, and if we want to do justice to these various forms of thought, we shall have to invoke some such category as 'style', since 'habit-making' will not carry us far enough.

It is, indeed, the history of art which provides us with a term capable of doing justice to the special nature of history of thought. There, too, the concept of 'style' has always played an important role, in that it made possible the classification of both the similarities and the dissimilarities of different forms of art. Everyone will accept the notion that art develops in 'styles', and that these 'styles' originate at a certain time and in a certain place, and that as they grow their characteristic formal tendencies develop in a certain way. Modern history of art has developed a very thorough method of classifying the principal 'styles' of art, and of reconstructing, within these styles, the slow process of change in which small modifications gradually culminate in a complete transformation of style. The method has become so exact that it is now nearly always possible to date a work of art accurately, simply by analysing its formal elements. The trained historian of art will always be able to say, even if a work of art is unknown to him: 'This must have been painted at such and such a date by a painter of such and such a school.' That a statement of this kind will not be mere guesswork is guaranteed by the fact that art does in fact develop in 'styles', and that within the styles there is a gradual change from one phase to another which makes it possible to 'place' an unknown work of art.

Now it is our contention that human thought also develops in 'styles', and that there are different schools of thought distinguishable by the different ways in which they use different thought patterns and categories. Thus it should be just as possible to 'place' an anonymous piece of writing as an anonymous work of art, if we only took the trouble to reconstruct the different styles of a given epoch and their variations from individual to individual.

Although the very rough division of thought into 'medieval', 'Renaissance', 'liberal' and 'romanticist' schools, as familiar in the history of philosophy or literature, may give the impression that the concept of 'styles of thought' is already generally accepted, we are for the most part prevented from recognizing their existence by two assumptions. One is that Thought is one, the same for all men, except for errors or deviations which are of only secondary importance. At the other extreme, there is the assumption (which in fact contradicts the first one) that the individual thinks independently and in isolation from his fellows. Thus the unique qualities of each individual's thought are overemphasized, and the significance of his social *milieu* for the nature of his thought is ignored. Applied to the history of art, this would mean either on the one hand that there is nothing but art as such, or on the other hand, that the individual artist is an absolutely unique, self-contained unit. Although we can neither deny the value of thinking about art in general, nor, on the other hand, ignore the differences between individual artists or the particular contributions made by each of them, the most important unit must nevertheless be the *style* of an epoch, against the background of which the special contribution of each individual stands out and acquires its significance.

But this intermediary level between the most abstract and the most concrete is just what is lacking in the history of thought. We are blind to the existence of styles of thought because our philosophers have made us believe that thought does not develop as part and parcel of the historical process but comes down to humanity as a kind of absolute entity; and our literary historians who have written monographs on the great literary personalities like to persuade themselves that the ultimate fountainhead of all thought is the personality of the individual. The former school makes the history of thought appear artificially homogeneous and indiscriminate, while the latter atomizes it. It is due to this lack of interest in this intermediary level that our tools for distinguishing styles of thought are not developed. We do not notice vital differences in styles of thought because we do not believe in their existence. Were we to take the trouble to watch the innumerable slight changes in the development of the mode of thought of a group throughout its history, the artificially imposed homogeneity or the indiscriminate atomization would give way to a proper differentiation.

This is exactly what we want to try to do in the pages which follow. We want to look at the thinkers of a given period as representatives of different styles of thought. We want to describe their different ways of looking at things as if they were reflecting the changing outlook of their groups; and by this method we hope to show both the inner unity of a style of thought and the slight variations and modifications which the conceptual apparatus of the whole group must undergo as the group itself shifts its position in society. This will mean that we shall have to examine all the concepts used by the thinkers of all the different groups existing in any particular epoch very carefully, in order to see whether they do not perhaps use identical terms with different meanings. Thus the *analysis of meanings* will be the core of our technique. Words never signify the same thing when used by different groups even in the same country, and slight variations of meaning provide the best clues to the different trends of thought in a community.

2. *The relationship between styles of thought and their social background*

Before developing further our method of demonstrating that styles of thought exist as relatively independent units, we must say a few words about the social 'carriers' of these styles. Just as a style of art cannot be fully described without an account of the artistic school and of the social group it represents, so we can never really understand changes in a style of thought unless we study the social groups which are the carriers of these changes. This relationship between a style of thought and its social carrier is not a simple one. It may be true that ultimately great changes in the class stratification of society are responsible for the broader changes in styles of thought; but when it comes to more detailed changes this general hypothesis needs modification. The main indication that there is some connection between the existence and fate of social groups on the one hand, and certain styles of thought on the other, is that the sudden breakdown of a style of thought will generally be found to correspond to the sudden breakdown of the groups which carried it; similarly, to the amalgamation of two styles of thought there corresponds an amalgamation of the groups. But there are reasons for thinking that this link between styles of thought and their carriers exists not only at the turning points of history in times of great social crisis. The fate of the group is apparently reflected in even the smallest change in the development of a style of thought.

3. '*Basic intentions*'

Any study in styles of thought characteristic of the first half of the nineteenth century must start with the fact that the French Revolution acted as a catalysing agent both in relation to different types of political action and to different styles of thought.

What we have so far said implies that a style of thought embraces more than one field of human self-expression; it embraces not only politics, but art, literature, philosophy, history, and so on. It implies further that the dynamic force which is behind its changing character lies deep below the concrete surface of the various ways of self-expression.

The history of art became a scientific discipline when it became the history of *styles of art* (*Stilgeschichte*). An exact description of each different style of art only became possible when Riegl introduced his concept of 'art motive,' or *Kunstwollen*, by which he meant the striving for a certain form of art, of which every style is the expression. This concept permitted him to refer all the works of art of a particular period to a basic and for the most part completely unconscious conception, in the spirit of which all the artists of the period appear to have created their works. He did not describe these art motives, these strivings behind the different styles of art, in a vague subjective way. He showed them at work in the different works of art of the period. He analysed them carefully, showing their growth, development and decay, and showing how they sometimes fused and inter-mingled with each other.

The concept which we wish to introduce here of a *basic intention* lying behind each style of thought is in many ways similar to that of Riegl's art motive, although different in certain important respects. In the first place it does not refer to art, but it expresses the idea that different ways of approach to the world are ulti-mately at the bottom of different ways of thinking. This basic drive determines the character of a style of thought. It manifests itself in the documents and utterances characteristic of that style. But whereas to Riegl this principle of style (this art motive) is something which needs no further causal explanation and has no particular social roots, the sociologist cannot assume that the basic intentions at work in the different styles have come 'out of the blue'. We must take it as axiomatic that they are themselves 'in the making' so to speak, and that their history and fate is in many ways linked up with the fate of the groups which must be con-sidered as their social carriers. Riegl was aiming at a pure '*Geistesgeschichte*'—a history of ideas and nothing more. Whereas in his view it was an unattached spirit which by some miracle communicated its decrees to us, the contention put forward here is that although the basic art motive can be detected in immanent analysis as the formal principle (*Gestaltprinzip*) of certain schools, it also can be shown as something ultimately born out of the struggles and conflicts of human groups. It can be used on occasion as an immanent principle to demonstrate that the mind does not work in an atomistic way, piling up shapeless experiences; but we must realize that, even in the process of experiencing, certain determining principles derived from the group are at work in the individual which shape his potential experience and knowledge. These determining principles can be approached by asking ourselves what are the social causes (lying outside pure *Geistesgeschichte*) which have produced them.

4. *A concrete example: German conservatism in the first half of the nineteenth century*

The next task is to find suitable material on which to try out this new method. We have chosen the development of conservative thought in Germany in the first half of the nineteenth century. This choice above all presents us with a limited task, as it focuses the analysis upon one period, one country, and one social group. This has the major advantage that it is possible to acquire all the published and otherwise accessible utterances of the group in question. Thus the continuity of the thought style can be fully and accurately reconstructed, and its connections with the social groups behind it can be more easily revealed. This choice is further justified by the fact that after the French Revolution, there developed what we may call a 'polarizing' tendency in thought—that is to say, styles of thought developed in very clear-cut extremes. The dividing issue was the political differences which developed under pressure of the events of the French Revolution. Different styles of thought developed along party lines, so that we can speak of 'liberal' and 'conservative' styles of thought, to which we shall later have to add the 'socialist' style. Now this polarizing tendency was especially marked in Germany. In Germany there has always existed a tendency to go to extremes in pushing logical arguments to their ultimate conclusions—a tendency which has not existed in such a marked fashion in the European countries outside Germany. This difference will be made clear by the example of romanticism.

Romanticism is a European phenomenon which emerged at approximately the same time in all countries. It arose partly as a reaction to identical circumstances and identical problems presented by a rationalized capitalist world, and partly as a result of secondary ideological influences. Thus the basic cause of this widespread historical factor is a common one—viz. the general similarity of the total situation in the various occidental countries. But it is never exactly the same in any two countries and always varies according to the social and cultural peculiarities of the different nations. It is striking to note, even in a comparison of different romantic writers, that, for instance, whereas the movement developed in France through the medium of poetry, in Germany it obtained its special expression in philosophy. Romantic poetry is less characteristic of German romanticism than is German romantic philosophy. This is merely a symptom of the fact that in Germany reactions on the philosophical level to changes in the social and intellectual substructure are far more intense than in other countries. As Marx already pointed out, the key to the understanding of modern development lies in a realization that Germany experienced the French Revolution on the philosophical plane.[1]

Just as the centre of gravity of German romantic idealism was its philosophy, German counter-revolution, or the 'opposite of the revolution' (to use a French traditionalist term)[2] developed its challenge to liberal-revolutionary thought in its logical and philosophical implications more completely than in any other country. If France played the role of radical reconstructor of all the enlightened and rationalistic elements in consciousness, and thus became the acknowledged bearer of 'abstract' thought, it is also possible to say that Germany played a complementary role in so far as she turned conservative, organic, historical thought into a weapon, giving it at the same time an inner consistency and logic of its own. Even this ideological difference between the two countries is rooted in certain social and historical factors.[3] It is usual to consider England as the typical home of evolutionary development, and the Romantics especially have impressed us with the conservative aspect of this gradualism by presenting England as both evolutionary and conservative. This is doubtless correct to a certain extent—especially if England is contrasted with France, which is in fact the typical radical revolutionary country of the new era. But these evolutionary features are also characteristic of the development of Germany. In Germany there has been no revolution (in the radical French sense), but at most internal growing pains and temporary disturbances. However, gradualism in England is based on the fact that the conservative strata possessed an enormous elasticity and adaptability to new circumstances, and could therefore always ensure in advance the maintenance of their power. The evolutionary character of German development, on the other hand, rested on the strong pressure of the ruling groups on the lower strata, preventing revolution. The existence of this strong barrier against internal disturbances of all kinds is almost certainly connected with the fact that the military set constituted the nucleus of the German social body. (This in its turn is connected with the geographical

1 Cf. *Zur Kritik der Hegelschen Rechtsphilosophie*, vol. I, pp. 389 ff., posthumous works by Marx and Engels, ed. Mehring.
2 Cf. de Maistre, 'Nous ne voulons pas la contre-révolution mais le contraire de la révolution.'
3 Cf. Ernst Troeltsch, *Der Historismus und seine Probleme*, vol. 1, Tübingen, 1922; *Naturrecht und Humanität in der Weltpolitik*, Berlin, 1923; P. R. Rohden, 'Deutscher und französischer Konservativismus', in *Dioskuren*, vol. 3, pp. 90–138.

situation, especially of Prussia between two enemy countries, which naturally led to the formation of a military state). And this meant a strong backing for both the conservative movement and its intellectual and emotional development.

This difference in the character of the development of the two societies, evolutionary in both cases, in so far as it was free from sudden eruptions, yet so essentially different in reality, must have had an effect on the form and structure of their respective ideologies. It is most clearly reflected in the political antagonisms as we noticed them emerge at the beginning of the period with which we are concerned. For a very long time in Germany, liberalism had no hold on conservatism, and influenced it very little. We have to wait until Stahl before we can detect the first traces of any liberal influence on conservatism. Up to that time, the two currents stood in sharp contrast to each other. On the other hand, the relations between Whigs and Tories in England up to 1790 were such that it is hardly possible to express them in German terms at all. In particular, what were known in Germany as the 'Liberals' in no way corresponded to the English Whigs. That the basic intention, the practical social motives behind conservatism were manifest in so sharp and pure a form in German thought, must be partly attributed to this almost antithetical structure of German political life, which produced a situation in which even the partial interpenetration of parties and social strata as it occurred in England was impossible. Further, of even greater importance was the ability of German conservatism to maintain itself intact in doubtful periods, and the fact that whereas, for a long time, conservatism developed quite independently of liberalism, liberalism allowed itself to be penetrated by conservative elements. So far as we are in a position to judge, England never showed such a sharp polarization into extremes, even in the later period when the French Revolution had played its part in sharpening social relations there.

Further, in Germany, quite half a century of uninterrupted intellectual development stood behind conservatism. It had therefore had time to educate itself and to equip itself philosophically without having to cope with the demands of a parliamentary life which, by continually embroiling it in factional strife, would certainly have interfered with its purity and consistency.[1] As soon as parliamentary life begins, the definite contours of *Weltanschauungen* and ideologies rapidly lose their sharpness. That they can still, though faded, penetrate through to the present, is due to the fact that the incubation period, so to speak, was a very long one, so that there was time for the ideology to

[1] A Conservative Parliamentary Party first appears at the Prussian Diet in 1847.
E.S.—6

develop thoroughly and consistently according to its own logical principles. The magic of the French Revolution provided just the right stimulus to induce people to occupy themselves with these political and philosophical matters, while the hard facts of reality were not yet mature enough to demand action which inevitably leads to compromise and logical inconsistency.

This then is the situation: under the ideological pressure of the French Revolution there developed in Germany an intellectual counter-movement which retained its purely intellectual character over a long period and was thus able to develop its logical premises to the fullest possible extent. It was 'thought through' to the end. The counter-revolution did not originate in Germany; but it was in Germany that its slogans were most thoroughly thought out and pursued to their logical conclusions.

The main stimulus actually came from England—much more politically developed than Germany at that time. It came from Burke. Germany contributed this process of 'thinking through to the end'—a philosophical deepening and intensifying of tendencies which originated with Burke and were then combined with genuinely German elements. Even the way in which Burke is received and dealt with is characteristic, however. Burke was anything but what his first German translator Gentz and his friend A. Müller believed him to be.

Müller makes him a reactionary, whereas Burke, although increasingly conservative as he got older, still retained so much of the concept of Liberty, that even the modern English liberals can quote him to their own advantage.[1]

In other words, Germany achieved for the ideology of conservatism what France did for the Enlightenment—she exploited it to the fullest extent of its logical conclusions. The Enlightenment started in England, in the most forward and progressive area of capitalist development. It then went over to France—there to achieve its most radical, abstract atheistic and materialist form. Counter-revolutionary criticism of the French Revolution originated in the same way in England, but achieved its most consistent exposition on German soil. The really basic elements of thought, for instance of 'historicism,' are to be found in embryo in Burke. Yet 'historicism', as a method and a philosophical outlook, appears to be a product of German conservative thought and when it ultimately appears in England, it is as a result of German influence. Maine, in his *Ancient Law* (1861), is the disciple of Savigny.[2] That conservatism in Germany was worked out to

[1] Cf. Fr. Meusel, *Edmund Burke und die französische Revolution*, p. 141, Berlin, 1913; Friedrich Braune, *Edmund Burke in Deutschland*, Heidelberg, 1917.
[2] Cf. Ernest Barker, *Political Thought in England*, pp. 161 ff.

its logical conclusions, and that the antitheses in the predominant *Weltanschauung* of the time are so easily visible, can be attributed partly to the lack of an important middle class, able to maintain an independent social balance and thus to pursue an independent intellectual synthesis between the two extremes. In so far as such a middle class existed at all, it either developed intellectually *within* the framework of conservatism, where it played a moderating role of which we shall have to speak again later; or it lapsed into an extreme, liberal scholastic dogmatism which again only went to sharpen the extremes.[1] To this already existing impetus to separation into extremes was added another geographical one. Whereas the Rhineland and South Germany came under the direct influence of France, and were thus the seat of German liberalism, Prussia and Austria were the main citadels of conservatism. This geographical difference, to say nothing of the economic differences, also went to sharpen the antithesis.

Thus it is clear, taking all these factors together, why the antithesis between liberal and conservative thought is to be found in its sharpest and most logically consistent form in Germany in the first half of the nineteenth century, and why sociological forces here enabled a social development which remained at a complex and confused stage in France and England to achieve the greatest logical and structural consistency. This is why it is just in this German period that we can follow in the sharpest outline the impact of social forces upon the very logical structure of thought, and why we chose this topic as a starting-point of our analysis of the significance of political elements in the development of thought.

Our choice has the disadvantage, however, that it suggests that political action is always the centre around which styles of thought crystallize. This is not necessarily the case. Our contention is only that in the first half of the nineteenth century politics gradually became the centre around which the differences in both the fundamental attitudes and the *Weltanschauungen* of various social groups developed. In other periods, religion might have been the crystallizing agency, and it only requires further explanation to show why in this period politics were so decisive in the formation of

[1] It is not correct to say that 'German thinking' as such is conservative, or that 'French thinking' as such is oppositional and liberal. What can be maintained is only that conservative thought was most consistently developed in all its implications in Germany, owing to certain peculiarities in the German sociological situation; the same applies, *mutatis mutandis*, to rationalism and libertarianism in France. A. de Tocqueville already pointed out that the predominance of general ideas and deductive systems in French pre-revolutionary political writings was due to the particular sociological position of the French *literati* of that period, rather than to some intrinsic quality of the '*esprit français*' (cf. *L'Ancien Régime et la Révolution*, 8th ed., p. 217, Paris, 1877).

styles of thought. In spite of this, however, it would be wrong to draw too clear-cut a distinction between politics and philosophy and to regard political thought as socially determined but not philosophy or other types of thinking. Such distinctions between philosophy, politics, literature, etc., only exist in textbooks and not in real life, since, given that they belong to the same style of thought, they must all emanate from a common centre. If only one penetrates deeply enough, one will find that certain philosophical assumptions lie at the basis of all political thought, and similarly, in any kind of philosophy a certain pattern of action and a definite approach to the world is implied. From our point of view, all philosophy is nothing but a deeper elaboration of a kind of action. To understand the philosophy, one has to understand the nature of the action which lies at the bottom of it. This 'action' which we have in mind is a special way, peculiar to each group, of penetrating social reality, and it takes on its most tangible form in politics. The political struggle gives expression to the aims and purposes which are unconsciously but coherently at work in all the conscious and half-conscious interpretations of the world characteristic of the group.

We do not mean that every philosopher is nothing but a political propagandist, or even that he himself is necessarily committed consciously to a certain political point of view. A philosopher, or even an isolated thinker, may be quite unaware of the political implications of his thought, and yet develop attitudes and categories of thought, the social genesis of which can be traced to a special type of political activity. Kant, for example, is the philosopher of the French Revolution, not primarily because he was in full sympathy with its political aims, but because the form of his thought (as reflected for example in his concept of the *ratio*, in his belief in gradual progress, in his general optimism, and so on), is of the same brand as that which was a dynamic force behind the activities of the French revolutionaries. It is the same form of active penetration into the world. It is this which unconsciously produces the categories and ways of interpretation common to those who are bound by the mutual bond of a common style of thought.

SECTION 1
Modern Rationalism and the Rise of the Conservative Opposition

Social differentiation reflects itself not only in different currents of thought but also in a differentiation, on a more general plane, within the mental climate of the age. Not only thought, but even the ways in which people experience things emotionally, vary with their position in society.

It has often been pointed out that the most characteristic feature of modern thought is its attempt to achieve a thorough rationalization of the world. The growth of natural science is nothing more than a consistent pursuit of this aim, which no doubt existed in earlier times. No one could deny the presence of some rational element in medieval Europe or in the civilization of the Far East. But rationalization in those cases was only partial, since it tended to merge too readily into irrationality. The characteristic quality of capitalist bourgeois consciousness is that it knows no bounds to the process of rationalization.

Modern rationalism as a method of thought finds its clearest and most radical application in the modern exact sciences. In that form it mainly arose in opposition to two main streams of thought—medieval Aristotelian scholasticism on the one hand, and the philosophy of nature of the Renaissance on the other. There is no better way of understanding the novel element in the rationalism of modern science than to investigate the aspects of these two streams of thought which it chiefly opposed.

The Aristotelian conception of the world was opposed because of its qualitative approach, because it held that the form of a thing is determined by a teleological aim which inheres in it. The new thought strove for a conception of the world which would explain the particular in terms of general causes and laws and present the world as a mere compound of physical mass and physical forces. It was their desire to overcome qualitative thinking that impelled modern scientists to turn to mathematics and to make it the basis of their analysis of nature.

The philosophy of nature of the Renaissance which at first continued to exert a considerable influence on the pioneers of scientific rationalism was opposed because of its magical elements and its tendency to think in terms of analogies. This side of the struggle reveals another aspect of modern rationalism. Rationalization as an opponent of qualitative thinking and rationalization as an opponent of magical and analogical thinking are two fundamentally different phenomena which were then only accidentally united.

But behind both there stands a basic attitude which holds them together. It is the desire not to know more about things than can be expressed in a universally valid and demonstrable form, and not to incorporate them into one's experience beyond that point. One tries to exclude from knowledge everything that is bound up with particular personalities and that can be proved only to narrow social groups with common experiences, and to confine oneself to statements which are generally communicable and demonstrable. It is therefore a desire for knowledge which can be socialized. Now quantity and calculation belong to the sphere of consciousness which is demonstrable to everyone. The new ideal of knowledge was therefore the type of proof which is found in mathematics. This meant a peculiar identification of truth with universal validity. One started out from the wholly unwarranted assumption that man can know only where he can demonstrate his experience to all. Thus, both anti-qualitative and anti-magical rationalism, from a sociological point of view, amount to a dissociation of knowledge from personalities and concrete communities, to its being developed along wholly abstract lines (which, however, may vary among themselves).

The characteristic of this conception of knowledge is that it ignores all concrete and particular aspects of the object and all those faculties of human perception which, while enabling the individual to grasp the world intuitively, do not permit him to communicate his knowledge to everybody. It eliminates the whole context of concrete relationships in which every piece of knowledge is embedded. The theory, in other words, takes into account only general experience, an experience which is general in a twofold sense. It relates to many objects and is valid for many subjects. The theory is interested only in the general aspects of objects and appreciates in man only that which 'generalizes', i.e. socializes him, that is to say, Reason.

This 'quantitative' rationalist form of thought was possible because it arose as part of a new spiritual attitude and experience of things which may be described as 'abstract' in a related though not altogether identical sense.[1] A symptom of this change is the decline, or eventual repression of pantheism which accompanies the tendency to 'quantify' nature.

It has often been pointed out that the rationalism of modern natural science has its parallel in the new economic system. With the substitution of a system of commodity production for a subsistence economy there takes place a similar change in the attitude towards things as in the change-over from qualitative to quantitative thinking about nature. Here too the quantitative conception of exchange value replaces the qualitative conception of use value. In both cases therefore the abstract attitude of which we have been speaking prevails. It is an attitude which gradually comes to include all forms of human experience. In the end, even the 'other man' is experienced abstractly. In a patriarchal or feudal world the 'other man' is somehow regarded as a self-

[1] For an analogous 'quantifying' tendency in ancient thought, see Erich Frank, *Plato und die sogenannten Pythagoreer*, pp. 143 ff., Halle, 1923.

contained unit, or at least as a member of an organic community.[1] In a society based on commodity production, he too is a commodity, his labour-power a calculable magnitude with which one reckons as with all other quantities. The result is that as capitalist organization expands, man is increasingly treated as an abstract calculable magnitude, and tends more and more to experience the outside world in terms of these abstract relations.

The psychological possibility of approaching men and things differently of course remains, but now the possibility exists of treating the world abstractly in a systematic and consistent manner. As to the sociological factor which accounts for the growth of this consistent rationalism, the common view is no doubt correct, that it is the rising capitalist bourgeoisie. This must of course not be taken too crudely. It is not that every individual bourgeois approached the world in this way continuously and at all times, but merely that the social aims of the bourgeoisie as the propagators of capitalism made such a consistently abstract and calculating form of experience possible. Other social strata could of course share and absorb this attitude to the world and to their environment. But it became really overwhelming and repressed all other tendencies, in those social strata whose daily life and work was immediately bound up with relations of this kind.

Most attempts to describe the general development of modern thought tend to pay exclusive attention to the growth of rationalism. The result is a picture quite incompatible with historical facts and the world as we know it. In fact, this mechanized world, this abstract form of experience and thought by no means exhaust what we know of our surroundings. A complete view of the present situation will reveal the falsity of a one-sided emphasis upon rationalism; it will lead us to recognize that the intuitive, qualitative, concrete forms of thought which rationalism repudiates have by no means disappeared altogether.

Our problem begins at this point and the study of conservative thought takes on a practical importance. We want to know: *what became of all those vital relationships and attitudes, and their corresponding modes of thought, which were suppressed by the rise of a consistent rationalization?* Did they merely sink into the past, or were they in some way conserved? If they were conserved, in what form have they been handed down to us?

As one might expect, they did in fact persist, but as is usually

---

[1] Cf. Marx on human relations in the Middle Ages: 'The social relationships of persons engaged in production appear, at any rate, as their own personal relationships, and not disguised as social relations of things, of products of labour' (*Das Kapital*, 9th ed., p. 44, Hamburg, 1921'

the case in history, they were submerged and became latent, manifesting themselves at most as a counter-current to the main-stream. They were taken up and developed further, at first by those social and intellectual strata which remained outside the capitalistic process of rationalization or at least played a passive role in its development. The personal concretely human relations which previously held sway were kept alive in varying forms and degrees primarily in the peasant strata, in the petit-bourgeois groups which had descended directly from the handicraftsmen of earlier times, and in the aristocratic tradition of the nobility.

In particular, we find that the unbroken tradition of the religious sects like the Pietists[1] maintained ways of life, attitudes and ways of experiencing things, particularly in their spiritual life, which were bound inevitably to disappear from the lives both of the bourgeoisie as it became more and more drawn into the capitalist process and of the industrial working class.

Even these strata, however, bound up as they necessarily were with the rationalizing process of capitalism, did not entirely lose their original way of life. It merely disappeared from what we may call their *public* and *official* life. Their *intimate* relationships, in so far as they remained untouched by the capitalist process, continued to develop in a non-calculable, non-rationalized man-ner. They did not become abstract. In fact, the phenomenon to which Max Weber also refers, the gradual *recession into privacy* of certain spheres previously public (the spheres of life in which personal and religious feelings prevail), is in the nature of a com-pensation for the increasing rationalization of public life in general —in the workshop, in the market-place, in politics, etc.

Thus the irrational and original relation of man to man and man to things is driven henceforth to the periphery of capitalist life—and this in two senses. In the first place it is driven to the periphery of the individual's life in so far as in contrast to the increasingly rational development of the more representative spheres of life only the more intimate and private of human re-lations remain vital and alive in the old sense. Secondly, from the narrower point of view of social stratification: it is the repre-sentatives of the new social order, the bourgeoisie and the pro-letariat, which become more and more immersed in the new modes of life and thought, and it is only at the periphery of the new society—among the nobility, the peasants, and the petit-bourgeois—that the old traditions are kept alive. Here, at the peri-phery in both these senses, slumber the germs of a style of thought and life which at one time dominated the world. For a long time these germs remained hidden, and did not emerge as a 'trend',

[1] Cf. G. Salomon, *Das Mittelalter als Ideal der Romantik*, pp. 118 ff.

as something conspicuous, until they became relevant to the social struggle and were adopted by the counter-revolutionary forces, who inscribed them on their banner.

The sociological significance of romanticism lies in its function as the historical opponent of the intellectual tendencies of the Enlightenment, in other words, against the philosophical exponents of bourgeois capitalism. It seized on the submerged ways of life and thought, snatched them from oblivion, consciously worked them out and developed them further, and finally set them up against the rationalist way of thought. Romanticism took up just those spheres of life and behaviour which existed as mere undercurrents to the main stream of bourgeois rationalism. It made it its task to rescue these elements, to lend them new dignity and valué and to save them from disappearance. 'Community' is set up against 'society' (to use Toennies' terminology), family against contract, intuitive certainty against reason, spiritual against material experience. All those partially hidden factors at the very basis of everyday life are suddenly laid bare by reflection and fought for.

It is well known that romanticism developed from the Enlightenment as antithesis to thesis.[1] No antithesis escapes conditioning by the thesis it sets out to oppose, and romanticism suffered the same paradoxical fate; its structure was fundamentally conditioned by the attitudes and methods of that very movement of Enlightenment in opposition to which it originally developed.

Romanticism tried to rescue these repressed irrational forces, espoused their cause in the conflict, but failed to see that the mere fact of paying conscious attention to them meant an inevitable rationalization. Romanticism achieved a rationalization which the bourgeois Enlightenment could never have carried through, not only because its methods would have proved inadequate to the task, but also because the psychic material in question would never have been significant enough for it to pay lasting attention to it. Irrationalism, like everything else in a given period, can only be understood in terms of the prevailing intellectual climate. When this general climate is rationalist, then even irrational elements have to be submitted to rational reflection if they are to be understood. Thus romanticism may be interpreted as a gathering-up, a rescuing of all those attitudes and ways of life of ultimately religious origin which were repressed by the march of capitalist rationalism—but a gathering-up and conserving *at the*

[1] Franz Oppenheimer calls romanticism an 'intellectual counter-revolution' and explains its genesis in terms of an *'imitation par opposition'* in Tarde's sense (cf. *System der Soziologie*, vol. 1, pp. 4 ff., Jena, 1922). Romanticism, however, was no mere negation of the revolution; it had a positive content of its own.

level of reflection. What the romanticists did was not to reconstruct or revive the Middle Ages, religion, or the irrational as the basis and foundation of life; it was something entirely different: a reflexive and cognitive comprehension of these forces. This was by no means the original aim of romanticism; but, as it happened, it worked out suitable methods, modes of experience, concepts and means of expression for all those forces which were for ever inaccessible to Enlightenment. Thus all those ways of life and attitudes to men, things, and the world, which for almost a whole epoch had been largely invisible were once more brought to the surface. They were brought to the surface not, however, in their old form as the natural basis of social life, but as a task, as the content of a programme.

Sociologically, these factors, once brought to the level of reflection, tended to link themselves up with certain anti-capitalist tendencies.

All those social strata which were not directly interested in or were perhaps even menaced by the capitalist process and were, moreover, bound by tradition to the lost ways of life of the various pre-capitalist stages of social development, made use of their discoveries against the bourgeoisie and industrialism. The historical alliance of the enlightened monarchy and the entrepreneur meant that both were interested in rationalism, while the feudal powers, small peasant proprietors and the petit-bourgeois strata which sprang from the old craft-guilds were all interested in varying degrees in romanticism.[1] As these romantic elements emerged in a conscious, reflexive form, these strata all contribute something of their own to them. Especially, however, when it comes to a struggle round cultural questions in which these elements are consciously exploited, these strata invariably plunder romanticism for certain elements which they then incorporate into their own ideology.

The task of our investigation then is as follows. We have to show how the political and social 'right-wing opposition' not merely took up arms against the political and economic domination of rising capitalism, but how it opposed it intellectually too, and gathered up all those spiritual and intellectual factors which were in danger of suppression as the result of a victory for bourgeois rationalism, even to the extent of working out a 'counterlogic'.

It is generally believed that the socialists were the first to criticize capitalism as a social system; in actual fact, however, there are many indications that this criticism was initiated by the right-wing opposition and was then gradually taken over by the left opposition; we must, of course, try to find out what shifts of

[1] Cf. G. Salomon, *op. cit.*, p. 111, pp. 118 f.

emphasis made this reception of 'right-wing' *motifs* by the 'left-wing' opposition possible.

In fact, the type of thought which arose in conjunction with the proletariat and its social aims has much in common with the type associated with the right-wing opposition, but the essential structural differences between them must not be overlooked. The proletariat has grown out of capitalism; it is its own peculiar creation and has no tradition behind it outside capitalism itself. The 'fourth estate' is no estate but a class. Its adherents have become blended into a unified class by having been torn out of the old background of 'estates' and 'organic groups' in which their ancestors had lived. With the rise of the new world, estates tended to be eclipsed by classes, which increasingly took over the function of articulating collective action. Yet many groups, especially those with strong local, non-urban roots, performed the transition only gradually, and among urban groups, artisans retained many features of the old guild-mentality. The proletariat alone, herded together in factories, developed from an inchoate mass into a completely new class with its own traditions. In so far, however, as this new social entity emerged within the rationalist epoch itself, it tended to exhibit rational characteristics of thought to a greater degree perhaps even than the bourgeoisie. Yet it would be a mistake to see in proletarian rationalism nothing but a variant of bourgeois rationalism.

Its own dynamic, the logic of its own position, easily impels this type of rationalism to transform itself into a peculiar kind of irrationalism.

The proletarian mode of life is essentially rational because its position in the world compels it to plan revolution on a calculatory basis even more than the bourgeoisie had done. The proletariat makes even revolution a matter of bureaucratic administration and transforms it into a 'social movement'. Yet its brand of rationalism and bureaucratic management has very little in common with that desire for calculability characteristic of the successful bourgeoisie. Proletarian rationalism in fact, so long as it is in opposition, can never do without the irrational element at the basis of all revolutionary action. The utopian ideal of the bourgeois is to make every enterprise so calculable that every element of risk is completely eliminated. That this ideal is not realized, and that risk and uncertainty still adhere to capitalist enterprise, is due simply to the fact that the capitalist world is only partially rationalized, only partially based on a planned economy.

On the other hand, even when the percentage chance of success can be assessed, say in the case of a strike, by the use of strike statistics, and similar analyses, action is still not wholly dependent

on a favourable outcome to the calculations, since the chances of
defeat are not really determinable in so far as revolutionary *élan*
always remains an uncertain factor.

At this point it becomes quite clear that the social position of
the proletariat forces it into irrationalism. The attempt at revolution, however planned and 'scientific' it may be, inevitably
produces an irrational 'chiliastic' element. Here lies its essential
affinity with the 'counter-revolution'.

Proletarian thought has in many ways a significant affinity
with conservative and reactionary thought. Although deriving
from entirely different basic aims, this affinity nevertheless unites
the two modes of thought in opposition to the aims of the bourgeois capitalist world, and the abstractness of its thought. A
further investigation—which cannot here be undertaken—of the
fate of these inherently irrational 'chiliastic' elements in proletarian thought would have to show that they derive in the last
resort from what may be called the 'ecstatic consciousness'. One
would have to show how from their beginning in the peasant
revolts of the sixteenth century they became the germ of all
revolutions, and how they were even retained as part of the otherwise extremely highly rationalized proletarian outlook on the
world. Here then we are confronted with a combination of the
most extreme rationalism with some of the most extreme irrational
elements; this shows that the 'irrational' proves on closer observation more complex than we are at first inclined to imagine.

An exhaustive analysis would need to show the very fundamental difference between the irrational elements produced by
the 'ecstatic consciousness', and that other type which we have
hitherto for the sake of brevity described as the remains of the old
religious tradition and frame of mind, and towards which Romanticism tended in a later epoch.

At yet another point, however, the proletarian revolutionary consciousness is directly connected with the conservative tradition—i.e.
in dialectics. There was an inner necessity in Marx's taking over
the idea of dialectic from the conservative Hegel. The concept of
dialectic—the logical sequence of thesis, antithesis, and synthesis—
seems, on the surface, extremely rationalist, and indeed it was an
attempt to condense the whole process of development into a single
logical formula, and to present the whole of historical reality as
rationally deducible. Yet this type of rationalism is nevertheless
completely different from that other type which finds expression in
the bourgeois ideal of the natural sciences. The latter seeks to establish universal laws of nature; it is a democratic, non-dialectical type
of thought. It is not surprising, therefore, that the latest, democratic and 'scientifically minded' generation of socialists did

their best to eliminate the dialectical element from Marxism altogether.

Thus, closer observation of rationalism shows that it has different variants which we have to keep apart, just as we above found it necessary to distinguish between 'chiliastic' and contemplative mystical (romantic) irrationalism.

As a matter of fact, as we shall see more clearly later on, the dialectic in Hegel serves to solve problems which are really romantic problems, and which live on in the historical school.

The chief function of the dialectic is to provide a rational understanding of the 'historical individual'—i.e. of the individual in all his historical diversity and uniqueness. In the rational search for universal laws and generalizations the individual tends to be lost altogether; but the dialectical approach restores him as a component part of a unique process of historical growth and development. Thus the attempt to understand the essentially irrational, historically unique individual in rational terms constitutes a paradox within dialectics, since it produces a form of rationalization which must involve the supersession of rationalism itself.

The second function of all dialectics which relates to its inner meaning rather than to its external formula is to trace the 'inner line' of growth of a civilization. Here again, therefore, it rationalizes what is essentially irrational and foreign in every way to non-dialectical, naturalist thought.

In the third place, dialectics is a form of approach which seeks to find a meaning in an historical process. It is a philosophical rationalization of history. It therefore involves a form of rationality which it is very difficult to reconcile with the positivism of natural science, to which all ethical evaluations and metaphysics in general are completely alien.

Taking all this into consideration, we are forced to admit that already through Hegel a close alliance is effected between rationalism and conservative thought—notwithstanding the fact that the latter is far removed from that form of naturalist rationalism which considers everything as calculable. That Marxism could go such a long way with the Hegelian school of historical thought, that it was at all possible that it should oppose the natural-law tradition in bourgeois thought in the same way as did the historical school, although from a different point of view, indicates that both had factors in common which must not be overlooked.

Nevertheless, in spite of all these affinities and similarities between proletarian and conservative thought, the basis of the proletarian mentality is strictly rational and fundamentally related to the positivist trend of bourgeois philosophy. This positivist basis is clear in the way in which the proletarian philosophy of history derives the dynamic of events from the social and economic spheres and interprets the movement of ideas in terms of a social movement centred round the economic organization of society. At this point, proletarian thought therefore embodies the gradually developed bourgeois concept of the primacy of the economic sphere. Proletarian thought is therefore rational in so far as it must pass through capitalism as a necessary phase in historical development; in a certain sense it is even more rational in that it has not merely to accept the process of capitalist development, but actually to accelerate its tempo. To the same extent, it is, however, irrational in so far as it is forced to rely on a 'self-reversing' tendency in capitalism; this self-reversal represents an element of irrationality or even 'super-rationality' as opposed to the directly traceable particular causal relations of bourgeois rationality.

However, it is not our task here to follow all this out in detail. We found it necessary to refer to proletarian thought in order to be better able to understand our historical period.

Our own field now narrows itself down. We shall be dealing with a strictly delimited phase in the development of thought. Our problem then is to trace the development of conservative thought in the first half of the nineteenth century in Germany, and to relate this development to the social background of the time.

SECTION 2

The Meaning of Conservatism

1. *Traditionalism and conservatism*

Let us begin by analysing more exactly what we mean by 'conservatism.' Is conservatism a phenomenon universal to all mankind, or is it an entirely new product of the historical and sociological conditions of our own time? The answer is that both sorts of conservatism exist. On the one hand, there is the sort that is more or less universal, and, on the other hand, there is the definitely modern sort which is the product of particular historical and social circumstances, and which has its own peculiar traditions, form and structure. We could call the first sort 'natural conservatism',[1] and the second sort 'modern conservatism', were it not that the word 'natural' is already heavily burdened with many different meanings. It will perhaps be better therefore if we adopt Max Weber's term *'traditionalism'* to denote the first

[1] Cf. Lord Hugh Cecil, *Conservatism*, Home University Library of Modern Knowledge, pp. 9 f., New York and London.

type; so that when we speak of 'conservatism' we shall always mean 'modern' conservatism—something essentially different from mere 'traditionalism.'

Traditionalism signifies a tendency to cling to vegetative patterns, to old ways of life which we may well consider as fairly ubiquitous and universal. This 'instinctive' traditionalism may be seen as the original reaction to deliberate reforming tendencies. In its original form it was bound up with magical elements in consciousness; conversely, among primitive peoples, respect for traditional ways of life is strongly linked with the fear of magical evils attendant on change.[1] Traditionalism of this kind also exists today, and is often similarly connected with magical hang-overs from the old consciousness. Traditionalism is not therefore necessarily bound up, even today, with political or other sorts of conservatism. 'Progressive' people for instance, regardless of their political convictions, may often act 'traditionalistically' to a very large extent in many other spheres of their lives.

Thus, we do not intend the term 'conservatism' to be understood in a general psychological sense. The progressive who acts 'traddi tionalistically' in private or business life, or the conservative who acts 'progressively' outside politics, should make the point clear.

The word 'traditionalist' describes what, to a greater or less degree, is a formal psychological characteristic of every individual's mind. 'Conservative' action, however, is always dependent on *a concrete set of circumstances*. There is no means of knowing in advance what form a 'conservative' action in the political sense will take, whereas the general attitude implied in the term 'traditionalist' enables us to calculate more or less accurately what a 'traditionalist' action will be like. There is no doubt, for instance, what the traditionalist reaction to the introduction of the railway will be. But how a conservative will react can only be determined approximately *if we know a good deal about the conservative movement* in the period and in the country under discussion. We are not concerned here to enumerate all the different factors which go to produce a particular type of conservatism in a particular country at a particular period. This much is clear, however, that acting along conservative lines (at any rate in the political sphere) involves more than automatic responses of a certain type; it means that the individual is consciously or unconsciously guided by a way of thinking and acting which has its own history behind it, before it comes into contact with the individual. This contact with

[1] Cf. Max Weber, *Wirtschaft und Gesellschaft*, p. 19, Tübingen, 1922. (This 'traditionalism' obviously has nothing to do with the French 'traditionalism' of a de Maistre or de Bonald.)

the individual may under certain circumstances change to some extent the form and development of this way of thinking and acting, but even when the particular individual is no longer there to participate in it, it will still have its own history and development apart from him. Political conservatism is therefore an *objective mental structure*, as opposed to the 'subjectivity' of the isolated individual. It is *not* objective in the sense of being eternally and universally valid. No *a priori* deductions can be made from the 'principles' of conservatism. Nor does it exist apart from the individuals who realize it in practice and embody it in their actions. It is not an immanent principle with a given law of development which the individual members of the movement merely unfold—possibly in unconscious fashion—without adding anything of their own. In one word, conservatism is not an objective entity in any rightly or wrongly understood Platonist sense of the pre-existence of ideas. But as compared with the *hic et nunc* experience of the particular individual it has a certain very definite objectivity.

In order to grasp the peculiar nature of this objective mental structure, we must first draw a careful distinction between eternal validity and objectivity. A content may be objective in the sense that it exists apart from the *hic et nunc* experience of the individual —as something intended by him—and yet it need not be a timeless content. A structure may be objective—it may transcend the individual which it has temporarily caught up in the stream of its experience—yet it may at the same time be restricted in its validity, subject to historical change, and merely reflect the development of the particular society in which it is found. An *objective* mental structure in this sense is a peculiar agglomeration of spiritual and intellectual elements which cannot be regarded as at all independent of the individuals who are its carriers since its production, reproduction and further development depend entirely on the fate and spontaneous development of these latter. The structure may nevertheless be objective in the sense that the isolated individual could never produce it alone, since he can only belong to some one phase of its historical development, and in the sense that it always outlives its individual carriers. Both nominalism and realism miss the essence of the objectivity of a mental structure in this sense. Nominalism never gets to the root of the matter because it always tries to dissolve the objective structure into the isolated experiences of individuals (cf. Max Weber's concept of 'intended meaning'), while realism never gets there because by 'objectivity' and 'validity' it understands something merely metaphysical, entirely independent of the nature and fate of the particular individuals and carriers, something constant and normative (pre-existing). Between these extremes there is, however, a third alternative which is neither nominalism nor realism. This is what I call a dynamic, historical structural configuration; a concept implying a type of objectivity which begins in time, develops and declines through time, which is closely bound up with the existence and fate of concrete human groups, and is in fact their product. It is nevertheless a truly 'objective' mental structure, because it is always 'there' 'before' the individual at any given moment, and because, as compared with any simple range of experience, it always maintains its own definite form—its *structure*. And although at any given moment such an objective mental structure may show the existence of some ordering principle in the way in which the experiences and elements of which it is composed are related, it must on no account be regarded as 'static'. The particular form and structure of these related experiences and elements can be indicated only *approximately* and only for certain periods, since the structure is *dynamic* and constantly changing. Moreover, it is not merely dynamic, but also historically conditioned. Each step in the process of change is intimately connected with the one before, since each new step makes a change in the internal order and relationships of the structure *as it existed at the stage immediately before*, and is not therefore entirely 'out of the blue' and unconnected with the past. Thus we can speak of a growth, of a development. It is a development the inner meaning of which, however, can only *subsequently* be grasped.

Within every dynamic historical structural configuration, we can discern a distinctive 'basic intention' (*Grundintention*), which the individual makes his own in the measure that his own experience becomes determined by the 'structural configuration' as such. Even this 'kernel', this basic intention, however, is not eternally valid regardless of time and history. It too has arisen in the course of history and in close connection with the fate of concrete, living human beings.

Conservatism is just such an historically developed, dynamic, objective structural configuration. People experience, and act, in a 'conservative' way (as distinct from a merely 'traditionalist' way) in so far, and only in so far, as they *incorporate* themselves into one of the phases of development of this objective mental structure (usually into the contemporary phase), and behave in terms of the structure, either by simply reproducing it in whole or in part, or by developing it further by adapting it to a particular concrete situation.

Only when the peculiar nature of the objectivity of a dynamic structural configuration has been grasped can one be in a position to distinguish 'conservative' from 'traditionalist' behaviour.

Traditionalist behaviour is almost purely reactive.[1] *Conservative behaviour is meaningful,* and moreover is meaningful in relation to circumstances which change from epoch to epoch. It is therefore clear why there is no necessary contradiction in the fact that a politically progressive man can react in an entirely traditionalist way in his everyday life. In the political sphere, he lets himself be guided more or less consciously by an objective, structural configuration; in his everyday life, his behaviour is merely reactive. Two points now arise. Firstly the term 'conservatism' must not be, assumed to be a purely political one, although on the whole, as we shall see, its political aspect is perhaps the rather more important one. Conservatism also implies a general philosophical and emotional complex which may even constitute a definite style of thought. Secondly, conservatism as an objective historical structural configuration must not be assumed to include no traditionalist elements within itself. Quite the contrary. We shall see, in fact, that conservatism takes a particular historical form of traditionalism and develops it to its logical conclusions.

Nevertheless, in spite of this apparent overlapping of the two phenomena, or maybe even because of it, the distinction between merely traditionalist and conservative behaviour is a very clear one. Precisely because of its purely formal, semi-reactive nature, traditionalist behaviour has practically no traceable history, whereas conservatism, on the other hand, is an entity with a clear historical and social continuity, which has arisen and developed in a particular historical and social situation, as the best of all guides to history—language—clearly demonstrates; the very word 'conservatism' is a new one of comparatively recent origin.

It was Chateaubriand who first lent the word its peculiar meaning when he called the periodical he issued to propagate the ideas of the clerical and political Restoration, *The Conservative.*[2] The word entered into general use in Germany in the thirties,[3] and was officially adopted in England in 1835.[4] We can take the emergence of a new terminology to indicate the emergence of a new social phenomenon, although of course it tells us little about the latter's actual nature.

2. *The sociological background of modern conservatism*

Modern conservatism differs from traditionalism primarily in that it is a function of *one particular* historical and sociological

[1] *Ibid.*, p. 2.
[2] Cf. the article 'Konservativ' by Rackfahl in *Politisches Handwörterbuch*, ed. P. Herre, Leipzig, 1923.
[3] *Ibid.*
[4] Cf. Lord Hugh Cecil, *op. cit.*, p. 64.

situation. Traditionalism is a general psychological attitude which expresses itself in different individuals as a tendency to cling to the past and a fear of innovation. But this elementary psychological tendency may attain a special function in relation to the social process. What was formerly merely a psychological characteristic common to all men, under certain circumstances becomes a central factor lending coherence to a *particular trend* in the social process.

This development of the traditionalist attitude into the nucleus of a definite social trend does not take place spontaneously: it takes place as a response to the fact that 'progressivism' had already constituted itself as a definite trend.

Traditionalism is essentially one of those dormant tendencies which each individual unconsciously harbours within himself. Conservatism, on the other hand, is conscious and reflective from the first, since it arises as a counter-movement in conscious opposition to the highly organized, coherent and systematic 'progressive' movement.

The emergence of a conscious conservative movement is therefore already an indication that the modern social and intellectual world has developed a particular structure of its own. The mere existence of conservatism as a coherent trend means that history is developing more and more in terms of the interaction of such comprehensive 'trends' and 'movements', some of which are 'progressive' and further social change, while others are 'retrogressive' and retard it.

That such 'trends' can arise is explained by the fact that society today is gradually achieving a new dynamic unity, at the expense of all the old, scattered, self-contained provincial feudal units which are increasingly absorbed into national units; these latter may later coalesce further into supra-national ones. Although at first nations remain to a large extent socially and culturally autonomous, the fundamental economic and social problem in all modern states is so structurally similar that it is not surprising that parallel social and intellectual divisions are reproduced in them all.

These structural problems common to all modern states include the following: (I) the achievement of national unity, (II) the participation of the people in the government of the country, (III) incorporation of the state in the world economic order, (IV) solution of the social question.[1]

They appear to be of such importance for the social as well

[1] Cf. L. Bergsträsser, 'Geschichte der politischen Parteien in Deutschland', *Schriftenreihe der Verwaltungsakademie Berlin*, No. 4, 2nd ed., p. 5, Mannheim, Berlin and Leipzig.

as for the intellectual life of the community that there is a marked tendency for all divisions within it to develop in close relation to the tensions arising from attempts to solve these fundamental problems of social structure. Religious struggles have gradually been transformed into political struggles, and in the English Revolution political divisions can already be clearly seen through the guise of religious divisions. The nearer we approach the nineteenth century, the more does this become true of other intellectual phenomena as well, and the more easily can they be described along party lines, in terms of their direct or indirect relation to social and political problems.

Accordingly, at the same time as a conscious, functionalized, political conservatism emerges as a distinct political force, conservatism transcends the political sphere proper and comes to imply also a *particular form of experience and thought*. At approximately the same time as, or perhaps even a little earlier than, political conservatism, there emerged a corresponding *Weltanschauung* and conservative mode of thought. 'Conservative' and 'liberal' in our terminology, in relation to the first half of the nineteenth century, signify something more than different political aims. The terms imply in each case a quite specific affinity with quite different philosophies and therefore also imply quite different modes of thought. Thus the word 'conservative' connotes, so to speak, an entire, comprehensive world structure; the sociological ·definition of this word (which necessarily includes more than its historical political definition) must therefore take into account that historical configuration which brought forth a new term as the expression of a new fact.

To find out why 'modern conservatism' emerged so late in history, we must turn to the various historical and social factors the conjunction of which provided the prerequisite conditions for its development. The following factors occurring together would appear to create the necessary historical and sociological conditions for the rise of conservatism:

(i) The status of historical-social forces must cease to be a static one. It must become a dynamic process of oriented change. Individual events must to an increasing extent in every sphere point to the key problem of the growth of the social body. At first this will happen unwittingly; later, however, it will become conscious and voluntary, and at the same time the exact importance of each element for the development of the whole will become clearer. The number of isolated self-sufficient social units which previously existed will also diminish accordingly. The most commonplace action, however unimportant in itself, will now contribute something to the general process of development, and either further or hinder it[1]: and it becomes increasingly possible to describe every event and every attitude in terms of its function in relation to the development of society as a whole.

(ii) Further: the dynamics of this process must to an increasing extent derive from social differentiation. Different classes must arise ('horizontal' social groupings, reacting to events in a more or less homogeneous way). Some will tend to push social development forward, while others will hold it up, or even consciously work to set it back.

(iii) Further: ideas must also be differentiated along these lines, and the major trends in thought, whatever mixtures and syntheses may be produced, must correspond to the broad lines of this social differentiation.

(iv) Finally: this social differentiation (into groups with different functions in relation to the social process—some forwarding and others retarding it), must take on an increasingly political (and later even a purely economic) character.[2] The political factor must be autonomous, and must become the primary nucleus around which new groupings crystallize.

To put it briefly, the development and widespread existence of conservatism, as distinct from mere traditionalism, is due in the last retort to the dynamic character of the modern world; to the basis of this dynamic in social differentiation; to the fact that this social differentiation tends to draw the human intellect along with it and forces it to develop along its own lines; and finally to the fact that the basic aims of the different social groups do not merely crystallize ideas into actual movements of thought, but also create different antagonistic *Weltanschauungen* and different antagonistic *styles* of thought. In a word—traditionalism can only become conservatism in a society in which change occurs through the medium of class conflict—in a *class society*. This is the sociological background of modern conservatism.

[1] In medieval times, too, there existed progressive centres, bearers of a dynamic principle: the towns. They were, however, isolated within a static world. So far as we can see, the international culture of the Middle Ages, as represented by the Church, lacked this element of 'oriented change' in which every event assumes a function affecting the whole. On the difficulties of forming parties in a feudal world, cf. K. Lamprecht, *Deutsche Geschichte*, Suppl. II, second half-volume, p. 53, Freiburg im Breisgau, 1904.

[2] Cf. Emil Lederer, 'Das ökonomische Element und die politische Idee im modernen Parteiwesen', in *Zeitschrift für Politik*, vol. 5, 1911. Intellectual life in Germany is definitely split up into a liberal and a conservative current only after 1840. The existence of a conservative and a liberal 'style of thought', however, had been apparent much earlier (in fact, from the French Revolution onward). Ideological trends in Germany somehow antedated the emergence of the corresponding social structures.

3. *Morphology of conservative thought*

Conservatism can be studied from two points of view. Either one can regard it *as a unit*, as the relatively self-contained and fully developed result of an evolutionary process, or one can emphasize its dynamic aspect and study the genetic process which gives rise to that final product.

We shall have to utilize both approaches. For the moment, however, our task is to arrive at a general descriptive characterization of the style of thought underlying German conservatism, and we shall therefore take its historical development for granted, and consider it in its final form. We shall deal with its historical development in the next section, but this historical analysis cannot be attempted before we have examined certain fundamental factors, which determine the process.

Our first task then, to which we now turn, is to give a relatively undifferentiated description of early nineteenth-century German conservative thought. This must be divided into two stages. Firstly we must deal with the inarticulate group experience which provides what we have called the *basic intention* out of which the style of thought first grows. Then we can turn to the fully articulated theoretical statements expressing the conservative style of thought, and try to work out that *key problem* which gives this style of thought its theoretical unity, determines its growth, and makes its interpretation possible.

(a) *The basic intention behind conservative thought*

One cannot help pushing one's analysis of a style of thought right back to this basic intention, and there is only one safeguard against arbitrary constructions with no basis in reality. As far as possible, we must always adhere strictly to the authentic manifestations of the trend of thought which we are analysing.

This inner core, this drive at the heart of conservative thought, is undoubtedly related to what we have called traditionalism. Conservatism in a certain sense grew out of traditionalism: indeed, it is after all primarily nothing more than traditionalism become conscious. Nevertheless, the two are not synonymous, since traditionalism only takes on its specifically conservative features when it becomes the expression of a very definite, consistently maintained way of life and thought (which first develops in opposition to the revolutionary attitude), and when it functions as such, as a relatively autonomous movement in the social process.

One of the most essential characteristics of this conservative way of life and thought seems to be the way in which it clings to the immediate, the actual, the *concrete*. The result is a quite new, very definite feeling for the *concrete* which is reflected in the modern use of the term 'concrete' with anti-revolutionary implications.[1] To experience and to think 'concretely' now comes to mean to desire to restrict the range of one's activities to the immediate surroundings in which one is placed, and to abjure strictly all that may smack of speculation or hypothesis.

Non-romantic conservatism always starts with the particular case at hand, and never broadens its horizon beyond its own particular surroundings. It is concerned with immediate action, with changing concrete details, and therefore does not really trouble itself with the *structure* of the world in which it lives. On the other hand, all progressive activity feeds on its *consciousness of the possible*. It transcends the given immediate present, by seizing on the possibilities for systematic change which it offers. It fights the concrete, *not* because it wants to replace it merely by another *form of the concrete* but because it wants to produce another *systematic starting-point* for further development.

Conservative reformism consists in the substitution of individual factors by other individual factors ('improvements').[2] Progressive reformism tends to do away with an undesirable fact by reforming the entire surrounding world which makes its existence possible. *Thus progressive reformism tends to tackle the system as a whole, while conservative reformism tackles particular details.*

The Conservative only thinks in terms of a system as a reaction, either when he is forced to develop a system of his own to counter that of the progressives, or when the march of events deprives him of all influence upon the immediate present, so that he would be compelled to turn the wheel of history backward in order to regain influence.

This contrast between concrete and abstract thought, which is primarily one of the ways of one's experiencing his environment, and only secondarily one of thought as such, together with the fact that in its modern form it is based on a difference of fundamental political experience, supplies a crucial instance of styles of experience becoming socially functionalized.

The emergence of a specifically modern society seems to depend on whole classes devoting themselves to the disintegration of the

[1] On Burke's definition of 'abstractness', see Meusel, *op. cit.*, pp. 12, 137. Hegel characterized 'abstract' freedom as 'negative freedom', the freedom of (mere) rationality, and ascribed a destructive tendency to it (*Philosophie des Rechts*, § 5). Cf. also Fr. J. Stahl, *Die Philosophie des Rechts*, 4th ed., vol. 2, p. 38, Heidelberg, 1870. The socialist 'left' later adopted the category of the 'concrete' as a basic category for the interpretation of society; for this group, the 'concrete' coincides with the class struggle.

[2] As a Prussian jurist, Bekker, expressed it: 'We placed a good administration above the best constitution.' Quoted in G. v. Below, 'Die Anfänge der konservativen Partei in Preussen', in *Internationale Wochenschrift für Wissenschaft, Kunst und Technik*, 1911.

existing social structure. Their thought is necessarily abstract—it lives on the potential and possible; whereas the thought and experience of those who seek to preserve the present and retard progress is necessarily concrete, and fails to break through the existing structure of society.

The peculiar nature of conservative concreteness is perhaps hardly more clearly to be seen than in its concept of *property*, as contrasted with the ordinary modern bourgeois idea of it. In this connection there is a very interesting essay of Möser's in which he traces the gradual disappearance of the old attitude towards property and compares it with the modern concept of property which had already begun to show its influence in his own time. In his essay 'Von dem echten Eigentum'[1] he shows that the old 'genuine property' was bound up with its owner in an entirely different way from property today. Before, there was a peculiarly vital, reciprocal relationship between property and its owner. Property in its old 'genuine' sense carried with it certain privileges for its owner—for instance, it gave him a voice in affairs of state, the right to hunt, to become a member of a jury. Thus it was closely bound up with his personal honour and so in a sense *inalienable*. When, for example, the owner of the property changed, the right to hunt did not go with the property to the new owner, and the retention of the right to hunt by the original owner was a living testimony to the fact the new proprietor was not the 'real' one. Similarly, a man of ancient nobility who might purchase property from a mere *homo novus* was equally unable to transfer to his newly acquired estate the character of 'true' property merely by virtue of his own fund of personal nobility. Thus there existed a completely non-transferable, reciprocal relationship between a particular piece of property and a particular owner.

In Möser's time the feeling for this relationship still existed, although all linguistic trace of it had long since disappeared. He laments its loss when he says: 'How imperfect is the language and philosophy that no longer has any special way of expressing these fundamental distinctions.'

Here we see clearly what a wealth of pre-theoretical, inarticulate experience, embodying relationships of a most concrete kind between person and property, there was in feudal society, in place of which the abstract concept of bourgeois property emerged, suppressing the old concreteness of experience. Later theories, especially the romantic-conservative type, all reach back towards this feudal conservative concept of property, the essence of which Möser caught, so to speak in its last moments.

[1] Cf. Justus Möser, *Sämtliche Werke* (Complete Works), ed. B. R. Abeken, vol. 4, pp. 158 ff., Berlin, 1842-43.

A. Müller[1] regards possessions as extensions of the limbs of the human body, and he describes feudalism as the amalgamation of person and thing. He attributes the decline of this relationship to the adoption of Roman law, and speaks of a 'Roman French revolution' (*op. cit.*, vol. 1, p. 281) on which he lays all the blame.

These are all mere echoes of the past in an openly partisan vein. Their significance lies in the fact that such living relationships extending to things did once exist. This emphasis on the 'intimacy' between property and owner continues right down to Hegel.

For Hegel the essence of property is that 'I make a thing the vehicle of my will',[2] and 'the rationale of property consists, not in that it satisfies our needs, but in that it helps personality become something more than mere subjectivity.'[3] It is also interesting to note here something which we shall have occasion to observe again later—how the Left opposition to bourgeois capitalist thought learns from the Right opposition to bourgeois thought. The abstractness of human relationships under capitalism which is constantly emphasized by Marx and his followers was originally the discovery of observers from the conservative camp.

We are not suggesting that this distinction between the concrete and abstract approach was never known in earlier times: we are merely pointing out that two quite different ways of experiencing history have gradually developed at opposite extremes and have been embodied in the general form of experience characteristic of different groups according to their position in the dynamic social process.

Another key concept for any analysis of different styles of thought and ways of experiencing is that of *Liberty*.

Revolutionary liberalism understood by liberty in the economic sphere the release of the individual from his medieval connections with state and guild. In the political sphere they understood by it the right of the individual to do as he wishes and thinks fit, and especially his right to the fullest exercise of the inalienable Rights of Man. Only when it encroaches on the liberty of fellow citizens does man's freedom know any bounds according to this concept.[4] Equality, then, is the logical corollary of this kind of liberty—
—without the assumption of political equality for all men it is

1 Cf. Adam H. Müller, *Die Elemente der Staatskunst* (1809), ed. J. Baxa, vol. 1, pp. 156, 162 f., Vienna and Leipzig, 1922.
2 *Philosophie des Rechts*, ed. Lasson, p. 302.
3 *Ibid.*, p. 297.
4 Cf. the French 'Declaration of the Rights of Man and of the Citizen': 'Liberty consists in doing anything that does no harm to others; thus, the only limits to the natural rights of any man are those which guarantee the same rights to the other members of society. These limits can only be fixed by law.'

meaningless. Actually, however, revolutionary liberalism never thought of equality as anything more than a postulate. It certainly never took it as a matter of empirical fact, and indeed never demanded equality in practice for all men, except in the course of economic and political struggles. Yet conservative thought twisted this postulate into a statement of fact, and made it appear as if the liberals were claiming that all men were in fact and in all respects equal.

Nevertheless, out of this sociologically determined misunderstanding there grew, as often before, a new insight into the actual differentiation of trends of thought. Just as in the case of the concept of property, conservative thought once more rescued an earlier, almost submerged way of thinking and experiencing things, and, by making it explicit, enabled it to play an active role in the dynamic process.

Political necessity compelled the conservatives to develop their own concept of liberty[1] to oppose that of the liberals, and they worked out what we may call the *qualitative idea* of liberty to distinguish it from the revolutionary equalitarian concept. The counter-revolutionary opposition had a sound enough instinct not to attack the idea of freedom as such; instead, they concentrated on the idea of equality which stands behind it. Men, they claimed, are essentially *unequal*, unequal in their gifts and abilities, and unequal to the very core of their beings. Freedom therefore can only consist in the ability of each man to develop without let or hindrance according to the law and principle of his own personality. A. Müller[2] for instance says: 'Nothing could be more inimical to freedom as I have described it . . . than the concept of an external equality. If freedom is simply the general striving of the most varied natures for growth and development, nothing more contradictory to this could be conceived than a false notion of freedom which would remove all the individual peculiarities, i.e. all the heterogeneity of these natures.'

This is also the romantic conservative idea of liberty, which now acquires political point. The revolutionary liberal, thinking abstractly in terms of the possible and not the actual, clings with an 'abstract optimism' to the principle of universal equality, or at least of equal opportunity among men, and conceives of no bounds to an individual's liberty except those set by the existence of other men. But the romantic thinker sees freedom limited by what Simmel called 'the individual law' of development within which

---

[1] Cf. Müller, *op. cit.*, vol. 1, pp. 156, 313, also Baxa's note in his edition of Müller, vol. 2, p. 334. Further see E. Rothacker, 'Savigny, Grimm, Ranke', in *Hist. Zschr.*, vol. 128, pp. 440, 1923.

[2] *Op. cit.*, vol. 1, p. 151.

each must find defined both his potentialities and his limitations.

This kind of liberty, vested in the nature of individuality, is typically romantic, and hence dangerously close to a kind of anarchistic subjectivism. Although the conservatives succeeded in subjectivizing the problem of liberty (thus blunting its revolutionary edge), the subjective anarchy with which they replaced the external *political* anarchy created by the liberal concept still contained a potential menace to the security of the state. The realization of this caused an immediate tendency in romantic thought (then in the process of becoming conservative) to detach the concept of 'qualitative liberty' from the individual and to transfer it to the so-called 'true bearers', the 'true subjects' of liberty, namely the larger collectivities, 'organic communities', *the estates*. Henceforth the estates became the bearers of that inner principle of growth, in the unrestricted development of which lies liberty. This makes it clear that the qualitative concept of liberty derives at least in part from feudal thinking. The 'liberty' of the different estates under feudalism which meant their 'privileges', and the distinctly qualitative and non-egalitarian flavour which was contained in the medieval concept, is here revived once more.[1] Even in its new form, however, the concept is still fraught with danger to the state and the position of the ruling groups within it, as later conservatism is well aware. Hence, an attempt is later made to select qualitatively different individual or corporative 'liberties' in such a way that they can subordinated to a higher principle, representing the whole of society. The historical school, Hegel, Stahl and others, differ among themselves only in their conception of this overarching totality; the formal structure of their various solutions to the problem is the same.

The solution was to make liberty a matter concerning the private, subjective side of life only, while all external social relations were subordinated to the principle of order and discipline. But then comes the problem: what is to prevent a collision between the two spheres, subjective Liberty and external Order? A solution is found in the assumption of a kind of 'pre-established harmony' which is either guaranteed directly by God, or by the natural forces of society and the nation. Here conservatism has clearly learned something from liberalism, from which it has taken over both the concept of 'separation of spheres' and of the 'hidden hand' which makes for universal harmony.

The historical school uses primarily the concept of 'the nation'

---

[1] Cf. A. v. Martin, 'Weltanschauliche Motive im altkonservativen Denken', in *Deutscher Staat und deutsche Parteien, Festschrift für Meinecke*, p. 345, Munich and Berlin, 1922.

or 'national spirit' to provide that necessary wider whole which prevents the liberty of the individual or group from degenerating into mere anarchistic caprice. Rothacker has shown how in Ranke's writings the concept of the state gradually overshadowed that of the nation.[1] In any case, the solution of the problem offered by Ranke and Savigny is to shift this qualitative freedom from the individual and the estates to the nation and the state respectively. Only the state, developing freely according to its own laws of growth, is ever really free. The individual is bound, and can only achieve usefulness within these wider units.

The tension between order and liberty is at its greatest in Hegel, who, as always, tries to preserve both factors. For him, what he calls the revolutionary, abstract concept of freedom becomes an intermediary stage in the progress towards truth: 'Negative freedom, or freedom of mere rationality, is one-sided. Yet this one-sidedness contains an essential feature, it is not to be discarded. But the defect of mere rationality is that it mistakes a partial and one-sided characterization for the final and comprehensive one.'[2] What he means by 'negative abstract freedom', however, becomes rapidly clearer if we follow him further: 'A more concrete manifestation of this freedom is the fanaticism of political and religious life. Of this nature was the terroristic phase of the French Revolution, which sought to slur over all distinctions in talent and authority. That was a time of tremor and commotion which was intolerant of anything that set itself off against the general. Fanaticism seeks abstract equality rather than differentiation; wherever it encounters distinctions, it finds them antagonistic to its indefiniteness and levels them down.'[3] Hegel then arrives at a third principle which holds the middle way between 'abstract freedom' and mere 'heteronomy'. This principle is that of 'concrete freedom'.[4] He says: 'The third step is that the will, while limited by the other, should yet remain by itself. While it limits itself, it yet remains with itself and does not lose its hold of the universal. This is then the concrete conception of freedom, while the other two aspects may now be seen as thoroughly abstract and one-sided.'[5]

Stahl also had to struggle with the romantic concept of liberty.[6] He, like Hegel, tried to incorporate the whole conservative tradition, and based his solution of the problem on the principle of

---

[1] *Op. cit.*, p. 433.
[2] *Philosophie des Rechts*, Addition to § 5, ed. Lasson, p. 287; cf. footnote 1, p. 103. Müller (*op. cit.*, vol. 1, p. 313) also speaks of 'negative freedom'. Cf. G. Rexius, 'Studien zur Staatslehre der historischen Schule', in *Hist. Zschr.*, vol. 107, p. 499, 1911.
[3] *Op. cit.*, p. 288.
[4] *Ibid.*, addition to § 7, p. 288.
[5] *Ibid.*, pp. 288 f.   [6] *Op. cit.*, vol. 1, pp. 143 f.; vol. 2, pp. 26 ff.

authority (*Obrigkeitsgedanke*). Hence the following conclusion: 'Freedom is not the ability to act in this or that way according to fundamentally arbitrary decisions; freedom is the ability to behave and live in accordance with one's innermost self. Now the innermost self of man is to be sure his individuality which accepts no external law and regulation. Nevertheless, individual rights such as those safeguarding an independent private sphere,[1] as well as those granting the individual a share in determining state policy, are an essential ingredient of political freedom. But the innermost self of man is not only his individuality but also his moral essence.'[2] This, then, leads to Stahl's final solution of the problem of freedom: 'The aim of politics, then, is to ensure this material [as against merely formal] freedom. It must not separate the individual from the physical power or from the moral authority and the historical tradition of the state, so as to found the state upon mere individual will.'[3]

Enough examples for the present. All these solutions of the problem show the same fundamental tendency, the same drive towards the 'concrete' and 'qualitative': The terms used are always 'material freedom' (Stahl), 'concrete freedom' (Hegel), 'positive freedom' (A. Müller), just as in the case of property. 'Concrete' and 'qualitative' are nevertheless expressions which by no means adequately describe the basic intention lying behind all these sequences of thought. The examples we mentioned merely serve to adumbrate something fundamental of which they are the manifestations: a harking back to an earlier way of life.

There is another pair of contrasts besides 'concreteness' and 'abstractness' (and a closely related one), which is also relevant to basic conflict between progressivism and conservatism. Progressive thought not only sees the actual in terms of its potentialities, but also *in terms of the norm*. Conservative thought on the other hand tries to see the actual as the product of real factors; it also tries to understand the norm in terms of the actual.[4]

[1] Note the infiltration of liberal ideas into the conservative system of thought.
[2] Fr. J. Stahl, *Die gegenwärtigen Parteien in Staat und Kirche*, pp. 5 f., Berlin, 1863.
[3] *Ibid.*, p. 10.
[4] Cf. Hegel's comment in the Preface to the *Philosophy of Law*: 'To understand what is, is the task of philosophy, since what exists *is* Reason. As to the individual, every one is a son of his epoch anyway; and thus philosophy, too, is nothing but the epoch grasped in thinking. It is just as foolish to imagine that a philosophy can reach beyond its contemporary world as to believe that an individual may skip over his own time—beyond Rhodes, so to speak. If a theory goes beyond the existing world and builds up a world *as it should be*, then this world will exist, to be sure, but its existence will be a purely mental one,—it will exist in a yielding medium in which anything may take shape.' In contrast to this, Hegel in his revolutionary youth wrote to Schelling: 'With the idea of how everything should be gaining universal acceptance, the indolence of settled people who take everything as it is will disappear' (quoted in F. Rosenzweig, *Hegel und der Staat*, vol. 1, p. 31, Munich and Berlin, 1920). In Stahl, Justification of the 'existing' rests on a religious basis; in *Philosophie des Rechts*, vol. 2.

Here too, in the last resort, we are faced with two ways of experiencing things and the environment out of which subsequently two styles of thought arise. One has a quite different attitude to things, persons, and institutions, if one always looks at them *with a demand*, with a 'So it *should* be', at the back of one's mind, instead of treating them as the finished and inevitable products of a long process of growth. If we adopt the first attitude, we shall find ourselves barely glancing at the given realities of our surroundings, never achieving any attachment which would make us indulgent towards their imperfections, nor any feeling of solidarity which would make us concerned with their survival. But the second attitude will lead us to accept the present, with all its defects, uncritically. The first attitude means that one always experiences and judges institutions *as a whole*, the second always involves losing oneself in a mass of detail. To understand the significance of these attitudes, we must first be clear that it is one of the characteristics of mental phenomena that they cannot be understood in isolation, but only as functional parts of a wider whole. If, however, we want to interpret something in terms of what it means—and all mental phenomena *are* only in so far as they *have meaning*—we must grasp it as a phase in some goal-directed endeavour.

The conservative, with his fundamental attachment to the principle of *quieta non movere*, would like to avoid recognition of meanings in this sense,[1] by looking at the actual simply as something that exists; this results in a streak of fatalism.[2] The conservative interpretation or imputation of meanings arises as an antagonistic reaction to the revolutionary mode of conceiving the meaning of things. The conservative, too, can only impart meaning to a thing by 'rounding it out' and fitting it into a wider whole. *But the process, the 'method' of rounding it out is entirely different from that used in liberal revolutionary thought and experience*, which is another indication that in this sphere, ways of experiencing things also develop in close connection with the social background. The peculiarity of the conservative way of putting things into a wider context is that it approaches them in some way *from behind*, from *their past*. For progressive thought, everything derives its meaning in the last analysis from something either above or beyond itself, from a future utopia or from its relation to a transcendent norm. The conservative, however, sees all the significance of a thing in

[1] In Ranke's 'Political Dialogue' Friedrich, the spokesman of conservatism, declares: 'I hope I did not express myself as if I had wanted to describe the ideal state. I merely wanted to characterize the one we have' (*Das politische Gespräch*, etc., ed. Rothacker, p. 29, Halle, 1925).
[2] This fatalism may assume various forms; it appears successively as theological scientific and historical fatalism.

what lies *behind* it, either its temporal past or its evolutionary germ. Where the progressive uses the future to interpret things, the conservative uses the past; the progressive thinks in terms of *norms*, the conservative in terms of *germs*.

This idea of 'the past which lies behind' can thus be interpreted in two ways: as a temporal past, or as an antecedent evolutionary phase which can account for any particular detail of the actual. Looked at from the former point of view, everything has meaning because it has arisen out of a temporal process of development; from the latter point of view everything that exists historically has meaning because it exhibits the same fundamental drive, the same basic trend of mental and spiritual growth.

Thus the particular thing in this latter case is understood 'physiognomically', as the manifestation of a basic intention, as a particular 'aspect' of a totality represented by a germinal beginning. Both these conservative ways of 'rounding out' an object and giving it meaning thus tend to a total view, and the wider whole which is reached in this way is usually *an intuitively reached whole*.[1] On the other hand, the wider wholes into which the progressive places things are derived from a rational utopia, and this leads to a *structural* view of existing and developing society. A simile may help to make matters clear. The conservative picture of things as a whole is like the inclusive sort of picture of a house which one might get by looking at it from all possible sides, a concrete picture of the house in all its detail from every angle. But the progressive is not interested in all this detail; he makes straight for the ground plan of the house and his picture is suitable for rational analysis rather than for intuitive representation. And within this difference of ways of fitting individual things into their wider context, there lies a further radical difference between progressive and conservative patterns of experience—this time *a difference in the way of experiencing time*.[2]

Briefly, this difference may be expressed as follows: the progressive experiences the present as the beginning of the future, while the conservative regards it simply as the latest point reached by the past. The difference is the more fundamental and radical in that the linear concept of history—which is implied here—is

[1] Cf. F. C. v. Savigny on law, language, customs, constitution as integral wholes; in his work *Vom Beruf unserer Zeit für Gesetzgebung und Rechtswissenschaft* (1814), new ed. 1892, p. 5. Hegel praises Montesquieu for having seen legislation and laws as 'an independent phase of a totality in correlation with all the other characteristics of a nation and an epoch; they will receive their true significance and their justification from this context only' (*op. cit.*, p. 21).

[2] It is not meant, of course, that every conservative experiences time in a different fashion from a liberal; such an assertion would be completely unverifiable. What we do say is that in conservative utterances time as a category appears in a role different rom the one it plays in progressive utterances.

for the conservative something secondary. Primarily, the conservative experiences the past as being one with the present; hence, his concept of history tends to be spatial rather than temporal; it stresses co-existence rather than succession. We may understand this better, if we recall that for typically feudal groups (aristocrats and peasants) history is rooted in the soil; the individuals are nothing but passing Spinozistic 'modi' of this eternal 'substance'.

Land is the real foundation on which the state rests and develops, and only land can really make history. The transient individual is replaced by the more durable factor, land, as the foundation of events. As Möser says in the important introductory sentences of his *Osnabrückische Geschichte:* 'In my opinion, the history of Germany would take an entirely new turn if we traced the fate of the landed estates as the real component parts of the nation through all its changes, considering them as the body of the nation, and their incumbents merely as good or bad accidents as they may happen to the body.'[1]

Every isolated individual and event is regarded as purely incidental and fortuitous as against this compact, territorial substructure. This space-like ordering of events in time is evident in A. Müller, who with the linguistic virtuosity characteristic of all romantics coined the conservative counter-term 'conspatiality' as against the democratically coloured term 'contemporaneity'. In his answer to the question, 'What is a nation?', he repudiated the concept that a given nation, say, the French, consisted of 'the beings with heads, two hands and two feet, who at this insignificant moment happen to be standing, sitting or lying on that part of the Earth's surface which is called France.' As against this, he defined the nation as 'the sublime community of a long succession of past, present and future generations . . . having its tangible appearance in a common language, in common customs and laws, in a host of beneficial institutions . . . in long-lived families and, finally, in the one immortal family . . . of the ruler. . . .'[2] Here he emphasizes the participation of past generations in the present, and he regards the cross-section of time we call the present as a quite unimportant phase in the development of history. This use of time-transcending, spatially determined, material entities as the basis of history is a characteristic which conservative thought has in common with the proletarian and socialist thought which developed later. Proletarian thought also rejects the idea that the individual is the real basis of historical development, and introduces instead entities like 'conditions of production' and 'classes'. There is also a good deal

1 Works, vol. 6, pp. ix f.
2 *Elemente der Staatskunst,* I, pp. 145 f.

of sociology in Möser's statement, if we mean by 'sociology' the ability to understand individual happenings in terms of the more comprehensive factors lying behind them.

But these two 'non-individualistic' interpretations of history differ essentially from each other in that the conservative tends to trace history back to *organic* entities (of which the family is the prototype), whereas the proletarian sees newer forms of collective entities which are primarily, though not exclusively, *agglomerative* rather than organic in character, i.e. classes, as the motor forces of history. The place occupied by the family and corporation in conservative thought is occupied by classes in socialist thought; and in the same way, industrial and productive relations take the place of land.

Only bourgeois thought, standing midway between the two, and starting at that point in history where the old associations are already in dissolution, while the new stratification is still in its infancy, sees society in terms of the isolated individuals of which it is composed, and achieves a picture of the whole which is merely the sum of its parts. The bourgeois-democratic principle which corresponds to this view of society dismembers time in the same way: it experiences movement, but is only able to master its dynamic in so far as it is able to split the movement up into cross-sections of time (*Momentanquerschnitte*). What the 'general will' is is indicated, for each moment in time, by a ballot taken. Thus, in the bourgeois-democratic society, the temporal continuity of the existence of society is atomized in the same way as the national 'community' is broken down into individual atoms; we can reconstruct both only by approximation if we add together the various cross-sections representing successive temporary states. No 'totality' of the collective existence of society can be grasped, except as a sum.[1]

Thus, conservative thought concentrates upon the past in so far as the past lives on in the present; bourgeois thought, essentially devoted to the present, takes its nourishment from what is new now; and proletarian thought tries to grasp the elements of the future which already exist in the present, by concentrating upon those present factors in which the germs of a future society can be seen.

At this point, we at last reach the root of the difference between conservative and progressive forms of experience. It becomes increasingly clear with every case one analyses, that there are at present many different attitudes in the light of which one can experience and understand historical and social events. Each of

---

[1] On other characteristics of the democratic mind, see Carl Schmitt, *Die geistes-geschichtliche Lage des heutigen Parlamentarismus*, p. 15, Munich and Leipzig, 1923.

us can view them, so to speak, from a different point in the stream of history itself. There are ways of acting in the present which are based upon patterns of response appropriate to past conditions but still surviving today. Others have arisen during the struggle for mastery of the present situation, while yet others, although generated in the bosom of the present itself, will only become dominant formative factors at some future time. The important thing is which of these attitudes determines our evaluation of the historical process.

So far then, we have gathered together a number of characteristic features of the conservative form of experience and thought. We have discussed its *qualitative* nature; its emphasis on concreteness as against abstractness; its acceptance of enduring actuality, as compared with the progressive desire for change; the illusory simultaneity it imparts to historical happenings as compared with the liberal linear conception of historical development; its attempt to substitute landed property for the individual as the basis of history; and its preference for organic social units rather than the agglomerative units such as 'classes' favoured by its opponents. All these individual traits, however, are not meant to add up to a concept which will represent 'conservatism' as such. They are merely examples which somehow adumbrate one basic intention, the fundamental impulse lying at the roots of this style of thought. Our aim is to look beyond the examples at this basic intention itself, to follow up its unfolding, and finally to understand its functional importance in relation to the general social process. For the main thing is that this insistence upon 'concreteness', along with all the other features we have described, is a symptom of the conservative's experiencing the historical process in terms of relationships and situations which exist only as hangovers from the past, and that the impulses to act which spring from this way of experiencing history also are centred upon past relationships still surviving in the present. To see things authentically as a conservative, then, is to experience events in terms of an attitude derived from social circumstances and situations anchored in the past,[1] an attitude which changed comparatively little right up to the birth of modern conservatism, because the groups cultivating it had not yet been affected by the specifically modern trends of social evolution. Authentic conservative thought derives its rele-

[1] Cf. the following phenomenological distinction between 'recollection' and 'tradition', made by Max Scheler: 'In effectively "traditional" behaviour, the past experience is not present in its individuality; its value and meaning, however, appear as "present" and not as "past", as is the case with "recollection"' (*Vom Umsturz der Werte*, vol. 2, pp. 202 f., Leipzig, 1909). Similarly, 'progressive' behaviour, for Scheler, is distinguished from 'expectancy': in the former, the future pattern of events becomes effective without explicit anticipation (*ibid.*).

vance, its dignity as something more than mere speculation, from the fact that vital attitudes of this character still survive in various sectors of our society.

These older ways of experiencing the world alone impart to conservatism its distinctive character. Hence, we can best study authentic conservatism in those social spheres where the traditional continuity of the concrete groups with a naturally conservative way of life is not yet broken. On the other hand, conservatism first becomes conscious and reflective when other ways of life and thought appear on the scene, against which it is compelled to take up arms in the ideological struggle. This is the first stage in the formation of a definitely conservative ideology; it is also a stage of methodological deliberation in which conservatism tries to become conscious of its essence. Subsequently, it becomes the destiny of conservatism that it can increasingly maintain itself only on the plane of conscious reflection. Möser, who marks this first stage in the development of conservatism in Germany, still lives entirely within the bounds of tradition; nevertheless, he does try to grasp the nature of this authentic conservatism in a reflective manner.

In the measure, however, that specifically modern social structures not merely co-exist with old ones but draw them into their orbit and transform them, authentic conservative experience tends to disappear. The simple habit of living more or less unconsciously, as though the old ways of life were still appropriate, gradually gives way to a deliberate effort to maintain them under the new conditions, and they are raised to the level of conscious reflection, of deliberate 'recollection'. Conservative thought thus saves itself, so to speak, by raising to the level of reflection and conscious manipulation those forms of experience which can no longer be had in an authentic way.

Here, at the stage where experience based on mere tradition began to disappear, the meaning of history was first consciously discovered, and every effort was bent towards the development of a method of thought by which the old attitude towards the world could somehow be rescued. This method of reviving old attitudes gave rise to an entirely new way of interpreting the genetic process of history. Our position, then, is that old ways of life and thought do not become superfluous and merely die off, as would be assumed by someone thinking in purely 'progressive' terms. On the contrary, in so far as these elements of the past are really alive and have a real social basis, they will always transform and adapt themselves to the new stage of social and mental development, and thus keep alive a 'strand' of social development which would otherwise have become extinct.

In order, therefore, that modern conservatism could develop as a conscious political philosophy opposed to the liberal philosophy of the Enlightenment, and play a dynamic role within the modern struggle of ideas, its germinal 'basic intention' had to exist as an authentic style of experience within certain traditional groups. Hence, we cannot neglect the task of exploring the conservative 'basic intention' in its unconscious, unreflective form; this is why we often return to the writings of Justus Möser who represents authentic conservatism, not yet at the level of 'recollection' and reflection, a conservatism—in fact, rather a kind of feudal 'traditionalism'. Only when this authentic conservatism is uprooted and detached from its original social foundations and takes on a reflective character, does the problem arise of its transformation into an urban current of thought with fixed maxims and methodological insights of its own.

(b) The theoretical core of conservative thought

Now comes the second stage in our analysis. We have described the basic impulse behind conservatism in its pre-theoretical, primitive form. We must now ask whether there is not some theoretical core, some problem at the centre of conservative thought in its more developed form, an analysis of which will provide us with a clear view of its major methodological characteristics.

Such a key problem for conservatism does exist. Conservative thought emerged as an independent current when it was forced into conscious opposition to bourgeois-revolutionary thought, to *the natural-law mode of thought*. What had up to this point been a more or less latent impulse in thought now found a theoretical nucleus around which it could crystallize and develop. Its opponent had a 'system', and conservatism was thus compelled gradually to develop its own 'counter-system'. It is important, of course, not to fall into Stahl's error by thinking that two distinct cut-and-dried systems of thought now confronted one another. Conservative and liberal-bourgeois thought are not ready-made 'systems' in this sense; they are *ways of thinking* in continuous process of development. Conservatism did not merely want to think 'something different' from its liberal opponents; *it wanted to think it differently*, and that was the impulse which provided that extra touch which turned it into a new form of thought.

The key problem for conservatism was opposition to natural-law thought. We shall therefore classify all the features which distinguish natural-law thought in the eighteenth century as a style of thought, and compare them with the corresponding characteristics of conservative thought. Our classification is divided into features of content and features of form, or methodology.

A. *The contents of natural-law thought*

    i. The doctrine of the 'state of nature'.
    ii. The doctrine of the social contract.
    iii. The doctrine of popular sovereignty.
    iv. The doctrine of the inalienable Rights of Man (life, liberty, property, the right to resist tyranny, etc.).

B. *The methodological characteristics of natural-law thought*

    i. Rationalism as a method of solving problems.
    ii. Deductive procedure from one general principle to the particular cases.
    iii. A claim of *universal validity* for every individual.
    iv. A claim to universal applicability of all laws to all historical and social units.
    v. Atomism and mechanism: collective units (the state, the law, etc.), are constructed out of isolated individuals or factors.
    vi. Static thinking (right reason conceived as a self-sufficient, autonomous sphere unaffected by history).

The most satisfactory way to get at the essentials of conservative thought is to see how it opposed each of these aspects of natural-law thought in turn.

The conservatives attacked the *content* of natural-law thought, questioned the idea of a 'state of nature', the idea of a Social Contract, the principle of popular sovereignty, and the Rights of Man.

They attacked it methodologically along the following lines:

(i) The conservatives replaced Reason with concepts such as History, Life, the Nation.

This produces philosophical problems which dominate the whole epoch. In their abstract formulation, these philosophies deal with such old problems as that of 'thinking' and 'being'; but it is possible to interpret this discussion in a thoroughly concrete fashion, that is, in terms of the overwhelmingly powerful experience of the French Revolution. Sociologically speaking, most philosophical schools which place 'thinking' above 'being' have their roots either in bourgeois revolutionary or in bureaucratic mentality, while most schools which place 'being' above 'thinking' have their origin in the ideological counter-movement of romanticism and especially in the experience of counter-revolution.

(ii) To the deductive bent of the natural-law school, the conservative opposes the *irrationality of reality*. The problem of the irrational is the second great problem of the period; it too, in the form it assumed at the time, has its sociological roots in the French Revolution. The problem of the relation of genesis to validity attains its modern significance in these ideological struggles.

(iii) In answer to the liberal claim of universal validity for all, the conservative poses the problem of *individuality* in radical fashion.

(iv) The concept of the social *organism* is developed by the conservatives to counter the liberal-bourgeois belief in the universal applicability of all political and social innovations. This concept has a special significance, since it arose from the natural conservative impulse to stem the spreading tide of the French Revolution by pointing out the impossibility of transferring political institutions arbitrarily from one nation to another. The emphasis on the qualitative which is so characteristic of conservative thought also arises from the same impulse.

(v) Against the construction of collective units from isolated individuals and factors, the conservative opposes a kind of thought which starts from a concept of a whole which is not the mere sum of its parts. The state or nation is not to be understood as the sum of its individual members, but the individuals are to be understood only as parts of the wider whole (cf. the concept of 'folk spirit'). The conservative thinks in terms of 'We' when the liberal thinks in terms of 'I'. The liberal analyses and isolates the various cultural fields such as Law, Government, Economy; the conservative seeks a synoptical and synthetic view.

(vi) One of the most important logical weapons against the natural-law style of thought is the *dynamic conception of Reason*. At first, the conservative merely opposed the rigidity of the static theory of Reason with the movement of 'Life' and history. Later, however, he discovered a much more radical method of disposing of the eternal norms of the Enlightenment. Instead of regarding the world as eternally changing in contrast to a static Reason, he conceived of Reason and of its norms themselves as changing and moving. In this way, the impulse to oppose natural-law thought had really contributed something new, had achieved new insights which played a momentous role in later evolution.

As we have already mentioned, nowhere do we find any conservative thinker making a systematic attack on natural-law thought as a whole; each deals with and criticizes certain aspects of it only. Thus it is impossible to juxtapose two static, completely developed systems of thought. All that can be done is to demonstrate the two ways of thinking, the two ways of tackling problems. The analysis of its pre-theoretical and theoretical elements which we have given is in our view the only legitimate substitute for a definition of conservative thought.

In the following section we leave this general description of conservative thought and turn to a more detailed historical and sociological analysis.

SECTION 3

The Social Structure of Romantic and Feudalistic Conservatism

Having described the general character of a certain historical mode of thought, our next task is to investigate its concrete development, in all its different currents, from the point of view of its social structure and stratification.

The most important aim of such an analysis is to find out how far any new trend of thought that may happen to arise reflects the sociological characteristics of the group or individuals who stand behind it and through whom it finds expression. Phenomenological and logical stylistic analysis and sociological analysis must be used as complementary methods.

Here again—as has already been mentioned—not more than one selected section of a complex historical situation will be presented. From the numerous currents which can be distinguished in the general flow of conservative thought, the romantic and feudalistic trend has been chosen for this purpose.

We can best give an overall characterization of the mental climate of a country at a given time, without entering upon a detailed analysis, by indicating the way in which it absorbs and transforms foreign cultural influences.

An investigation, from this point of view, of the intellectual atmosphere of Germany in the period which has been selected, viz. the decades following the French Revolution, shows as the most significant fact that the revolution produced in Prussia, the outstanding centre of conservative thought, an antagonism between the older feudalistic tendencies and the bureaucratic rationalism of the eighteenth-century monarchy. The French Revolution no doubt had a revolutionary influence on the Prussian bourgeoisie. But perhaps even more significant was its effect in weakening, for a time, the spiritual and political alliance between the absolute monarchy and the nobility which Frederick the Great had made one of the corner-stones of his social policy.[1] Not that the middle classes were inaccessible to the liberal ideas of the

---

[1] Frederick the Great wrote in his Political Testament of 1752: 'One object of the policy of the king of Prussia is the preservation of nobility. For, whatever changes may come about, he may perhaps find a richer, but he will never find a more courageous and loyal nobility. In order to assist the nobility in maintaining their property, commoners should be prevented from acquiring titled estates. They should be encouraged

revolution; we know very well the enthusiasm with which the widest circles of the German intelligentsia greeted the outbreak of the revolution in France.[1] The careers of most conservatives and reactionaries show revolutionary periods in their youth. We know also that there was a surprisingly large number of men with liberal ideas among the higher officials, and that the 'reforms from above' which were carried through after the battle of Jena were due to these influences. Yet this liberal response to the revolution was in the main ideological in its nature; it was largely reversed by the subsequent development of the real historical factors.

That fact in itself need not surprise us. The complex intellectual pattern of any age is historically and socially conditioned. It is therefore one of its characteristics that it reacts to external ideological influences in a definite manner which reflects its own specific structure, and that it re-moulds them to fit the direction of its own development. The ideas of 1789 demanded, in contrast to the theory of royal absolutism, that the state should be constructed 'from below' instead of 'from above'. When they penetrated into Germany, they could only set in motion and bring to life those elements of the German, and more specifically the Prussian, body politic which happened to exist there as historically and socially relevant forces. They were the estates of which in turn one alone was politically effective, the nobility.[2] Every other influence was at that time bound to remain merely 'ideological'.

We may see in the first decades of the nineteenth century in Prussia a sociological experiment, as it were, which shows what happens when ideas which have genuinely grown up in a more advanced stage of social development enter a socially backward but culturally mature society. Germany, and especially Prussia whose fate was decisive for conservative thought, were many decades behind the Western countries in the economic development towards capitalism. We need not accept Frederick the Great's estimate of Germany's backwardness in his time.[3] But

to invest their capital in trade so that only a nobleman may buy an estate, should another be forced to sell' ('Friedrich der Grosse, Die politischen Testamente', *Klassiker der Politik*, ed. Meinecke, Oncken, vol. 5, p. 33, Berlin, 1922). For the later development, *vide* F. A. L. v.d. Marwitz, *Ein märkischer Edelmann im Zeitalter der Befreiungskriege*, ed. F. Meusel, 2 vols. (in 4 half-vols.), vol. 2, pp. 80 ff.

[1] Cf., for example, Venedey, *Die deutschen Republikaner unter der französischen Republik*, Leipzig, 1870.

[2] Cf., for example, E. Jordan, *Die Entstehung der Konservativen Partei und die preussischen Agrarverhältnisse vor 1848*, pp. 9 f., 1914. Also G. Kaufmann, *Geschichte Deutschlands im 19. Jahrhundert*, p. 48, Berlin, 1912.

[3] Cf., for example, E. v. Meier, *Die französischen Einflüsse auf die Staats- und Rechtsentwicklung Preussens im 19. Jahrhundert*, vol. 1, p. 6, Leipzig, 1907. Meier considers Frederick the Great's remark that the intellectual condition of Germany corresponded to the condition of France under Francis I correct if applied to the early years of Frederick's life.

Marx's view is probably correct; and he held that the social condition of Germany in 1843 corresponded roughly to that of France in 1789.[1] At the time of the French Revolution neither Germany nor *a fortiori* Prussia possessed a real equivalent to the third or fourth 'estate'. The transformation of the feudal society of estates into a class society was still in its early stages. The proletariat consisted of handicraftsmen who still lived to all intents and purposes in a system of guilds and did not react to external pressure as a class. Nor did the '*Mittelstand*' really correspond to the '*tiers état*'; as Sombart has shown, it was as yet by no means a bourgeoisie.[2] Socially and politically immature, it still lacked clearly defined aims and a conscious purpose; it was at the mercy of a variety of ideological currents and cross-currents. The *Mittelstand* had as yet no precise place in the social system, a place defined by its own interests. As a result, most of its members were politically indifferent. They were quick to welcome new ideas; but also unstable and ready to change their moods when things went wrong or not in accordance with their abstract expectations. All these characteristics were clear symptoms of the fact that the diverse interests of the *Mittelstand* were not yet integrated along class lines. The reason for the relatively weak revolutionary influence of the French Revolution is therefore that it evoked a purely ideological response: the bourgeois element was at that time less capable of political action than any other social stratum in Germany.

An active response to the revolution came only from those strata in Prussia which their own history and the nature of the social order enabled to be politically effective, the nobility and the bureaucracy. If we may put it in an exaggerated form: For our purposes, the most important effect of the French Revolution is that the French conflict between king and people is here reproduced on a 'higher' level. It takes the form of a struggle between the estates (the nobility), which form and build up the state 'from below', and the monarchy, ruling the state 'from above' and represented in Prussia by its bureaucracy. The result is a curious interplay of influences. The revolutionary impulse proper in the French upheaval gives life and meaning to the aims of the

---

[1] K. Marx, *Zur Kritik der Hegelschen Rechtsphilosophie*, vol. 1, p. 385.

[2] 'The *Mittelstand* united in those days everyone who did not belong either to the nobility or to the lower classes. It did not have the character of a class in our sense of the term. Sometimes it appeared as the group which comprised all the moderately well-to-do; sometimes more as the educated sections of the population' (Sombart, *Die deutsche Volkswirtschaft im 19. Jahrhundert*, p. 444, Berlin, 1921). Cf. also K. F. Moser's frequently quoted remark: 'We lack that mediatory power which Montesquieu considered the support and defence of a good monarchy: le *tiers état*.'—For reasons of space we cannot enter upon a more thorough-going economic analysis of the social system of the time.

nobility who wish to form and rule the state 'from below', insists upon the privileges of the estates, and seeks an 'organic' society, a desire to revive the corporative structure of medieval society.[1] The mechanistic, rationalist, and centralizing impulse in the French Revolution, on the other hand, finds its exponents in the bureaucracy and is used by them as a weapon against the nobility. What complicates the situation further is the fact that in Prussia the revolution was at first really imposed 'from above'. (The expression 'revolution from above' was coined by von Harden-berg.) Reforms which the development of the state towards capitalism required were carried out by the absolutist state, supported by its bureaucracy. They were carried through only partly in the interests of the masses. To a certain extent they were directed against the nobility.

In France the revolution had brought about a defensive alliance between the nobility, the monarchy, and the Church. In Prussia the *real* pressure from below was negligible. The result was there-fore a partial weakening of the alliance between the nobility and the bureaucracy. The situation found its ideological expression in a feudalistic reaction. It was a movement which in its thought and ideas belonged to the nineteenth century. With the most advanced ideological weapons it fought for aims which were determined by the social position of the nobility. It expressed therefore in modern terms purposes which had their social basis and justification in an age long gone by. The ideological reaction to the Enlightenment was combined with the social reaction of the nobility. Romanticism took on a feudalistic character; the feudalistic conservatism of the nobility assumed a romantic colouring. From this combination arose the peculiar features which to the present day characterize the 'German' mind.[2] What

[1] The following sentences from v. d. Marwitz may serve as an illustration : 'However active and benevolent a government may be, it is useless to the state, unless the governed understand and share [*miterleben*] its activities' (*op. cit.*, vol. 2, p. 58), or (*ibid.*, footnote) : 'The state does not consist of men who *live side by side*, and of whom some rule and the others obey; it consists of men who live *within each other*, it is the *unified* spiritual direction of their will'. ('Der Staat ist nicht ein *Nebeneinandersein* von Menschen, deren einige befehlen, die anderen gehorchen, sondern das *Ineinandersein* dieser Menschen—die *gemeinschaftliche* geistige Richtung ihres Wollens . . .').

[2] We cannot accept the view of those who think of national ways of thought as ultimate and unanalysable data which are to be deduced directly from 'national characters' and who speak in that sense of the 'French', 'German' or 'English' mind. It is possible that sociological study may in the end come up against some irreducible residuum of national character, although even that residuum could not be considered as unchangeable in the course of time. But one must first take into account all those factors which can be deduced from the history and social structure of the nation. Once one adopts this approach, one will realize that those who speak of a 'national' way of thought are in fact thinking of the thought of a particular period of national life, and within that period only of the thought of a particular social stratum which happens to have a decisive influence on the national culture in that period. They take this socio-logically and historically closely definable way of thought for the way of thought of

strikes us as the 'German' way of thinking is the predominance of these 'romantic' elements, supplemented by 'historicist' ones which arose at the same time and in the same constellation of historical forces and which became a powerful factor in the alliance between romanticism and feudalistic conservatism.

In order to understand this peculiar combination it is necessary to look more closely at the social character of the strata which took part in this ideological struggle. Let us begin with the romantic opposition. It consists, first, of the nobility, and secondly, of the 'idéologues', middle-class literati and literary aristocrats, who became the spokesmen of the movement.

The romantic movement, considered as an *ideological* force, began as a reaction against the Enlightenment. Its *social* basis seems to have been—especially in the period of *préromantisme*—in social strata which stood apart from the general current towards modern capitalism. They may perhaps be defined as the petty bourgeoisie (*Kleinbürgertum*). In this connection the Protestant parsonage seems to have played a particularly important part.[1] It is especially the son of the Protestant parson in whom the Enlightenment stirs doubts of the traditional religion, but who does not therefore succumb to the opposite extreme of an abstract rationalism. He experiences a transformation of his religious attitude. All his traditional habits of thought and emotional reactions which were fostered by the religious life in the parsonage survive the impact of the Enlightenment. Deprived of their positive content, they are directed with redoubled strength against the rationalist atmosphere of the time. The new approval of irrationality for its own sake was made possible by the preceding tendency to concentrate and emphasize the rational elements of the mind. A compact

---

the whole nation at all times. In this form the view is mistaken. What is true is that certain epochs and in these epochs certain social strata may have a lasting effect on the habits of thought of a nation, especially if the epoch is a decisive one for the development of national history and culture. In this sense, A. de Tocqueville (*L'ancien régime et la révolution*, 8th ed., p. 217, Paris, 1877) deduced the French tendency towards abstract thinking quite correctly from the sociological importance of the pre-revolutionary era—and the mentality of that era, in turn, from the cultural predominance of an intelligentsia which was excluded from the government and administration of the country. To the same extent, but in the opposite direction, the years of the Napoleonic wars and of the subsequent period of reaction have been decisive for the character of German thought. The 'German' mind has ever since been so completely romantic and historicist that even its own opposition which grew up in that atmosphere could never quite free itself from its habits of thought. Heine was a romantic despite his opposition to the romantic school; Marx a historicist despite his opposition to the historical school; etc.

[1] Cf. the thorough investigations of H. Schöffler in his *Protestantismus und Literatur*, 'Neue Wege zur englischen Literatur des achtzehnten Jahrhunderts', Leipzig, 1922.— For the precursors of the romantic movement see also Paul van Tieghem, *Le Préromantisme*, 'Études d'histoire littéraire Européenne', Paris, 1924; and A. Weise, *Die Entstehung des Fühlens und Denkens der Romantik auf Grund der romantischen Zeitschriften*, Diss. Leipzig, 1912.

ideological counter-movement of irrationalism could only arise because the Enlightenment had carried the tendency towards rationalization to the utmost extreme. It had managed to conceive the world in a radically and consistently rational manner. It thereby excluded at every point irrational factors; but with them it threw out elements of human nature which by that very process of exclusion were welded together and became the nucleus of a counter-current. They became the object of special attention and affection to all those who by reason of their personal history and social tradition were still able to think and feel in such terms— just as in the opposite camp the rationalist current had found its exponents in the progressive bourgeoisie, the monarchy, and the bureaucracy.

With the political trends of the time the romantic movement was at first but loosely connected. All we can say is that revolutionary sympathies prevailed in harmony with the predominant mood of the pre-revolutionary period. After the French Revolution the various national sections of the romantic movement went their own ways, each in accordance with the social structure of the country. The special conditions of Germany explain why German romanticism turned to conservatism and reaction.[1] In any case, this development meant a reinforcement of all those trends within the romantic movement which were from the beginning opposed to the new world of capitalism and liberalism. The peculiar characteristic of German romanticism is therefore that it increasingly unites the ideological and the political opposition against the modern world.

This ideological and political antagonism against the basic forces of the modern world must, however, not be allowed to conceal the fact that the romantic movement is not just a purely retrogressive reaction. The romantic mind has already absorbed and neutralized the contribution of modern rationalism. It is not adequate to think of romanticism simply as a diametrically opposed and entirely heterogeneous counter-movement to rationalism. It should rather be compared to the swing of a pendulum —a sudden reversal from an extreme point reached in one direction. The change-over from rationalism into irrationalism— both in the emotional life and in the intellectual activities of the individual—occurs even among the chief representatives of the Enlightenment itself. Thus in Rousseau and Montesquieu an extreme rationalism and its opposite exist peacefully side by side.[2]

[1] For the situation in France cf. C. Schmitt-Dorotic, *Politische Romantik*, Munich and Leipzig, 1919, especially the introduction.
[2] A. Wahl, 'Montesquieu als Vorläufer von Aktion und Reaktion', in *Historische Zeitschrift*, vol. 109, 1912.

In Germany the precursors of the romantic movement, the men of the 'Sturm und Drang', Hamann and Herder appear already in the heyday of the Enlightenment. Only the swing of the pendulum which derives its impetus from the same forces as the rationalist movement explains why—in spite of undeniable radical contrasts—romanticism shows qualities which recall the rationalism of the eighteenth century: among them, its excessive subjectivism, admittedly a form of subjectivism very different from the subjectivism of the Enlightenment; also, its tendency—co-existing with a pronounced programmatic irrationalism—to rationalize all those irrational forces of the mind which the rationalism of the Enlightenment with all its abstract methods could never really have apprehended.

By the time this romantic current takes on the form of a 'movement' its exponents are to be found chiefly among the 'socially unattached intelligentsia'.[1] Thus, it has its social basis in the same stratum as the Enlightenment. But there is also a difference. In the Enlightenment, that stratum and its philosophical spokesmen were still, as it were, in touch with their social and historical origins. The bourgeois writers of the Enlightenment could still lean on the ideological support of the bourgeoisie. The conversion to romanticism meant for the intelligentsia an increasing social and philosophical isolation.[2] Nowhere is it more apparent to what extent the intelligentsia constitutes a distinct sociological phenomenon whose place within the social organism is so difficult to determine just because of the instability of its social condition and its lack of a secure economic position. The German intelligentsia, as far as it was socially unattached, was indeed very badly off during that period. Newspapers in our sense there were none, and the last years of Kleist's life show what it meant to keep alive a journal like the *Berliner Abendblätter*.[3] One could try to exist as an independent writer, a profession which was then of but recent origin. Klopstock, Lessing and Wieland were in fact the first German writers who tried to make a living by literary production alone.[4] In view of these difficulties which life as an independent intellectual involved it is not surprising that the lives of most literary men of the time show, after a period of violent youthful

[1] An expression of Alfred Weber's.
[2] The son of the parson becomes an independent writer, etc.
[3] Cf. the vivid account in R. Steig, *Heinrich v. Kleist's Berliner Kämpfe*, Berlin and Stuttgart, 1901.
[4] Cf. Lamprecht, *Deutsche Geschichte*, vol. 8 (I), p. 209. Lessing's other literary contemporaries, Weisse, Engel, Moritz, Dusch, soon took refuge in safer means of earning their living. Compared with Lessing's time conditions had improved only at the time of Schlegel and Novalis. Cf. W. Dilthey, *Leben Schleiermachers*, vol. 1 (2nd ed.), pp. 193, 255, Berlin and Leipzig, 1922.

opposition to the world and their environment, the tendency to take refuge in the haven of officialdom.

This combination of an unstable economic position with an intellectual horizon which went far beyond their own narrow sphere of life produced in the romantic writers an enormous sensibility coupled with moral uncertainty and a constant readiness to become adventurers or mercenary pamphleteers. They cannot earn a living by their own unaided effort in their 'unattached' state. They sell their pen to one government or another[1]; they oscillate between Prussia and Austria, many of them landing at that time with Metternich who knew well how to make use of their services. Never properly employed as officials, chiefly used for secret or propaganda services, their thought assumes that semi-concrete quality which stands halfway between the idealist's remoteness from the affairs of the world and the official's exclusive concentration on concrete tasks. They are neither abstract dreamers, nor narrow-minded practical men. They are characteristically interested in exploring the specific marks of their age[2]; they are born philosophers of history. This, in fact, is the positive side of their activity, for there must and should always be men who are sufficiently free from the ordinary ties to shoulder cares other than that for the common routine of life[3]; and the more involved the social process becomes, the greater the need for such men who are in a position to throw light on its course. At the beginning, or at least at an important juncture of that development, which represents, as it were, the creation by history of an organ of self-observation, stand the speculations of the Enlightenment on the philosophy of history. Romantic thought fulfils the same function, although the value standards it applies are diametrically opposed to those of Enlightenment. From this source, too, German sociology has derived its predilection for problems of the philosophy of history, a predilection which, in contrast to Western sociology, it still maintains as its characteristic quality. This is the positive element in romantic political thought. Its negative quality is its readiness to justify any cause and any condition.

[1] Adam Müller even makes an offer to Hardenberg to edit, in the service of the government, a government *and* an opposition paper at the same time.

[2] An essay by Friedrich Schlegel was entitled 'Die Signatur des Zeitalters'.

[3] If one attempted to speculate *a priori*, without taking historical experience into account, at which point in the social structure a philosophy of history (in other words an interest in the totality of the process of history) is likely to arise, one would think it probable that those would reflect on these general aspects who, by their social position, are responsible for the whole—high officials, diplomats, kings. Experience, however, shows that this conjecture is only partially correct, if at all. High civil servants possess the necessary practical experience and knowledge of the forces at work; but their general point of view tends to see society in terms of administration or

These unattached intellectuals are the typical advocate-philosophers, *ideologues* who can find arguments in favour of any political cause they may happen to serve. Their own social position does not bind them to any cause, but they have an extraordinarily refined sense for all the political and social currents around them, and the ability to detect them and enter into their spirit. By themselves they know nothing. But let them take up and identify themselves with someone else's interests—they will know them better, really better, than those for whom these interests are laid down by the nature of things, by their social condition.

Sensibility is therefore also the peculiar quality of their thought. Their virtue is not thoroughness but a flair for events in the spiritual and intellectual life of their society. Their constructions are therefore always false or even deliberately falsified. But there is always something that is astutely observed. Herein lies the fruitfulness of the romantic movement for the social sciences.[1] It threw up problems for discussion; it discovered whole new spheres of study. But it was left to later research to sift the facts from mere

power politics. Such a perspective can never give rise to a philosophy of history or sociology. The 'unattached intelligentsia' is no doubt liable to hatch out empty speculations. Yet the best chance for the achievement of comprehensive views of the whole course of history appears when intellectuals who are gifted with an instinct for concrete matters and who are, to start with, socially unattached, ally themselves with the aims of real existing social forces. (It is, in this context, at first irrelevant whether the real forces which they join show society from above, as with Ranke or Treitschke, or from below, as with Marx.) The first generation of the romanticists still lacked this sense of the concrete. Even in its later period (Fr. Schlegel, A. Müller) abstract speculation and awareness of real forces are to be found side by side but unrelated. Ranke, Treitschke, Marx show a much more powerful fusion of both faculties; it is almost possible to speak of progress. How much even the 'first servant of the state' is prevented by the peculiar character of his social position from reaching a proper philosophical or sociological insight into the general structure of society—even where he is personally endowed with a gift for 'philosophy'—some sentences from Frederick the Great's Political Testament of 1752 may serve to illustrate. He writes: 'Too ambitious and complicated political schemes are no more successful than excessively ingenious movements in a war. . . .' He gives some historical examples and then continues: 'All these examples show that grand schemes which are tackled too soon never come off. Politics is too much subject to accidents. It gives the human mind no power over future events and over anything that belongs to the realm of chance. The art of politics consists more in utilizing favourable opportunities than in bringing them about by careful planning in advance. For this reason I advise you not to conclude treaties which refer to uncertain events in the future, but to preserve your freedom of action so as to be able to take your decisions in accordance with time, place, and the state of your affairs: in one word, as your interests will require at the time' (pp. 61 f.). Even the 'political reveries' which follow do not break through the 'tactical approach'. The agent himself stands much too close to be able to see behind the appearances of men and affairs and to penetrate to the structural relationships.

[1] For the importance of romanticism for historiography, cf. v. Below, *Wesen und Ausbreitung der Romantik*, supplement to his book *Über historische Periodisierung* (*Einzelschriften zur Politik und Geschichte*, ed. by H. Roeseler, no. 11, Berlin, 1925). Also v. Below, *Die deutsche Geschichtsschreibung von den Befreiungskriegen bis zu unseren Tagen*, 2nd ed. (*Handbuch der mittelalterlichen und neueren Geschichte*, Munich and Berlin, 1927).

intellectual constructions. The 'enlightened' intellect of the French *philosophes* had to substitute wit and *esprit* for the scientific foundation which it lacked. With the romanticists this wit becomes a specific form of sensitiveness—a faculty for detecting fine shades of quality, supreme mastery in the art of emotional sympathy and appreciation. Thus the intellectual current of literary *esprit* and romanticism produces one component of what one might call 'qualitative thinking'. Its other component sprang at the same time, though in a wholly different way, from the attitude of feudalistic conservatism.[1] It was due, as we have seen, to their lack of any firm roots in the social structure that the romanticists were excluded from an understanding of ultimate ends, that their thought was full of direction but without starting-point, that they defended causes which had their social basis elsewhere—in strata of greater social vitality. Their fate is typical of the fate of the intelligentsia in the modern world—clearly traceable since the eighteenth century. The fate of the world of thought is in the care of a socially unattached, or barely attached, stratum whose class affinities and status in society cannot be precisely defined; a stratum which does not find the aims it pursues within itself but in the interests of strata with a more definite place in the social order. This fact is of the greatest importance for modern thought, because the ultimate directions and aims of ideological movements are determined by their social background. If even these ultimate aims were surrendered into the hands of that socially unattached intelligentsia they would soon be scattered and frittered away. If, on the other hand, there were no such stratum of socially free and unattached intellectuals, it might easily happen that all spiritual content would disappear from our increasingly capitalistic society and leave nothing but naked interests. For it is the latter which are at the basis of ideas as well as ideologies.

If one wants to carry the description of the peculiar character of the thought of these romantic writers beyond the two qualities which have already been mentioned (their interest in the philosophy of history and their sensitiveness to qualitative differences) one could hardly find a better definition of the romantic element than that which was given by Novalis himself. He declares: 'The world must be romanticized. That is the way to its original meaning. Romanticizing means nothing but *raising to a higher level of quality*. Through that operation the lower

1 When two currents of thought merge into each other, it is the task of the sociology of knowledge to discover those elements in both which showed an inner resemblance even *before* the synthesis and which thus made the synthesis possible. This is one of the guiding considerations in this part of our analysis. The methodological problem has been suggested previously, in a similar sense, by Max Weber, in his *Religionssoziologie*, vol. 1, p. 83.

self is identified with a higher self, since our soul consists of a series of qualitatively different levels. This operation is still completely unknown. *In giving a noble meaning to the vulgar, a mysterious appearance to the commonplace, the dignity of the unknown to the known, the semblance of infinity to the finite,* I romanticize it.'[1] We should like to redefine this 'technique' of thought by saying that it finds a higher level of cause and meaning for the facts of a given situation than is usually associated with them. We believe that this merely expresses in different words what Novalis said in the above quotation. It shows, at the same time, that the facts of a situation are not created or discovered by the romantic thinker. He merely receives them from somewhere. A typical instance of this method of 'romanticizing' is the romantic treatment of Catholicism or of the nobility. The existence of the nobility is an empirical fact. Assuming all the historical faults and virtues of the nobility as known and given, romantic thought contributes its share by discovering a 'principle', and representing the historical development of the nobility as a struggle between conflicting principles. The facts which in themselves are merely parts of a causally interrelated situation, especially in the eyes of a person with a positivist approach, are thereby given a new interpretation as aspects of a meaningful whole. Such 'romanticizing' no doubt sheds new light on the facts ('something is always astutely observed') but it conceals the real relationships.[2]

It would not be necessary to spend much time on this method of 'romanticizing' if it were confined to the political sphere. The peculiar thing is, however, that this method led to the re-discovery and understanding of an older *mode of thought* which would otherwise have remained latent. Just as romantic thought failed to find its political aims within itself, so it took over, at a certain

---

[1] Novalis, *Schriften*, ed. by J. Minor, vol. 2, pp. 304 f., Jena, 1907. My italics.

[2] We emphasize in the text the concealing character of romantic thought. It could, however, be shown that the romantic method of thought is fruitful in fields where interpretation is appropriate. The reason is that the spiritual sphere may be penetrated to varying 'depths'. The positive meaning of Novalis's remark and of the whole romantic mode of thought lies in the fact that, in contrast to the Enlightenment, it was aware of these different depths. For reasons of space we have to refrain here from a phenomenological analysis which would show this in detail. But such an analysis would also have to show that the romantic preoccupation with these 'depths' was not a true one. The predominance of the subjective approach introduced an arbitrary element into its interpretations and prevented the thinker from getting really inside his subject. This also explains the possibility of abuse to which the method of 'romanticizing' lends itself: the tendency to interpret, or understand 'from within', causally interrelated situations which, by their objective nature, are incapable of such interpretation, and to dignify mean and brutal power relationships by 'interpreting' them. Significantly enough, the possibility of a twofold interpretation is already contained in Novalis's definition : one which attempts to sound the 'depths' of the soul, and a second which leads to an ideological dressing-up of things as they are. The romantic movement realized both possibilities.

stage of its development, certain fundamental ideas opposed to the Enlightenment from the inventory of ideas of *feudalistic conservatism*. It 'romanticized' certain tentatively elaborated conservative theses into a full-fledged methodology, and adapted them to political purposes.

At the important juncture in the history of German social thought where the romanticism of the intellectuals (as the ideological reaction against the Enlightenment) joins hands with the current of feudalistic conservatism stands Adam Müller with his *Elemente der Staatskunst* (Elements of Politics). Adam Müller is not an author who deserves attention on account of his creative originality or the solid worth of his achievement. But he is one of those historical figures who have done a great deal to shape the thought of their age, or at least of one of its predominant movements. He is the born *ideologue* and romanticist in the sense which has just been defined; receptive rather than creative, but at the same time a connoisseur, endowed with an exquisite flair for gathering up what belongs together from the teeming welter of contemporary ideas.[1]

Since we are here concerned only with the main trends of thought, we cannot discuss in detail the beginnings of political romanticism, and little need be said about the early political writings of Novalis and Friedrich Schlegel. Everything they contain that became relevant for the subsequent development of thought is somehow or other worked into Adam Müller's system. Novalis's beautiful essay 'Christendom or Europe' (1799) stands out, but it is a poetic dream rather than political thought.[2] Its ideological point was discovered by Müller: its criticism of Protestantism and its praise for the Catholic hierarchy. With Novalis came into the open that curious Protestant longing for the deserted Church which led to a considerable movement of

1 The literature on romanticism is too extensive to be given here in full. Some of it is collected in J. Baxa, *Einführung in die romantische Staatswissenschaft*, pp. 176 ff., Jena, 1925, and in the second volume of Baxa's edition of Adam Müller's *Elemente der Staatskunst*. The relevant chapters in Meinecke, *Weltbürgertum und Nationalstaat*, and Troeltsch, *Der Historismus und seine Probleme*, are useful. Of recent works may be mentioned, for example, the special volume on romanticism of the *Deutsche Vierteljahrsschrift für Literaturwissenschaft und Geistesgeschichte*, 2. Jahrg., Heft 3, Halle, 1924; R. Aris, *Die Staatslehre Adam Müllers in ihrem Verhältnis zur deutschen Romantik*, Tübingen, 1929; I. Petersen, *Die Wesensbestimmung der deutschen Romantik*, Leipzig, 1926; S. v. Lempicki, *Bücherwelt und wirkliche Welt*. 'Ein Beitrag zur Wesenserfassung der Romantik', in *Deutsche Vierteljahrsschrift für Literaturwissenschaft und Geistesgeschichte*, pp. 339 ff., 1925; G. A. Waltz, *Die Staatsauffassung des Rationalismus und die Romantik und die Staatsidee Fichtes*, Berlin, 1928. The best brief account in English of the political thought of the German romanticists is to be found in R. Aris, *History of Political Thought in Germany 1789–1815*, part 2, London, 1936.

2 There is an early English translation by J. Dalton, London, 1844. For Novalis, see R. Samuel, 'Die poetische Staats- und Geschichtsauffassung Fr. v. Hardenbergs, (*Deutsche Forschungen*, vol. XII), Frankfurt, 1925.

conversion and which had its sociological basis in the interests of Austria, in the Holy Alliance, and in ultramontanism.

One element of the early period of romantic thought was taken up by Adam Müller and acquired an immense importance for the formation of the romantic attitude. It is the element of *pantheism* which, as an intellectual attitude, formed a curious contrast with the hierarchic structure of the Catholic conception of the world and of Catholic thought.[1] Pantheism appeared for the first time in the modern world in the Renaissance, whose philosophy of nature was an intellectual reflection of the pantheist attitude to life. As a wide stream of thought it was vanquished by the growth of natural science. But there were apparently thousands of small rivulets in which it had survived. The *Sturm und Drang* period marks its first powerful reappearance. It is well known how much it colours Goethe's thought.[2] This attitude to life became part of early romantic thought, and there seems to be some truth in the epigram: when Protestantism becomes atheist it tends to turn to pantheism; when Catholicism becomes atheist it turns into materialism.[3] The pantheist attitude dominates the early period of romanticism and lends it a special colour. As its most pronounced feature appears the feeling or idea that God not only stands at the beginning and is not experienced only as the Creator, but lives in every particle of nature.[4] In a sense, both the generalizing, inductive, and positivist thought of natural science and the conceptions of Catholic dogma are opposed to this type of thought, however much they may differ from each other.

For the Catholic Church and scientific positivism resemble each other in that both conceive the immanent world as rational and therefore as rationally intelligible. They are, for that reason, well able—as has often been observed before—to join forces. The miracle (the irrational) stands for Catholic thought at the beginning as the creator and the act of creation; for natural science the irrational has either completely disappeared or it has been relegated to a kind of transcendental sphere of things-in-themselves—at any rate, both systems of thought possess a purified

[1] For the history of pantheism cf. W. Dilthey's essays in vol. 2 of his *Gesammelte Schriften*, Leipzig and Berlin, 1914; and the relevant portions of his Life of Schleiermacher; see also H. Ritter, *Die Halbkantianer und der Pantheismus*, Berlin, 1827.

[2] Cf. F. Bulle, 'Zur Struktur des Pantheismus: Die Kategorie der Totalität in Goethes naturwissenschaftlichen Schriften', in *Euphorion*, vol. 21 (1914), pp. 156 ff.

[3] This connection was already noticed by Fr. Schlegel ('Signatur des Zeitalters', published in *Concordia*, a journal edited by him .pp. 45 f., 1820–23). Also Stahl, *Gegenwärtige Parteien*, lecture 27; cf. v. Martin, *Weltanschauungsmotive*, pp. 374 f.

[4] A passage may be cited which illustrates the mood as well as the structure of pantheist thought: 'Feel how a spring day, a work of art, a loved one, how domestic bliss, civic duties, human deeds weave you, in all the dimensions of the globe, into the Universe, where one art follows the öther and the artist lives for ever . . .' (A. Müller, *Die Lehre vom Gegensatz*, book 1, 'Der Gegensatz', p. 92, Berlin, 1804).

sphere which is thoroughly amenable to rational analysis. In contrast to all this, the pantheist feels Life and God everywhere. He feels a vitality which is inaccessible to the rigid intellect with its abstract generic concepts. Thought, where it plays a part at all, undergoes here a change of function. Its task is no longer to recognize and register the rules of the game, the general laws which govern the world, but to move in harmony with the growth and fluctuations of the world. Two tendencies of thought arise from that pantheism. One is the tendency to think in terms of analogies[1] which existed already in medieval alchemy and astrology, reappeared later in the romantic speculations on nature, and was finally introduced into political philosophy. This mode of thought conceives the world as thoroughly alive, but it assumes that one can find in it hidden sequences and analogies. The tendency to think in terms of analogies is still not wholly opposed to the ordinary method of thought which looks for generally valid laws in the world, since—in its own curious way—this form of thought, too, endeavours to find general laws—that is, morphological laws of succession. This thought becomes really pantheistic when it abandons even the analogy as a pattern of regularity—when it experiences every moment as something unique and incomparable, any genesis as the manifestation of a life force, and assigns thought the task of following the rhythm of the world. Thought must not *portray* the world; it must *accompany its movements*. From this tendency arises everything that we call 'dynamic thinking'. The pantheism of the nineteenth century represents a special form in that it became a historical pantheism—as the highest experience of the essence of life appeared the experience of history.

We shall later on pursue in detail the varied fate of romantic pantheism. For the present it is enough to state that the pantheist dynamic style of thought was the most important heritage which Adam Müller received from the early period of romanticism. At the same time, it is interesting to observe the struggle which takes place in his thought between the hierarchic and static principle of Catholicism and the new dynamics. It is almost possible to put one's finger on the exact spot in the *Elemente der Staatskunst*[2] where the pantheist conception of things gradually dies down and gives way to the hierarchic mode of thought. Later on, we shall have to consider two other influences which

[1] Carl Schmitt, in his *Politische Romantik*, analyses that tendency to think in terms of analogies and the technique of 'removing dualities by means of a higher *tertium quid*' very cleverly from the Catholic point of view. We feel that Schmitt does not do justice to the essential dynamic element which is contained in this type of thought.

[2] Cf. A. Müller, *Elemente der Staatskunst*, half-vol. 1, p. 218, and Baxa's marginal comment to the passage.

left their mark upon the *Elemente:* Edmund Burke and Justus Möser.

Before turning to the analysis of these additional influences, it is necessary to investigate the concrete sociological situation in which the *Elemente der Staatskunst* were written and which alone entitles us to consider the work as historically representative. As the title-page announces, the book consists of lectures which had been delivered in the winter of 1808–9 in Dresden 'before His Highness, Prince Bernard of Saxe-Weimar, and a gathering of statesmen and diplomats', and were printed in the same year in lecture form. It anticipates a state of mind which did not find expression in practical politics until the rise of the aristocratic opposition against Hardenberg in 1810–11.[1] The main theme of the book is a plea for the nobility and the whole feudalistic attitude. This is the nucleus around which the author develops a whole system of political philosophy—with much brilliant argument and unrivalled intellectual virtuosity. The immediate occasion for the choice of the subject was a pamphlet by the liberal writer Buchholz, 'Concerning the Hereditary Nobility', which, according to the testimony of Gentz, aroused immense consternation among the older nobility.[2] We do not wish to linger on the much-discussed fact that Gentz encouraged Müller in his letter to write a refutation of Buchholz's book and promised him an 'exceedingly pleasant existence' as the reward.[3] For us that fact is important only because it shows clearly that the alliance between romantic and feudalistic thought was causally determined by real social relationships. Two currents of thought which already possess an inherent affinity are here induced to merge and coalesce by the influence of external social conditions.

After these comments on the real sociological situation we may now return to the analysis of the two non-romantic contributors to Adam Müller's thought we have mentioned, Burke and Justus Möser. The influence of the former is much more obvious, not only because Müller frequently refers to him and praises him to the skies, but because there is material evidence of his influence, i.e. one can show without difficulty that certain ideas are derived from Burke. The influences of the feudalistic element on Müller's work, on the other hand, lie much deeper; and that is perhaps the

---

[1] Cf. W. Steffens, 'Hardenberg und die ständische Opposition 1810–11', in *Veröffentlichungen des Vereins f. Geschichte d. Mark Brandenburg*, Leipzig, 1907; also F. Lenz, *Agrarlehre und Agrarpolitik der deutschen Romantik*, Berlin, 1912; H. Sultan, 'Rodbertus und der agrarische Sozial-Konservatismus', in *Zeitschrift f. d. ges. Staatswissensch.*, vol. 82, pp. 71 ff., 1927; A. Lewy, *Zur Genesis der heutigen agrarischen Ideen in Preussen*.

[2] Cf. *Briefwechsel zwischen Friedrich Gentz und Adam Heinrich Müller, 1800–29*, p. 140, Stuttgart, 1857.

[3] *Ibid.*

reason why they are much harder to establish by 'positivistic' methods. Adam Müller does not quote Möser once.[1] Yet, reading Müller after Möser, one cannot help noticing how the former reproduces Möser's attitude on a romantic plane; and that Möser's writings contain, in a naïve (unromantic) form, modes of thought and older feudalistic ideas which reappear on a romantic 'level' in Müller. That influence is so fundamental that the individual does not matter. In other words, what matters is not whether Müller derived that attitude from Möser himself, but whether Möser does not represent a type of thought which was so common in his time that it may have acted on Müller through quite different intermediaries.

We will begin with the less problematic of the two influences, with Burke.[2] Here again the first thing to do is to determine his sociological position. The importance of Burke lies in the fact that he was the first influential author who attacked the French Revolution. He was the initiator of modern anti-revolutionary conservatism, and all those who later on criticized the French Revolution from the conservative side were somehow influenced by him. It was Burke who, more than anybody else, supplied the anti-revolutionary camp with ideas and slogans. His 'Reflections on the Revolution in France' was published as a pamphlet against the pro-revolutionary societies and clubs which which were growing up in England. His comments are therefore the spontaneous outgrowth of that definite historical situation. That nonetheless—and in spite of the speed with which they were written—so many points of principle, so much that was to recur again and again, became visible to Burke can only be explained by the fact that he was already able to look at the revolution from a vantage point which virtually forced fruitful insights on the spectator. For a proper political understanding of the revolution England offered so favourable a perspective that every particular observation turned of itself into a statement of principle, it became 'philosophical'—even for a mind which was, by any serious standards, so essentially unphilosophical as Burke's. Herein

---

[1] Cf. Baxa, 'Justus Möser und Adam Müller', in *Jahrbuch für Nationalökonomie und Statistik*, series 3, vol. 68, Jena, 1923. Baxa confines himself chiefly to an elaboration of the similarity of *ideas*, while we must attempt to discover much more fundamental similarities, viz. in the general mode of thought.

[2] It is impossible to give here a comprehensive survey of the literature on Burke. For our purposes the most useful works are: A. Cobban, *Edmund Burke and the Revolt against the Eighteenth Century*, London, 1929; J. MacCunn, *The Political Philosophy of Burke*, London, 1913; M. Einaudi, *Edmondo Burke e l'indirizzo storico nelle scienze politiche*, Torino, 1930; F. Meusel, *Edmund Burke und die französische Revolution. Zur Entstehung historisch-politischen Denkens, zumal in England*, Berlin, 1913; also *Early Life, Writings and Correspondence of Edmund Burke*, ed. by A. R. I. Samuels, Cambridge, 1923; J. Morley, *Burke*, London, 1888; R. H. Murray, *Edmund Burke*, Oxford, 1931.

lies the peculiar feature of that 'philosophy' (and this is the only real point of resemblance between Burke and Möser as opposed to Müller), that in the case of the former it is an involvement in political practice which yields philosophical insights, whereas, in the case of Müller, philosophical principles are to be applied so as to master practical problems.

It is in itself an interesting spectacle to observe how England provides the first impressive picture of revolutionary France, a picture which guided whole generations. It is as if England takes revenge for the conventional portrait of herself which the Frenchman Montesquieu originally painted and which was, for a long time, decisive for the judgment of England abroad.[1]

To the question, which aspects of Müller's thought are already present in Burke's, the answer must be that it is simply the specifically conservative attitude which Müller took over from Burke. It is primarily the idea of 'history', if it may be so called. Looking at it more closely one finds that 'history' in Burke's thought is not yet that complicated, profoundly romantic, transcendental construction which confronts us in the writings of Müller, and also of Savigny. It is only one element of this complex whole, though an important one, the element of 'continuity.'[2] Burke profoundly stimulated conservatism to think about the

[1] The German idea of England naturally changed in the course of time. The Anglomania of the young Adam Müller emphasized the feudal structure of English society. The same Adam Müller characteristically abandoned his favourable attitude towards England as a result of the changes in English foreign policy. (Cf. F. Engel-Jánosi, 'Die Theorie vom Staat im deutschen Oesterreich 1815-48', in *Zeitschrift f. öffentl. Recht*, p. 386, footnote 3, 1921.) It is interesting to observe the widespread appeal which England made at that time to the minds of contemporary Germany. At the time when capitalist England experienced its first crisis (1815-19), risings of the working classes, the agitation for parliamentary reform, and the first wave of serious criticism of its social and political system, German contemporaries were still full of praise for England, although each for different reasons. Thus the young Adam Müller sees in England the example of an anti-revolutionary organic social order; F. J. Stahl praises the English constitutional system; Fr. List, the economist, looked at England as the *nation prédominante*; the liberals from Kraus to Prince-Smith glorify England as the home of Locke and Adam Smith; and even Marx takes English development as the pattern for his analysis.

[2] Some characteristic passages from the 'Reflections' may be quoted: 'You will observe, that from Magna Charta to the Declaration of Right, it has been the uniform policy of our constitution to claim and assert our liberties, as an *entailed inheritance* derived from our forefathers, and to be transmitted to our posterity' (Burke, *Works*, vol. 5, pp. 77 f., London, 1801-27). 'The policy appears to me to be the result of profound reflection; or rather the happy effect of following nature, which is wisdom without reflection, and above it. . . . The people of England well know, that the idea of inheritance furnishes a sure principle of conservation, and a sure principle of transmission; without at all excluding a principle of improvement' (*ibid.*, p. 78). 'You [the French] had all those advantages in your ancient states; but you chose to act as if you had never been moulded into civil society, and had every thing to begin anew. You began ill, because you began by despising every thing that belonged to you. You set up your trade without a capital' (*ibid.*, p. 82).

historical nature of society. But his is not yet the attitude to the
historical factor which gives rise to refinements of historical
method, which attributes an unchangeable place in the historical
scale of values to every product of organic growth. He does not
yet realize all the complications of the problem of value standards
and fails to grasp the fruitfulness of the relativistic method which,
arising out of historicism, makes even the position of the observer
a relative one within the general process of historical development.
He is unaware of the depth of the organic conception of society
and of the synoptic view of the whole. All he sees is that one will
achieve more useful results if one allows institutions to grow
gradually than if individuals set about to construct them in a day.
He is aware of the continuity, the gradualness of historical
development; he stresses the gradual accumulation of the historical
forces of the past (compare the typically English simile of
'capital'). He shows that reverence towards the past which one
feels in a gallery of ancestral portraits. 'By this means our liberty
becomes a noble freedom. It carries an imposing and majestic
aspect. It has a pedigree and illustrating ancestors. It has its
bearings and its ensigns armorial. It has its gallery of portraits; its
monumental inscriptions; its records, evidences, and titles. We
procure reverence to our civil institutions on the principle upon
which nature teaches us to revere individual men; on account of
their age; and on account of those from whom they are descended.'[1] All these, however, are relatively unemotional statements of principles, rather than expressions of a new fundamental
attitude. At most, one can consider them as the first appearance of
the phenomenon which may be called a 'positively historical'
conception of history, as opposed to the 'negatively historical'
conception of the Enlightenment.[2] To the Enlightenment the
gradual continuity of historical development appeared as a purely
negative element. It would not be true, then, to say that conservatism discovered history as such; but it did discover a specific
meaning of growth, viz. its aspects of tradition and continuity. This
example clearly shows the value 'social attachment' has for the
understanding of history. Historical thinking is fructified by the
vital relationship in which the knowing subject stands to the
historical process. One cannot understand history without wishing
something from history. The sympathetic[3] grasp of the nature
of historic growth which Burke achieved would never have been

---

[1] *Ibid.*, p. 80.
[2] Cf. G. Rexius, 'Studien zur Staatslehre der historischen Schule', in *Historische
Zeitschrift*, vol. 107, p. 500, 1911.
[3] Gentz, in the comments to his translation of Burke's 'Reflections', speaks of an
'affectionate return to the past' (Burke, *Betrachtungen über die französische Revolution*,
transl. by Fr. Gentz, new ed., vol. 1, p. 408, Hohenzollern, 1794).

possible had not certain strata felt that their social position was threatened and that their world might perish.

Historicism is, as we have seen, an exceedingly complex and many-sided phenomenon, both in its internal structure and in its sociological foundation. But in its chief points it is of conservative origin. It arose everywhere as a political argument against the revolutionary breach with the past. A mere interest in history becomes historicism when historical facts are not merely lovingly contrasted with the facts of the present, but where 'growth' as such becomes a real experience. This is the common meaning of Burke's 'continuity', French traditionalism[1], and German historicism. This fundamental experience, as the common element, on the other hand, is accompanied by several more complex factors which account for the detailed ramifications.[2] With the fact of growth, of continuity as such, as the basic experience of the historicist, there goes always, as a second element, the preference for a particular epoch and a particular social stratum in history. Here again Burke set the example for Müller in his preference for the Middle Ages and his conception of the nobility as the chief makers of history.

An analysis of the significance of the historical phenomenon 'nobility' was an important problem for the conservative forces after the revolution. But only in exceptional circumstances are the outlines of a form of social life visible to those who are born into that form. Sociology, even a sociology which serves merely to 'interpret' and to bolster existing institutions, needs a suitable perspective, involving a certain 'distance' but also a certain amount of solidarity with some of the factors involved. We have mentioned before the value of a 'socially unattached' intelligentsia for making the structure of society transparent. The

[1] Rohden, in his introduction to the German edition of J. de Maistre's *Considérations sur la France* ('Betrachtungen über Frankreich', *Klassiker der Politik*, ed. by Meinecke and Oncken, vol. 2, p. 24, Berlin, 1924), analyses the fundamental experience of the French traditionalists, the '*durée*', and goes on to show that it is conceived, not 'dynamically' but 'statically'. Following up this idea, we see the essence of German historicism in the fact that it had become 'dynamic' and was able to take full advantage of the fruitful potentialities of conservative thought.

[2] The historical and sociological explanation of the 'dynamic' character of historicism in Germany is probably (I) that in Germany conservatism in its chief trends and in the historically decisive period under discussion, had no need to become reactionary since there was after all no revolution in its own country. For a counter-revolution has to confront reality with an ideal just as rigidly utopian as that of a revolution. The revolutionary attitude, on the other hand, favoured the growth of a 'dynamic' historicism. (II) The German middle class with its static natural-law conceptions had no part in German conservatism for the simple reason that it had not yet become politically relevant. (III) German historicism was able to develop to a large extent independently of Roman Catholicism and could therefore also avoid the static approach of the latter. (This independence of Catholic influence has also been pointed out by Rohden.)

example of Burke merely confirms that view. Burke was not a member of the nobility himself, he was a self-made man who sought admission to the inner circle of the aristocracy; his own social status thus was a mobile one. For that very reason he was able to determine in an exemplary fashion—although with an apologetic intention—the social significance and peculiar character of the nobility. In Germany, too, a member of the middle class, Adam Müller, became the interpreter of the nobility. France alone provides an example of a nobility who themselves became aware of the significance of their social position.[1] The explanation is, of course, to be found in their emigration during the years of the revolution. The detachment from their accustomed mode of existence which fate forced upon them gave them also historical and sociological insight. It is during ascent or descent in the social scale that the individual achieves the clearest view of the social and historical structure of society. In the ascent one understands what one is aiming at, in the descent what one is losing.

What is true of the evaluation of different social strata is equally true of the evaluation of different epochs of the past. With the defence of the nobility goes an apologia for the Middle Ages—focused less upon the medieval status and guild system or upon medieval mysticism than upon the element of chivalry.[2] Burke, however, achieved little more in this respect than a sympathetic treatment of the Middle Ages at a time when they were simply the 'Dark Ages'. Nothing in his writings betrays that emotional sympathy which is characteristic of historical thinking, as opposed to a mere 'attribution of positive value' to historical facts. Nor do they show that urge to rekindle the embers of the past that are still aglow in the present which alone makes possible a socially relevant revival of the past. In Burke's thought the defence of continuity, of the nobility, of the Middle Ages has too much of a rhetorical flavour. All these things are indeed only of the nature of 'reflections', they do not yet constitute a distinct mode of thought.

To turn now to Möser[3]—a writer who may be considered a

---

[1] Rohden points out that French traditionalism had its origin without exception in the landed nobility and he attributes a special importance to that fact (introduction to 'de Maistre', *loc. cit.*, p. 14).

[2] Cf., for instance, the famous passage from the 'Reflections': 'The age of chivalry is gone. That of sophisters, economists, and calculators has succeeded; and the glory of Europe is extinguished for ever. Never, never more shall we behold that generous loyalty to rank and sex, that proud submission, that dignified obedience, that subordination of the heart, which kept alive, even in servitude itself, the spirit of an exalted freedom' (Burke, *Works*, vol. 5, p. 149). The guild system of the Middle Ages found its apologists in Tieck and Wackenroder.

[3] For Möser, cf. the introduction by K. Brandis to the selection from Möser in the series *Der deutsche Staatsgedanke*, first series, vol. 3, Munich, 1921. A detailed bibliography of Möser, *ibid.*, pp. 265 ff. Cf. also H. Baron, 'Justus Mösers Individualitätsprinzip in seiner geschichtlichen Bedeutung' in *Historische Zeitschrift*, vol. 130, 1924.

good representative of the feudalistic trend of thought. The first thing that strikes one is the great difference between his general attitude and that of the romanticists. One might call his conservatism a 'primitive' conservatism, implying by that term that it is the first stage in the transition from a mere traditionalism into a self-conscious conservatism.[1] There is here none of the reflectiveness and introspectiveness of romantic conservatism. The frontal attack of the French Revolution against the inherited, traditional attitude is still in the future. The *leitmotiv* of Möser's reflections is, first of all, praise of the 'good old days'.[2] Somehow he stands completely in the atmosphere of the Enlightenment. His grandfatherly wisdom is sober, practical, rational. Yet his rationalism—and here we realize that there are also several variants of rationalism —is not the calculating, abstract rationalism of the bourgeoisie.

As long as planned economy has not yet unified the world, capitalism will always show a double mentality.[3] One representative type of capitalism is the meticulous keeper of accounts; the other is the pioneering adventurer who takes incalculable risks. Möser's sober wisdom has much more of the rationality of the peasant farmer. It is not a constructive calculation of abstract factors. It is the method of carefully reckoning up the concrete factors of a situation. It has its origin in caution and a mental agoraphobia which refuses to face any dynamic factors. This rationality refuses to leave for one moment the sphere of direct experience, it revolts against any invasion by elements from other worlds. It is afraid of the disintegration of the conventional moral ties which make the environment what it is. It is a conservatism which does not want to engage in experiments beyond its ken. That this primitive conservatism becomes reflective at all in Möser is due not to any sudden shock, but to the gradual infiltration from France of 'new-fangled' ideas and attitudes. It does become reflective. But Möser never 'romanticizes' what has happened. He may, and in fact he constantly does, interpret history involuntarily in the light of his own aims[4]; but he never tries, consciously or unconsciously, to justify something by means of far-fetched and extraneous arguments, or to save it by investing it with a 'higher' meaning.

The romanticists were full of enthusiasm for the Church, for the Middle Ages, and for the nobility, because something in their

[1] Cf. Sec. II, p. 116, above.
[2] Cf. 'Die Spinnstube', a local story in *Works*, 1, p. 24.
[3] Sombart distinguishes the 'mentality of the entrepreneur' from the 'middle-class mentality' ('Victorian') and analyses the two separately as component parts of the 'mentality of the bourgeoisie' (Sombart, *Der Bourgeois*, Munich and Leipzig, 1920).
[4] The *Osnabrückische Geschichte*, though based on original sources, is largely a tissue of more or less gratuitous explanations.

own wish-dreams had brought these things nearer to them. They sought in them compensation for some of their own troubles. The relation between the romanticist and his ideal is never one of intensive study. Led on by a wish-dream inside him he merely grazes the surface: 'Those were lovely, glorious times when Europe was a Christian country; when *one* Christendom inhabited this human corner of the world; when *one* great bond of common interest joined the remotest provinces of this far-flung spiritual realm'—these are the opening lines of Novalis's essay 'Christendom or Europe'. They suggest the fundamental mood, and in the remainder of the essay it is that mood, not the subject, that is developed.

Möser's attitude is completely different. He does not *approach* his subject, he *lives* in it. He does not go back to the past, he lives in the remnants of the past which still exist in the present. He lives in them and his thought arises out of them. The past is not something that lies behind him; it is an integral part of his life, not as a memory and a return, but as the intensified experience of something that he still possesses and is merely in danger of losing.

This type of conservatism which still lives in the heritage of the past, for which the past is not yet a memory and an object of reflection, has already been mentioned in our general discussion of the conservative attitude. We pointed out that Möser exhibits it in its purest form. It merely remains to illustrate that assertion.

The following passage serves well to characterize Möser's standpoint. 'When I come across some old custom or old habit which simply will not fit into modern ways of reasoning, I keep turning around in my mind the idea that, "after all, our forefathers were not fools either," until I find some sensible reason for it. . . .'[1] Now compare this with Novalis. Möser starts out from the concrete datum, an old custom, an old habit, and tries to discover its meaning. In the case of the romanticists the thinker is, so to speak, the starting-point, and all his efforts are directed to discover, if possible, a world that will satisfy him. 'Turning around and around' an object is as characteristic of Möser's thought as is his peculiar rationalism which must somehow find a 'sensible reason' for the behaviour of the forefathers.[2] Only the blind reliance on everything old and inherited is irrational, not a reluctance to attack traditions. Moreover, he looks for a 'sensible reason', not for some 'higher' far-fetched, metaphysical justification. Of course, one may keep 'turning around' real objects and yet arrive at romantic or paradoxical conclusions. Of the French traditionalists, it has been well said that they were 'rationalists

1 *Works*, vol. 5, p. 260.
2 Cf. also H. Baron, *op. cit.*, p. 49.

with irrational axioms.'[1] A writer like Kierkegaard, for instance, also practises some of that paradoxical sophistry which makes use of a trenchant rational logic to demonstrate an irrational position. Möser is paradoxical only in order to surprise,[2] not in order to invent irrational explanations. He merely intends to recover the lost 'sensible reason' for the inherited traditions. What is irrational in his thinking is only his conviction that the ancients must have acted sensibly, not, however, the explanations he is trying to find.

Bourgeois calculation is always abstract. Things and human beings appear solely as figures in an intellectual operation. Möser's 'reckoning' is always concrete. He really *reckons* with things, not simply by counting them or treating them as functions in a calculable process, but because he believes that they demand his attention as concrete parts of a definite social context.

From that attitude arises also the concept of 'practice', as he calls it, the eternal praise of practice as opposed to theory (a feature, by the way, which we shall find again, on an entirely different level, with the romanticists). He wrote an unfinished polemical essay against Kant with the title 'Theory and Practice'. Its salient passage runs: 'Real events often form a sounder basis for correct conclusions than far too exalted [*gar zu hohe*] premises.'[3] He fights against constructive thinking from 'far too exalted premises' in the name of concrete thinking which holds on to the data of experience: 'Practice which clings to each individual circumstance and knows how to use it must surely be more competent than theory which in its high flight is bound to overlook many circumstances.'[4]

The purpose of the essay is a justification of serfdom. It is of special interest because it shows clearly how the immediate occasion, the desire to defend an old institution, gives rise to a struggle between two methods of thought and thus brings out in full relief the differences between them which were to engage conservative thought for a long time to come. It is the contrast

---

1 Rohden says: 'If the traditionalist asks the question: "What is a nation?" the naïve reader necessarily expects the answer, which to de Maistre represents the banal solution, "The totality of all citizens." The traditionalist answer, on the contrary, is: "The king and the bureaucracy." The art of the traditionalist thinker consists in taking a problem from the armoury of the adversary and connecting it by a logical argument with the solution which is supplied by his own attitude to life. The discrepancy between the expected "enlightened" answer which is constantly present in the reader's subconsciousness and the answer which he in fact receives produces a state of anxious tension' (Rohden, introduction to his edition of 'de Maistre', *loc. cit.*, p. 23).
2 The above-quoted sentence from Möser is taken from a fragment of his entitled 'The Right of Man: Serfdom'. Referring to that title the fragment begins: 'Indeed a paradox! many a reader will think when he reads this title.' To that extent Möser, too, uses the method mentioned by Rohden.
3 *Works*, vol. 9, pp. 158 f.
4 *Ibid.*, p. 168.

between the method which starts out from normative and constructive premises and that which proceeds concretely from the
given data. The tension is increased by the fact that Möser, in his
justification of serfdom, still thinks in terms of natural-law ideas,
since he starts from an original contract. Underneath that justification in terms of natural law, however, works the fundamental
intention to deduce the validity of the institution, not from
normative premises, but from the living, practical interplay of
social and historical phenomena.

Another example may be mentioned which illustrates how
much Möser is constantly occupied with the tension between
concrete and abstract thinking. He wrote a short essay called
'The Moral Point of View'.[1] In it he tries to show, from an entirely
different angle—in the moral sphere—that the value of a thing
cannot be grasped on the basis of general principles, because
measured by such excessively high standards everything must
appear imperfect. Instead one should realize that everything
carries within itself the point of view from which it can be adequately apprehended: 'Can you tell me one single beautiful object
of the physical world which retains its beauty under the micro-
scope? Does not the most beautiful skin get knolls and furrows?
the loveliest cheek a horrible mildew? the rose quite a wrong
colour? Everything therefore has its own point of view from which
alone it is beautiful.' And at the end of the essay he says: 'Let us
be honest, and see the virtue of a thing only in its usefulness or
its inherent quality. In this sense, a horse, and iron, have their
virtues, and so has the hero who has his due share of steel, hard-
ness, coldness, and heat.'

Möser's thought contains still further elements which became
the intellectual heritage of conservatism and were taken over
by romanticism as parts of the feudalistic trend of thought. One
is generally inclined to consider the tendency towards extreme
individualization, the demand that every man and every thing
should themselves provide the clue for their understanding, as a
typically romantic trait. An analysis of Möser's thought shows,
however, to what a large extent that tendency is already inherent
in the aims of feudalistic thought. It displays already the preference for 'qualitative thinking' as a method of thought. It is
already concerned with the problem of making the individual
element accessible to thought. Already we find a close connection
between such reflections on the method of thought and political
aims. Our task is therefore to show that the feudalistic conception
which still constitutes the framework of Möser's point of view

---

[1] *Works*, vol. I, pp. 196 f.

produced modes of thought which were just then being attacked by the bourgeois world; and that it was due to that attack that this thought became reflective and aware of its own character.

Some examples may now be quoted which disclose the *political* significance of Möser's desire to experience every thing as individual, to understand it in terms of its specific 'usefulness'. In his essay which bears the title 'The Modern Taste for General Laws and Decrees is a Danger to Our Common Liberty' (1772)[1] the feudalistic origin of the emphasis on individuality, as opposed to the generalizing tendency of the bureaucracy, is clearly apparent. Right at the beginning he declares: 'The gentlemen of the *Generaldepartement* [central administration], it seems, would like to see everything reduced to simple principles. If they had their way, the state would let itself be ruled according to an academic theory, and every councillor would be able to give his orders to the local officials according to a general plan. . . . That means in fact a departure from the true plan of Nature who shows her wealth in variety; it paves the way for despotism which wants to force everything by means of a few rules and in doing so loses the wealth of variety.'

One can see here quite clearly how the political struggle against the centralizing and rationalist bureaucracy gives rise to insights into problems of method. Möser clearly recognized the spiritual affinity between the centralizing bureaucracy and the enlightened monarchy, and saw the essence of despotism[2] in that it wants to force everything by means of a few rules. He calls the tendency towards uniformity and generalization a 'new-fangled way of thinking'[3] which may be used as a technical expedient but never as a standard of judgment in a concrete case. Every native inhabitant should be judged according to the laws and customs of his locality. In fact, he sees the meaning of liberty in the observation of these local differences. Voltaire had made fun of the fact that someone lost a case by the law of one village which he would have won by the customs of the neighbouring village. Möser has something to say even for that paradox: 'Voltaire need not have troubled to think the difference between two neighbouring villages ridiculous; he could have found the same diversity between two families living under the same roof.'[4] If the decrees of the state are not obeyed the reason is that 'we are trying to cover too many things by *one* rule and deprive Nature of her wealth rather than change our system.'[5] Having observed the sense for variety

1 *Works*, vol. 2, pp. 20 f.
2 This goes back to Montesquieu.
3 *Works*, vol. 2, p. 21.
4 *Ibid.*, pp. 23 f.
5 *Ibid.*, p. 26.

and diversity, individuality and peculiarity arising from a feudalistic and particularist conception of the world (which becomes merely reflective in Möser) we are not surprised to hear that, in his opinion, every little town should be given a constitution of its own.[1]

Nor is it surprising, in view of that tendency which had its roots deep in the thought and experience of feudalistic conservatism, that the Prussian nobility were slow in their appreciation of the idea of the nation state; and that, for a long time and even during the high tide of national patriotism in the first decades of the nineteenth century, their path to it was beset with difficulties and antagonistic emotions. Not until one has got to know the incredible particularism of the feudalistic attitude in its original form does one realize that, compared with the provincial particularism of that period, nationalism is already a stage in the transition to internationalism. Here is a passage from v. d. Marwitz which illustrates the *Prussian* variety of this particularist individualism: 'Prussia is not a nation which has always been what it is now, uniform in language, customs and laws. It is a conglomerate of provinces each of them very different from the other in its laws and habits. Nor can it ever become a nation. For every province has for its neighbours other provinces which are not part of its own state but to which it feels at bottom more closely related than to the remote and unknown other provinces of the Prussian state—Brandenburg, for instance, to Saxony, Silesia to Bohemia and Moravia, East Prussia to Courland and Lithuania. To propose to merge them into one means depriving them of their peculiar character, turning a living body into a dead carcass.'[2] There are many sociological differences between v. d. Marwitz and Möser apart from the interval of two generations.[3] There is first the fact that v. d. Marwitz was a *Junker*, landlord of Friedersdorf, and spokesman of the nobility of one of the oldest provinces of Prussia (Kurmark). Möser's father, on the other hand, had been a councillor in the chancellery of Osnabrück who had done so well later on as a middle-class lawyer that he had actually governed the country for a time side by side with the aristocratic 'privy councillors'. As the son of a patrician Möser showed no more sympathy towards the nobility than was necessary in his position.[4] He believes in the corporative feudal state, even though

---

[1] Cf. the essay 'Sollte man nicht jedem kleinen Städtchen seine besondre politische Verfassung geben?', *Works*, vol. 3, p. 67.

[2] Quoted by W. Steffens, *Hardenberg und die ständische Opposition*, p. 30. Cf. also *ibid.*, footnote 2, where it is pointed out that there was *some* national feeling, however overlaid by antagonist emotions.

[3] Möser was born in 1720, Marwitz in 1777.

[4] 'Too many princes, too many noblemen, too many scholars, are the ruin of the state' (*Works*, vol. 5, p. 37).

he may date back his Golden Age to the days of ancient liberty and common property.[1] But just because he does not defend the nobility but rather the medieval social system with its relatively high degree of integration, with its hierarchic stratification[2] and feudal structure, as a whole, and takes a special interest in the attitude of the old peasant strata, we may accept the agreement between the two as typical. It confirms the assumption that at least one of the roots of Müller's emphasis on individuality, quality and peculiarity is to be found in the older 'feudalistic' trend of thought. Similarly, the emphasis on 'life' and variety, as the elements which a bureaucratic rationalism is bound to neglect, anticipates a line of thought which is crystallized as a definite trend, at first in opposition to bureaucratic centralization, later in opposition to revolutionary natural-law thought—and points to later 'philosophies of life'. The older forms of thought and experience were being subjected to an attack from all sides by bourgeois, absolutist, and bureaucratic forms of rationalism and were in danger of dying out. They were saved by their meeting and alliance with romanticism which revived them and equipped them with a modern theoretical foundation.

The earliest stage of conservative thought, represented by Möser, is no longer a primitive traditionalism. It has assumed a social function in the shape of its antagonism against the 'enlightened' tendency towards bureaucratic centralization. Under the direction of romanticism its political significance changes. Its enemy is now the natural-law thought of the revolutionary bourgeoisie.

To their conservative adversary the two variants of modern rationalism now appear interlocked. Under the influence of the French Revolution conservatism begins to acquire some insight into the character of bourgeois thought as well. The times called for resistance to it too. In their efforts to lay bare the ideological roots and causes of the revolution the French traditionalists concentrated on the metaphysical and religious premises of the eighteenth century, and made them bear the brunt of their attack.[3] In Germany, in contrast, romanticism tends rather to

[1] Cf. the introduction by Brandis to his selection from Möser's works, p. xxi; also O. Hatzig, 'Justus Möser als Staatsmann und Publizist', in *Quellen und Darstellung zur Geschichte Niedersachsens*, vol. 27. For v. d. Marwitz, see the essay by Fr. Meusel in vol. 1 of his edition of v. d. Marwitz's works; also W. Andreas, 'Marwitz und der Staat Friedrichs des Grossen', in *Historische Zeitschrift*, vol. 122, pp. 44 ff., 1920.

[2] Cf. 'Der Staat mit einer Pyramide verglichen. Eine erbauliche Betrachtung' ('The State Compared to a Pyramid, An Edifying Reflection') (1773), in *Works*, vol. 2, p. 250.

[3] A typical example of the character of the campaign against revolutionary thought which was carried on by the French traditionalists may be seen in de Bonald's interesting essay 'De la philosophie morale et politique du 18e siècle' (1805), in *Œuvres de M. de Bonald*, pp. 104 ff., Paris, 1819. He tries to draw parallels between theism,

make the logical and methodological aspects of liberal thought the objects of its criticism. The reason is that in France the counter-revolution found its metaphysics ready-made in the dogma of Roman Catholicism; whereas in Germany—as often has been observed before—the schism between Protestant and Catholic dogma rendered the metaphysical foundations heterogeneous and therefore unsafe. As a result, one withdrew into considering problems of method. Moreover, since the revolution was not taking place *intra muros*, one could afford to thresh out differences of *Weltanschauung* on this very abstract plane. As soon as the socio-logical situation became more critical (after 1830) and conserva-tism, even in Protestant Prussia, had to retire to the stronghold of theism, considerations of dogma and metaphysics came again into the foreground. There was a feeling that the pantheist and methodological ground of romanticism was no longer safe. It is Stahl's achievement to have satisfied that demand by establishing the monarchical principle once more on theistic foundations.

For the time being, however—during the first decades of the nineteenth century—the pantheistic and methodological variant of counter-revolutionary thought was still able to develop freely, and thus to determine the character of German conservatism for a long time to come. Adam Müller can claim to have drawn on both the feudalistic and romantic sources and thus to have given internal consistency to the ideological struggle. His *Elemente der Staatskunst* reveals, for the first time, the full importance and force of the fight against natural-law thought. Here grows up that phenomenon which, under the name of 'philosophy of life' (*Lebensphilosophie*), has ever since, and today with renewed vigour, assailed rationalism in all its diverse forms.[1]

atheism, deism and the various forms of government. A few passages may be quoted which indicate his conclusions: 'Democracy furiously casts out from political society all visible unity and focus of power; it sees the sovereign only in the *subjects*, or the people: just as atheism rejects the original and prime cause of the universe, and sees it only in its effects, in matter. In the system of the latter, matter has done everything; in the system of the former, the people have the right to do everything. In fact, one might call the democrats the atheists of politics, and the atheists the *madmen* or *jacobins* of religion' (pp. 128 ff.). 'Royalism' has its counterpart in 'theism or Christianity', and this is what he says about the centre: 'The "*impartial*" moderates and constitutionalists of '89 take their stand between the democrats and the royalists, just as do the deists be-tween the atheists and the Christians; one might therefore reasonably apply to the constitution which they have invented the name "*monarchical democracy*". They want a king, but a king without a will of his own, without the right to independent action; and a king who, as the scholar of the party, Mably, told the Poles, *receives the highest respect but has only the barest shadow of authority*. By these signs one can recognize the ideal and abstract God of deism, without will, without action, without presence, without reality' (pp. 129 ff. De Bonald's italics).

[1] Cf. Baxa's comments to the *Elemente der Staatskunst*, vol. 2, p. 293. Rothacker points out the roots of the concept in the historical school (*Einleitung in die Geisteswissenschaften*, pp. 62 ff., especially p. 71, footnote 2, Tübingen, 1920).

Having analysed one by one the most important currents which converge in the thought of Adam Müller we may now inquire which new and comprehensive political impulses brought about the ideological unification of all these different tendencies in a single *Weltanschauung*.

At this stage, conservative thought derives its impulse to emphasize Life, as opposed to concepts, no longer, as in the case of Möser, from the reaction against bureaucratic rationalism alone, but also from the reaction against the other contemporary variant of rationalism, the rationalism of the bourgeoisie.[1] If we were to speculate *a priori* about which group emphasizes Life and which builds on abstract, unchanging concepts, we should answer: it is obviously the progressives who favour Life, the conservatives who rely on rigid norms and abstractions. But if we look at history empirically, we see that it was the other way round. The reason is that the revolutionary thought of the bourgeoisie arose in alliance with rationalism. The reaction therefore naturally adopted the contrary ideology for the sake of mere opposition if for no other reason. But interpretation can penetrate even deeper. Revolutionary thought derives its force from the desire to realize a rationally well-defined pattern of perfection of the social and political order. Conservative thought, opposed to the fulfilment of that utopia, is forced to consider why the actually existing state of society fails to correspond to that rational pattern.[2] This impulse which is primarily anchored in self-interest at the same time renders conservatism sensitive to all those factors which revolutionary thought—again in its own vital interest—overlooks, viz., the non-rational factors of organic reality. But whereas revolutionary thought conceives such irrationalities—where it sees them at all—as imperfections of reality when measured by the standard of reason, conservative thought—indulging in one of its favourite means of expression, the paradox—attributes to them the character of super-rationality.[3] It is, however, not merely a question of inverted values, but rather of different categories of life and experience. This is shown, for

[1] Concerning the nature of modern rationalism cf. the works of Max Weber (especially his remarks on rationalism in legal thought in *Wirtschaft und Gesellschaft*, pp. 394 f., and on the form of rationalism which is produced by the socialization of the market and by the institution of the contract, *ibid.*, p. 394), Sombart, Simmel (*Philosophie des Geldes*, Leipzig, 1900), Lukács (*Geschichte und Klassenbewusstsein*, Berlin, 1923, especially the essay on 'Die Verdinglichung und das Bewusstsein des Proletariats').
[2] That is the stage which German conservatism has reached, for example, in Hugo, *Lehrbuch des Naturrechts, als einer Philosophie des positiven Rechts, besonders des Privatrechts*, 1st ed., 1798.
[3] It is not our task as sociologists to decide whether interpretation in terms of 'supra-rational' categories is objectively correct or not. *Our* opinion on the value of irrationality must be left aside.

instance, by the fact that definition of irrationality as super-rationality leads to that class of philosophical systems which might be called in a word 'philosophies of Life', the philosophies which put forward, in opposition to mere reason, sometimes 'history', sometimes 'life' or sometimes 'the spirit'. The great polarities of nineteenth-century philosophical thought: 'reality' and 'thought', 'concept' and 'idea', 'theory' and 'practice', often arose as integral parts of philosophical systems. But they were always nourished and their sociological significance was preserved by the corresponding political polarities of liberalism and conservatism.

The most primitive form of the struggle against destructive rationalism through the appeal to Life consists in contrasting the 'written constitution' with a reality richer and more alive than the written word.[1] Frederick William IV's phrase about the 'mere scrap of paper' which was coined to ridicule the idea of the constitution goes back to this most primitive form of the fight against 'rationalization'. But if we look more closely, we notice that it expresses a contrast which can be defined in philosophical language as the contrast between 'norm' and 'being'. What conservative thought objects to in this context is that such reflections, as for instance in the Declaration of the Rights of Man, start out from the 'rights of man as such'.[2] The conservative is shocked by this procedure, by the application of the deductive

---

[1] This was formulated in a typical manner by de Maistre in his *Considérations sur la France* (1796): 'No constitution has its origin in a mere decision. The rights of the people have never been written, or at least, the articles of the constitution and the written fundamental laws are never more than plain declarations of previously existing rights of which nothing more can be said than that they exist because they exist.' Or: 'A written constitution of the kind that rules France today is nothing but a mechanism which appears to be alive.' In his struggle for the idea that it is impossible to construct anything according to a rational plan from the beginning he works out for himself the difference between 'creating' and 'changing': 'In his sphere of action man can change everything but he creates nothing.' Here again the emphasis on 'growth'. He goes so far in his aversion to planned creation as to prophesy: 'I do not believe in the durability of the American government; nor do I trust the peculiar institutions of English America. The cities, for instance, have not been able to agree where the Congress should sit; none of them would leave that honour to another. They therefore decided to build a new city which should become the seat of government. The most favourable situation by a broad river was chosen and it was decided that the city should be called Washington. The site of all public buildings is already fixed, building operations have begun, and the plan of the "queen of cities" already circulates throughout Europe. There is nothing in the idea as such which is beyond human power; it is certainly possible to build a city. But there is too much deliberate decision in the thing, too much that is human; and one could offer a bet of a thousand to one that the city will not be built, that it will not be called Washington, that Congress will not sit in it.' It is fortunate for de Maistre that he did not make that bet. Cf. for the struggle against 'artificial creation' also Burke: 'The very idea to manufacture a new government is repulsive to us Englishmen', quoted in A. Wahl, *op. cit.*, p. 550.

[2] 'The constitution of 1795 is, like its predecessors, made for men. But there is on earth no man as such. I have seen in my lifetime Frenchmen, Italians, Russians, etc.

method, and the idea that a perfect state can be developed in this fashion; he casts about to find a different method. In the course of his search, in his opposition to the oppositional forces, he remembers how hitherto the state and society, law and regulations, have come about. He realizes that now it is discussion and the vote which decide matters, that now 'reason' wants to make reality, whereas formerly everything grew gradually and was preserved by custom. With that realization the logical and the historical starting-points fall apart. In natural-law thought logical and historical origins were still conceived as identical; the theory of the social contract was at once a logical construction and a historical fiction. Not until Kant were the two quite clearly separated. Once the separation was made, the relation between being (growth) and norm became a vital problem for the collective thought of the whole epoch.

The feudalistic opposition was faced with the bureaucratic form of rationalism; hence, the aspect of modern rationalism it criticized was mainly its questionable tendency towards generalization and mechanization. The appearance on the scene of a more radical form of rationalism in the shape of the revolutionary rationalism of the bourgeoisie widens the basis of attack of the anti-rationalist campaign. Bureaucratic rationalism consists, on the whole, of little more than the tendency to 'equalize' (the abolition of territorial and later of feudalistic social differences). Apart from that, it does not advance beyond a narrow sphere. Bourgeois rationalism, on the other hand, is revolutionary and radical just because it wants to rationalize the whole social order right from the beginning in a systematic manner. It opposes to the world as it has grown up a single rigid and static political system (in the form of written plans or constitutions). In reply, conservatism puts into the foreground, next to the struggle against generalization, the struggle against systematic thought, against thought as a static system.[1]

Thanks to Montesquieu I even know that one can be a Persian, but I declare that never in my life have I seen a man—unless indeed he exists unknown to me' (De Maistre, *Considérations sur la France*, Germ. ed., p. 72). Here again the intellectual attitude is transferred to the left-wing opposition: 'But man is no abstract being, sitting outside the world' (K. Marx, *Zur Kritik der Hegelschen Rechtsphilosophie*, ed. Fr. Mehring, vol. 1, p. 384).

[1] The paradox that the progressive, the liberal, who after all proved in fact surely more open to the new elements of growth than the conservative, appeared to his contemporaries as 'rigid', while the conservative and the old traditional forms of development appeared as mobile and 'alive', is due to an illusion to which those who took part in the process (the contemporaries) were bound to succumb. Lukács (*Geschichte und Klassenbewusstsein*, p. 109) tries—with reference to law—to suggest a solution to a similar paradox: 'Thus arises the apparently paradoxical situation that the law of primitive forms of society which has hardly changed for hundreds, in some cases even for thousands, of years possesses a fluid irrational character, continuously reborn in udicial decisions, whereas modern law which undergoes continuous and violent

Rigid and immobile thought having been confronted with dynamic Life there were now two possibilities: Either one renounced all thought, denied its significance and returned to irrationality; or distinguished a rigid from a mobile form of thought, the latter being able to keep step with the mobility of life because it is itself dynamic. The historical school chose the first path by combining the experience of dynamics with a thorough-going irrationalism. Adam Müller, on the other hand, combined the dynamic experience he derived from practical politics with certain sociologically related trends he observed in contemporary philosophy, and thus came to conceive the idea of '*dynamic thinking*'. In this mobile thought he saw the solution to the political problems of the time. This leads us to a fundamental methodological conception, the distinction between 'idea' and 'concept'.

The antithesis between 'idea' and 'concept' which Adam Müller elaborates in the *Elements of Politics* is in his case the fruit of earlier reflections on logic the beginnings of which are to be found in his work *The Theory of Antithesis* (1804). The development of his thought brings out most clearly the consecutive stages of the elaboration of 'dynamic thinking'. The most important stages might be described as (*a*) thinking in terms of antitheses, (*b*) dynamic thinking, and (*c*) dialectical thinking.

The first stage is the attempt to oppose to linear deduction from an axiom the method of thinking in terms of polarities.[1] The rigidity which lies in the method of linear deduction is here overcome by dissolving all positions into antitheses. The thought of the Enlightenment proceeded in straight lines[2]; where an

transformations appears rigid, static and complete. The paradox proves illusory when it is realized that it only arises from the fact that the same situation is seen, in one case, from the standpoint of the historian (who stands outside development as far as his method is concerned), in the other, from the standpoint of the person who stands within the process, from the standpoint of the impact of the existing form of society on his consciousness.' To this undoubtedly correct observation may, however, be added that the thought of the complete, static system is *in fact* more rigid than that which its romantic opponents opposed to it as more 'alive'. If conservative thought proved none the less more impervious to the 'new', the reason must be sought not in the *forms* of conservative thought but in the fact that this current closes its eyes to the new *contents*. That is the other aspect of the paradox which has just been discussed: the contemporaries paid attention to the manner of thought (the forms of thought), whereas we as historians concentrate on the contents.

[1] Here is an example for the early stage: 'The listener is the true counter-speaker; which of the two we call the active, which the passive partner or counter-agent in the process, who is called object and who subject, is completely arbitrary. One thing alone is essential: if one of them is called object, the other must be called subject' (A. Müller, *Die Lehre vom Gegensatz*, pp. 38 f.).

[2] The excessively 'unilinear' form of rationalism itself gives rise, at a certain late stage, to a tendency towards antithetical thinking. Since 'unilinear' thought splits up everything into sets of exclusives, it contains within itself the elements which eventually carry evolution beyond it. In this sense Lublinski points out correctly that at a late

attempt was made to construct a philosophy of history, development was always conceived as the unfolding of a single principle. The idea of progress has its roots in a 'unilinear' construction—just as, in another sphere, the rights of man are to be deduced from a single idea, the 'idea of man'. Such a construction, however, is remote from reality, because the world cannot be understood in terms of a single principle. To try to think from more than one position and to comprehend the world by means of several principles increases the efficacy of thought and is therefore the first step towards improvement. This method of thinking in terms of antitheses and polarities is a romantic heritage. It is a method of thought which endeavours to reach some degree of mobility while remaining within the static framework.[1]

Adam Müller demonstrates the possibility of the two alternative methods of thought by two alternative methods of definition. He calls the first (the rigid one) the 'atomistic', the second the 'dynamic' definition. The former consists in describing 'the nature of the thing to be defined in isolation, its qualities, the parts of which it is composed, the symptoms by which it is recognized. The dynamic definition consists in mentioning some other known

stage of the Enlightenment a position beyond mere Enlightenment was sought and found in the Enlightenment itself. He shows how both Kant and Schiller attempted, in different spheres, to overcome 'unilinear' thought by means of the category of 'interaction'. In Lublinski's view, Schiller's endeavour to portray the hero as bound up with his environment by mutual relations and 'interaction' represents the same emergence of a new attitude as Kant's endeavour to establish the category of interaction in thought. In both cases, the point is that instead of merely placing correlated entities side by side, thinking sees the elements of experience as interrelated. Here once again it appears that new forms of thought are emanations of a more comprehensive factor, of new forms of experience. Cf. S. Lublinski, *Literatur und Gesellschaft im neunzehnten Jahrhundert*, 4 vols., vol. 1, p. 57, Berlin, 1899–1900.

[1] Metzger (*Gesellschaft, Staat und Recht in der Ethik des deutschen Idealismus*, pp. 260 f., Heidelberg, 1917) points out the romantic roots of this dynamic thinking. He mentions Friedrich Schlegel's *Ironie und antithetische Synthesis* (*ibid.*, footnote 1). Meinecke (*Weltbürgertum und Nationalstaat*, p. 131, footnote 2) refers to Fichte for its origins. H. Heller (*Hegel und der nationale Machtstaatsgedanke in Deutschland*, pp. 139 f., Berlin, 1921) tries to establish Hegel's influence on Müller through Schelling, on the one side, and Gentz, on the other. The only influence which is certain is that of Schelling's philosophy of nature which is mentioned by Metzger (*ibid.*, footnote 2) who follows A. Friedrich's book *Klassische Philosophie und Wirtschaftswissenschaft* (Gotha, 1903). Müller himself acknowledges this influence when he writes about antithesis in his essay on 'The Nature of Definition' (published in the review *Phoebus*, ed. by H. v. Kleist and A. Müller, and republished in *Neudrucke romantischer Seltenheiten*, 1924, p. 37) : 'It was in 1803 when I succeeded in the chief step of constructing a dynamic logic, the need for which I had felt in the name of the philosophy of nature.' (Cf. also *Die Lehre vom Gegensatz*, pp. 9, 11.) For the sociologist the determination of priority does not possess the cardinal importance that it has for the pure historian of ideas. For isolated discoveries are for him always expressions of general social trends. It is not important for us whether the dynamic logic which was achieved at about the same time by Hegel, Schelling and Müller, was arrived at independently or under mutual influence. What is important is to find the sources in the social and intellectual life of the time from which arose the impulse to search for a dynamic logic.

thing which stands in direct opposition to the thing to be defined',[1] e.g. heat through cold, love through hatred, masculinity through femininity. Nature herself is, on this view, nothing but 'a whole [organism] composed of an infinite number of antitheses'.[2] This type of dynamic thinking remains, in any case, still deeply bound up with the speculations of pantheism and the philosophy of nature. The element of analogy competes with the intention to think dynamically and the dynamic quality of the method does not really come to life until this type of thought turns from the philosophy of nature to historical reality.

The second stage of the dynamic conception of thought finds expression, in Adam Müller's system, in the correlation between *concept* and *idea*. One of the most important passages in the *Elements of Politics* runs: 'The State and all great human affairs have the characteristic quality that they can in no way be enveloped or compressed in words or definitions. . . . Such stiff forms, designed once for all for the State, for life and for man, as the ordinary sciences carry and hawk around are called *concepts*. But there *is* no concept of the State.'[3] One asks, what *is* there of the State? He answers promptly: 'If the thought which we have entertained of such a sublime object expands; if it moves and grows, as the object moves and grows; then we call the thought, not the concept of the thing, but the *Idea* of the thing, of the State, of life.'[4] The difficult question of how to treat thought once it has become evident that there is a discrepancy between flowing reality and rigid thought is thus not solved here by simply rejecting thought altogether. The solution consists rather in calling only one type of thought rigid and hence inferior, and opposing to it the idea of a mobile form of thought (the 'Idea'). The Idea too is a product of rationalization, but of a dynamic rationalization. It is admitted—and the above-mentioned sentences show that Adam Müller realized this—that thought need not necessarily comprehend the live object under a rigid concept fixed at a given moment of time. The single concept may always be static and rigid. But thought is a process, and this process can participate in the changes of the object. The theory demands that thought should move and grow—a demand which already goes far beyond the first step towards dynamic thinking,

[1] A. Müller, *Vom Wesen der Definition*, p. 37.
[2] *Ibid.*
[3] A. Müller, *Elemente der Staatskunst*, vol. 1, p. 20.
[4] Cf. S. T. Coleridge, who developed the theory of the Idea which he had probably taken over from Schelling in a manner very similar to that of Adam Müller and who gave it a very important place in his philosophy. He defines the notion of the Idea as 'that conception of a thing, which is not abstracted from any particular state, form or mode, in which the thing may happen to exist at this or that time; nor yet generalized from any number or succession of such forms or modes; but which is given by the knowledge of its ultimate aim' (*Church and State*, pp. 11 f., 1852).

the method of merely thinking in terms of polarities. It is no longer a question merely of grasping the object through its no less rigid opposite. The wish to make thought just as mobile as life itself breaks through here.

The difference between this solution and the solution of the same problem by Savigny and the historical school is that the romantic solution does not destroy the eighteenth-century faith in reason. It merely modifies it. The faith in the power of reason, in the achievement of thought, is not abandoned. Only one type of thought is rejected, the immobile thought of the Enlightenment which argues deductively from one principle and simply puts together rigid concepts. Only as compared with that type of thought does a widening of the horizon of potential thought take place. Here again romantic thought (unintentionally perhaps) merely continues, though more radically, and with new methods, the same process which the Enlightenment had already hoped to complete—the thorough rationalization of the world.

What is rational and what is irrational is, after all, really a relative question, or rather—and this is a point which we have to get clear—the two terms are correlative. Under the rule of the generalizing and rigidly systematic thought of the Enlightenment the limit of the rational had coincided with the limit of that thought. Everything that lay beyond had been conceived as irrational, as Life, as a residuum which, from the point of view of the Enlightenment, was irreducible. The idea of dynamic thinking pushed the limit of the rational a good deal further. Romantic thought therefore solved a task of the Enlightenment which the latter with its own instruments could never really have solved. Adam Müller acquired access to the dynamic experience, partly from the pantheistic sources of romanticism, but also largely from a revived experience of the old conservative attitude to the world. He saved this old mode of thought from decay by equipping it with new instruments of thought which corresponded to the most modern stage of consciousness—with instruments of thought, in other words, which not only incorporated but also made considerable advance on the thought of the Enlightenment. He helped to raise to a modern stage of consciousness a mode of experience and thought which historically preceded the Enlightenment.

It would none the less be one-sided to pretend that the above quotation adequately represents Adam Müller's conception of idea and concept. It presents only the dynamic intention of thought, clear and freed from romantic oddities. If further passages are adduced in order to observe the method of thinking with 'ideas',[1]

---

[1] Cf., e.g. Müller, *Elemente der Staatskunst*, vol. 1, pp. 351, 354, 355, 356.

it becomes apparent that he relapses again and again into the romantic tendency to think in terms of analogies. Every concrete event is understood by him only by presenting it as an 'interplay' of several forces which are mostly opposed to each other on the analogy with the sexes.

In one place he himself gives a good brief description of the method which he actually uses: 'I had to show the nature of the State. Without any definitions which are the poison of science, I described the interplay between the four eternal estates, the clergy, the merchants, the nobility and the professions [*Bürgerschaft*]; I mediated [!] between the necessary differences of age and sex, and there developed—more clearly and precisely than would have resulted from the astutest analysis, and now moreover alive—the nature of the State.'[1]

It is a matter of portraying the interplay of living forces as the 'mediation' between differences. Everything that lives is conceived as alive by presenting it always as a tension between several antagonistic principles. Every moment, every situation in life is on that view nothing but a momentary mediation, a neutralization of ever-present tensions. The following sentence from Adam Müller stands wholly under the influence of that conception; at the same time it reveals the political point, the political origin, of that mode of thought: 'The social contract is therefore not a contract concluded at some definite time in some definite place; it is the Idea of a contract which is continuously and at every point being concluded, a contract which is at every moment renewed by the new freedom that begins to stir at the side of the old, and which is thus preserved.'[2]

Here again it is quite apparent that the desire to think dynamically has its sociological roots in the opposition to bourgeois natural-law thought and hopes to overcome the latter not only as to its content but also as to its method of thought. Nowhere else can the fundamental difference between the two forms of thought be seen more clearly. In bourgeois natural-law thought the state is established by a settlement (contract) between the contracting parties recognized for all time as just. In feudalistic, romantic thought the state is an ever-fluctuating dynamic settlement between antagonistic groups. Something in that conception sounds familiar to us. Today we are quite accustomed to interpreting the historical process in terms of such polar and counteracting factors, and to conceiving any one situation of the present as a synthesis (mediation) of co-existing but dynamically changing factors. This mode of

---

[1] *Ibid.*, vol. 2, p. 178.
[2] *Ibid.*, vol. 1, p. 147. Cf. Coleridge who speaks of the Idea of an 'ever-originating contract' (*The Friend*, 2 vols., vol. 1, p. 191, 1863).

thought which has become almost axiomatic for us arose here in reaction to the 'unilinear' construction of eighteenth-century rationalism. In the method of thinking with Ideas (to use Adam Müller's terminology) romantic and feudalistic 'philosophy of life' did indeed create an instrument for the orderly arrangement of flowing historical growth and for the understanding of history as a totality.

The third stage in the development of conservative dynamic thought is represented by the stage of the dialectic. It must be analysed in connection with Hegel, whose complex sociological position leads to a very special intellectual solution.

We must now turn to a third important category of Müller's thought which can only be understood in relation to the contrast between 'concept' and 'idea'.

In the discussion of Müller's dynamic conception of the Idea we have several times come across a favourite concept of his, the concept of 'mediation'. 'Mediation' is a category characteristic of the romantic-feudalistic synthesis. All thought is, however reluctantly, analytical; and it has the task to reunite the parts of reality which it has broken to pieces. But the peculiar character of a mode of thought is never more apparent than where it is faced with the task of synthesis. The rationalist thought of the Enlightenment analysed by taking to pieces and atomizing things. Its synthesis accordingly consists in addition. Feudalist-romantic thought, as it has just been described, analysed by dividing a living totality, life or the state, into polar movements of its various parts. The question would have to be: How can one reach a living dynamic synthesis? The answer to the problem lies in the concept of 'mediation'.

The word recalls sometimes the common Christian idea of the 'mediator', sometimes the specifically Catholic idea of the mediating role of the Church.[1] But here it is really rather a special romantic creation which receives its peculiar modern meaning from the fundamental tendency of romanticism which has already been described, the striving for dynamic thinking and for an intellectual comprehension of the polyphony of life. But at the same time the concept contains also the other component which is derived from the feudalistic attitude, the antipathy to the subsumption of the individual and particular under one general principle. Feudalistic conservatism somehow strives for some other definition of the relation between whole and part, between particular and universal, than those of subsumption and addition. This impulse is here incorporated in Müller's solution.

[1] One passage in the *Elemente* (p. 175), recalls the religious context. Cf. for the religious origin of the term 'Mediator', P. Kluckholn, *Persönlichkeit und Gemeinschaft. Studien zur Staatsauffassung der deutschen Romantik*, p. 17, Halle, 1925.

In order to understand the meaning of the concept of 'mediation' in Adam Müller's system—its meaning in connection with
the fundamental notions of 'concept' and 'idea'—one has to return
once more to the basic attitude which holds that every living
totality is always developing and unfolding itself, that it is a
dynamic product of antagonistic forces and principles. Sometimes,
as has been seen, the antithesis lies between the different estates that
fight each other, sometimes it is the conflict between the family
and the individual,[1] or between eternity and the moment.[2] It is
the task of the agent, of the judge or of the thinker, not to conceive
any given concrete situation as the special case of a general rule or
or a general concept, but to experience the constantly changing
situations as the neutralization of the changing elements of the
process, and to understand them and deal with them as such.
Rationalistic, generalizing thought works with the correlation:
general law—particular case. Its methodology is based upon the
category of subsumption. Dynamic thinking grasps the Idea, i.e.
the inner aim and purpose of the concrete whole, and conceives the
particular as a part of this dynamically changing whole. Its methodology is based upon the category of 'mediation', as illustrated by
the role of the judge who 'mediates' between a law and a concrete
case under dispute. 'The highest judge of your land', says Adam
Müller, 'should represent, not the whole as such, but the aim and
purpose of the whole. In a small way and within his own limited
sphere he should stand—like the Sovereign in his large and wide
sphere—between the demands of the forefathers and the needs of
the contemporaries, between law and dispute, carrying out a vital
mediation, not making lifeless comparisons and calculations.'[3]

The sociological root of this tendency of thought to which we
have already alluded is here clearly visible. The threatened patri-
monial jurisdiction of the lord, for example, is contrasted as a
higher form, a 'mediation', with the jurisdiction of the bureaucratic administration which merely subsumes individual cases
under the general law.[4]

It is not an accident that the judicial decision is here taken
as the model. Rationalism was implicitly concerned with the
purely thinking, theoretical, contemplative, inactive individual
who makes no decisions, who merely assents or denies (which is
not the same as making decisions). The model of dynamic thought,

---

[1] Müller, *Elemente der Staatskunst*, vol. 1, p. 179.
[2] *Ibid.*
[3] *Ibid.*, p. 143.
[4] For further passages containing the term 'mediation', see *ibid.*, pp. 148, 205.
Note in the latter passage the expressions 'calculating wisdom', and 'not only weighed
and decided by quantity . . . mediated'; also pp. 206, 286, 305 ('continuous peace-
making'), and again applied, by analogy, to money (p. 361).

in contrast, is the man who decides, judges, mediates. The purely contemplative, theoretical, individual subsumes under general rules. The individual who stands in the midst of the conflicting polarities of life decides and mediates. The concept of dynamic synthesis, 'mediation', therefore contains already a *breach with the contemplative attitude*.[1] Dynamic thinking grasps the particular by decision and mediation. It should gradually become clear that the manifold forms of thought which the levelling effect of the written word has largely blurred for us are here still visible. 'Thought' is not always the same thing; thinking differs from thinking, depending on the living function which it fulfils. Both the man who subsumes and systematizes and the judge who decides *think*; yet, 'thinking' as a function in the judicial decision is something completely different from contemplative subsumption.

For a proper understanding of the difference between the inductive rationalism of the Enlightenment and the dynamics of feudalistic romanticism it is not sufficient merely to elaborate the dynamic quality. One has to penetrate to those ultimate sociological foundations which in practice determine the varying forms of the relation between theory and practice. By the way, the adherents of both modes of thought also reflect on this very problem of the relation of theory to practice, and they reach, of course, different conclusions.

Before turning to this problem of the relation between theory and practice, it is, however, necessary to say a word or two about the subsequent fate of the category of 'mediation'. Already in the *Elements of Politics* (where, as has been mentioned, the pantheist and dynamic begins, at a certain point, to fade before the Catholic and hierarchic element) there are passages which represent mediation not as an automatic mutual combination of dynamic polarities, but in the new meaning of *reconciliation*. The tribunal of reconciliation which is set up above the dynamic elements is the Catholic clergy. The clergy is said to be a 'mediatory apostolic estate' whose task it is to provide a bond between the various national states, to mitigate the contrast between poverty and excessive wealth within the states, and to preserve the spirit of 'moral equilibrium'.[2] The function of mediation is therefore here assigned to a special institution. That this is the Catholic clergy follows naturally from the pro-Catholic tendency of romanticism which began with Novalis.

[1] Here again a far-reaching agreement between the 'left' and the 'right' opposition to the bourgeois rationalist world. Cf. for instance the condemnatory reference to the calculating and contemplative character of the capitalist attitude also in the legal sphere in Lukács, *op. cit.*, p. 109.

[2] Müller, *Elemente der Staatskunst*, vol. 1, p. 288.

Once again we can observe clearly that even the most fundamental categories of thought, the special forms of synthesis, differ
as and when the conditions of thought change in their sociological
and historical structure. The same thinker constructs different syntheses on a romantic-feudalistic and on a Catholic foundation.
Even the formal categories of the synthesis change with his answers
to the main problems. As long as thinking remains pantheist in
inspiration, the antagonistic poles reach a synthesis by themselves,
without an extraneous mediating force. Now the Catholic tradition also contains philosophies based upon the idea of polarity, as
the Jesuit scholar Przywara[1] has penetratingly shown. In Pascal
one finds a philosophy of polarities, the same as in Newman's
doctrine of 'opposite virtues'. Genuinely Catholic thought, however, has the tendency to join the polar elements by means of some
higher factor to which they are subordinated. Originally it was
God. But his place may also be taken by the Church. With Novalis
romanticism already shows this hierarchic junction of polarities:
'It is impossible that mundane forces should of themselves find
their equilibrium; a third element, at once mundane and super-
mundane, can alone solve this task.'[2]

The more this feudalistic, romantic and pantheist thought
moves across into the Austria of Metternich with its largely
Catholic traditions the more the first layer of dynamic ideas is
overlaid by a second Catholic layer which may briefly be called
hierarchic. The Idea and 'mediation' receive a new meaning.[3]
Since we are here concerned only with romantic and feudalistic
thought, the subsequent fate of 'mediation' cannot be dealt with
here, and we must resume the analysis of the problem of the relation between theory and practice in feudalistic romanticism.

The respective attitudes of bourgeois rationalism and feudalistic
conservatism to this problem have been discussed in connection
with the polemic between Möser and Kant.[4] The former takes

[1] Cf. his preface to A. Müller's *Schriften zur Staatsphilosophie* (Theatiner-Verlag,
Munich), pp. vi f.
[2] Novalis, 'Die Christenheit oder Europa', in *Schriften*, ed. by J. Minor, vol. 2, p. 42,
Jena, 1907.
[3] Hence, Baxa (see his Comments on the *Elemente der Staatskunst*, vol. 2, p. 292 f.)
is wrong when he tries to interpret the notion of Idea in the *Elemente* by means of
quotations from Müller's later works, such as the *Theologische Grundlagen*; for in the
latter the 'Idea' has already received a platonistically 'archetypal', theological meaning. A similar mistake was committed by Gentz, who tried to explain the 'Idea' of the
Elemente simply on the basis of Müller's work of 1804 (cf. Fr. v. Gentz, *Schriften*, ed.
by Schlesier, vol. 4, p. 359, 1838–40). The point is to see even the thought of a single
author dynamically. It must always be the task of the sociologist of knowledge to
observe how the thought of the same thinker is modified when it moves from one
sociological position towards another within the same social environment. On the
other hand, it will be necessary to observe in what forms certain fundamental concepts
like 'Idea' and 'mediation' appear in other currents of conservative thought.
[4] Cf. Sec. III, p. 141, above.

practice as his guiding principle and makes theoretical reasoning follow practice; the latter separates the two spheres and subsequently establishes a relation between them. It has also been seen that the 'practice' which Möser contrasts as the living element with theory is not only free from all mystic elements but that it is something exceedingly sober—just as his custom and habit, religion and tradition are in no way the irrational factors which they became in the hands of romanticism and the historical school.

From feudalistic conservatism romantic conservatism derived merely the denial of the autonomous nature of theory and the conception of thought as embedded in life. The peculiarly irrational, fluid element is an independent contribution of urban middle-class romanticism. Thus the romanticism of Adam Müller possesses, in place of Möser's sober 'practice', a concept of 'life' in which the 'practical' element is mingled in a peculiar manner with emotional elements and with remains of the contemplative mystic consciousness.

The mere men of practice can satisfy Müller just as little as the mere theorists, because the former 'are confined to such narrow spheres of action, are oppressed by such petty conditions, and shut up in such narrow-minded localities that they find it just as hard to escape pedantry as it is for our theorists to escape visionary enthusiasm [*Schwärmerei*].'[1] Whereas for Möser a narrow sphere of action had still meant living contact, Müller sees in the man of practice the danger of pedantry. He now begins from two sides the process of mystifying, irrationalizing, 'romanticizing' practice. On the one hand, he stresses that aspect of practical thought which later on came to be admired as 'the sureness of instinct'. He sets out to prove that 'principles are of no use, only the feeling for what is advisable and good which has been gathered by long experience'.[2] Möser, too, had been aware of this—but his conception of practice was a different one. The second aspect under which he introduces irrationality is that of pure change and becoming, the protean quality which according to him characterizes Life and Practice or whatever else he may call the antagonist to rigid systematic theory: 'The kind of politics to which I refer should treat of the State as *flowing, living, moving*, not merely throw laws into it and then wait leisurely to see what is going to happen. The statesman should be the ever-present soul of civil society and act at once martially and peacefully.'[3]

Thus there is superimposed on the sober 'practice' of Möser the experience of the dynamic factor. It is the sheer flow and movement

---

[1] Müller, *Elemente der Staatskunst*, vol. i, p. 15.
[2] *Ibid.*, Introduction, p. xii.
[3] *Ibid.*, vol. i, p. 11. (My italics.)

in the concept of life which Müller wants to grasp.[1] Practice is characterized not only by the factors of concrete circumstance and locality (a concept, by the way, which appears both in Möser's and Müller's thought). For the romanticist, 'practice' does not mean day-to-day activity but that pure 'becoming' which can only be experienced from within. The emphasis upon the concrete by which the conservatives reacted to the revolution is here made an 'internal' affair and at the same time combined with a form of experience which in a religious age appeared as mysticism and in an atheistic or pantheistic one as pure dynamism.

This conception of life (a mixture of 'practice', 'concreteness' and 'pure movement') is none the less related to Möser's conception. For it too gives absolute value to something that stands outside theory and in relation to which theory is seen as something secondary. Thought is here a function of life and practice, and not vice versa; practice a mere application of theory to the immediate situation. It is not the case that the theorist decides and the practical man carries out the decision, but the decision actually lies in the comprehension of the concrete; this is the mediation performed by the living, practical participant and agent. Cognition is action and at the same time the knowledge that arises out of action. While, therefore, the consciousness of the Enlightenment which concentrated on theory was inclined to conceive even action as a kind of subsumption (in other words, concealed even action under the categories of 'theory') it is now possible that a vital concept will serve for the understanding of the concrete object. The synthesis is not a matter of joining or adding, but a mediation carried out from within.

The most important phases of feudalistic romanticism thus complete a circle: a special conception of thinking in terms of Ideas, of the relation between theory and practice, and the concept of mediation mutually explain each other as parts of dynamic thought and experience. At the same time one can isolate the dynamic element in Adam Müller's thought (which, as we have seen, is clearly distinguishable from 'practice' in Möser's sense), and thus grasp the conservative origin of the modern idea of 'life' which has its roots in the conservative's experiencing of 'pure becoming' as an Absolute.

In Müller's case, we can often observe how he strains to grasp the concrete object in its concreteness; yet he never achieves a proper realism. At the point when he should become really concrete he goes off into declamations about 'life', 'becoming', the 'Idea', and his discussions are no less abstract (though in a different

---

[1] For further examples of the pure experience of dynamics see *ibid.*, pp. 4, 144, 115, 193, 348, 365 f.

way) than the 'normative' abstractions of the Enlightenment to which they were supposed to be the reaction. And yet, this forced and at first merely programmatic striving for dynamics gave rise to an important aspect of the modern philosophies of Life.

The realism of the second half of the nineteenth century included a romantic conservative element which corresponded to this intense preoccupation with Life. This dynamics was at first experienced in isolation; in its German development it later took a twofold direction. In its romantic direction it gets more and more 'internalized'. In Adam Müller's thought it is—in intention at least—still in alliance with the desire for the concrete, practical and sober. Later, however, it becomes more and more separated from it and is experienced by itself in all its purity. There arises a kind of realism which does not look for 'reality' in the empirical object, in 'everyday life', but in pure 'vital experience'. This new direction, after having been temporarily eclipsed by materialism, especially during the capitalist boom of the eighteen-seventies, received a new impetus from the vitalist philosophy of Bergson, whose notion of '*durée réelle*' is really a revival of the romantic conception of pure dynamics. Many currents from the history of German thought find their way to Bergson, and German intellectual life received back from him, though at a later stage of development, much that had formerly been its own.[1] The impulse that came from Bergson combined in Germany, on the one side, with currents which converged in the *phenomenological* school; on the other, it entered into an alliance with the revived historicism of Dilthey.

The peculiar qualities of the different variants of modern philosophies of life can be defined in accordance with the different tendencies which they have absorbed. However much the various forms of this 'vitalism' may differ from each other, they all betray their origin in (counter-revolutionary) romanticism by their common opposition to both Kantianism and Positivism, the two variants of bourgeois rationalism which both endeavour to preserve and uphold as the exclusive model of all thought general concepts and the inductive method of natural science, though on different epistemological foundations. All philosophies of life are romantic in origin, because they keep alive the opposition against general concepts and because they look for reality in 'pure experience', free from conceptual constructions and rationalization. Today[2] one can no longer speak of them as counter-revolutionary,

[1] For the existence of the conception of '*durée*' in French traditionalism, see P. R. Rohden, *J. de Maistre als politischer Theoretiker*, p. 217, Munich, 1929; see also Brinckmann's review in the *Deutsche Literatur-Zeitung*.

[2] This was written in 1925. Since then, various counter-revolutionary movements in Germany and elsewhere have made use of 'vital' categories in building up their ideologies.—Ed.

since they have mostly become politically indifferent. But the aims of their thought and experience originally sprang, in the romantic period, from the basic aims of conservatism. Just because this originally romantic current lost its political foundation (and with it all immediate efficiency, all concrete touch with its real environment) it could isolate the 'life' and 'pure dynamics' of romanticism from Möser's 'practice' and give it a more and more 'purely internalized' meaning.

The great importance of the philosophies of Life consists in their constant emphasis on the limitations of bourgeois rationalism which in its expansion threatens gradually to obscure and devitalize everything that is alive in the world. The philosophy of Life is never tired of pointing out that whatever passes for 'real' in our rationalized world is merely a reflection of the specific categories of Reason of which modern man has made an idol;[1] in other words, that this world of alleged reality is merely the world of capitalist rationalization. As such it conceals behind it a world of pure 'vital experience'. But even today the philosophy of Life betrays its conservative origin in that it constitutes a latent opposition to the rationalist world which surrounds us. But, having lost all political interest and significance, it can find no direct way of changing things; it exalts the idea of 'becoming' in the abstract but has severed all connection with the actually 'becoming'—though rationalized—world. Nevertheless, philosophies of 'Life' are an integral part of present trends of evolution—in fact, a very important part. They serve to keep alive a certain form of experience; it is an open question to what social trends they will ally themselves in the future.[2] As a position from which to understand the world, the philosophy of Life is a useful counterpart to the currents of thought which stand under the spell of an absolute rationalism. For it teaches us again and again to put aside the rationalizations which conceal the real nature of things and to avoid shaping our consciousness to the pattern of the theoretical attitude alone. It always splits up and relativizes what we believe to be 'rational' and 'objective'.

The romantic experience of pure dynamics followed another path in the hands of Hegel. Opposed to the method of 'internalization' he sought an 'objective' standpoint and thus combined the dynamic element with the concrete problems of the political and

[1] Here again parallels, though of a very different structure, can be found in the left opposition; cf. Lukács, *op. cit.*, *Das Problem der Verdinglichung*, *passim*.

[2] As far as it is possible to judge at present, it has the tendency—when it regains political significance—to provide an ideological foundation for the modern eruptive activist currents (whether in a reactionary or progressive sense). This at any rate is true of the Bergsonian trend which provided the impetus both for Fascism and for the direct action of syndicalism (Sorel).

historical world. That meant that he gave up the purely 'internal' experience of dynamics; by means of a new process of rationalization, he transformed it into 'dialectics'. But at the same time he preserved the lasting conservative discovery of movement by turning it into a method of understanding the growth of history. The dilemma, rigid thought-irrational dynamics, which appeared in the open at the beginning of the new century, he solved by the answer: There is a higher order of rationality than that of abstract, rigid thought; there is *dynamic thinking*. That answer constituted the final triumph of the tendency which has been observed before in Adam Müller, i.e. the tendency to extend the sphere of potential rationalization and to use the new method for the understanding of history. That Hegel succeeded in this, that he did not, like the romantics, lose touch with the real world and take refuge in mere 'internalized' experience, was due to the fact that he clung, with indomitable perseverance,[1] to the historical reality which was then the basic reality for conservatism.

Adam Müller's type of romanticism developed at first in alliance with the feudalistic opposition; but, since the latter could not maintain itself in the long run, it was soon left without any real social backing and had in part to escape into the Austrian camp in order to keep alive at all. That, however, meant the destruction of all that had arisen organically out of it, that gave it meaning and derived its meaning from it. As a visible 'movement', it did not even last as long as Metternich. For as a living influence in intellectual life, it had been done with in the forties; a critic like Heine had completely seen through it as early as in 1833, and still more in 1839.[2]

But in turning the mere experience of dynamics into a rational method of thought of a higher order, Hegel at the same time sets the problem of dynamic thinking and the whole complex of questions concerning truth and a standard of value, which occupy us to the present day. We cannot here describe this whole range of problems and analyse the social background of Hegel's thought. It is important only to show that it is the 'objective dynamics' of Hegel which is absorbed in the synthesis of Marxism. Marxist proletarian thought has therefore also a dynamic and dialectic conception of reality. Hegel and Marxism have this in common with

---

[1] The following passage from the *Rechtsphilosophie* (add. to § 13, p. 290) sounds like a confession in this direction: 'A will which decides nothing is no real will. . . . Only by means of decisions does man enter reality, however hard it may be. For laziness will not venture beyond a state of solitary brooding in which it keeps open an unlimited possibility. But possibility is not reality. A will which is sure of itself is not therefore lost in the thing it determines.'

[2] Cf. for instance Heine's *Romantische Schule* (1833), or the essay 'Der Protestantismus und die Romantik. Zur Verständigung über die Zeit und ihre Gegensätze', a manifesto publ. in the *Hallische Jahrbücher für deutsche Wissenschaft und Kunst*, 1839.

the philosophy of Life, that they, like the latter, are able to relativize 'everyday', 'static', 'abstract' thinking, and to do so on a dynamic basis. But whereas in the 'internalized' philosophy of Life the dynamic foundation is something that precedes all theory (i.e. the pure '*durée*', 'pure vital experience'), in Hegel's philosophy the dynamic basis in respect of which he relativizes 'ordinary', 'abstract' thinking is an intellectual basis (rationality of a higher order), and in proletarian thought, it is the class war and the economically determined social process itself.

It is not necessary to go into all the details which might be mentioned. Our purpose was merely to show that not only the content of thought, but even the conceptions of reality of the twofold opposition against bourgeois rationalism were formed in direct reaction against it; that the product of the struggle was a concept of life which was characterized by movement, by dynamics; and that both the vitalist and Marxist conceptions of reality developed in clear continuity from this romantic opposition.

Apart from these two directions in which the romantic-feudalistic element developed there is a third path which was chosen by the historical school. It solves in a specific way of its own the conservative problem of the relation between norm and history, between thought and existence. The determination of its sociological position presents quite a distinct problem; it occupies a place between romanticism and Hegel. But a discussion of this important current of conservative thought must also be left aside.

CHAPTER III

The History of the Concept of the State as an Organism:

A sociological analysis

M Y aim in this paper is to analyse the history of a concept against the changing social and cultural background. Owing to limited space I can hardly do more than discuss some cross-sections in the development.

My first question will be whether there is any give and take between the natural sciences and politics as far as this problem is concerned: or whether instead of a simple borrowing of the concept its meaning changes when it is transferred from natural science to the sphere of politics.

Perhaps I had better give the answer at the very beginning. Both in the history of science and of politics we find a growing antagonism between the concepts of mechanism and organism.[1] At a certain stage of history this antagonism between the individual concepts developed into two different styles of thought. By 'style of thought' I understand not only a set of concepts linked together by a coherent *Weltanschauung*, but also a specific approach to reality which tends to influence the method of thinking and the presentation of the facts. Both concepts, mechanism and organism, originally emerged from the field of everyday thought, but the history of the emancipation of our thought pattern from ordinary use varies considerably in science and in politics. As far as the

---

[1] For general orientation consult, besides the books to be quoted later, the following:
A. Th. van Kricken, *Über die sogenannte organische Staatstheorie: Ein Beitrag zur Geschichte des Staatsbegriffes*, Leipzig, 1873; E. Th. Towne, *Die Auffassung der Gesellschaft als Organismus, ihre Entwicklung und ihre Modifikationen*, Diss. Halle, Philos. Fak., 1903; F. W. Coker, 'Organismic Theories of the State: Nineteenth Century Interpretations of the State as an Organism', *Studies in History, Economics and Public Law*, vol. 38, No. 2, Columbia University, 1910; J. M. E. McTaggart, *Studies in Hegelian Cosmology*, Cambridge (University Press), 1918 (1st ed. 1901); G. Busse, *Die Lehre vom Staat als Organismus: Kritische Untersuchungen zur Staatsphilosophie Adam Müllers*, Berlin, 1928; O. Hertwig, *Die Lehre vom Organismus und ihre Beziehung zur Sozialwissenschaft*, Frestrede, Jena, 1899; R. H. Wheeler, 'Organismic and Mechanistic Logic', *The Psychological Review*, vol. 42, No. 4, July 1935; Kurt Lewin, *Der Übergang von der aristotelischen zur galileischen Denkweise in Biologie und Psychologie*, Erkenntnis, vol. 1, 1930.

evolution of concepts and methods in the sciences is concerned, we are able to state the factor which governs their differentiation. It is the handling of objects, the practical technique of the work-shop and later on the laboratory which compels us to recast our concepts and our theories.

If we agree that it is the changing nature of practice which is ultimately responsible for the growth of scientific concepts, and that practical activities in the workshop and in the laboratory were responsible for the growing precision of our scientific lan-guage, it is all the more urgent to raise the same question with regard to the nature of political thought. The next task in the history of political thought is to relate the changing forms of con-cepts to the changing practice of political life. Whenever possible, I shall hint at the pattern of practice which probably stood behind the evolving pattern of thought. Thus I hope to show that although there was a constant interchange of ideas between the natural sciences and politics, it was ultimately always the change of poli-tical practice which shaped the concepts of political science.

I shall try to trace four stages in the development of organic thinking.

I. Organic thought as it first emerged on a scientific level.

II. The seventeenth- and eighteenth-century use of the term organic, when it is not yet clearly distinguished from the term mechanistic.

III. The romantic and mainly conservative use of the term in German philosophy.

IV. The discussion of the same problems in terms of modern '*Gestalt* theory' and 'logical positivism'.

The emancipation of scientific patterns from the background of everyday thinking[1] can best be observed in the political theory of Plato and Aristotle. Had I time to embark upon details I would show how in Plato's theories he very often draws on current analo-gies. When he regards the state as a man on a large scale (*Republic*, 434 D) or says that the state may be just in the same sense that a man is just (*Republic*, 441) or when he makes the three classes of which the city is composed correspond to the three parts of the soul (*Republic*, 441 C–D), we have an instance of what one may call primary analogy.

Explaining in terms of primary analogies is commonly practised in everyday thinking because the process of abstraction is still undeveloped. Whenever one meets a new object one naturally tries to refer it to more familiar things. But instead of stating

[1] For the problem of pre-scientific thinking cf. D. Essertier, *Les formes inférieures de l'explication*, Paris, 1927; J. Schultz, *Psychologie der Axiome*, 1899.

exactly in which respect the two things are alike, there is a tendency at this stage to consider them as similar in every respect.

In Aristotle's thought the emancipation from everyday analogy has reached a further stage. He already describes the state in more abstract terms, but still the image of the human body is always in his mind. Right at the beginning of his *Politics* he wishes to apply the method which analyses the composite whole into its uncompounded elements (*Pol.*, I, 1, 1252 A 20 f.). He thinks in abstract terms when he comes to realize that the state is a whole although its elements, through the passing of generations, may be continuously replaced (III, 3, 1276 A 35). But when he describes the nature of interdependence between these parts, the analogy with the living organism comes to the fore.

The significance of Aristotle, however, from our point of view is not limited to the fact that he compared the state with the human organism; his system also furnished the most important concepts which later became associated with the idea of organic thought. Among others the ideas that the whole is prior to the parts and the state to the individual, and that things develop from within, since they contain the source of motion in themselves, found their classical expression in his system. His concept of entelechy has continuously remained in the centre of the discussion.

The more one realizes that most of the elements of a future organic theory of the state were already foreshadowed in his philosophy, the more striking it becomes that the term *organ* in his terminology is still quite simple: it does not mean more than an *instrument*, and *organic* corresponds to *instrumental*.

When one asks oneself what kind of practice, which types of reality are reflected in the underlying patterns of Aristotle's thought, one has primarily to refer to two different fields. First there is the rural background of contemporary thought which still focuses the attention on living beings, especially on animal life, so that any comparison with them will appear natural and obvious. Besides that, there are the simpler operations of craftsmanship. The concept of the organ and teleological thought correspond in many respects to the stage of handicraft. The organ is the tool and teleology is, at least partly, the expression of an age when there was little division of labour and the same man both planned and executed the work. As his mind was steadily fixed upon the purpose of his actions, it was natural to think that purpose was the driving force behind everything that happened in the universe.

Owing to the prevalent conception of the tool as equivalent to the organ, organism at this stage does not mean more than 'the combination of diverse parts in a joint production'.[1] The term organism has not yet become a slogan representing the principle of life. It will be a long time before it becomes the nucleus of a style of thought.

This special style of thought could not appear until its opposite, the mechanistic style of thought, established itself in the scientific world. Before this could happen, the medieval social order had to be dissolved. For, owing to the general prestige of Aristotle and to its agrarian environment, medieval thinking preserved his patterns of thought and the technique of organic analogy.[2] Even in Renaissance thought the organic pattern was predominant. The turning point in the history of philosophy in spite of the many forerunners one could name is still Descartes.[3] In his mechanistic thought the new style of experience finds its philosophical expression. The essence of scientific method consists for him in breaking up the wholes and complexes of everyday experience into homogeneous units. This ultimately leads him to conceive of nature as a machine. This is likewise the origin of modern mechanistic psychology[4] and sociology which is pushed to its farthest extreme in modern behaviourism.[5]

Whereas the concepts of organ and organism are ultimately the product of a society which is largely made up of peasants and craftsmen, familiar with animal life and skilled in the use of tools, the mechanistic theory reflects the life of early industrialism and the use of the simpler types of machine. The artefact, the automaton, the clock are fascinating inventions and give rise to a new interpretation of the universe which tends to translate everything into mechanical terms.[6] To this perhaps there is to be added

[1] Cf. E. Barker, *The Political Thought of Plato and Aristotle*, London, 1906, p. 281; note also A. Espinas, 'Organisation ou la machine vivante en Grèce au IVe siècle avant J.-C.', *Revue de Métaphysique et de Morale*, vol. 11, pp. 709, 712, Paris, 1903; cf. also his book *Les Origines de la technologie*, Paris, 1897.

[2] Cf. O. Gierke, *Political Theories of the Middle Age*, transl. by F. W. Maitland, ch. IV, 'The Idea of Organization', pp. 22–30, Cambridge, 1900; also H. Schmalenbach, *Das Mittelalter, sein Begriff und Wesen*, 1926.

[3] Some of the stages in the development are traced by Pierre-Maxime Schuhl, *Machinisme et Philosophie*, ch. II, Paris, 1938.

[4] Recently attention was drawn to the fact that even within the School of Descartes certain trends were at work which led to a transgression of the pure mechanistic principle in the sphere of psychology. So it was Malebrauche himself who in certain passages is compelled to admit a kind of auto-regulation within the organism which is in contradiction to the theory of animals being machines. Cf. H. Pollnow: 'Reflexions sur les fondements de la Psychologie chez Malebranche', *Revue Philosophique*, 1938, Nos. 3/4, pp. 81–84. Cf. also Bréhier, E.: 'Sur la nouvelle édition de Malebranche', *Revue Philosophique*, 1939, Nos. 1/2, p. 22.

[5] Cf. also to the latter the survey given by P. Sorokin: *Contemporary Sociological Theories*, ch. I, 'The Mechanistic School', pp. 3 ff., N.Y. and London, 1928.

[6] G. Canguilhem gives an interesting account of the technical inventions to which Descartes refers in his works as examples. Cf. G. Canguilhem, 'Descartes et la technique', in *Travaux du IXe Congrès International de Philosophie, Congrès Descartes*, vol. 2; *Etudes Cartésiennes 2me partie*, pp. 77–85, Paris, 1937.

another hypothesis: that it is also the specialization of labour in the early industrial period which forms the background of mechanistic thought.[1] The specialization of labour went a step further and the dismemberment of the product into its parts is more familiar to this age than to the age of craftsmanship. Thus current economic practice also lends its support to a mode of thought in which the only way to understand how anything works is to take it to pieces.

We might be inclined to think that the appearance of the mechanistic mode of thought in the political philosophy of the seventeenth century is a mere imitation of the pattern of thought current in the natural sciences. But this would mean that one can assimilate the patterns of thought which originate in another field without the corresponding change in attitude in one's own field.

As long as man's primary attitude to society was that social reality is something which has to be taken for granted just as it is, the new idea that social institutions are artefacts which originally were made and not created could not be developed. In that frame of mind one could make war and stir up rebellion, but this did not yet involve the conscious reconstruction of the social order.

Of course this new attitude is not universal in this age, but it is gradually growing up in those groups which played an active part in the rise of state absolutism. Both the princes and the thinkers who gave theoretical expression to the new kind of practice were perfectly capable of conceiving political reality in terms of an artefact. It was natural that a social group which built up the modern state out of the ruins of feudalism, which deliberately organized a new type of army and bureaucracy, and created a new industrial system to finance them, should think in mechanistic terms. This social and mental type gradually developed and expressed itself in the new theories of the state which are represented, for example, in Machiavelli and Hobbes. To the former accession to power and the maintenance of power is mainly a technical problem, to the latter the construction of a state is not unlike the working of an automaton. One has only to think of the existing social relationships in real life to realize that those who framed the absolute state were bound to think of their subjects in terms of homogeneous units. For them the citizens only exist in order to be taxed—thus in terms of a purely abstract financial relationship. Once the practical attitude towards society had changed, and one

---

[1] Cf. F. Borkenau, *Der Übergang vom feudalen zum bürgerlichen Weltbild*, Paris (Alcan), 1934; H. Grossmann, 'Die gesellschaftlichen Grundlagen der mechanistischen Philosophie und die Manufaktur', in *Zeitschrift für Sozialforschung*, pp. 161–231, Paris, 1935.

dared consciously to mould the social order, the thinkers who had
to cope with the task could become analytical, breaking up wholes
into their elements and thinking of individuals as of homogeneous
atoms whose relationships were regulated by eternal laws.

The mechanistic concept did not stand by itself but was supplemented by the theory of social contract[1] by these thinkers. Contract seems to be the only bond which unites isolated individuals
so that they form a political unit. Nothing is more natural than
that such a theory should have appealed to the legists and jurists of
the absolutist state. It is clear that anyone who focuses his attention mainly on barter and legal contracts is apt to lose sight of
the older forms of social integration such as customs and habits.
This is exactly what happened to these thinkers who took as their
model the legal regulations of the new state and the competitive
framework of the new commercial society, and applied it to society
in general.

At this stage, although the term 'organism' was very often used,
it really meant mechanism. To Descartes organ and instrument
are synonymous, and to Leibniz the organism is a natural mechanism which differs only quantitatively from the artificial one.[2]

In the early phase of their development the rising classes,
among them the new bourgeoisie, also thought in mechanistic
terms, when they tried to explain to themselves the essence of the
state. They likewise start from the idea that society can be moulded
by man, and the idea of contract is always at the back of their
mind together with the assumption that society must be constructed out of homogeneous atoms. The reason why the rising
bourgeoisie could have so much in common with the rationalism
of the absolute state is obvious as soon as we realize that what
animated them beyond all the differences was the conscious
desire to rebuild society on the basis of rational analysis. The
main difference between the bourgeois philosophers and the
bureaucratic mind is clearly apparent in the role they attribute
to the atoms out of which the great mechanism of society is built.
Whereas in the absolutist theory the great watchmaker has to
wind up the clock from outside, the atoms of the new theory
gradually become alive, make contracts of their own free will and
have full powers of decision. One has only to think of Locke in this
context to see the main changes in the approach. Thus the
equilibrium which makes for order in society will ultimately be the
product of their spontaneous relationships. This is the point where

---

[1] For the legal doctrine and history of contract cf. also Roscoe Pound's article on
'Contract' in the *Encyclopedia of the Social Sciences*.
[2] Cf. R. Eucken, *The Fundamental Concepts of Modern Philosophic Thought, critically and
historically considered*, p. 183, transl. by M. S. Phelps, N.Y., 1880.

the image of the machine gradually changes into the analogy with the living organism[1] in which the spontaneity of life is present in all the elements and out of their vitality follows the organic harmony of the whole. It is to Kant's credit that he synthetized these trends[2] and realized their ultimate logical consequences. In the 65th paragraph of his *Critique of Judgment*[3] he establishes the theoretical differences between organism and mechanism in three main statements. When defining the organism he emphasizes that in the latter the parts are reciprocally cause and effect of each other, which means their spontaneity and mutual interaction. Then, he points out that the parts in an organism are only possible through their reference to the whole; and, thirdly, that the whole is an end in itself and has its own causality. Kant's achievement was to formulate the ultimate logical consequences of a new type of thought which completely corresponded to the democratic pattern of action which was spreading so rapidly in England and in France. It was through Rousseau that the new spirit reached him, and we have a most valuable document in his fragments where he confesses that the French philosopher taught him that the crowds were not just crowds but the living protagonists of the Rights of Humanity. 'There was a time when I believed that all this [i.e. the thirst of knowledge] might contribute to the honour of humanity, and I despised the crowd that knows nothing. It was Rousseau who set me right. That dazzling privilege disappeared and I should think myself far less useful than common artisans if I did not believe that my line of study might impart value to all others in the way of establishing the rights of humanity.'[4]

Each of Kant's three aspects of the concept of organism was later to become the starting-point of new political principles. His conception of the living parts and their mutual interaction supported the claims of the subject against the state, and the rights of the smaller units. The theory that the parts are determined by the whole paved the way for a new understanding of the growing

[1] For the trend in the development of economic theory cf. H. Denis, 'Die Physiokratische Schule und die erste Darstellung der Wirtschaftsgesellschaft als Organismus: Der Kreislauf des Blutes und der Kreislauf der Güter', in *Zeitschrift für Volkswirtschaft, Socialpolitik und Verwaltung*, 1897.

[2] Cf. Erich Kaufmann, *Über den Begriff des Organismus in der Staatslehre des* 19. *Jahrh.*, pp. 3 ff., Heidelberg, 1908; and Eucken, *op. cit.*, p. 184.

[3] Kant's *Critique of Judgment*, transl. by J. H. Bernard, 2nd ed., pp. 276–7, London, 1914.

[4] 'Fragmente', *Werke* (Schubert-Rosenkranz) ii, 240, quoted by R. Fester, *Rousseau und die deutsche Geschichtsphilosophie. Ein Beitrag zur Geschichte des deutschen Idealismus*, p. 69, Stuttgart, 1890. The above quotation is given in Bosanquet's translation. Cf. also K. Fischer, *Immanuel Kant und seine Lehre*, 3rd ed., 1889; Chapter 14 in his *Geschichte der neuern Philosophie*, vols. 3–4; B. Bosanquet, *The Philosophical Theory of the State*, 3rd ed., p. 217 ff., 1920; M. Levy-Bruhl, 'De l'influence de Jean Jacques Rousseau en Allemagne', in *Annales de l'Ecole libre des Sciences Politiques*, July, 1897.

community spirit, in which even the spontaneous parts only exist with respect to the whole. The idea of the whole as an end in itself foreshadows the growth of the spirit of nationalism and the theory of the '*Volksgeist*'. The great builders of philosophical systems such as Fichte, Schelling and Hegel could only free themselves from the spell of the eighteenth-century mechanism by starting with Kant's seemingly dry and abstract definitions.

The question arises: how was it possible that the philosophical implications of a new type of political experience could be worked out in a country which was still untouched by the revolutionary movement and the new spirit of democracy? The answer is to be found—in my view—in the empirical rules which govern the transplantation of ideas into new social surroundings. General experience proves that when intellectual groups take over new ideas which they cannot put into practice, these ideas tend to vary in two different directions:

1. Either they are projected on to a higher plane of abstraction. Since there is no scope for practical application, instead of working out concrete details, they are bound to turn their attention to the purely logical implications. In this way the ultimate principles underlying the new thought are laid bare.

2. Or the new modes of thought may again be projected on to a higher plane but by quite a different method. This is precisely what happened to the democratic patterns of thought when they were transferred from Western politics to the realm of German philosophy where there was no opportunity of putting them into practice. Kant represents the first type: of the projection in forms of a search for ultimate implications. Fichte, Schelling, Hegel and the romantics like Adam Müller represent a projection of political experiences on to the metaphysical or aesthetic plane.

Let us observe in two special cases what happened to the new type of democratic experience and to the corresponding patterns of thought when they were handed over to German thinkers. As Schelling and more particularly A. Müller are perhaps less known in this country, I shall take them as representative exponents of the organic theory of the state in that age. Schelling in his famous lectures 'The Method of Academic Study' (*Vorlesungen über die Methode des akademischen Studiums*, 1803)[1] already builds upon Kant's achievement, but whereas Kant was very cautious in framing his abstract definitions of organism, Schelling uses the new concept as the basis of a new style of thought. He makes a

[1] F. W. J. Schelling, *Sämmtl. Werke. Erste Abteilung*, vol. 5, pp. 207–352, Stuttg.-Augsburg, 1859. Cf. especially the 10th Lecture on the 'Study of History and Jurisprudence', pp. 306–16. Cf. also W. Metzger, *Gesellschaft, Recht und Staat in der Ethik des deutschen Idealismus*, p. 245, 1917.

systematic attack on the eighteenth-century concept of natural
Right and on the whole set of attitudes underlying its arguments.
It is interesting to note his objections as to the latter. He points out
that for one thing they were too formalistic, secondly that they
were too analytical, thirdly that they had too deterministic a conception of the state, and last he criticizes them for having constructed the state too exclusively out of the egoistic instincts of the
individuals. To Schelling the state should be thought of on the
level of philosophical construction as 'the objective organism of
freedom and a work or art within reality' (als einen objektiven
Organismus der Freiheit und als ein reales Kunstwerk).[1]

If we look at this definition of the state as the objective organism
of freedom, we have an example of what we have called projection
of empirical ideas on to a higher plane. When Schelling is speaking
of the state as an organism, he never thinks of it as a biological or
social organism but as a mental and spiritual one. It is obvious
that the problems of practical organization of society which were
troubling the minds of French revolutionary thinkers were, in
his concepts, projected on to a higher metaphysical plane.
He definitely creates a gulf between the plane of the philosophical construction of the state and the pragmatic writing of
history.

Although his metaphysical theory of the state is completely out
of the line of our present-day thinking, it would be wrong to suppose that the problem as such is an entirely fictitious one. His
contempt for the realistic elements of the state blinded Schelling,
but the fact that he was blind to the social factors should not blind
us to his superior sense of spiritual integration.

1. He realized that the social organism is bound to differ from
the biological one, its parts, unlike those of the individual organism, being made up of conscious beings which are also free in their
decisions. Thus, on the level of legal regulations, where the
empirical state establishes itself, we cannot really grasp the
genuine forms of integration in spiritual life. Legal regulations,
being only negative in nature, will be, even in their sum, an
inadequate picture of the integration which takes place in intellectual history. The state therefore, as we empirically conceive of
it, represents only one aspect of the integration of human activities
into a whole. It presents the life of the spirit only in those aspects
in which freedom is limited. The state on this level is therefore
only a kind of 'second nature', mechanistic and deterministic.
One has therefore to surpass that level if one wants to see the whole
as an organism of freedom. Just as, when dealing with biological

<hr />

[1] Schelling, *op. cit.*, pp. 307, 312.

organisms, the deliberate limitation of our approach to some causal sequences in mechanistic terms does not reveal their real nature, the pragmatistic, purely empirical approach to the state prevents us from seeing the metaphysical organism standing behind it. Although this projection of the solution of the problem on to a metaphysical plane which, in his philosophy, immediately leads us to the concept of the world soul (in Hegel's case to the world spirit) cannot satisfy us, one cannot deny that he saw the problem clearly. The pattern of integration which is to be applied to human beings endowed with consciousness and freedom is bound to differ from that which is used in natural science where the fusion of consciousness is not yet a problem.

2. Another merit of Schelling's philosophy was that he thought of nature in evolutionary terms long before Darwin[1] and that for him and even more for Hegel the spiritual organism of which the state was just an aspect was not a static but an evolving phenomenon.[2] Although their philosophy was too speculative, by these very concepts they laid the foundations of a new kind of study in Germany which was later called *Geistesgeschichte* (cf. Dilthey and his followers), an entirely empirical study, based upon detailed documents of the transformation of the human mind during the course of history.

But the concept of the state as a spiritual organism is, as I said, only one aspect of the changing style of thought in the German romantic movement. What I wish to convey through an analysis of A. Müller's thought is that this movement moulded nearly all the concepts dealing with historical experience, and only against this background can the changing concept of the state be fully understood.

In Schelling's case we have seen how empirical concepts are transformed when they are projected on to a metaphysical plane— A. Müller in his *Die Elemente der Staatskunst*, Dresden, 1808–9, provides another instance of this projection, but in addition his work shows how completely revolutionary concepts can be transformed by a traditional and conservative attitude.

Here we have to remember that the romantic movement in

[1] L. Roth, 'Schelling und Spencer. Eine logische Kontinuität', in *Berner Studien zur Philosophie und ihre Geschichte*, vol. 29, ed. by L. Stein; C. Ihmels, *Die Entstehung der organischen Natur nach Schelling, Darwin, Wundt. Eine Untersuchung über den Eutwicklungsgedanken*, Leipzig, 1916; E. W. Quarch, 'Zur Geschichte und Entwicklung der organischen Methode in der Sociologie', in *Berner Studien*, vol. 28, 1901.

[2] On the other hand, Kuno Fischer pointed to some of the main achievements in the natural sciences which stimulated the philosophic speculations of Schelling. Cf. Kuno Fischer, *F. W. J. Schelling*, 2nd ed., 2 vols., 1894–5, pp. 332 ff. (In his *Geschichte der neueren Philosophie*, vol. 6.) Cf. also W. Pagel, 'Religious Motives in the Medical Biology of the XVIIth Century', in *Bulletin of the Institute of the History of Medicine*, vol. 3, No. 4, pp. 295–6, April 1935.

Germany was not, as most people think, originally a conservative movement. The early romantic thinkers were like most members of the German intelligentsia[1] in full sympathy with the French Revolution. But the Terror horrified them, the Napoleonic wars aroused their nationalist spirit, and the restoration period stiffened them into rigidity. These changes are reflected exactly in the changing meaning of their concepts and in their ways of thought, as I tried to show by my studies on conservative thought.[2] This is the reason, among others, why the originally progressive, revolutionary meaning of most of the terms, although it never disappears entirely, is remoulded and transferred to a new plane.

A. Müller, like Schelling, fully realized that he was creating a new type of thought when he attacked the mechanistic theories of the Age of Enlightenment. He goes so far as to say that this type of thinking was responsible for the Revolution. His target is the 'declaration of the rights of man' and the idea of a written constitution. A written constitution means that people imagine that a state could be thought out, that one could *make* it, whereas a state grows. Making and growing are two completely different things— and the core of this organic theory is the principle of growth. The state grows, and as Burke,[3] by whom he is deeply impressed, has shown, it is through the medium of slow traditional changes that the really valuable elements in social life develop. Whereas the bureaucratic mind of the seventeenth-century thinkers was focused upon those parts of society where contracts and legal regulations are the only bond, it is the achievement of the post-revolutionary, conservative thinkers to have directed our attention to those spheres of social life where the integration of society takes place without the conscious interference of some organizing agency. It is against this background that we have to understand A. Müller's statement that the essence of history and of the state is a kind of inner vitality, the opposite of which is the rigidity of abstract concepts. What he is aiming at, therefore, is the creation of a new type of thought which is based upon ideas which are dynamic and thus are capable of coping with the ever-changing nature of reality. It is interesting to notice in which direction the principle of vitality (which for the revolutionary thinkers was

---

[1] Cf. A. Stern, *Der Einfluss der französischen Revolution auf das deutsche Geistesleben*, Stuttgart-Berlin, 1928; also M. Levy-Bruhl, *op. cit.*

[2] K. Mannheim, 'Das Konservative Denken. Soziologische Beiträge zum Werden des politisch-historischen Denkens in Deutschland', in *Archiv für Sozialwissenschaft*, vol. 57, 1–2, 1927 (translated in this volume, pp. 74 ff).

[3] As to Burke and his influence in this respect cf. A. Cobban, *Edmund Burke and the Revolt against the Eighteenth Century. A Study of the Political and Social Thinking of Burke, Wordsworth, Coleridge and Southey*, London, 1929.

identical with the spontaneity of the atoms of society) is being transformed. To Müller vitality, life, is either represented by the slow spontaneous growth of traditions and customs or by the irrational elements in our mind, and is diametrically opposed to mere theory based upon rigid analytic concepts. It is impossible not to see how this romantic antithesis between the life stream and the mechanic rigidity of concept leads through invisible undercurrents ultimately to Bergson's philosophy.

The organic type of thought is also present in his interpretation of the state as the result of continuous struggle between antagonistic forces. In his remarkable early study 'On Antithesis'[1] (*Die Lehre vom Gegensatze*, Berlin, 1804), he laid the logical foundations of a new pattern of thought which, when applied to history, enabled the romantic thinkers to discard the idea of progress. Most styles of thought have a hidden symbol behind them. The age of Enlightenment thought in terms of a straight line. This is gradually replaced by another symbol of current and counter-current. Although this thinking in terms of antagonistic forces will later become the basis of the dialectical principle in Hegel and Marx, in A. Müller's phrasing thesis and antithesis is not yet completed by synthesis. Instead of the term synthesis he makes use of mediation (*Vermittlung*), the task of the statesmen being continuous mediation between the antagonistic tendencies in the state.

The deepest element in romantic thinking is reached when, as a result of the dynamic concept of the historical organism, many of the romantic thinkers come to realize that time, as conceived in history, is utterly different from time as it is measured by the clock. The idea of historical time means that not every moment in the course of events is of equal significance.

Taking time seriously was the great endeavour of all the traditionalist post-revolutionary philosophers. The bitter experience of the Revolution that those who put abstract schemes into practice, irrespective of the historical circumstances, are bound to fail, made these thinkers aware of the historical configuration in which they lived. The time of which they suddenly became aware was the time in which an historical community lives. The time based on common inner experience is qualitatively different in two historical groups, even if the chronological date should be the same.

Thus the time which the historian deals with is concrete and unique, every moment contains a completely different historical

[1] In the romanticist doctrine of polarity an old thought pattern is transferred by way of natural philosophy into the field of political thinking. The doctrines of Paracelsus as further developed in Robert Fludd's (1574–1637) teachings overflow into medical biology and constitute a peculiar blend of religious motives and scientific hypotheses. Cf. W. Pagel, *op. cit.*, part 5.

configuration, in which every institution depends on the rest, and it would change its meaning if it were transplanted into another historical community. Even the political organization, the state or a constitution is a living product of one's community; one cannot successfully transplant it into another social organism. What suits the French, does not suit the German. Here the conservative interpretation of the individualistic aspect of the organism becomes apparent. The organic concept here means the uniqueness of living configurations and is therefore wholly opposed to the idea of generalization and to comparative studies. Anyone who realizes that the dominant tendency in the writing of history in Germany originated in the logic of the romantic school will understand why these historians even later repudiated any attempt to generalize about history.

The logical foundations of the 'Historical School' were closely related to the organic style of thought. They not only stressed the uniqueness of the time element and that of historical situations but emphasized the individuality of every nation as a whole. The nationalism aroused by the Napoleonic wars is reflected in the uniqueness of the *Volksgeist*,[1] which is conceived of as a kind of emanating force which manifests itself in every element of national life. In connection with the concept of emanation the technique of knowing is being gradually shifted from causal explanation to intuitive understanding. It is the latter alone which ultimately helps us to penetrate into the core of the unity of the *Volksgeist* and to interpret the meaning of every cultural product in terms of national self-expression. Although in the Historical School the emphasis was not so much laid upon the state as upon *Volk*, the organic state as represented in its law is only genuine if it naturally evolves from the silent growth of its institutions, 'die stillwirkenden Kräfte' (Savigny). The idea of artificially setting up a systematic rational legislation like that of the Code Napoleon was strongly attacked by Savigny, who is to be considered the founder of that school, the teachings of which penetrated into all the branches of historical studies and produced scholars like Eichhorn, K. F. Boeckh, Ranke and the Grimm brothers.

The elements of which the romantic and conservative style of thought was composed (the theory of the spiritual organism, of historical growth and inner vitality together with the principles of antagonism, the historical concept of time, the uniqueness of any historical configuration and the individuality of the *Volksgeist*)

[1] Cf. H. Kantorowicz, 'Volksgeist und Historische Rechtsschule', in *Histor. Zeitschrift*, vol. 108, 1911; G. Rexius, 'Studien zur Staatslehre der historischen Schule', in *Histor. Zeitschrift*, vol. 107, 1911; E. Rothacker, *Einleitung in die Geisteswissenschaften*, Tübingen, 1920; E. Troeltsch, 'Der Historismus und seine Probleme', *Ges. Schriften*, vol. 3, Tübingen, 1922.

were not biological; the organic patterns have been genuinely transformed. Emerging from an utterly new approach to history, they helped us to realize social phenomena which formerly passed unnoticed.

This is how the romantic adaptation above all differs from a later penetration of the pattern of organism into the social sciences as represented in the writings of Spencer, von Lilienfeld, Schäffle, Worms, Fouillée during the second half of the nineteenth century. Limited space prevents me from dealing with them, but the most important criticism should be stated here, that by being too subservient in the application of the pattern borrowed from biology, they failed to do justice to the genuine problems of the social sciences proper. They very often stated mere generalities and stretched the analogies too far.

Our history of the concept 'organism' would remain incomplete, were we not at least to hint at its contemporary form as it presents itself in the modern *Gestalt* theory. We have—even if very briefly—to deal with the modern form of the old controversy between the mechanistic and organic theory as it was carried on between the logical positivists and those who have worked out the *Gestalt* theory, because without their analysis it is impossible to understand the real meaning of the whole process so far described. Although the main classification of concepts and methods this time took place in the natural sciences and in philosophy, the names like those of von Ehrenfels, Köhler, Wertheimer, Bertalanffy, Woodger and Schlick are the most important in the controversy, the *Gestalt* theory has already been applied to the theory of the state as in the recent writings of A. Menzel and A. Vogel.[1] That the *Gestalt* theory is nothing but the modern variation of the organic theory can be seen from the following facts: It emerged in Germany, and has only lately been transferred to the Anglo-Saxon world. It is likewise opposed to the mechanistic style of thought and very often uses the old arguments. As is known, the new variation of organic thought, the *Gestalt* theory, emerged mainly in the field of experimental psychology, but it was very soon applied to physics, biology, and, as I have said, recently even to the study of the state.

To put it very briefly, its essence is the emphasis upon the whole, *Gestalt*, which is always considered a new entity as compared with the sum of its elements. As the oft-repeated example shows, the melody is entirely different from the sum of the single notes. In

[1] A. Menzel, *Zur Psychologie des Staates*, Vienna, 1915; 'Die energetische Staatslehre', in *Archiv für Sozialwissenschaft und Sozialpolitik*, vol. 66; W. Vogel, 'Rudolf Kjellén und seine Bedeutung für die deutsche Staatslehre', in *Zeitschrift für die ges. Staatswissenschaft*, vol. 81, 1926.

every field we find such wholes. As Köhler has shown, there are in physics systems of energy which are not simply the sum of individual forces. In this field, in an electrostatic system the elements are dependent on each other and on the whole system, and they always try to restore this equilibrium if it happens to be disturbed by external interference. Thus a mechanistic analysis of the constituent parts and forces cannot tell us much about the nature of the whole.

What, then, is new in the *Gestalt* theory as compared with the organic theory? I think it has the merit of being more carefully stated than the organic theory and less overburdened with metaphysical implications. It speaks of wholes and systems of which the organism is merely one. By speaking in more abstract terms it avoids the projection of inner hidden force into the objects. What still remains of the age-old antagonism between mechanism and organism is the absolute gap, the leap between mechanical sum and the *Gestalt*, the latter being conceived as something completely new.

But even this gulf has been bridged in the recent discussion between the modern representatives of the old traditions where the mechanistic point of view has been adopted by the logical positivists.

According to Schlick, for example, there is no leap, no inherent difference between the mechanistic sum and the *Gestalt* integration. In his words: 'Were I to know everything about a people and its history, were I in the position to gather information about all the possible activities of an individual in minutest detail, there would be no need to enlarge my existing knowledge by making statements about wholes like the "general will" or about the "nation as such".'[1]

The advantage of this interpretation is that it avoids splitting up the realm of science into two incoherent fields—that is to say one which is governed by the mechanistic method and the other by the *Gestalt* integration. In the same way it avoids creating two different spheres of reality in the very same object: as if the sum of the people were utterly different from the nation. But a great *rapprochement* is shown when the logical positivist no longer

[1] M. Schlick, 'Über den Begriff der Ganzheit', in *Erkenntnis*, vol. 5, 1935, p. 55. Cf. also K. Duncker, 'Behaviorismus und Gestaltpsychologie,' and R. Carnap, 'Erwiderung', both in *Erkenntnis*, vol. 3, 1932–33; K. Grelling and P. Oppenheim, 'Der Gestaltbegriff im Lichte der neuen Logik', *Erkenntnis*, vol. 7, 1937; Ludwig von Bertalanffy, *Modern Theories of Development, an Introduction to theoretical Biology*, translated and adapted by J. H. Woodger, ch. VIII, 'The Organismic Theories', London (Oxford University Press), 1933; 'Tatsachen und Theorien der Formbildung als Weg zum Lebensproblem', *Erkenntnis*, vol. 1, 1930; J. H. Woodger, *Biological Principles, A Critical Study*, New York (Harcourt, Brace), 1929.

rejects the *Gestalt* integration. To him the *Gestalt* is one of many possible methods of integration and the practical aim decides which method would be the more appropriate one.

As soon as this stage is reached, I can advance my own hypothesis:

Whether the same reality (natural or social) presents itself in terms of a mechanistic total or of a *Gestalt* depends on the practical purpose. Man seems to approach the very same reality from different levels of action, and so the very same world may appear to him as a mechanistic total in which the individual elements are still clearly visible, or as a *Gestalt* where the parts themselves are fused, but some of the relationships between them are unconsciously emphasized.

In the experimental sciences these different levels of approach, these methods of handling the object can often be clearly defined. Thus in biochemistry attention is focused on the elements and their sums, whereas in biology proper, this method would lose sight of many connections which only become visible when they are studied, so to say, from a greater distance. Thus even in the natural sciences a definite distance is created between oneself and the object and there are different levels of manipulation. Biology proper mostly makes use of a *Gestalt* perspective, concentrates on the relationships between and configurations of the parts rather than the parts themselves.

If we were to apply the same hypothesis to the study of the state and society we should arrive at the same results. Whether the mechanistic or the organic (*Gestalt*) approach was more successful depended, as we have seen, on the practical purposes to which they were applied by certain groups. The philosophers who thought in terms of the absolutist monarchy or the rising bourgeoisie (thinkers who hoped to remake the state by recombining its elements) naturally chose the mechanistic view. Among them again those who aimed at rebuilding society not from above but through the spontaneous will of the atoms which composed it, unconsciously transformed the mechanistic conception into that of an organism. In order to realize that in the social organism the whole was an independent entity as compared with the sum of the parts it was necessary to wait till the rise of nationalism. In the same way we had to await the arrival of the conservative thinkers who wanted to stop revolutionary interference in order to make us realize the meaning of growth and time in history and in the life of the state.

Thus it is obvious that the patterns of social activity are ultimately responsible for the transformation of the patterns of thought, and our next task should be to give a clear definition of the different levels of social action and their effect on the changing models of thought in social theory.

The history of political science will only become a real contribution to the Cosmos of learning if it is capable of explaining the history of political thought with continuous reference to the changing political practice out of which the changing concepts emerge.

The philosophy of the natural sciences has reached a stage at which it is evident that even the most empirical approach to reality corresponds to the practice out of which it evolves. There was a phase in which we believed that the explanation of the same fact in organic and mechanistic terms would lead to complete relativism, either view being equally valid in every case. We see now that the difference between the organic and the mechanistic explanation consists in a different level of approach to the object, a different perspective, and ultimately a different method of handling it. Which conception is likely to be the more fruitful and adequate depends on the nature of the object examined.

The same applies, *mutatis mutandis*, to the study of the social sciences and politics. Here again the different patterns of thought correspond to the different forms of political action and to the different levels of political approach. These various approaches, in their turn, are very often but not always evolved from different social classes and groups.

Let me sum up in a few statements the main results of the inquiry.

1. In the development of the patterns of thinking there is a continuous interchange between the ways of thinking in the natural sciences and political thought.

2. But the nature of that process cannot adequately be understood if we confine our observation to causal influences and only think in terms of reciprocal causation. Behind the development of the two concepts, mechanism and organism, there stood the development of two corresponding styles of thought.

3. Thus the origin, unity, dissemination and decay of these styles of thought is a problem in itself and has to be investigated with the same accuracy as the various styles in the history of art or literature. This does not mean that scientific thinking is nothing but a kind of artistic activity, but only that our approach to the various spheres of reality does not emerge out of the vacuum, that it does not proceed in terms of mere accumulation, but that there is a kind of cohesion, an inner unity in the changing patterns of thinking.

4. On the other hand this is only the subjective aspect of the process. The unifying *Weltanschauung*, the styles of thought in their

turn are not absolute entities. They do not appear out of the blue, they are somewhere connected with social history.

5. Once this has been agreed the next task is to find the connecting link with social history. This cannot be found simply in the social classes themselves, as Marxism asserts. There is nothing in the concept 'class' which would immediately explain the fact that the underlying symbols and modes of thought and the methods of inquiry should change. The key to changes in our thought patterns is to be found—as I have tried to show—in the changing practice both of science and politics. If the main patterns of action are disclosed, then we can further inquire whether this was brought about by the rise of some new class or group, and its changed attitudes towards society.

6. Through the Sociology of Knowledge a new approach to the problems of political science becomes possible. A careful analysis of the specific nature of political practice and of its various forms might disclose the main changes in its modes of thought.

This also might throw light upon the deeper unity which underlies scientific and political development.

PART TWO

★

GERMAN AND WESTERN SOCIOLOGY

CHAPTER IV

American Sociology[1]

Methods in Social Science,[2] edited by Stuart A. Rice, Chicago
(University of Chicago Press), 1931

I CONSIDER it my task to convey to you the ideas awakened in a German sociologist by the reading of the 'case book' on methods in social science edited by Stuart A. Rice. Of course I do not mean to say that German sociology is a single, homogeneous unit. On the contrary, the most antagonistic schools of thought are lined up against each other in that country. However, even their differences reveal something common in all German conceptions of sociology, a common train of ideas which might profitably be compared with the typical American approach to the subjects of social science. I believe that *Methods in Social Science* furnishes a welcome occasion to confront our different mental habits.

In so limited a space, however, only the fixing of a first impression is possible, without any pretension to finality. Questions of detail must be left aside. The only purpose of this review is to show the difference in the fundamental attitudes of German and American scholars towards the problems of social science.

To speak of the *Methods* of Rice, I must begin with the confession that a European sociologist is bound to feel agreeably surprised by the vast and comprehensive plan of the work and even more by the successful realization of this plan, aiming at a methodological survey by eminent scholars of the latest products of social research in America as well as of historically or theoretically important European works. This example of scientific co-operation reminds us of the excessive individualism prevailing in German sociology. In Germany, almost every author believes it necessary to start from a new beginning, and most scholars take pride in having

[1] From *The American Journal of Sociology*, vol. 38, no. 2, pp. 273–282, September, 1932.
[2] *Editorial Note.*—The editors of the *Journal* have felt that this important volume in social science literature could scarcely be given adequate treatment by a single reviewer. For this reason, they have arranged a series of reviews by a number of scholars, which would present a variety of points of view. The following review by Professor Karl Mannheim, of the University of Frankfurt, Germany, is the first in this symposium.

systems of their own, overlooking the fact that division of labour and organization of scientific research are perfectly feasible in sociology and that central guidance could be of very great profit.

A second fact calling for approval is that the methodological subject matter of the work is treated in close connection with concrete examples of practical study. The problem of method is not examined *in abstracto*, but all methodological questions are exposed as they present themselves to the practical worker. A similar book written by Germans would probably begin with a general treatise on the difference between natural and social sciences, between 'understanding' and 'explanation', and on other such questions of principle, while the American work soundly confines itself to the methodological requirements of concrete tasks. Methodology of this kind embraces in the first place problems like these: 'What should one do to find out this or that? How should this or that problem be set forth? Where are the possible sources of error, and what was done, and must yet be done, to eliminate them? (Cf. the exemplary work of Park, p. 165 and *passim.*)

As I said, this approach to methodology from the practical aspect is very sound and effective. There is nothing ambiguous about it; all criticism assumes the form of conferences in a workshop where the opinion of a foreman on a piece in construction is immediately understood by everyone.

However, not only methodological criticism has this character of directness, but the sociological research work under examination also shows a similar quality. Each work starts from a practical problem, from a social task calling for immediate solution. The sociologist is called upon to help in finding this solution.

The typical problems of American sociology arise from the immediate necessities of everyday life. They assume the form of convergent planning and concerted action aiming at overcoming the difficulties threatening the progress of collective work. This explains the fact that most of the subjects treated fall under the heading of what in Germany is called 'social policy'. Such problems are those of juvenile delinquency, juvenile gangs, ghettos, immigration policy, etc., to which excellent studies are devoted. This sort of work brings help where help is needed without devoting much time to elucidating intricate problems of evolution and to defining exactly the historical place of the phenomena in the process of social evolution. It is also characteristic of this kind of research that it is based on ready documentary evidence, focusing on just those matters on which life itself accumulates such evidence. Thus the authenticity of factual observation is guaranteed in advance.

Limitation to practical problems of this kind tends to segregate single phenomena from the social fabric with which they are interwoven, thereby disintegrating the whole of social 'life. An endeavour towards clarity and exactness, evidenced by the choice of well-defined and concrete subjects, is accentuated by the use of notion-patterns ready for use by anyone. Every phenomenon will be subjected to an analytical treatment laying bare its correlations with these notion-patterns. Thus the variety of problems and aspects will be reduced to a single set of terms. The appreciation of a scholar will depend on his skill in handling the technique of research and on his ingenuity in experimentation.

In fact, nothing else could be expected. Collective research, that is to say, research which may be continued by anyone from the point where it has been interrupted, demands a certain simplification of the phenomena. The embarrassing multiplicity of living facts must be broken up and articulated so as to lend itself to a mental treatment from which all ambiguity and subjectivity is banished and by which the exactness of all terms is guaranteed.

The above seems to me to be typical not only of the contributions to Rice's compendium but also of most of the representative specimens of American sociology. However, after having rendered justice to the high merits of this scientific attitude, I feel obliged to point out some of its shortcomings. It seems to me that the scientific outlook which I have characterized above necessarily misses some essential points, not so much in the treatment of its problems as in its fundamental conception of social life and social science.

The more one approves the empirical outlook of American science—agreeing with its motto that science, after all, is not called upon to reassert the supremacy of all the irrational factors which tend to thwart an effective and intelligent control of social phenomena—the more significant is the uneasiness with which one reads some, though not all, specimens of this kind of scientific research.

To confine ourselves to Rice's compendium, we must admit a very ·marked and painful disproportion between the vastness of the scientific machinery employed and the value of the ultimate results. The subject and title of most of the contributions evoke the highest expectations; yet, after having reached their conclusions, one is tempted to ask, disappointedly: 'Is this all?'

It need not be repeated that this does not apply to all papers contained in the book. However, in order to make our attitude clear, we have to over-emphasize a little all the typical traits, meritorious as well as defective, which in our opinion distinguish American sociology from our own.

Now it may be worth while to ask what is wrong in a scientific attitude which, on the whole, is so sound and well founded. What is to blame for the inability of works of such flawless methodical integrity really to satisfy us?

The essential seems to me to be this: American social science of the kind which I regard as typical has the defects of its qualities; indeed, the defects which we have to point out are almost inseparable from the qualities which we praised.

1. The first reason why we are left unsatisfied by this type of science is the limited scope of the questions to which it confines itself and the character of the social knowledge towards which its efforts are directed.

It is certainly worth while to examine the conditions responsible for the neglect and delinquency of juveniles. It is equally useful to know which type of immigrant will adapt himself best. A couple of the best contributions are devoted to these themes. However, if such problems are treated in isolation while the totality of social problems remains neglected, if the scholar examining details does not aspire towards a comprehensive view of social reality or shrinks from generalizing hypotheses out of mere caution or owing to methodical asceticism, then the most excellent work of detail is bound to remain in a vacuum. Society at a given stage of its evolution is no mere agglomeration of exactly observable individual data, of sparse events and relationships all of which, added together, in some way produce the picture of the whole, but a combination of interdependent phenomena, and even more: a structured whole or *Gestalt* (a term used here in a general, not merely psychological, sense). If we divide this whole into its parts, and focus attention on the individual functioning of each part, then we shall necessarily overlook a very important aspect of the functioning of the parts, namely, their relation to the whole to which they belong. An individual event or a social phenomenon is adequately described only if it be characterized as a manifestation of the life and functioning of society as a whole. The observation of individual tasks and their analysis are both necessary to attain scientific truth, but once this task is done, the scholar must turn to the whole of social life and interpret the detail from the aspect of the whole.

Nothing could be learned on the economic laws of exchange if one were to confine one-self to the psychological and empirical analysis of so many hundreds of thousands of individual acts of barter without formulating the principles of economic circulation. These principles are never exactly represented by facts; yet they form the mental pattern to which the individual facts are referred. The same applies to all empirical observations. They must be confronted with constructive principles. Empirical data are only useful if they are enlightened by a constructive hypothesis, by a theory of social processes in general.

It seems to me that American sociology suffers from an excessive fear of theories, from a methodological asceticism which either prevents the putting forth of general theories or else keeps such theories as exist isolated from practical research.

To have nothing but theories without verifying them, to discuss theoretical dicta as a kind of mental sport serves no useful end whatsoever. On the other hand, it is a misunderstanding of positivism to try to know reality without having theories. Finally, to have theories but not to apply them to reality may be attributed to an excessive love of security which must lead to sterilization.

2. This ascetic attitude towards theories seems to be based on a mistrust of 'philosophy' or 'metaphysics'. Unwillingness to discuss basic questions, however, does not benefit positive research. In conversations with American scientists one often hears the criticism that German sociology is still lingering at the 'philosophic' stage, and has yet to make some progress before attaining the 'scientific' one. Correct as this criticism may be as regards many German authors who indulge in metaphysical escapades under cover of sociology, it would still be a mistake to overrate the antagonism between philosophy and science, and to brand as 'philosophy' in a defamatory sense every theory, every constructive hypothesis penetrating beyond immediate and tangible experience and outlining a comprehensive system of social and historical phenomena. We must distinguish between 'speculative' and 'constructive' mind; the latter is as indispensable to any empirical research as the former is detrimental. To think speculatively is to sit at a desk and conceive casual and uncontrolled ideas on all things on earth and in heaven. To think constructively means to build up, by an effort of constructive imagination, a structure which is embedded in the phenomena themselves but cannot be detected by direct observation of any individual fragment of reality.

It is possible that many American scholars will admit the importance of theoretical construction. However, the main thing, in the field of methodology, is not to have a right opinion but to act according to it. Now, it seems to me that the most valuable specimens of 'empirical' sociology show a curious lack of ambition to excel in the quality of theoretical insight into phenomenal structures. They reveal a greater anxiety not to violate a certain, very one-sided, ideal of exactness. One almost ventures to say, such works aim in the first place at being exact, and only in the second place at conveying a knowledge of things. Now, as to this,

I believe that it is much better first to seek to have some knowledge of a vitally important matter, and only afterwards to worry about the method assuring the highest possible degree of exactness.

American sociology seems to yield too much to the fascination of natural science. Although it is admitted that all social phenomena are not measurable, still numerical proportions are the ideal of exactness toward which most scholars are striving. However, before adopting a specific ideal of exactness, one should inquire which ideal suits best the particular field of phenomena to which research is to be devoted. In the field of philological and historical science where interpretation plays a foremost part the criteria of exactness are quite different from those prevailing in experimental psychology, physics, etc.

Exaggerated 'methodological asceticism' often results in the drying-up of the sources of scientific inspiration and invention. In order to know social reality one must have imagination, a particular brand of imagination which I should like to call 'realistic' because it does not create fiction but exerts itself in binding together apparently unrelated facts by means of a vision of structural correlations which alone enables us to see the framework into which every fact, even the most casual one, is fitted. Like other qualities required for science, such as self-criticism, control of methods, etc., this realistic imagination must be cultivated through generations.

Harmful as the excessive philosophical tradition dominating intellectual life in Germany may be (such tradition is always harmful when it dominates exclusively, without confronting speculation with the facts) philosophical training is useful whenever it is tinged with the yearning for the knowledge of real things. Then it may evolve into a realistic imagination which makes for increased constructive power. Such philosophical training, acquired in many generations, is responsible for a greater capacity of recognizing connections between things, for the development of a comprehensive view of the social process as a whole, instead of mere isolated treatment of sporadic facts which can be mastered in a division of jobs. Comprehensive vision will put every fact in its place within the framework of a broad hypothesis embracing the whole of society.

It is true that, according to Comte's fundamental conception, the survivals of the old philosophical and metaphysical stage must be eliminated once the empirical stage is reached. However, these survivals cannot be eliminated by simply sacrificing everything reminiscent of philosophy, or of a philosophical conception of history, but only by applying to the facts and fructifying in empirical research that gift of consistent questioning and comprehensive vision which humanity for the first time developed in its philosophy.

3. While on the one hand American sociology lacks a certain courage in outlining broad theories, or rather shrinks from inquiring into the structural aspects of social life as a whole at a given stage, out of fear engendered by the common identification of theory as such with theory in the sense of pure, causal, metaphysical speculation—on the other hand there is another reason why our claims on social science are not satisfied by typical American contributions to this science, interesting and valuable as they may be in themselves. This reason is that typical American studies start from questions in nowise connected with those problems which arouse our passions in everyday political and social struggle.

In one respect, American sociology is nearer to reality than German—namely as regards the solution of everyday problems. The American scholar is no bookish person; he maintains contact with criminal courts and social welfare institutions, lives with gangs, in slums and ghettos. However, as soon as political and social problems impose themselves we notice an immense reserve, a lack of social atmosphere. It looks as if science had no social background; as if groups devoted to social research cultivated no exchange of ideas on matters social and political; as if no conventicles existed in which the practical attitude of science towards such problems were discussed.

Science, in these parts, serves the purpose of reforming or reorganizing society. Scientific interest centres on the dynamic forces determining the process of transformation of society, although, of course, political viewpoints differ very widely. As to myself, I shall always regard it as one of the most important questions to know how human consciousness is shaped and determined by the social struggle; a question which may not only be asked in connection with the present situation, but also applied to history and to the psychic and intellectual changes wrought in the past by social revolutions and by the shift in class dominance. It may be objected to this that such enormous questions do not lend themselves to empirical analysis. Our reply is that, naturally, these problems cannot be solved by one or two works; if, however, every study of detail is carried out in clear consciousness of these comprehensive questions (whether they directly guide the research or merely act as a background), then even such central themes might successfully be tackled.

Just as there is a certain arrogance in the attempt of pure speculation to solve the Gordian knot of big problems at one stroke, there exists a certain false modesty of the empirical scholar whom his 'exactitude complex' prompts to ignore the genuine basis of his own questioning, which alone makes a scientific occupation worth while. In our opinion, methodological criticism of sociological studies (as it was undertaken in Rice's compendium) should in each case inquire whether the work in question is devoted to a genuine problem. In America, the inverse method seems to be practised: one concludes from the existence of ready documentary evidence, of statistical material, etc., that social research is worth while. This is nothing but an 'exactitude complex' which canonizes every fact, every numerical certitude just because they are factual and controllable.

In view of the growing amount of the material of science it would be dangerous further to accumulate facts without choice. The loss of command over the material at this juncture has become a serious menace to science as such. The desire to bring order into this chaos is at least as justified as the attempt to isolate and exactly to define individual fragments of it. Genuine problems, real scientific tasks are only those which impose themselves on the basis of the general trend of science, that is to say, questions which emerge from the group consciousness of society struggling for its existence and its livelihood.

In the introduction to the volume under discussion (p. 10), the question is asked whether Marx and Carlyle would have been unable to envisage their problems had they known the statistical method. If the answer is in the affirmative, then we do not hesitate to confess that we would rather renounce statistical exactness than forego seeking answers to those questions which seem important to us. Should it not be possible to save these questions, then the cruel name of a 'science of that which is not worth knowing', which was originally applied to academic, dry classical philology, would befit our science.

4. We know that a closer contact with central political problems involves the danger that judgments of value creep into science, reducing it to mere political propaganda. In fact, this danger constantly threatens German sociology just because it is closely in touch with political problems. However, if we know about this danger, we can take precautions against it, evolving methods which help to detect and eliminate political bias. One of the greatest German sociologists, Max Weber, has shown how we can discuss the political *nervus rerum* without making propagandistic judgments of value. The desire to treat politically important problems without being a victim to bias was responsible for the development in Germany of a new branch of social science, *Wissenssoziologie*. This new branch of research, intended to be an organ of critical self-control, has already succeeded in

detecting and subjecting to control important groups of sources of error.[1]

The absence of the viewpoint of *Wissenssoziologie* from a methodological analysis seems to us to be a defect inasmuch as this branch of sociology claims to have discovered that science itself is embedded in the stream of social and historical reality, wherefore even in cases when the sincere effort towards unbiased objective knowledge cannot be denied, the available supply of terms, the technique of questioning, the articulation and grouping of problems may be responsible for distortions which can only be detected by means of an intimate historical acquaintance with the correspondence between the development of science and the evolution of society. Only a scholar well acquainted with these facts of human evolution is able to construct those systems of perspective which necessarily introduce an element of partiality into all human consciousness.

Thus, we miss in Rice's compendium, in which we recognize a serious effort towards objectivity and towards the perfecting of the methods of observation, an element of self-control. A critic who himself shared the American approach to social science would not miss it. If, however, there is any reason for asking for the opinion of foreign critics, the reason is not that the foreigner might make suggestions regarding this or that detail but that he should unreservedly and with all possible frankness convey his impression of the work as a whole.

It is possible that such a general survey will not do justice to every detail, and that it expresses contrast too sharply. However, it may have the merit (if it has any) of making us look from a new angle at things to which daily intercourse and too much familiarity have dulled our senses.

In this review I have abstained from the usual compliments regularly bestowed by foreigners on foreign works. I have done so, in full awareness of the risk that I may shoot wide of the mark in my criticism; however, I deliberately run this risk because I think that the future of American sociology means something to us, just as America is not indifferent to the fate of German sociology. One thing shown by such a discussion more than anything else is that there were hardly ever two different styles of study so fit to supplement each other's shortcomings as are the German and American types of sociology. These two schools can become very useful to each other, just because their approach to their subject is so fundamentally different. We must learn from American sociology

[1] Cf. the author's article 'Wissenssoziologie' in Alfred Vierkandt's *Handwörterbuch der Soziologie*, which also contains a bibliography of the subject.

that science must remain in contact with real life and its exi-
gencies; on the other hand, American sociology may gain if its
studies on questions of practical detail are alive to the great
theoretical problems which pervade and co-ordinate with each
other all the scattered empirical facts.

CHAPTER V

The Place of Sociology[1]

I AM inclined to side with those who aver that whereas the by-gone two hundred years have witnessed revolutionary changes in the technical and natural sciences, the centuries to come should be dedicated to the moral and social transformation of mankind. For it is surely a striking commentary on the age in which we live, that while should anyone try to repair his car without knowing the first thing about its machinery he would by common consent be dubbed a fool, yet no such derision is displayed towards those who, possessing no clear knowledge of cause and effect, believe that hitches in the mechanism of society can be set right by emotional resentments or irrational movements against social forces. In my view, therefore, very much depends upon whether we can—before it is too late—succeed in building a science of society.

It must be admitted that the attempt to build such a science is confronted by many difficulties. The causal sequences which lead up to results in the sphere of the social sciences are far more complex than are parallel sequences in the natural sciences. Again, the isolation of single causal tendencies by the experimental method is well-nigh impossible in the social sciences. Thirdly, there is the difficulty of co-ordinating the divergent conclusions which are the fruit of specialized research in the different branches of the science of society.

Of these difficulties, I propose in this paper to focus attention solely on the last named—the difficulty of co-ordination; because it is in this respect particularly that, it seems to me, there is readiness in this country to improve the situation. For in England, as in America, France and Germany,[2] we find today the most diverse branches of the social sciences increasingly working on questions that lie on the periphery of their respective specialized

[1] Paper presented at a conference held under the auspices of the Institute of Sociology and World University Service, British Committee, London, 1936.
[2] For the setting of the problem in different countries see *inter alia* Ogburn and Goldenweiser, *The Social Sciences and their Interrelations*, 1927; Bouglé, *Bilan de la Sociologie française contemporaine*, 1935; L. v. Wiese, *System der Allgemeinen Soziologie*, pp. 1–100, 1933; K. Mannheim, *Die Gegenwartsaufgaben der Soziologie. Ihre Lehrgestalt*, 1932; and recently, A. Löwe: *Economics and Sociology. A Plea for Co-operation in the Social Sciences*, 1935.

spheres. Merely by following-up consequentially the separate
links in the long chain of causality they are inevitably brought up
against facts and problems of other specialized branches of the
science of society, or, to put this more precisely, from their specific
field they get to see the functioning of *society as a whole*.

Let us take political science for instance. In the long run it is
impossible to restrict the problems of this branch of learning to the
faithful description and classification of the political institutions of
different countries. For, sooner or later, one is confronted with
the question *why* do countries at the same period and on the same
plane of development have wholly different types of constitutions
and forms of government, and *why* when the technique of government and constitution belonging to one country are taken over by
another do they change their form in the adopting country?
Democracy is not the same thing in England, France, and America;
and the German Fascist dictatorship differs in fundamental
respects from that of Italy or Turkey. Thus the political scientist
is thrown back on certain unknown entities, which—according to
his particular disposition and tradition—he labels 'the national
spirit' or the 'cultural heritage' of a people. Or he may seek the
causes of these variations in the differently articulated social and
economic structures of different countries. Or, again, he may
attribute those variations to forms of power-integrations in society
which exist outside the state (e.g. workmen's unions, employers'
unions, political parties, the church, the family) and which in
their turn resist or support a particular form of constitution and a
definite organization of power in the state. There may be other
cases in which the psychological foundations of different societies
can be called forth to explain the differences in the forms of
domination in these societies. The political scientist, therefore,
turns in such cases to the history of culture for enlightenment
concerning the development of the particular moral standards
which prevail in a given country. From the history of the family
and education he seeks an explanation of the fact that the peoples
of different countries and the members of different social strata
have developed psychologically in a manner which causes men in
one country to delight in going about in uniform and in obeying
officers' orders, whilst for the nationals of another land spontaneity
and self-help in the individual or in small groups is, both in
political and day-to-day association, a matter of course. In this
connection, nothing could be more instructive than to map out
exactly those minute educational influences, mostly unobserved,
by which the different forms of loyalty and spontaneity are fostered
in different countries. What are the attitudes of commendation
and reprimand in family, in school, and in public life which

determine the different behaviour patterns predominant in different nations? But if our political scientist is a man who likes to go to the bottom of these problems, then he will not consider these mental differences, brought about by various systems of education, as ultimate data. The different educational systems, with their varying ideals and methods, are themselves products of a certain structure in which only definite types of domination and obedience may occur.

Once the question is put in that way our political scientist is brought back again to the problem of the social structure and to the element of domination in it. He realizes that the greater part of the statements which are made in his field rests upon the validity of a general theory of 'power and domination' which in spite of its fundamental character is only in a state of everyday wisdom.

But if he would study the neighbouring branches of learning, psychology, history, etc., he would to his great astonishment discover that it is not the lack of substantial knowledge which prevents us from building up such a general theory of 'power and domination' on scientific lines, but rather the fact that there is so far not enough consistent endeavour to bring together out of the detached results of the social sciences those elementary facts which are fundamental to all of them.

Simply by co-ordinating the facts already collected we are today in a position to build up a theory which contains all that knowledge of human nature, in its relations to social institutions, which is necessary for a deeper understanding of social life.

Even today such a general theory of power and domination would be able to start investigations into such questions as: Is there such a thing as the striving for power as an unalterable instinct fundamental to all human activities? If not, how wide is the range of possible modification, so far observed, in the so-called 'power instincts' of man? What are the main forms of its mutability? By what external influences, created by life opportunities and education, has this striving been so far fostered, repressed, sublimated, or even turned into its opposite, into a desire for humiliation? What have been so far the typical social channels through which that craving for power could find release? Then, taking more and more into account the totality of social structures presented by history, one might ask why in different constellations these power impulses accumulated at different points of the social texture, and what was the role of those particular social institutions in which they were released. How did the institutions ensure that the individual could satisfy his craving for power in different ways? Can we make conscious the principles by means of which institutions have always unconsciously moulded the character of peoples and could we not reorganize these institutions with the help of this knowledge on new and more humanistic lines?

This tendency of political science to reach gradually beyond the confines of its own field of specialized research has been discerned also in the case of economics. The economist has for a certain time primarily been concerned to elaborate a theory of 'pure economics'. In this task he has proceeded—legitimately—by a process of abstraction, and since all his 'data' were non-economic in origin he, without further inquiry, simply accepted them as 'given'. But, today, he wants to know why those data vary—even if this curiosity should lead him away from his own sphere and into the domains of the sociologist.

It is for instance becoming increasingly evident that—as Dr. Hicks has told us—the choices made by individuals in their capacity as consumers are not fortuitous, but conform to certain collective standards which, either in a particular epoch or in certain social strata, are fairly homogeneous and are determined by non-economic 'social' factors. *What* social factors? To be able to answer this and similar questions, the economist, like the political scientist, seeks as it were a theory of the constants and variables in the formation of human wants; historical and theoretical studies of the collective ductibility of wants, an account of the factors through whose influence different scales or standards of wants came to be established in different social strata.

A similar problem arises when the individual is studied not as consumer but as entrepreneur or worker. Let me put but one question: what working-incentives characterized the different stages of economic development, and the different occupational and social strata in each of these stages? For it must be remembered that the various strata work, on an average, from different motives.[1] Between the physical coercion which drives the slaves to toil and the alternative of working or starving which is the typical working-incentive of the worker in the so-called 'free market', there are numerous more or less differentiated types of motive.

In the higher strata of society where, unlike in the lower, the bare necessaries of life are already met, the working-incentives no longer centre round the primary instinct of self-preservation but round other, more sublimated, motives, the specific characteristics of which vary with profession and social standing. The

[1] In connection with points to be raised in the following discussion, I should here like to refer to my article 'Über das Wesen und die Bedeutung des wirtschaftlichen Erfolgstrebens', in *Archiv für Sozialwissenschaft und Sozialpolitik*, vol. 63, 1930, where this whole problem is treated in greater detail. Cf. also Max Weber, 'Wirtschaftssoziologie', in *Wirtschaft und Gesellschaft*, and *Grundriss der Sozialökonomik*, vol. 3, part I, ch. 2, section 14, 1922.

aims which the functionary strives to satisfy are, on an average, quite different from those of the entrepreneur; those of the artisan, again, different from those of the peasant or soldier. Once the minimum needs of subsistence are met, the attraction of additional material consumption as the motivation towards an additional expenditure of effort often recedes behind the sublimated incentive based on the idea of 'honour', a social attribute lent *inter alia* to the status of the civil servant and, for a time, also to the liberal professions. It recedes, that is to say, behind the incentive offered by certain positions in society to exercise power over subordinates. With the officer and the 'captain of industry', for instance, this is the typical stimulus to extra exertion in their work. In the case of the inventor, the scholar, the teacher or the administrator, the corresponding motivation is the chance of manifesting their knowledge.

How very important it is to be more intimately acquainted with the possible kinds of working-incentives will be readily realized by anyone who appreciates the effects of chronic unemployment in sapping the will-to-work; or who is alive to the fact that the Russians, by partly successful and partly unsuccessful experiments, are endeavouring to replace the old individualist incentives of capitalist society, namely the escape from insecurity and the wish to become rich, by new incentives, planned, guided, and instilled by the state, such as 'socialist competition'. But it is impossible to understand either the infinite historical variability of working-incentives or the mutations that are taking place in them today unless, besides direct empirical observation of specific cases, one can give to the phenomena studied a theoretical foundation. For there can be no real empiricism without theory.

The reason, for instance, why from time to time the conception of 'honour' impinges differently on the human will-to-work, which itself is differently constituted at different times, can be understood only if it is remembered that different types of men have a differently constituted and differently articulated 'sense of personal worth'. In this connection the sociologist distinguishes between two important types. First, there is the type of individual who feels mentally at ease if his 'sense of personal worth' is socially guaranteed by circumstances beyond his control. The type, in other words, which seeks a 'borrowed prestige' such as, for instance, the 'nobleman', the 'patrician' who considers himself distinguished because he is the descendant of a distinguished family; or the black-coated worker in a government office or industrial concern, who feels important because his state or company is strong and powerful. In contrast to this 'borrowed prestige', we can speak of a 'prestige acquired through independent, personal achievement', of a sense of 'personal worth' founded on the fruits of individual effort when, in a mobile society, individuals improve their position through their own effort, such as the merchant adventurer in a freely competitive world, or the scholar whose outward and inner recognition centres in the results of his own work. The former type will, when at work, develop a hierarchy of wishes and of corresponding expenditures of energy, a hierarchy which becomes intelligible only when the welfare of the particular corporate body which vests him with prestige is taken into account. The latter type can be understood only if the pains he takes with his work are set in the immediate contexts of his personal interest and of the heightening of his personal prestige.

These examples of specialized fields of social inquiry have, I hope, served to show that, by tracing a particular chain of causality in any of those inquiries, or by becoming aware of the tacitly assumed premises from which those inquiries proceed, one is brought closer and closer to a psychological and sociological theory of man and society. But as these examples have made manifest, the specialized social sciences are no longer in a position themselves to elaborate and complete the theory which underlies their particular investigations, or to follow up the historical diversity of the phenomena they encounter. From this dual embarrassment they have extricated themselves by considering for a time psychology and history as the sciences basic to them. For some time psychology seemed entitled to the claim of being fundamental because every human activity is a product of the mind and rests therefore upon the laws inherent in the latter. History's claim to be fundamental was based on the fact that it is the record of the endless variability of human institutions and that their range of mutability can only be determined with its help.

Although these arguments are partly right and no foundation for the social sciences can be built up without combining the results of psychology and history, they themselves do not contain those points of view by which the principles of the changes in human life can be found, the latter being mostly based upon interaction and the laws of 'living together'.

If time allowed, it would not be difficult to show that the present state of history and psychology is not very different from that of the other specialized social sciences. Like the latter, both have of late tended more and more to transgress the boundaries of their respective fields, and like the other separate social sciences, psychology and history have through this process of expansion only come to discover the significance of sociological problems.

History, whose sole function was for a time deemed to be the study of specific historical constellations and causal sequences, has recently turned also to problems of comparative observation. In so doing, it has come to see the really important aspects of the process of the transformation of man, his history, and the social structures in which he and his fellow-beings live together. Ever since it has turned to these comparative problems history has felt the need to have as the basis of its inquiries a typology of social factors and social structures as well as a serviceable psychology which would do justice to the different historical types of human beings and to their understanding.

As regards such a psychology, it must suffice here to recall that Dilthey already drew attention to the fact that the older type of psychology, though it contains much that is valuable and important on the plane of experiment and analytical description, cannot in its present form be of very great assistance to the historian and sociologist. The reason why the philosophical and historical sciences (*Geisteswissenschaften*) have little use for the existing general psychology is that, owing to its present methods, it works to a pattern of man in general without taking sufficient account of the diverse forms in which historical and social factors impinge on the psychic life of the individual. What we need today is a psychology which studies not man in general but man in certain concrete historico-social situations. A psychology, in other words, which is sufficiently related to actual situations to be able to understand and explain the real psychology of existing types of human beings, as we encounter them in society and in specific stages of historical development. There is indeed among psychologists themselves a movement to correlate psychology and sociology. This movement aims at breaking with the old method of studying perception, sensation, will, feeling 'in general' and at analysing the behaviour patterns of individuals in direct relation to the actual, concrete social background of those individuals. It is, for instance, becoming increasingly recognized that the capacity for work which the individual will develop, the evolution of his whole mental constitution and outlook, etc., will differ according to the particular kind of industrial and educational community into which he is brought, and according to the manner in which the chance of individual initiative is approximated to collective discipline in the different kinds of social groups in which he moves. There is, therefore, in contemporary psychology a tendency to work out a theory of differentiated sociological types. In this theory, it is not the psychology of an abstract model called 'man in general' which is made the problem but the psychology of the *rentier*, the peasant, the unemployed. Or, in historical context, this theory of sociological types studies the particular psychology for instance of the hunters, of the pastoral nomads, the condottieri, the courtiers, the bourgeois, the intellectuals of the period of the French Revolution.

Thus neither history nor psychology answers the questions which are passed on to them from the other specialized social sciences. All they do is to enrich those questions from their own particular methodological approach with the specific kind of material at their disposal. And the more history and psychology, like the other specialized social sciences, become engrossed in their new tasks, the more they tend to develop new sociological facts and problems without, however, being in the position to combine these facts and problems into a general, unitary picture of society or to elaborate them into a system of ultimate, social elements.

What now are the conclusions that emerge from what has been said so far? In the first place surely that if the kind of division of labour we today tolerate in the social sciences were to make its appearance in an industrial concern, it would forthwith be abolished to the accompaniment of scornful jeers. For the division of labour in these sciences has little in common with that in a factory where everything is organized in terms of controllable efficiency and where, as the goods in process of manufacture pass along a moving belt, each operative adds his specific quota to their completion until they leave the packing room, ready for sale. Our division of labour is rather like that in a badly organized bureaucracy where a question which the officials of one department are unable to solve (and these are mostly the problems concerning the social foundations of given facts) is simply passed on to those of the next, with a brief covering note: 'wrong department. Refer to department——', so that having gone the round of the departments the question is as near solution at the end as it was at the beginning.

The present spontaneous movement on the part of the separate social sciences to combine the results of their respective inquiries into a synthetic picture of society as one whole, is to be welcomed. And the courage to acknowledge that every sociological statement rests on a more or less closed system of theoretical premises must also be deemed a big step forward. Without such a spontaneous movement from within the specialized social sciences, no coordination of problems would be possible at all. For while the course of investigation to be followed by the separate branches of knowledge cannot be dictated from above, one can undoubtedly make known the trend of the process which is taking place within those disciplines and draw attention to the inconsistencies and loopholes in their respective conclusions. It might, perhaps, be argued that sociology therefore exists in the shape of the separate social sciences. But the most casual reflection will show that, if this were so, we should have as many sociologists as there are separate social sciences, instead of a unitary sociological science.

The economist, the political scientist, the historian, the psychologist—to say nothing of the others—even when they do go outside their respective special fields, see nothing but a limited cross-section of society and see even this in their own way and in terms of their specific partial problems and special ideas. The sociology of the economist can at best explain only the sociology of economic behaviour and that of the social institutions strictly connected with the process of production and consumption. The sociology of politics again comprehends only the individual's power-impulses and the power-integrations in the political institutions of society. But how these attitudes and behaviour patterns exist side by side in the whole make-up of the individual, why this 'whole man' always behaves in quite a different manner according to the particular group of which at any given moment he forms a part (according to whether he happens to be in family surroundings, on the playground, in the market, in the army or in his club), to these questions political sociology supplies no answers. Still less can it elucidate the question how far this special psychology of different types of human groups reflects the particular social functions of those groups. These functions, in their turn, can be described only if one has a clear picture of the functioning mechanism and the social differentiation of particular societies and of society as a whole. But such a picture cannot be gained from the field of any of the specialized social sciences.

These considerations have, I hope, made it clear that co-operation between the social sciences can be established only if the co-ordination of the problems of those sciences and the comparison of the results reached by them is made the specific task of a scientific discipline which has as its *raison d'être* the construction of a consistent general theory of society—and that discipline be *Sociology* as the basic discipline of the social sciences. Just as it would be an absurdity to study the different parts of the human organism without a knowledge of biology, so also it is absurd to expect that there can be any organic division of labour in the field of the social sciences without general sociology as the basic social science.

What, now, is the task of such a sociology as the basic social science? What qualifies it to undertake the co-ordination of the problems and the comparative analysis of the results arrived at by the specialized social sciences? The fact that it is aiming at a *theory*, a complete theory of the totality of the social process, based as far as possible on the diversity and availability of all the social phenomena and causal factors to which from time to time we have obtained access. The fathers of sociology made the mistake of building theories on insufficient facts; but even for this error they cannot be lastingly reproached. For in that early stage it was precisely these generalizations ahead of facts and these rough and insecurely founded theories which gave the impetus to the emergence of specialized inquiries which pointed out the fallacies of those hasty generalizations and theoretical constructions. To the older, all too constructive, sociology, we can apply the saying which Max Weber coined in reference to Marx's work: 'An uncommon error is often of greater historical significance than a commonplace truth.' And Max Weber's own work is surely proof enough that a systematic sociology can be constructed on the basis of a plethora of empirical data; that we have passed beyond that stage of sociology when it was merely a philosophy of history; that we already have at our disposal an infinite number and diversity of separate facts; and that the only reason why these have not yet been fully explored is that our investigation of them has hitherto lacked a methodical basis, that the concepts we use are not clearly defined and that in our inquiries we do not keep the picture of the totality of the social process constantly before us.

Time prevents me from embarking on a description and discussion of the nature and problems of such a sociology outside of the separate social sciences. I shall confine myself to only a few observations on the special method of this sociology as the theoretical foundation of the social sciences.

Sociology as the basic social science has three important functions, and fulfils them on three distinct methodological planes.

1. As *systematic or general sociology* it must retrace the variability of social phenomena to those *basic elements* and *basic concepts* of a more or less axiomatic character which make society possible at all. There cannot be fruitful causal inquiries in the realm of the social sciences so long as we operate with those *ad hoc* concepts which everyday life holds out to us and which, though useful in the observation of social phenomena as a sort of 'first approximation', become completely useless as soon as the basis of comparison is widened. For the anthropologist, historian, and political scientist, for instance, a secret society of the so-called primitives, a 'guild' in the late Middle Ages, and a club, are totally dissimilar and non-comparable phenomena. For the sociologist, on the other hand, they have—despite tangible dissimilarities—*one factor* in common: they are 'closed groups'. Now the closing of a group tends, in all societies, to produce the same result—it creates what is called an *esprit de corps*, a complete change in the behaviour

pattern of the individual who is admitted to it as a member, and since the closing of the group to 'outsiders' prevents new ideas and behaviour patterns from penetrating, sooner or later it results in the entrenchment of a deadening, stultifying tradition within the group. But we could not discover such general, common causal factors in the maze of intermittent historical phenomena unless we had correspondingly abstract concepts to work with. If the general concepts 'closed' and 'open' group had not been coined, this common, causal factor—which is responsible for the common, basic, mental trait in all the members of such groups—could never have been singled out from amidst the plenitude of the other characteristics of specific historical phenomena. As Mr. Postan has rightly observed, the natural sciences would never have become sciences at all had they never managed to get beyond the stage of disjointed, disconnected observation. Their main results are due to the comparative method and abstraction.

2. The second methodological plane of sociology as fundamental to the social sciences is that of *comparative sociology*. General concepts in systematic sociology are fruitful only if they are not devised in a philosophical and speculative manner and do not originate in an *ad hoc* way from the phenomena of a narrowly delimited sector of observable society, but are based on the widest possible expansion of the field of observation, when alone it will be possible to see the various phenomena in their proper proportions and to reduce them to their basic and simplified characteristics. Therefore, the concepts of systematic sociology must grow out of the results arrived at in comparative sociological inquiry. For comparative sociology supplements the analysis of abstract, general social phenomena by a theory which explains how these same phenomena vary in different societies in history. A general theory of 'power', for instance, must, as we have seen, be supplemented by a comparative analysis of the various possible types of power-organizations and of the different forms which the craving for power has assumed as well as of the ways in which that craving has found release and satisfaction at different stages of historical development. Or, again, a comparative typology of the mutability of the family and the town must supplement a general theory of social integration through blood-relationship or local ties, etc. In all these instances it is through comparison only that that isolation of causal factors and the discovery of the tendency in which they will operate is possible. In the field of the social sciences, unlike that of the natural sciences, experiment is, by the very nature of the phenomena we study, impossible, but comparison based upon historical variety is a substitute for it.

3. But the isolation and abstraction of general factors is only

part of the functions of the social sciences. For these sciences seek to explain the general features of human behaviour patterns and the universally possible, ultimate elements of society not only *in abstracto*, but also the specific, separate constellations which from time to time they assume in different societies in history. Our science is concerned also to elucidate such concrete problems as these, for instance: How, in certain given types of society, e.g. feudal, early-capitalist, monopoly-capitalist society, do certain factors and groups of factors exist side by side and fit in with one another? How does each of these types of society mould its members (the burgher, the worker, the peasant, the functionary) in such a way that they acquire just those behaviour patterns which the smooth functioning of that particular social system requires? Here the importance lies, not so much in the often-debated question 'What is the prime cause of historical events?' but in the task of building up a simplified sketch of the circulation of events (*Kreislauf*) in different societies (in feudalism, capitalism, etc.). It is the task of *structural sociology* to work out the adequate scheme.

Structural sociology in its turn consists of two parts: statics and dynamics.

The theory of statics deals with the problem of the equilibrium of all the social factors (not only the economic ones) in a given social structure. It tries to show what makes different societies work. Which of the block-factors are responsible for the continuous reproduction of the main processes, which regenerate the same typical situations and the same structure again and again? For instance, to what causes is it due that the different social strata which are engaged in economic production are moved just by those respective working-incentives which are needed in a given society? What influences guarantee the constancy of the wants of the consumer, in the lack of which no prevision and therefore no continuous production would be possible? Or take other spheres of social life. What social mechanism has to answer for the fact that, both in the political and in the cultural sphere, we always get (as long as a system functions at all) as much personality reserve as is required for the reproduction of the leading élites, that there is neither an over- nor an under-supply of people who have the capacity, education, and will for the guidance of a society? How does it come about that partly by spontaneous adjustment and partly by regulation, the amount of aggressive and competitive energy is just sufficiently great and is found precisely in those fields where it fulfils the functions necessary for the preservation of the social mechanism in question? Vice versa, how does it happen that, chiefly by an unobserved self-regulation of the process, there is just as much compromise and solidarity as is required by the constantly varying nature of the co-operation and the division of social functions?

In this connection, even the working of the mind can be correlated with typical situations in the social structure. The latter works only if there is a definite amount of ignorance and acquiescence in the dominated groups, whereas the members of the leading groups have to become rationalized beings, capable of prevision at least in those spheres where their range of action requires definite calculation. Thus the social spreading of knowledge and enlightenment does not simply depend on the increase of organized educational opportunities, but on the limitations of the existing social structure which can only bear a certain amount of rationalization. Fear, anxiety, wrong judgments or ideologies are not only survivals, but must be explained by the sociologist in their actual significance in different societies.

In dynamic sociology we concentrate on those factors which are antagonistic in their respective tendencies. Here we stress the working of those principles which in the long run tend to a disequilibrium and thus bring about changes which transform the social structure.

Dealing, for instance, with the crisis or with the sociology of a revolution we do not simply describe the upheaval and its psychological symptoms, but we try to analyse the disproportion in the growth of the stimulating forces which necessarily lead to the outburst. As an illustration, the wish to rise in the social scale, if it spreads excessively among the different groups, may become the immediate reason for the outbreak of a revolution. Now it is important to know that this wish is, as a general striving, not present in all periods of history. That in modern times this striving is definitely present is due to the very general spread of another social principle, that of competition, whose first effect is that a man gives up his traditional attitudes and is more concerned with his personal welfare than with the common endorsement of standards accepted by the stratum of society to which he belongs. The point is that the very same force, namely competition (which is the creative principle of this social system and without which it could not work), if it produces more initiative and ambition than there is creative outlet, leads to the total destruction of the system. If there are more initiating forces at work than there are opportunities for spontaneous action or leading positions we shall witness that general dissatisfaction which leads to revolution. Then the task of the subsequent social system will be either to create new opportunities for the fulfilment of ambition or forcibly to suppress ambition. It is possible that the arrest of individualization in

Germany today, with its regressions to more primitive mental patterns and standards, can be explained as a reaction against too great an increase of the former mental vitality of the people, which has become disproportionate to the absorbing capacity of the existing social order.

In my examples in this paper, owing to lack of time, I have mentioned only those cases of equilibrium or disequilibrium where the interdependence between the dominant psychic attitudes and the social structure was in question. I want to add that structural sociology deals in the same way with all those phenomena of mutual adjustment between block-factors, which can be observed in the working of the economic, political and cultural spheres in concrete types of society.

My argument is that it is only structural sociology which is capable of a comprehensive synthesis of all these facts which are the outcome of the separate social sciences; because it is its especial task to deal continually with the elaboration and the comparison of the social structures as wholes. It is only the structural view of society which enables us to transcend the stage of a mere cumulative synthesis, by relating the data of the special sciences to our hypothetical conception, which views the functioning of societies as a continuous adjustment of all their parts to one another. But structural sociology could not present this wider hypothesis if it had not at its disposal the fruits of the analytical work done by systematic and comparative sociology, or if it did not keep in constant touch with the various specialized branches of knowledge.

Sociology, therefore, is—as you see—on the one hand a clearing-house for the results arrived at by the specialized social sciences and, on the other hand, a new elaboration of the materials on which they are based. This process of elaboration sociology carries out with the help of ascertainable and definable methods which, though available in the separate social sciences, have hitherto not been systematically co-ordinated and unified. In our field we, today, have at our disposal a tremendous wealth of scientific material and, instead of turning it to fruitful account, we appear to be emulating those imperialist powers which, instead of using the vast treasures that are already theirs, still strive to make new conquests.

Therefore I venture to assert that as long as in our research work and in our school and academic curricula we do not introduce sociology as a basic science, so long we shall not be good specialists —let alone be able to educate a generation of citizens on whose correct understanding of the functioning of the society in which they live it must depend whether the social process is in future to be guided by reason or by unreason.

CHAPTER VI

German Sociology (1918–1933)[1]

THE collapse, temporary or permanent, of anything significant calls always for a careful retrospective weighing of its
merits and shortcomings. In Germany we have just witnessed
the breakdown of one of the most important forms of culture, viz.
that of democratic culture, which had there attained a very high
stage of development. Gradually, therefore, a balance will have
to be struck of the achievements of that culture in each of its
several spheres. This paper seeks to strike such a balance for the
sphere of sociology only. But it is necessary to point out at the very
outset—and the point will be discussed at length later—that it is
precisely in the field of sociology that something of vital importance is reflected, for it was just in this particular field that the
spiritual and cultural forces of post-war Germany sought to shape
themselves. Both the everyday view of the world and the separate
sciences found their fulfilment through the new aspects of sociology
and, conversely, sociology honestly tried to embody all that
wealth of new knowledge which the separate sciences and everyday life proffered to it. The following analysis is in no sense to be
considered as a detailed account of the achievements of post-war
German sociology. We shall be concerned, rather, to present a
living picture of the most recent development of German sociology,
to explain the characteristics of that development in terms of its
social background, and to contrast, in rough outline, the nature
of the endeavours of German sociologists during the period since
1918 with the achievements of sociology in other countries. The
purpose of this paper, in short, is to bring a whole spiritual constellation, which has now vanished, nearer to the foreign public.
For we are convinced that in spite of the contemporary autarchic
tendencies, and partly, indeed, as a reaction against those tendencies, the feeling is in certain circles gaining ground that, because knowledge is the common property of the whole world, it is
the duty of the public to try to save what certain forces are, for
specific reasons, endeavouring to annihilate. Furthermore, we

1 I am indebted to Mr. R. Krammer (London) for valuable assistance in the com-
position of the English text of this paper.

believe that we are historically and socially so far advanced as to be able, if we wish, to save not only individuals but also, where they deserve it, whole spiritual constellations, and, if need be, to let them continue to take definite shape on different soil.

With such problems to the forefront, this discussion tries to draw a picture of the inward vitality of the sociological movement in Germany at the moment of its collapse and, because this is our guiding aim, we shall often give greater prominence to new works and to the names of young scholars who are not yet widely known, but who were just about to establish their reputation, than to such names as were already well known abroad.

I shall start (1) with a general characterization, shall then (2) touch upon the essential historical preconditions and shall conclude (3) with a discussion of sociological works, problems and personalities that have figured in the latest phase of development.

I

If I were asked to summarize in one sentence the significance of German sociology since 1918 I should say: *German sociology is the product of one of the greatest social dissolutions and reorganizations, accompanied by the highest form of self-consciousness and of self-criticism.* In order to understand this sentence it is necessary to analyse its implications in some detail. First we must be agreed that a process of social dissolution and crisis is not simply a negative process. For the significance of crises lies in the fact that they are not simply disintegrations but are, rather, the attempts which society makes to overhaul the whole of its organization, and in the course of these attempts the utility and value of every institution and of every form of spiritual and cultural relationship is put severely to the test under entirely new conditions. In this context, then, sociology is seen to be not only the product of this process of dissolution but also a rational attempt to assist in the reorganization of human society, to help in the reorganization and readaptation of the individual himself. What we read in textbooks and treatises on sociology is very often nothing else than a retrospective collection of new insights which were gained during such periods of social unrest. In the works of Saint-Simon and Comte, for instance, the impact of such direct experiences is still clearly visible. If the function of a period of crisis and upheaval is defined in this sense, then the period since 1918 may truly be described as the most dynamic period in the history of German society. It was the most dynamic period of society because these two decades saw a continuous and incessant shifting and displacement of social forces. But however highly we may rate the dynamic factor in social life, change by itself does not engender sociological science; otherwise every period of social instability ought to enrich that science. Only if changes are coupled with a highly developed capacity of objective scrutiny, and a genuine self-consciousness enables us to formulate and express our experiences, only then can we expect an impetus to fruitful sociological investigation. The content of the newer German sociology springs from the experiences of the last fourteen years, but the mental training necessary to formulate the problems arising from the events of those years is the fruit of a long process of historical development of which we shall treat later.

German sociology owes three debts to the dynamic forces of the last fourteen years.

1. The awareness that every social fact is a function of the time and place in which it occurs. Time and place in their turn, however, have meaning only when related to the totality of a given society. As a trite assertion this conception is not new. But so far it had only been a tentative hypothesis of the scientist; now, however, it was put to the test of experience in everyday life. People who live in a well-consolidated society with a fixed tradition do not realize the variability and interdependence of social phenomena; they see everything in isolation and imagine that everything has an isolated and independent existence. The further dissolution in society proceeds, and the more our habits change in conformity with altered situations, the more apparent does the functional interdependence of facts become. The import of a period of radical social dissolution for sociology, therefore, is:

(a) the gaining of a consistent view of the variability of social factors;

(b) an understanding of the inescapable interdependence of social factors;

(c) the habit of seeing each separate factor in its correct relation to the totality of a given society.

2. Not only the variability of the above-mentioned objective social facts, e.g. the institution of the family, political parties, political constitutions, etc., but the whole sphere of spiritual life appears in the new light of this constant variability.

The first and unavoidable consequence of this social instability is a general consciousness of the relativity of moral, aesthetic and intellectual values. A moral crisis is sooner or later inevitable, and there are only two ways of escape from it. The masses who cannot understand the significance of these changes insist upon a return to older forms of organization and to the ethical norms that seemed so reliable and behind which the individual found such secure shelter; this is one of the paths that lead the masses to

Fascism. The intellectual groups forming part of these masses, who can catch a glimpse into the nature of that uncertainty, but who are not naïve enough simply to want to put the clock of history back, defend the 'theory of decisionism'. Decisionism means, in essence, that any decision is better than no decision; hence their adventurous policy. Only a small group of persons can extricate itself from this moral dilemma, and the necessary fight with the changeability of values leads them eventually to a new moral position and at the same time to a new theory of social values.

The more progressive groups of individuals realize that 'in history bygones are for ever bygones', and the more they have lived through a period of constant social change the less security will they find in the notion of an external permanence of ethical and moral norms. The dynamic type of personality, i.e. an individual who has accustomed himself to constant change, will eventually, as the result of a process of intensive critical reflection, re-establish his moral equilibrium. Unlike the static type who finds the assurance of the validity of his moral behaviour in the notion of a permanence of social values, the dynamic type appreciates the fact that, even though the totality of values may change through time, certain values are inseparable from certain given situations. In the view of social dynamics moral values may change, situations may change, but any given situation is inseparably related to concrete norms. Hence the theory that is founded on this fact is called 'relationism' and not 'relativism' or 'relativity'. Relativism would mean that there are no objective values, *therefore* moral obligation cannot exist. Relationism, on the other hand, stresses the fact that there *is* a moral obligation, but that this obligation *is derived from the concrete situation to which it is related*. Sociology derives from this interpretation a clear understanding of the functional connection between social situations and moral values. Values and ideas are no longer considered apart, but are constantly related to social situations and social structures. The unceasing variability which is the characteristic feature of the history of moral ideas presents us with as many problems as there are problems in contemporary society. These problems arise from the struggles which the numberless small groups, each with its own group-morality, wage against one another. In sum: henceforth not only are the objective facts of social life observed in their relation to one another, but the mental forces too (i.e. norms and ideas) are watched in their relation to the social process.

3. Besides this visible interdependence between objective facts and ideas, this social mobility and dissolution reacts upon the human psyche; thus a period of social upheaval has its psychic aspect too. There is no social transformation without a change in

norms; but changing norms are mostly the expression of the changing habits and attitudes of man. In this state of instability the individual is increasingly thrown back upon himself, and the constant reflection to which, owing to the feeling of uncertainty in himself, he is driven, ends up in becoming habitual self-analysis. This psychic mechanism which in static periods works unconsciously becomes clear in periods of dynamic evolution.

The invisible sway of social forces and the continuous transformation of these into the subconscious of the individual and of the group becomes of much greater interest to the sociologist than the simple description and classification of the objective phenomena of social and cultural life. However problematical many results of psycho-analysis may be, the discovery of the psychology of the subconscious and the discovery of the sociology of knowledge (*Wissenssoziologie*) belong to the recent development of German sociology. Many of these problems are well known to English, American and French sociologists, but the germane difference between German sociology and the sociology of France, England and America seems to me to be that whereas French, American and English sociologists have treated several of these problems in isolation, German sociologists endeavour to treat every problem from the three approaches that I have discussed.

These three approaches, it will be recalled, are:

1. The viewing of each isolated objective factor as part of the changing totality of society.

2. The setting of each spiritual phenomenon and idea in its relation to concrete social situations.

3. To see in every mental attitude and in every form of human behaviour the adaptation of the unconscious to new situations.

II

So far I have been concerned to indicate the debt that recent German sociology owes to the contemporary process of disintegration and change in Germany. But I have also taken care to point out that although the facts and problems may be taken from the present their interpretation and theoretical formulation was only possible because sociological thought had behind it a long history. Social self-criticism and self-consciousness had already reached the high degree of perfection mentioned earlier when the cataclysm of social, political and economic convulsion occurred. From among the numerous preparatory trends of thought I wish to mention only three. (1) The contributions of the Hegelians and other schools of philosophy. (2) The significance of non-academic sociological thought which has only recently been incorporated into University curricula, such as Marxism. (3) The contributions of Dilthey and Simmel.

1. The ability to master facts and to view them in a theoretical light we owe to German philosophy, and mainly to Hegel. When I mention Hegel, I do not, of course, think of that large crop of unimportant philosophers who, instead of collecting and thoroughly investigating facts, give us their purely subjective and more or less insignificant impressions of them. Hegel is responsible both for the purely speculative phantasies of bad social philosophy and for the constructive power of genuine sociological investigation. For we must distinguish between the speculative and the constructive mind; the latter is as indispensable to any empirical research as the former is detrimental. To think speculatively means to sit at one's desk and to conceive vague and unverifiable ideas about all manner of things. Constructive thinking, on the other hand, implies the erection, by an effort of constructive imagination, of a structure which is embedded in the phenomena themselves, but cannot be discovered through the direct and bare observation of any isolated fragment of reality. Every sociology is ultimately derived from a philosophy of history; sociology in all countries is born as the result of trespassing beyond the confines of pure philosophy. But sociologies in all countries are distinguished from one another by the manner in which they have passed beyond those limits. American sociology trespassed them by overthrowing completely every philosophy of history and ended up in a body of empirical generalizations which can no longer embrace its multifarious facts. English sociology preserved from the philosophy of history, among other things, the theory of historical stages and the socio-psychological foundation. German sociology preserved from Hegelian doctrine the dynamic conception, even though the problem is not amenable to solution in such simple formulae as the philosophical formulation of dialectics would suggest. The gift of not seeing facts simply as they occur in everyday life without any relation to the dominant social forces and to the whole social situation existing at any given moment derives from Hegel. Those who assert that German sociology has not yet passed beyond the methodological and philosophical stages are unacquainted with its more recent developments; though it is true that many German sociologists still find themselves in those stages. Among the more representative members of the younger generation of German sociologists we can discern a real striving after empirical investigation, although this empiricism is a complicated conception.

2. The second event I enumerated was the reception and critical analysis of Marxism in academic discussion. Marxism is indebted to Hegel for the recognition of history as the development of

antagonistic forces. Marx and Lorenz v. Stein made this conception more realistic by stressing the economic aspect and the influence of class-clashes in historical development. Marx owes much in his philosophy to the development of economic thought in England, and Stein his ideas to the social movement in France, whose early theoretical formulation dates back to the more naïve speculation of Saint-Simon. Till the advent of the German republic, Marxian theory, like many other social theories, counted only as an 'opposition theory', i.e. academicians did not concern themselves with this branch of knowledge. This had the advantage that many urgent practical problems of everyday life and of political tensions were given a sociological interpretation in this non-academic discipline; but it had the disadvantage that those theories were abused for propaganda purposes and, since they were handled by laymen, an element of dilettantism inevitably crept into them. After the establishment of the republic the problems arising out of those theories found free discussion at the Universities. The consequence of this was that the non-Marxist, liberal professors first set themselves to select those aspects of Marxian theory which are the most important and then endeavoured to prove or disprove their validity empirically. Eventually a mere dispute over principles was turned into an advancement of knowledge. Recognized opponents of Marxism like Max Weber, Troeltsch, Sombart, Scheler, cannot be thought of without being coupled with the name of Marx.

3. This sketch of the early development of German sociology would not be complete without reference to the valuable contributions of the German cultural sciences, the so-called *Geisteswissenschaften*. In general we can assert that whatever fruitful results German sociology achieved, it owes largely to its co-operation with the different branches of science. The interpretative faculty of the German humanistic studies had attained a very high level of perfection. Dilthey, who had both an interpretative faculty and a knack of methodical reflection on the nature of humanistic studies, pointed out that there is a fundamental difference between the natural sciences and the non-experimental cultural sciences. Whereas we are wont to ascribe exactness only to the experimental and mathematical sciences, Dilthey insisted that the numerical exactness which psychology and the humanistic sciences can mostly not pretend to, is compensated for by the fact that they are able to gain an insight into and interpret their particular object of study: the human psyche. He distinguished between *explanation* (*Erklärung*) and *understanding* (*Verstehen*). The purpose of the exact sciences is to explain facts. The object of the humanistic sciences is the human psyche. The former are concerned with

calculable external facts, the latter endeavour to penetrate into the internal phenomena of the human mind, which are familiar to us in a different sense from external events. External events, which in the main constitute the subject-matter of the natural sciences, can only be observed in their outward relationships; on the other hand, the phenomena which constitute the subject of the cultural studies, as well as the outward expressions of the psyche, can be observed and explained as well as understood. By to 'understand', in contradistinction to 'explain', I mean, in this context, the ability either to grasp the meaning of a sentence or the meaning of a communicative act, such as a work of art, literature, music, etc., or to penetrate into the inner aspect and internal entanglements of the human mind. Professor Ginsberg[1] has suggested the phrase 'sympathetic intuition' which well expresses the modern sense of the German term *Verstehen*. Sympathetic intuition means the ability to have access to and to penetrate into the subject before us; natural science, however exact it may be, does not claim to pass beyond external cognition. Statistical data concerning, for instance, the frequency of suicides in different seasons of the year can at best indicate interesting correlations between objective events; with the help of such statistics we can in certain cases explain the facts to which they relate. But it is quite a different question when we want to obtain an understanding of the inner motivation that led to any of these suicides. It is interesting to observe that whilst Anglo-Saxon psychology, especially the American branches of the science, incline to the behaviouristic approach, i.e. are inclined to neglect the inner aspect of the psyche and to stress external behaviour so as to simplify the phenomena discussed, the leading German sociologist, Max Weber, insisted that sociology is a discipline of the *inner* understanding. Whereas it is a characteristic of the Anglo-Saxon mentality that it always tries to reduce phenomena to their most obvious contours, and to reduce the diverse impulses of human action to a few basic common factors in order ultimately to place them on a basis of mathematical exactness, the German mentality has a bent for the investigation of the complex nature of reality. Though sometimes this way of envisaging facts in their full complexity may lead to obscurity, nobody will deny that, once we proceed to a minute analysis of any isolated fact, that analysis is found to be inexhaustible. Especially when we attempt an exact description of the psychic life of the modern individual in terms of the social background to which he belongs do we find that it has so many aspects that an adequate interpretation of them is possible only if our

[1] M. Ginsberg, 'Recent Tendencies in German Sociology', in *Economica*, February 1933.

intuition is far developed and our psychological terminology is refined. Simmel, one of the most important precursors of recent German sociology, achieved both. Whilst Dilthey was responsible for evolving the theory of interpretation and understanding, Simmel knew best how to apply that theory in practice. He is one of the greatest masters of the interpretation of social facts. He used the same method for the description of everyday life that was previously used to describe pictures or to characterize works of literature. He had an aptitude for describing the simplest everyday experiences with the same precision as is characteristic of a contemporary impressionistic painting which has learned to reflect the previously unobserved shades and values of the atmosphere. He might well be called the 'impressionist' in sociology, because his was not an ability to take a constructive view of the whole of society but to analyse the significance of minor social forces that were previously unobserved. When he describes the social significance of the senses, for instance the human glance or the psychic position of the poor, or the various forms of sociability, the thousand hidden relationships which go to make up social life are suddenly revealed. His thirst for life finds its place in his contribution to German sociology, and since his day German sociologists have sought to combine a survey of all the constructive forces of social life with a refined analysis of minor details.

III

If, now, we summarize these trends of social thought, namely, the capacity for constructive thought that dates back to Hegel; the political realism that derives from Marx and Lorenz v. Stein; and the capacity for sympathetic intuition and interpretation that is found in the sociological works of Dilthey and Simmel, we have before us the mental equipment with which the modern sociologist has analysed the experiences that are met with in the present era of disintegration and dissolution. It was well that simultaneously with the growth and development of those political events, a systematic sociology was evolved. The names and works of Toennies, Oppenheimer, v. Wiese, Vierkandt, are sufficiently well known to obviate further reference to their contributions to sociology. Here we need only point out that what v. Wiese[1] attempted to do in the most abstract and general manner, namely to create a universal 'system' of sociology, Oppenheimer sought to achieve in a more realistic way. However highly the modern generation of sociologists rates the work of these men, it is convinced that now

[1] Cf. in English: Becker-Wiese, *Systematic Sociology on the Basis of 'Beziehungslehre'*; Abel, *Systematic Sociology in Germany*; Oppenheimer, *The State (Der Staat)*.

that the objectives of systematic sociology have been attained, the most urgent need of the moment is not for a closed system of sociology built by an individual but for an exact observation of social forces at work. Our need is neither for an abstract classificatory system nor for methodological reflections on the nature of sociology, but for a concrete analysis of past and contemporary events. The criticism levelled against Freyer[1] by the younger generation of sociologists is due just to this, that, though he gave to sociology the securest foundation, he did not fill in with empirical matter the framework he constructed.

The man on whose work the younger generation could fall back most safely is Max Weber,[2] whose formulation of problems and whose manner of empirical investigation have become representative. He does not study the past like an archivist, whose task it is to look after ancient documents and who sees a big hiatus between 'the yesterday and the to-day'; he investigates the most distant past, e.g. Chinese and Indian religion, or the economic system of Rome, relates all these historical data to the present, and is most concerned with the similarities and differences between the operation of social forces then and now. The great problem that engaged the attention both of Sombart and Max Weber, namely the rise and development of capitalism, was so worked out as to provide a diagnosis of the contemporary situation. What are the roots of Western society; whence do we come, whither are we going, and what is our place in the present crisis? These are the questions that are latent in Weber's empirical investigations. He was one of the first to see the dangers inherent in our social tendencies and in the *Kulturkrise* or 'crisis of culture'. He realized that the destiny of any society depends upon the texture of its organization and on the transformation and adaptation of the human mind. On this point there is a similarity between Max Weber and the greatest English sociologist, Hobhouse, who also was concerned to trace the development of the human mind and morals. But whereas the latter worked out his investigation with the help of a conception of general stages of human evolution, the former relates every change of the human mind to concrete social situations. Thus, for instance, he shows us how the mentality of man in different societies where bureaucracy plays a great part is moulded, e.g. in ancient Egypt or in the Prussian state. If he is an antisocialist, it is because he foresees the inevitable advent of

---

[1] H. Freyer, *Soziologie als Wirklichkeitswissenschaft*, 1930.

[2] See especially: Max Weber, *Wirtschaft und Gesellschaft*, 2nd edn., 1935; *Gesammelte Aufsätze zur Soziologie und Sozialpolitik*; *Gesammelte Aufsätze zur Wissenschaftslehre*, 1922; *Gesammelte Aufsätze zur Religionssoziologie*, 1920; *Gesammelte Politische Schriften*, 1921. In connection with Max Weber, reference must also be made to Ernst Troeltsch, *The Social Teaching of the Christian Churches*, trans. by O. Wyon, 1931.

an unprecedentedly vast bureaucracy. The different forms of the organization of power and the varying importance that attaches to different classes in society are decisive for the peculiar mentality that differentiates social groups and nations. In substantiation of the assertion that the mental attitude of a group is conditioned by its class character he takes numberless instances from all the eastern and western religions. In his compendious work, *Wirtschaft und Gesellschaft*, he proves that the religions of peasants at all times and in all societies closely resemble one another. They incline to an explanation of life that is based on magic, and to public orgiastic cults. The culture and mental outlook of feudal society is fundamentally different from that of a handicraft economy. We can thus explain the most important features of the early Christian religion by the fact that it was created and spread by handicraft journeymen. The religion of intellectuals differs from that of other social strata in that intellectuals are inclined to treat religion as a purely intimate and private matter. Marx pointed out the dynamic forces inherent in society, the character of economic growth and the social transformation resulting from the class struggle. The idealistic school of sociologists suggested that Marx overlooked the significance of the immanent transformation of the human mind which is a *sine qua non* of social change. They have utilized Max Weber's book on *Protestant Ethic and the Spirit of Capitalism*[1] to uphold the idealists' view that a change in the individual's character and outlook cannot at all be a function of general social and economic change, since the human mind develops *sui generis* and autonomously, and is itself the cause of a new economic system and of the concomitant social transformation. If we take into account the whole of Max Weber's work, and not only his previously mentioned book, then we come to that conclusion which constitutes the standpoint of the younger generation of German sociologists, namely that *the manner in which the question was formulated by the materialists and the idealists was wholly wrong*. We cannot separate spheres of economic and social change on the one hand from the sphere of a change in mental development on the other. The greater art of the sociologist consists in his attempt always to relate changes in mental attitudes to changes in social situations. The human mind does not operate *in vacuo*; the most delicate change in the human spirit corresponds to similarly delicate changes in the situation in which an individual or a group finds itself, and, conversely, the minutest change in situations indicates that men, too, have undergone some change.

It was realized that the older type of philosophy, psychology,

[1] M. Weber, *Die Protestantische Ethik und der 'Geist' des Kapitalismus* (English translation, *Protestant Ethic and the Spirit of Capitalism*, by T. Parsons, 1930).

pedagogy, economics, law, history of literature, etc., had per-
sistently fallen into the same error. They all started from an
abstract model of 'man in general', instead of observing human
beings and their spiritual life in their actual social setting. Here I
may mention that during my lectures I have endeavoured to make
a psychological study which should be of an entirely sociological
character. Its object was to watch, on a small scale, the behaviour
of individuals in relation to given situations, and to ascertain how
that behaviour changed in response to the most unobtrusive
change in their social situation. It was hoped thereby to elaborate
an accurate technique of situational observation with the help of
which—both for pedagogical purposes and for the study of history
—the individual could be observed and studied in the particular
situations that prevail in different social structures; situations
which create *en masse* the type of individual who is characteristic
of the new era. It was intended to find the point in the social and
economic system at which *Homo oeconomicus* sometimes changes
and the place in the political sphere where certain leading personalities arise and certain types of mass instincts are mobilized.
This new method for a realistic psychology was all the more welcome as hitherto the psychology of everyday life has not been the
strong point of Germans; they have always been either too abstract
or too metaphysical to notice the less obvious changes in the
behaviour of people with whom they come into daily contact.
They have seldom produced the 'man of the world' who was conspicuous in the aristocracies of France and England. This is evident also from the fact that the quality of the German novel
dealing with society could not, till recently, be compared with
French and English fiction. Now, however, all this has changed.
Successful attempts have been made at exact characterizations of
the lives of employees, young working girls, etc.[1] The same method
of exact situational observation of mental phenomena led not only
to the concept of an eternal super-temporal unity of the human
mind becoming highly suspect but also to the notion of the im-
mutability of human logic being challenged.

The most surprising event in the recent development of sociology has, perhaps, been the way in which *Wissenssoziologie* (the
sociology of knowledge) has described the differences in human
thought among different groups and at different times. Just as the
history of art describes and distinguishes between different styles
of art, so *Wissenssoziologie* describes and distinguishes exactly
between different styles of thought. What the school of Durkheim

[1] L. Franzen Hellersberg, *Die jugendliche Arbeiterin*, 1932; S. Kracauer, *Die Angestellten*,
1930; H. Speier, *Die Angestellten* (published in English in *Social Order and the Risks of
War*, Stewart, New York, 1952, pp. 68–85).

and Levy-Bruhl in France did in the way of pointing out the system of logic peculiar to primitive tribes, German sociology of thought began to do for the different groups and periods in western civilization. The results achieved by *Wissenssoziologie* became embarrassing when the investigation showed that not only does the manner of thought differ among different social groups in a given society, and not only is the mentality of different political parties different, but that these differences penetrate into the realms of philosophy and the different scientific disciplines. The realization of the fact that scientific research is coloured by the social and historical standpoint of the investigator led to an attempt at careful self-criticism. We know that in German theories, more than in those of any other country, the *Weltanschauung* (the philosophical interpretation of life) plays a too important role, and therefore *Wissenssoziologie* effected a great purge in the direction of a pure theory of society. But even when we have ostracized the influence of our *Weltanschauung* from all social sciences, we shall still find important traces of the fact that our thinking is largely conditioned by our social status and that our logic is a particular and not a general one. That is why every theory is preceded by a subconscious selection of the elements which shall penetrate our problems and theories. Not all elements of reality find their way into our consciously formulated theories, but only those which are admitted by the conscious control. This conscious control, again, is guided by latent wishes and forces. In this way not only is the content of the theory itself influenced, but the conceptions and logical categories of the mind of different groups are affected by social forces.[1] All this can be made clear by an example. For instance, every liberal theory lays stress on all those factors which tend to an harmonious balance of contradictory elements. Socialist theories, on the other hand, accentuate unduly those forces that work for the collapse of the present social and economic system; thereby they tend to overlook the elements of elasticity in this system. Thus the recent appreciation of the significance of those social forces, that up to a certain point influence all sciences, places the new problem of the theory of knowledge, on the one hand, and new tasks that have to be disposed of

[1] Those interested in *Wissenssoziologie* should for general information consult the works of M. Scheler, *Die Wissensformen und die Gesellschaft*, also my article on 'Wissenssoziologie' in the *Handwörterbuch der Soziologie*. For further examples of empirical investigations in this field, cf. also: G. Lukacs, *Geschichte und Klassenbewusstsein*, 1923; M. Scheler, *Die Formen des Wissens und der Bildung*, 1925; P. L. Landsberg, *Wesen und Bedeutung der Platonischen Akademie*, 1923; P. Honigsheim, *Zur Soziologie der mittelalterlichen Scholastik* (Erinnerungsgabe für M. Weber), 1923; K. Mannheim, 'Das konservative Denken', in *Archiv für Sozialwissenschaft*, Bd. 57; *Ideologie und Utopie*, 2nd edn., 1930 (Engl. trans., *Ideology and Utopia*); F Borkenau, *Der Übergang vom feudalen zum bürgerlichen Weltbild*, Paris, Alcan, 1934.

in the search for objectivity, on the other, on a higher plane. The merit of recent German sociologists lies, perhaps, in the fact that they have freed themselves from that exaggerated 'methodological asceticism' for which nothing that is not susceptible of measurement can be deemed to be exact, and, further, that they have successfully shown that the spiritual sphere has its own peculiar criteria of exactness which have hitherto not been noticed.

Since this branch of German sociology may prove especially helpful to those who come to sociological questions from the cultural sciences (*Geisteswissenschaften*), something should at this stage be said about the *sociology of culture*. The sociology of culture has turned to account all the methods and techniques which the cultural sciences have elaborated in the form of the *technique of interpretation*. Of these, the *morphological* method has become particularly conspicuous; Alfred Weber,[1] the head of the school at Heidelberg, used it in his *Sociology of Culture*. Cultural contents can be characterized in this form with very great exactness; witness, for instance, the perceptions attained to in the history of art by the method of style-analysis. This morphological description of cultural patterns and styles seems to me quite fruitful, so long as morphology is not made to serve as an end in itself or, as with Spengler, does not degenerate to a kind of play with analogies. To ascertain their morphological characteristics, a culture or cultures must also be *explained* in the light of their social background. Morphological analysis is a means of rendering the causal analysis more effective and richer, but is not a way of escape from historical empiricism. A. v. Martin[2] has made a valuable contribution to an empirically verifiable sociology of culture. He belongs to those historians who have been enterprising enough to venture from their special discipline into the sphere of sociology. Among the works on the sociology of literature, Schöffler's[3] contributions occupy a place of high importance. Coming to sociology from English philosophy, he has shown, *inter alia*, how the temper of an era can be explained in terms of an analysis of the social origin of individual poets from the ruling stratum of the intelligentsia. The early generation of English and German romantic poets came from the clergy, and their attitude to the world, their social surrounding, characterizes their work.

In general the problem of the historical evolution of *forms of life* (*Lebensformen*) and *types of inner experience* (*Erlebnisformen*) became

[1] A. Weber, *Ideen zur Staats und Kultursoziologie*. Also, 'Das Alte Aegypten und Babylonien', in *Archiv für Sozialwissenschaft*, vol. 55, p. 1, 1926.
[2] A. v. Martin, *Die Soziologie der Renaissance*; cf. also the different essays on the sociology of culture in Vierkandt's *Handwörterbuch der Soziologie*.
[3] H. Schöffler, *Protestantismus und Literatur*, 1922.

increasingly the problem which established the intimate contact between the history of literature, sociology, and philosophy. The dynamic conception of human beings, i.e. the idea that historical and social evolution always shapes the individual and his spiritual life anew, has rendered possible an historical examination of different aspects of spiritual life. Thus we have interesting analyses of the genesis of love,[1] of the meaning of the cult of friendship,[2] about the growth and social significance of ideals of civilization,[3] about the origin of the conception of genius,[4] about the social genesis of public opinion,[5] the social genesis of the *bourgeois*,[6] etc.

But sociology does not only derive stimuli from the history of literature. A very high degree of development has been reached in the sociology of law; though here it is interesting to observe that with the exception of M. Weber nearly all the important workers in this field were, at first, Austrians.[7]

Besides the sociology of law there was forming, especially among the younger generation, a *political sociology* and a scientific study of contemporary events (*Gegenwartskunde*) from which much was expected.[8] It bore an affinity to the English *political science*, except that its close association with sociology has certainly not been detrimental to it. Thanks to this intimate connection with sociology, political phenomena are seen in their relation to social events in general. As a starting-point it was endeavoured to obtain a sociological analysis of the stratification of German society, and into

[1] P. Kluckhohn, *Die Auffassung der Liebe in der Literatur des 18ten Jahrhunderts u. in der deutschen Romantik*, 2nd edn., 1931.

[2] A. Salomon, *Der humanistische Freundschaftskult* (unpublished).

[3] H. Weil, *Die Entstehung des deutschen Bildungsbegriffes*, 1930; Naumann-Müller, *Höfische Kultur*, 1930; N. Elias, *Soziologie des Hofes* (unpublished).

[4] Zilsel, *Die Entstehung des Geniebegriffs*, 1926.

[5] F. Toennies, *Kritik der öffentlichen Meinung*, 1922, and E. Manheim, *Die Träger der öffentlichen Meinung*, 1933.

[6] B. Groethuysen, *Die Entstehung der bürgerlichen Welt- und Lebensanschauung in Frankreich*, vol. 1-2, 1927-30; B. Guttmann, *England im Zeitalter der bürgerlichen Reform*, 1923. In the history of literature an ambitious attempt was made to estimate sociologically the debt owed by German literature to the influence of the various Germanic tribes and provinces. Cf. J. Nadler, *Literaturgeschichte der deutschen Stämme und Landschaften*. On the sociology of literature, cf. Kohn-Bramstedt, 'Probleme der Literatursoziologie', in *Neue Jahrb. für Wissensch. u. Jugendbildung*, 1931.

[7] E. Ehrlich, *Grundlegung der Soziologie des Rechts*, 1913; K. Renner, *Die Rechtsinstitute des Privatrechts und ihre soziale Funktion*, 1929; A. Menger, *Das bürgerliche Recht und die besitzenden Volksklassen*, 5th ed., 1927; A. Menger, *Neue Staatslehre*, 4th ed., 1930; further, H. Sinzheimer, *Grundzüge des Arbeitsrechts*, 2nd ed.; F. Neumann, *Koalitionsfreiheit und Reichsverfassung*, 1932; F. Dessauer, *Recht, Richtertum und Ministerialbürokratie*, 1928.

[8] Important essays in this field appeared in the various well-known journals of sociology. Cf. *Kölner Vierteljahrshefte für Soziologie*, ed. Wiese; Thurnwald's *Soziologus*, and the excellent *Archiv für Sozialwissenschaft und Sozialpolitik*, ed. E. Lederer, which has recently ceased publication. Cf. further: the interesting *Ztschr. für Sozialforschung*, ed. Horkheimer. For the Socialist standpoint of the two Socialist sociological journals, *Die Gesellschaft* and *Neue Blätter für Sozialismus*, cf. in the latter the essays by Heimann, Löwe, Tillich.

this question Geiger[1] has made an interesting investigation. A history of the political parties was attempted along the same lines.[2] Thus at the same time that numerous concrete and realistic analyses of the purely social aspects of present-day German society were made, the efficiency of the political form of that society was submitted to the searchlight of theoretical controversy and its fundamental import and implications were discussed in the light of and in terms of the new sociological perspective.[3]

In this connection attention must also be drawn to the very instructive contributions of Lederer and Marschak, Brinkmann and Götz Briefs,[4] on the social stratification in capitalist society. Reference should be made also to the numerous sociological contributions from the pen of the Catholic writers, and, *inter alia*, particularly to the works of Gundlach, Schwer, and Jostock.

The most instructive contributions by literature to the understanding of society are to be found in the numerous novels dealing with social life which have been published in post-war Germany. Mention should be made of the following, in particular: Hans Fallada, *Kleiner Mann, was nun?* (translated into English, *Little Man, What Now?*); Eric Reger, *Union der Festen Hand*; A. Döblin, *Alexanderplatz*; Ernst v. Salomon, *Die Geächteten, Die Stadt* (translated into English).

I should like to conclude this study with an attempt to suggest sociological reasons for the differences that exist between American, English and German sociology.[5] American sociology is

[1] Th. Geiger, *Die soziale Schichtung des deutschen Volkes*, 1932. Cf. also, J. Nothaas, *Sozialer Auf- und Abstieg im Deutschen Volk*, 1930; v. d. Gablentz-Mennicke, *Deutsche Berufskunde*, 1930; O. Demeter, *Das Offizierskorps*; E. Kehr, *Die preussischen Konservativen*, 1930.

[2] S. Neumann, *Die Deutschen Parteien, Wesen und Wandel nach dem Kriege*, 1932.

[3] Of especial interest is the controversy about State and Nation; cf. in this connection: R. Smend, *Verfassung und Verfassungsrecht*, 1928; also the well-known works of C. Schmitt, Kelsen, and the recently deceased Heller. Apart from the last-named political sociologist's work, *Die Souveranität*, 1927, his unpublished *Staatslehre* is also a noteworthy contribution. Cf. further: D. Schindler, *Verfassungsrecht und Soziale Struktur*, 1932, and G. Salomon, *Allgemeine Staatslehre; Probleme der Demokratie*, 1st and 2nd series, published by the Deutsche Hochschule für Politik, 1928–31; also the volume on *Politik als Wissenschaft*, 1931; M. H. Boehm, *Das eigenständige Volk*, 1932; H. O. Ziegler, *Die moderne Nation*, 1931; H. Marr, "Grosstadt als politische Lebensform,' in *Grosstadt und Volkstum*, 1927.

[4] In the *Grundriss der Sozialökonomik*, vol. 9, I (Die Gesellsschaftliche Schichtung im Kapitalismus).

[5] I am, of course, aware that it is possible here to give only the roughest outline of such a comparison. In the above analysis it has not been forgotten that sociology does not arise *only* from the sociological situation of a particular country and that the *history of ideas* itself carries its influence from one author to another and from one country to another. But it is my view—which can be substantiated by any fairly accurate analysis of the influence which the literature of one country exercises upon that of another—that in the process of understanding and assimilation those factors and elements are thrown overboard which are unimportant to the particular purpose and outlook of the recipient of alien influences, and that, conversely, those factors are stressed which derive from situations and attitudes similar to those of the recipient.

characterized by its peculiar delight in a form of empiricism which I should be inclined to call an 'isolating empiricism'; for, whilst the enumeration and description of facts becomes always more exact and refined, the constructive bases of social life are completely veiled behind the mass of secondary details. This, it seems, can only be attributed to the fact that the most urgent impulses to the growth of sociological investigation in the United States arose from the immediate problems of everyday life which present themselves in any colonizing society that spreads itself over an expansive territory and has to develop its social institutions in a relatively short span of time. In such a society the most difficult and vital problems crop up one by one, and social study concentrates on the solution of these isolated problems. Here we have one reason for the prevalence in American sociology of questions such as those of gangs, of delinquency, of the conflict of different races living in the same territorial region, of the psychic adjustment of immigrants, all of which are problems that arise from particular needs at particular moments. But, as has been pointed out above, the phenomena that do not become apparent are: the totality of society, the dynamic forces operating throughout society and the class problems that exist in society. The totality of society is veiled because of the general belief that if the difficulties of single institutions and particular situations are solved in the right way, the entirety of society will reveal itself through a process of integrating the solutions of individual social difficulties. Such a belief is possible as long as there are still vast expanses of territory unexploited and numerous possibilities unexplored; where this is the case it is always possible to find a way out of social dilemmas. The interdependent nature of the various gaps in the social structure does not become visible because the elasticity of the scope for action is so great that in most cases a way out of difficulties is found. The manifestation of the class-problem—as we shall have occasion to observe again later—very often depends on the particular position of the intelligentsia in society. Since it is the intellectuals who give theoretical expression to the class-problem, much in the character of their theory will depend on whether in their own struggle for existence they have had experience of class conflicts. In the United States the class-problem for a long time did not become noticeable because the élite of society and the groups of the intelligentsia had the chance to rise through individual initiative; where a rise in the social scale is possible through individual initiative alone, the existence of social classes and their nature is not apparent.

The English and German situations are similar in that in both cases a society has passed through a long historical process within the same territorial confines. But whereas the growth of the

English people, especially since 1688, has been evolutionary and reformist, that of the German people has been more difficult and uneven; recent German history especially has been one of convulsions. The essence of the rapid transformation that is now taking place is the dissolution of the older forms of society. As I pointed out earlier, we obtain our most important insight into the working of social forces in periods of rapid social disintegration such as that which Germany is now experiencing; for it is at such times that the latent elements operative in society are revealed. The class-problem was intelligible not only to the German socialists but to all the groups of the German intelligentsia, because in recent years the latter have become increasingly aware that their fate is closely linked up with that of the groups immediately next to them. It was impossible to remedy individual defects by mere reformist measures in a society where, owing to the narrowness of the field for action, no social element could be conceived of independently of any other element. All social and political groups were therefore struggling for the radical transformation of the whole social fabric; and each group was intent on transforming it exclusively according to its own ideal pattern. Because all social groups were anxious to change the whole face of society, they were forced to concentrate on the whole social organism at once, and not only on particular parts of that organism.

Turn now to English sociology. English sociological development, as indeed the nature of English sociology in general, reflects the even trend of recent English social and historical development.

It is an example of a discipline that can grow in a society whose development has, on the one hand, been continuous and free from the shocks and surprises which have characterized the recent history of Germany; and, on the other hand, has not developed by way of accidental leaps and bounds as has American society, where new institutions were generally added to existing ones, and sociology did not evolve its problems by reinterpreting the traditional view, but approached them in a naïve manner as if it were confronted with a completely new task. Because the development of English society has been more continuous, and because its progressive evolution consisted mostly in the reforming and reconditioning of old institutions, it was possible for the root conception of progress to be that of an even development by consecutive stages. Therefore English sociology was for a long time fitted into the framework of a conception of 'progress by stages'. In contrast to this, the conception of progress held by German sociologists is the dialectical conception; this embodies the primitive experience of man that history is an alternating process of progress, retrogression

and progress. English sociology has all the advantages of a traditional development. The first consequence of a continuous social
development is that academic science can pursue the even tenor
of its way, and single problems can be worked out and developed
with minute exactness. If new problems crop up anywhere they
can be fitted into the existing framework of the different academic
sciences. It is thus characteristic of English sociological thought
that it is found not only in sociology *qua* sociology but in the
different particular branches of science. The best of sociology is
often found in academic fields such as anthropology, social and
economic history, social psychology, political science, and social
science as distinct from sociology. This has the advantage that
much of sociology is scattered in the various branches of academic
knowledge; but it has also the disadvantage that an all-embracing
view of the whole field of sociology can be obtained only with
difficulty, and that no specialist in any of the previously mentioned
sciences will venture to work out constructive principles for integrating the results arrived at by each of those sciences. Whenever
the connections between the facts with which he is particularly
concerned and other facts are pointed out to him, the specialist
will retort that this transgresses beyond his special competence;
in so doing, however, he forgets that in reality the different facts
and factors are interlocked and that they do not do the specialist
the favour of developing in watertight compartments. If we look
upon the whole history of social development we can say that the
impulse to consider facts in their interrelation and not in isolation
is never due to science itself but to the actual needs and urgencies
of social life. These impulses penetrated only gradually into the
framework of the different parts of English sociology, and the
class-problem which, as I have shown, dominated German
society in times of crisis, did not take first rank in English sociology.
But in my view there is also another reason for this. The intelligentsia, as we have already mentioned, is nearly always the first to
see and to voice the existence of these problems in the light of its
own experiences. In England for a very long time it had no experience of the class structure because English society has always had
the valuable knack of absorbing the most gifted elements from the
lower classes. Thus, so long as this absorption continues the class
character of society and all its implications is felt to be something
fluctuating and unsubstantial.

Within recent years, however, the need for taking a connected
view of separate social occurrences has come to be realized in
England also. German sociology anticipated its sister-sociologies in
that it was forced by the social crisis to pay attention to problems
which sooner or later were destined to shake the rest of the world

too; and since it was the first to concern itself with these problems, German sociology devised methods for the observation and interpretation of complex general situations. An interest in the functional connection between the separate parts of the social organism is gradually being evinced in England, and in this connection the class-problem, too, is beginning to be seriously examined, and its significance in relation to that of the institutions and occupations previously alluded to is receiving increasing attention. This new interest in problems kindred to those with which recent German sociology has concerned itself makes it easier for us to exchange ideas and to compare our methods and experiences. Thus the rapidly growing similarity of the basic social problems with which different countries have to grapple finds its reflection not least in the *rapprochement* between the trends of sociological thought pursued in those countries.

PART THREE

★

SOCIOLOGICAL PSYCHOLOGY

CHAPTER VII

A few Concrete Examples concerning the Sociological Nature of Human Valuations [1]

With some theoretical remarks on the difference between the psychological and the sociological approach [2]

AFTER the penetrating and systematic remarks of our chairman, and after the broad synthesis of the main suggestions which have grown out of the papers and discussions of this conference carried out by Mr. Marshall (an unenviable task indeed), it only remains for me to add a few small items, more concrete in nature, which might provide in practice examples of such a co-ordination of the different approaches. Such a concrete approach has unavoidably the disadvantage of narrowing down the broader outlook of general discussion, but it might, perhaps, provide a foothold for the clarification of the prevailing differences.

Dr. Oeser, as a worker in the concrete field, presented us with a riddle of life. He observed, among other important things, that in Dundee, where he is working with a staff of five expert field-workers, the mill hand is socially looked down upon as compared with the factory hand; he asked what the origin of this strange fact could be. Thus he was, in his immediate observation of life, brought up against a problem which has the same roots as those philosophical problems which Professor Ginsberg dealt with in his illuminating remarks: the social factors making for change in valuations. Let us see if we can find examples of analogous things occurring in history which could serve to supplement our more local observations and also the theoretical analysis.

The Germanic tribes, in the course of their invasions during the great migration of peoples, show within a relatively short period a

---

[1] Paper presented at a conference held under the auspices of the Institute of Sociology and World University Service, London, 1936.

[2] As an excuse for the somewhat haphazard nature of these remarks, I must explain that they do not constitute a prepared paper, but are the substance of an improvisation. I was asked on the eve of the last session to take up some of the threads of the discussion, and in the short time at my disposal I had only my memory to rely on for concrete illustrations. I am here reconstructing my original remarks with the aid of my notes, only occasionally adding a few supplementary explanations and references where I thought necessary.

striking shift in their valuations; or to put it more exactly, with the first differentiation of groups and classes the respective valuation of these groups and classes becomes different. The original Germanic tribes, at the time of the beginning of their invasion, were, according to the present state of our knowledge (the subject, as you know, is a controversial one), cattle-breeding nomads who, when they had the chance of settling down, linked up their cattle breeding with agriculture. I do not want to enter here into detailed discussion as to what their exact anthropological and sociological category was: they were, at any rate, in a tribal stage, with tribal ethics, which makes for conformity, stereotyping of attitudes, aiming at co-operation and stressing the value of labour. Professor Chadwick has given us, in an admirable book,[1] a detailed description of how, in a very short time, owing to the weakness of the Roman Empire, an opportunity was given to adventurous groups for easy conquest. Under the leadership of princes, small groups of warriors split off and invaded foreign territories, setting up short-lived barbaric empires like the Gothic Empire. Now, this social differentiation within the community, the splitting up of the warrior group, rapidly brought about the creation of a completely different scale of values, and the prevalence of a new set of attitudes. Whereas, formerly, it was conformity guaranteed by magic, community standards, and the valuation of collective achievements which prevailed, now the heroic set of attitudes arose as the creation of the new warrior caste. It is spontaneity, initiative, aggressiveness that is appreciated, and if we take the social differentiation within the group, already pointed out by Tacitus, between the *princeps* and the *comitatus* (the princes and their warrior followers), we find that the princes are admired for their almost anarchic individualism, and the only thing demanded from the followers is their personal allegiance to the prince, a loyalty which is quite different from that to the tribe. The whole set of these values and attitudes challenges intentionally the tribal ethics of conformity and valuation of labour; it stresses individualism, bravery and pillage. The philologists have found reflected in the two gods Wodan and Thor the two social surroundings and their values and ideals, Wodan being the ideal of these small warrior courts of princes, and Thor a kind of old peasant. If we forget for a moment that we are concerned with princes, who set themselves above the established tribal order of society, and their followers, and regard them instead as gangs—occasional integrations under the personal guidance of one leader for the sake of pillage and hazardous invasion, we can understand the sudden

[1] H. M. Chadwick, *The Heroic Age*, Cambridge Archaeological and Ethnological Series, Cambridge, 1906.

change in values and attitudes in terms of so-called gang behaviour: individualism, bravery, enterprise, heroism, personal allegiance to the leader, are necessities of such a group organization, the maintenance of which is not so much based on continuous labour, as on sudden perilous but often well-rewarded raids. And in a book such as Thrasher's *The Gang*,[1] the author of which personally, as a sociological field worker, observed more than a thousand gangs in the area of Chicago, you will find, *mutatis mutandis*, the growth of the same set of heroic attitudes of leadership, personal allegiance, and all the other traits of gang behaviour, in our society.

That in the situation described in connection with the Germanic warrior tribes certain generalizations can legitimately be drawn concerning one type of society—society organized for conflict as against society organized for labour—can be partly shown by other parallels. As Chadwick himself points out, the very same situation and the corresponding values and attitudes occur in early Greek history during the so-called Homeric age, and in many other tribes among the Celtic and Slavonic peoples who have in the course of their history gone through a similar phase. And in fact we need not confine ourselves to instances from early societies, for in such a book as Bovet's *Fighting Instinct*[2] we are shown that not only the general attitudes and values, but the identical patterns of concrete situation occur as soon as we have individual fighting together with society organized for conflict. Bovet gives a detailed description and phraseology of fighting between young boys, and shows how this fighting does not simply follow instinctive outbursts, but is canalized in definite social patterns by typical phases of preliminaries, such as boasting, verbal provocation, and so on, the main object of which is to give the spectators time to form a ring about the fighters; Bovet goes so far as to speak of 'the phase of Homeric challenge'[3] in the fights of these boy-heroes, which proves it is not only a question of the spirit of the age, but that closely similar situations produce similar attitudes and values.

So the observation of living society complements many items in our historical studies, just as our present-day field-work lacks perspective if it is not supplemented by the historical approach.

For the set of values and attitudes prevailing in a society organized for labour, we can turn to Roman society, which never passed through the heroic phase. Here, in the earliest period

[1] F. M. Thrasher, *The Gang*, a Study of 1,313 Gangs in Chicago (with a map and bibliography), University of Chicago Studies in Urban Psychology, Chicago, 1927.
[2] P. Bovet, *The Fighting Instinct*, tr. into English by I. J. T. Greig, London, 1923.
[3] *Ibid.*, p. 21.

known to us, the *patres* themselves cultivate the soil, and correspondingly the social valuation of agricultural labour is very high; a sudden change, however, arises when the *patres*, in order to proceed to the conquest of Italy, are compelled to become soldiers and to leave the work to the slaves. Immediately the public valuation of agricultural labour is lowered, since the valuation of an activity seems to follow the social prestige of the group which engages in it.[1]

The next important shift in the valuation of labour in Roman society occurs with the growth of a leisured class, which not only despises any kind of manual work, but sets a moral premium on those achievements only which are unpaid and are carried out for their own sake or in the public service. The idea of the *artes liberales*,[2] of those professions which only are worthy of a free man, is the ideological creation of the Roman leisured class. But that this valuation is not bound to one historical setting can be proved by the fact that when a similar case occurred in English society, when the landed aristocracy became the new leisured class, they held that honorary work was the only fitting work for men of a higher order, and it is only that kind of work which has a real inner value.[3] In the English distinction between the professions and other vocations, a similar gradation of values concerning work is still maintained.[4]

This leads me to another set of facts which presents us with a very similar problem. In any society there is a group of professions considered as dishonourable or suspect. These occupations are

---

[1] With the instances quoted above, compare Ettore Ciccotti, *Der Untergang der Sklaverei im Altertum*, pp. 36 ff. (dealing with ancient Greece), pp. 110 ff. (dealing with ancient Rome), Berlin, 1910; Max Weber, 'Agrarverhältnisse im Altertum', in his *Gesammelte Aufsätze zur Sozial- und Wirtschaftsgeschichte*, pp. 2 ff., Tübingen, 1924.

The above-mentioned statement about the lowered valuation of agricultural labour has to be complemented by some of the observations of O. Neurath, who lays stress on the fact that in Roman society, with the growth of the latifundia, the big landowners and the intelligentsia for certain ideological reasons and according to prevailing romanticizing tendencies tend to praise agricultural work as contrasted with any other kind of manual labour. Neurath rightly points to the fact that these ideological documents should not be taken as a reflection of the really existing attitudes of Roman society.

Cf. O. Neurath, 'Beiträge zur Geschichte der opera servilia', in *Archiv für Sozialwissenschaft und Sozialpolitik*, vol. 41, Tübingen, 1916; 'Zur Anschauung der Antike über Handel, Gewerbe und Landwirtschaft', in *Jahrbuch für Nationalökonomik und Statistik*, 1906, 1907 (cf. especially p. 599 in vol. 87 (1906), and the very interesting quotation taken from Montesquieu, p. 600).

[2] Cf. S. Feuchtwanger, *Die Freien Berufe* (Im Besonderen: die Anwaltschaft. Versuch einer allgemeinen Kulturwirtschaftslehre), p. 21, München, Leipzig, 1922, and the literature quoted there.

[3] M. Weber, *Politik als Beruf* (Wissenschaftliche Abhandlungen und Reden zur Philosophie, Politik und Geistesgeschichte, 2nd ed., pp. 34 ff., München, Leipzig, 1936.

[4] A. M. Carr-Saunders, P. A. Wilson, *The Professions*, pp. 1 ff. and 287 ff., Oxford, 1933.

usually found, on examination, to be vital to the maintenance of the society, so that one cannot explain their social valuation on the basis of observation of their objective importance for society. I searched for a long time for a sociological description and explanation of these facts till Dr. Ernst Manheim and I found by chance in the Library of the British Museum an old brochure by a certain Beneke on the dishonourable professions.[1] In Beneke's time there was no sociology, but while working in the archives he was struck, as he says, by the fact that from the beginning of German society up to his own time some occupations—shepherd, miller, barber, weaver, hangman and others—are looked down upon and considered as suspect. He almost apologizes for dealing with such a doubtful subject, but he is so intrigued by this strange treatment of otherwise useful professions, that he can but devote himself to a more elaborate study. Indeed, if we think how vital to the existence of certain societies the hangman is, one cannot help blaming a society which accepts his services without their due appreciation. The value of Beneke's book is not so much in his theoretical explanations, as in his elaborate collection of current everyday evaluations of occupations in society. Nevertheless in certain passages he comes to the real reason for this strange valuation; it was that as the Germanic tribes for very long had to protect themselves, the armed members of the group had prestige and their valuations became predominant. As warriors they tended to despise those people whose professions (e.g. the shepherd and the miller) prevented them from fighting. Later the guilds set up professional standards and prevented suspect professions from becoming acknowledged.

One reason why I thought it necessary to bring together these examples was the hope that although these facts do not directly answer his question, Dr. Oeser's problem (why mill workers are looked down upon as compared with factory workers) might find a background against which it could be considered and perhaps more easily solved. At the same time I wanted to raise the question of the nature of empiricism in sociology. We have now at least reached a stage where it is agreed that society is worthy of careful observation, a stage that fortunately leads from empty armchair speculation to field observation. But there were already desires expressed in this conference to limit sociological work to the mere collection of facts, with the hope that when all the million facts are collected a theory will automatically spring from them. There is in this country a tendency to put a premium on pure description,

---

[1] O. Beneke, *Von unehrlichen Leuten* (Culturhistorische Studien aus vergangenen Tagen deutscher Gewerbe und Dienste mit besonderer Rücksicht auf Hamburg), Hamburg, 1863.

surveys, collections of statistical data, to the exclusion of theoretical and historical analysis of society. My historical examples may show you that Dr. Oeser's field-work would only become as efficient as he would like, if he had a historical sociology at his disposal to which his special experiences in Dundee could be related. The investigation in a certain area of the changing social prestige of occupations should presuppose a knowledge of their variability in history. But to learn from history we must be able to theorize; otherwise the historical facts mean nothing, and cannot even be compared or adequately related.

I feel like asking those who think the social sciences can get on without sociology and theoretical questioning, whether, if Newton had confined his field-work with apples to counting and describing them, he would have found his theory of gravitation. Only theory which keeps pace with the facts, and facts which are interpreted in the light of a theory, lead to knowledge. Similarly, it is not enough for Dr. Oeser, and those other field-workers who are doing indispensable research into our society, to be backed by a kind of historical sociology which broadens the perspective of their observations on the present day; they need at the same time a body of knowledge based on theoretical principles which helps them to relate their facts to a theoretical frame of reference. Thus all these shifts in valuations (a few of which I have tried to illustrate by my examples) reveal nothing, and are merely on the level of anecdotes, if nobody will risk formulating hypotheses concerning those social factors which make for changes in human valuations.

Perhaps I might put forward, quite tentatively, some such hypotheses, which in my opinion suggest themselves when one tries to solve the riddle of changing human valuations.

1. Valuations of human attitudes and activities (among which are the professions) are originally set by groups. The more one goes back into history the more it becomes evident that the real carrier of standards is not the individual, but the group of which he happens to be the exponent.

2. The standards of different groups reflect, in large part, their respective social structure, the nature of their organization, and of their fundamental needs and functions. Thus we have found the standards of a group of warriors to be fundamentally different from the valuations of agriculturalists, etc.

3. Valuation is originally not an isolated psychological act of an individual, and for the most part cannot be sufficiently explained in terms of subjective intention. This is the mistake of the introspective psychologists; the isolation of the individual's experience from the social and historical background, which gives

rise to the illusion that subjective motivation is the final and fundamental source of social acts. On the contrary, most social acts have a definitive social—mostly integrating—function in the life of the group. The valuations differ with different groups, between our warriors and peasants, for example, not because the fundamental psychological endowment of the individuals in these two groups is different at the beginning, but because the social functions these valuations have to fulfil are different in the two groups. In a society organized for conflict, for example, the fundamental valuations have set a premium on initiative, aggressiveness and adventure; in a society based on labour, the fundamental function of valuations is to guarantee steadiness, uniformity and co-operation.

4. A conflict in valuations usually arises when two or more different groups are co-ordinated or superimposed on each other. In such cases, the function of valuations is not only positive—the integration of the respective groups; the values are primarily *counter-values*, set up against the standards of competing or subjugated groups. I refer to the case Professor Chadwick mentions, in which the 'individualistic' attitudes and valuations of the warrior caste were consistently played off against the tribal rules of conformity.

5. When a society becomes differentiated, a social stratification of different classes or castes (for example, peasants and warriors) grows up. The forms of co-existence of their standards will tend to reflect the nature of co-existence of these social strata. If they do not communicate, their standards will be separated, as occurs in a caste society, where each caste has its own ritualized standards. If they do communicate, the originally different standards tend either to clash or to mix, depending on the nature of the social integration.

6. In a static society, which has reached a certain balance, there will always be some classes of leading groups (élites) the standards of which will become representative, and will be silently accepted even by those groups which are subjugated and essentially frustrated by these valuations. In the cases referred to in my examples, it was the warrior group which set the official pattern of values, and determined among them the social prestige of different occupations.

7. It is only when a society is becoming dynamic, when quick changes in the stratification take place, when a sudden rise and fall of individuals in the social scale is a matter of course, that the prevalence and the social prestige of the leading groups will be challenged.

8. But it would be wrong to relate social values exclusively to

social classes, although their dynamic function seems to be un-questionable. All groups—the family, the neighbourhood, the playground, the working team, the club, the secret society—set their peculiar patterns which compete with each other and clash in the consciousness of the individual who participates in their activities. Moreover, we should unduly narrow down the scope of sociology if we confined the value-generating function to social groups only. Changing valuations are very often engendered by one of the so-called 'social forces' or social processes which deter-mine and change the group-forms themselves. Such social processes are, among others, competition, organization, etc. Competition, whenever it is introduced in a sphere of social life, puts a premium on initiative; organization, in its turn, on 'institu-tional behaviour'.[1]

But I do not wish to go into detail and enumerate all those pro-cesses which are fundamental to the life of society and work behind the scenes when values change; what I want to show is that there is in sociology a field of theoretical investigation without which any field-work and social research is no more than a collection of bare facts or interesting anecdotes.

After this, I should like to venture a few remarks on another subject much discussed during this conference. It is possible that the example mentioned at the beginning of my contribution may throw a little light on the relationship between psychology and sociology. I think both belong inseparably together. In the long run it is impossible to conceive of a sociology which is not founded on psychology and of a psychology which does not follow up its social implications.

There is above all one fundamental error, found only too fre-quently, concerning the relationship of psychology and sociology; that is, to take psychology as dealing with the individual, socio-logy as dealing with the mass: one individual—psychology; the mass—sociology.[2] Nothing could be more erroneous than to adhere to this alternative; any individual can be considered from a sociological point of view, which means, as we shall see, that we observe the working of his mind not in isolation, but in its social setting; and on the other hand there is no mass social behaviour which is not confined to those possibilities of behaviour which are inherent in the mind of the individual. Instead of the equation single individual : psychology : : many individuals : sociology, I should prefer to say that both deal with the same material—the

[1] Cf. F. H. Allport, who uses this term in his book *Institutional Behavior* (Essays toward a Re-interpreting of Contemporary Social Organisation), University of North Carolina Press, 1933.
[2] Owing to lack of time I cannot discuss the problem of social psychology here.

psychic life of the individual, but whereas psychology tends to concentrate on the individual, thereby severing him more or less from the social context, sociology observes attitudes and behaviour with reference to this social context.

Even this alternative should not be exaggerated: there is no psychologist who, when fixing his attention on the individual, does not occasionally refer to the environment, to the most obvious representatives of human surroundings such as the father and mother, or to institutions like the family, neighbourhood, nation; but on the whole he does not consider it his task to follow up how these typical representatives of society and these social institutions are linked up with each other and how they react upon the individual in their unique constellation. On the other hand, although the sociologist will tend to start just with the analysis of these institutions and their configuration, observing how they react upon the individual, he will also occasionally be interested in the psychological peculiarities of the individuals concerned in order to see how they modify the general tendencies inherent in these institutions. On the whole they have, while dealing with the same material, a different approach and they follow opposite directions in the chain of causation. Psychology mainly stresses that concatenation of events which has (or seems to have) its source in the individual, which can be tracked back to original impulses. The guiding thread of its account is the inner life history of the individual, with which external influences may interfere, but the unity of which is guaranteed by the supposition that psychology takes the individual as a unit, as a closed organism.

The sociologist follows up the causal interlinkage in the opposite direction. He will emphasize that although all these individuals seem to be self-contained and self-determinate units, nevertheless if one concentrates upon the working of institutions like barter, mutual help, co-operation, division of labour or upon the main functions in the family or political party, the seemingly self-centred individuals tend on the whole to behave as if they were giving up their autonomy in order to adjust themselves to those objective functions, the sum of which makes the institutions. You may start with subjective motivations or personal intentions of a quite peculiar kind, but as soon as you take over a function in a given system of division of labour, or you act as a member of a family or a club, you will very probably tend to act according to certain traditional patterns or rationally established rules.[1]

We have so far stressed the similarity between psychology and sociology (that both deal with psychic acts of individuals); we shall now consider their differences. What I have said thus far

[1] Cf. also p. 241, last paragraph of the present paper.

could also be put in the following way. Psychology deals with the individual as if the ultimate origin of his behaviour lay with him, even if he always had to respond to challenges coming from his own surroundings. Sociology deals with the attitudes and acts of the individual as if his ultimate determinants were those objective institutions and functions the demands of which he has to answer.

Under these circumstances our next question must be: what are these 'objective' institutions which react upon the psychic act of the individual so strongly that they even deflect him from his original direction? Are these social institutions meta-psychological entities, 'reified' relations—to use an expression which occurred in the debate—or are they too, in the last analysis, subjective and psychological in nature? I think they are both, and in the correct analysis of the co-existence of these contradictory attributes consists the solution of the problem.

First of all, these 'institutions' are not superhuman entities. They are basically configurations of psychological acts and attitudes, as much as any other spontaneous human reaction. They differ from the latter in so far as they represent the network of *already established relationships*. Any fresh, spontaneously arising attitude, the driving force of which is centred in the primary impulses of the individual, runs up against the resistance of this network and is generally altered or deflected by this force. The life of the individual is in many ways nothing but the history of compromises and adjustments which the original impulses must make in order to fit in with the configuration of already established relationships.

On the other hand, the configuration of these established relationships is not a matter of chance. Although it looks very often as if it were the mere product of blind tradition and imitation, the elements of this configuration are more or less determined by certain objective necessities and functions which this interplay of human activities has to fulfil. At the bottom of these we generally find some kind of scarcity (i.e. scarcity of goods or time), the mastery of which compels society to limit the possibility of random or purely self-centred action. The collective mastery of this scarcity creates the various forms of struggle, co-operation, division of labour and organization. These in turn create the possibilities of an equal or unequal distribution of power, the interplay of which reacts at any moment upon the original direction of our primary impulses.

The unceasing interplay between our primary impulses which seek for satisfaction and their repudiation or remoulding by the counter-action of the already established relationships makes the theme of the history of mankind. If in the observation of this interplay one is more interested in the subjective origin of these psychic driving forces and in their concatenation in the life-history of the individual, one becomes a psychologist. If one is more interested in the power of these 'established relationships', and primarily wishes to know how they react upon the newborn individual from the very first day of his socialization; and if one follows up the existing configuration of these institutionalized activities viewed from their objective function in a given society, one becomes a sociologist.

Hereby the strange thing happens that any human attitude or activity can be considered from both angles, and accordingly reveals its double meaning. One can observe and define any human action:

(a) in terms of the psychological, purely subjective intentions or motivations which are implied in it, or

(b) one can define its meaning in terms of the social functions it consciously or unconsciously fulfils.

Any human activity can be observed as if it were the gratification of a subjective drive (psychology), or as if its *raison d'être* were only to fulfil certain functions with which it is presented by an already existing network of established relationships (sociology).

Take, for instance, my case. As psychologists you may concentrate on the subjective motives which have induced me to waste so much of your time. You may find various interpretations of this; let us take the most unfavourable of them, the subjective urge to self-display. If you approach the matter as a sociologist, you will at once realize that the above-mentioned subjective urge very soon clashes with certain objective established relationships, which unmercifully react on the purely subjective motivation. The already established relationships provide me with a definite role and function: I am here not only as an individual, but as a speaker with certain functions to fulfil and certain limitations on his activities. The same established relationships provide us also with a chairman, whose function it is to set a limit to the above-mentioned subjective urge. If as sociologists we inquire into the reason why the chairman is very soon going to bring into play the established rules concerning the length of contributions, we shall not find the answer in his personal motivation. It will be in the objective necessities (such as scarcity of time) which are simply reflected in the function he has to fulfil. This gives a better explanation of his interrupting behaviour than a subjective psychological analysis. Thus, although the two approaches supplement each other, there is a series of interesting problems implied in the continuous transmutation of subjective motivations into objective functionally determined behaviour.

But once having realized so clearly the objective necessities which will very soon induce our chairman to bring my remarks to a close, I think I had better refrain from expounding further this intricate subject.

CHAPTER VIII

On War-conditioned Changes in our Psychic Economy

In my opinion, the most urgent task at the present moment is to work out those methods of investigation on the basis of which psychologists and sociologists could work together. Hence, everything I am going to say refers in the last analysis to the methodological problem.

I am in agreement with most of what Dr. Glover has said— not only with his general conception of science, but also with his postulate that a new line of inquiry can be successful only if it is undertaken with a theoretical schema in mind which draws clear lines of demarcation both between the problems to be solved and between the fields of research assigned to the different groups of workers engaged in the study. A mere accumulation of facts cannot produce results. I also admit that we should do well to begin with the study of pathological cases, but I hasten to add this qualification: provided that one does not forget to devote equal attention to so-called normal behaviour. Further, I also agree that we should not start with such comprehensive concepts as 'society in general', or 'war in general'. Such large units do not lend themselves well to empirical study, partly because war, for example, has a different effect upon different groups, and partly because 'society in general' cannot be observed directly. Hence, it may be desirable to find smaller groups in which exact observation of the effects produced by war is possible, although, as will be made clear in the course of my argument, I am of the opinion that concrete groups are not the only units which can be subjected to observation. This enumeration of the points on which I agree with Dr. Glover would not be complete, should I fail to point out how much I appreciate his attempt to establish correlations between certain social institutions and certain psychic factors, e.g. in that he considers the Church and the Ethical Societies as organizations destined to guide the super-ego, while according to him social welfare agencies are primarily concerned with ego functions.[1] Such correlations, however, are valid only if they are not meant to state an analogy according to which society is to be considered as

[1] From *Internationale Zeitschrift für Psychoanalyse und Imago*, vol. 25, no. 3/4, 1940.

a psychic organism writ large, equipped with functions very much like those of the individual psyche.

Certain discrepancies between our positions begin to emerge only at the point where Dr. Glover makes it plain that he considers concrete groups, and these alone, as the truly representative social units, those which alone lend themselves to sociological investigation.

Two kinds of reasons, it seems to me, are responsible for this difference of approach. One has to do exclusively with the technical aspect of research, while the other is traceable to different methodological principles.

As regards the technical difficulties, it is not quite easy to explore the life of a group, such as a church or sect, unless one is satisfied with data about purely external behaviour, e.g. fluctuations in the number of churchgoers. Placed in a significant context, even data of this kind may represent a valuable addition to our knowledge, but they are assuredly not the kind of data we are interested in when we want to transcend the limits of a purely behaviouristic approach. Another drawback inherent in limiting our attention to concrete groups alone is that in this way we can never find out what we would like to know when our main problem is to ascertain how people react to events of national importance like the war. It is obviously in order to take small groups like cliques as our units of observation when the topic of our research is clique behaviour. And if we are examining behaviour within the family, there can be no objection to taking families as our experimental objects, since interaction within the family is the real source of the modes of behaviour we want to explore. But in the present case, we should like to learn things of an entirely different nature; we should like to find out something about the typical effects of social factors which exert their influence from a distant centre rather than at close proximity. Distortions would result if in such a case we were to limit our observation to small units. If we do this, we shall be tempted to look for causes in the immediate family environment rather than in society as such. In investigating the psychic effects of war, however, we have to isolate effects related to, and radiating from, a distant centre. Observation of war-conditioned responses among his patients, then, will give the psychoanalyst an opportunity to supplement his knowledge about the nature of the family with data revealing the psychic impact of the wider social environment. I am far from belittling the significance of the family situation and of early childhood experiences, but these represent only one, albeit decisive, chapter in the life of man.

If sociologically interested psychoanalysts still think exclusively in terms of small groups or concrete groups of whatever kind, the reason seems to me to be that their working concept of sociology is a perhaps deliberately simplified one. Adopting such an artificially simplified schema, one will consider sociological reality as consisting of small or large groups, or to be more concrete, one will analyse society into vocational groups and social classes—but the really decisive differentiations and variations in the picture of society will be overlooked.

Let us reverse our positions: what would psychoanalysts say if a sociologist attempted to treat all psychological problems in terms of three basic concepts alone, that is, thinking, feeling, and will, completely disregarding such fundamental categories as consciousness, the unconscious, the ego, id, and super-ego, as well as the effects of the various ego mechanisms? It is obvious that such a scanty theoretical equipment would hardly enable our sociologist to distinguish the various psychic processes, let alone to give an adequate explanation of the effects they produce.

I am particularly anxious to ward off any misunderstanding at this point. Nothing is further from my intention than to criticize the psychologist for using too limited a conceptual apparatus when dealing with society as a whole. It is not his task to go into the details of the social processes. As a result of an unsound division of labour, however, it has come to pass that each psychologist now has a private sociology of his own and perhaps each sociologist also has put together a similarly truncated psychology for his private use. Any attempt to work together must therefore begin with a mutual airing of differences like the present one, as they affect the problem at hand. In the spirit of such a mutual searching of our consciences, I bid fair to assert that to select concrete groups exclusively for purposes of observation would be tantamount to neglecting many other social factors which are equally involved. Coming from the consultation room, one will be easily led to look at things somewhat in this way: On the one hand, we have the individual with his exceedingly complex mechanisms; on the other, we have smaller or larger groups, that is, individuals multiplied ten-, a hundred- or a thousandfold. There are only two roads open to those who think in this fashion. For one thing, one could consider these hypothetical units, the groups, as mythical entities, and so develop constructs like that of the 'collective psyche'—and if one is a psychoanalyst, this 'collective psyche' will become more and more similar to the individual psyche. It will possess an ego and a super-ego, contain aggressive drives, and so forth. This was the error committed by those psychoanalysts who proposed to engage in a 'psychoanalysis of society'. The other possibility consists in avoiding such mystical analogies and defining the 'collective psyche' simply as the individual multiplied a million times. One will then conclude that certain responses observed in individuals may represent more or less frequent cases, and this will eventually lead to the assumption of statistically 'average' modes of response; these, to be sure, may be quite revealing in themselves but they are still totally incapable of telling us anything about the more complex processes which are the *real* causes underlying social change. Just as statistical correlations are of little help to the psychologist when he tries to reconstruct the dynamic structure of his patient's biography, a mere summation of individual cases will not satisfy the sociologist when he is chiefly interested in reconstructing the dynamic process underlying a series of events like the present war.

When, as in our case, the task consists in collecting observations relevant to a psychological and social history of the war, what one has to observe is not the rigid and limited group units as such, or the life of individuals in its relation to these groups, but rather the changing behaviour of individuals in correlation with the comprehensive mechanisms operating in the society.

If I had to choose units permitting the most direct observation of the dynamic nature of war in terms of the successive stages in which it unfolds and of its various effects upon the mind, I would start in the first place with *intra-group conflicts* as my subjects of investigation. Just as in the case of the individual an analysis of his intra-psychic conflicts contributes more to our understanding than isolated descriptive data (such as age, occupation, likes and dislikes) would, a successful investigation of the *social* dynamism will be easier if one starts with typical intra-group conflicts. Following through the way in which all relevant factors are affected by such conflict situations will tell us more about the interplay of social forces than a mere survey of abstract units—such as groups or institutions—would.

The real history of the war seems to me to be best reflected in a series of intra-group conflicts, each of which gives a most pregnant illustration of what group integration is and how it adds something new to the process taking place in the individual psyches separately.

Intra-group conflicts are responsible for the fact that—as Freud says—the peacetime ego is transformed into the wartime ego. Similarly, conflicts of this kind stimulate the revision of values, the reinterpretation of situations, and the initiation of new ways of action. New valuations, new ideologies, new ways of action do not originate exclusively in the depths of the isolated psyche (as one might assume in the consultation room)—they owe their existence to the integration process based upon reciprocal social action.

Hence, if we try to find an answer to the puzzling question, 'How does it come about that while each individual has his own system of values, the resulting social value system is so utterly different from these individual value systems?', we have to observe most carefully the nature of these reciprocal processes. Now the chief concern of the sociologist is precisely the study of reciprocal processes of this kind. He becomes interested in them because he cannot conceive of institutionalized public norms either as products of a mysterious collective psyche or as simply the sum or the average of typical individual experiences. What happens in these reciprocal processes is more than a summation of individual experiences: a gradual transformation is brought about by certain *social mechanisms* which the trained sociological observer can elucidate, just as the trained psychoanalyst can elucidate the effect of the various ego mechanisms.

The time has now come to give a concrete example. Were I to choose among the many problems raised by war that of the genesis of the wartime ego, I would obviously start by asking the psychoanalysts about their conclusions from the various cases of war neuroses and psychoses observed by them; in addition to this, however, I would also, as suggested by Dr. Glover, observe how such large 'groups' as the Church and the Ethical Societies go about influencing the super-ego. And I would supplement all this by directing the attention of observers to those areas in the social structure in which the spontaneous exchange of individual experiences takes place, and I would point out that radical re-evaluations are taking place in such areas. At this moment, for instance, there seem to me to be two groups in which the transformation of the peacetime ego is particularly conspicuous—the pacifists on the one hand, the Communists on the other. Intra-group conflict must necessarily arise in these groups, because their ideals have received a very rude shock; they must seek a new adjustment to the situation. For the pacifist, the very existence of war (and the ineffectiveness of passive resistance) in itself represents a challenge. The Communist, on the other hand, must find a way to overcome the shock caused by Stalin's support for the National Socialists. When I speak of a new adjustment, what I have in mind is obviously not that these groups now must make compromises and give up their old ideals, but merely that they must find a new answer that would fit the changed situation. In cases like these, in which war events cause intra-group conflicts, it would be possible to gather more exact observations about the nature of reciprocal processes and the mechanisms through which collective re-evaluations result from individual ones.

In this context, intra-group conflicts represent for the sociologist not simply 'quarrels' but a confrontation and competition among individual attempts to work out an emotional, intellectual and practical adjustment to a new situation. The first social mechanism which comes into play seems, then, to be competition as a method of finding those solutions which have the greatest survival value. We may consider these discussions and conflicts, in this sense, as a confrontation of the various opinions, attitudes and emotional responses, reflecting the varying personal experiences and character of the various individuals which these individuals, as it were, 'offer on the market'. In this as well as in every other case, sociological field investigation must above all try to ascertain how the many individual attempts to attain a new adjustment lead to new valuations, to a shift in our libido economy, to the discovery of new modes of self-realization; how the new form is being adopted, how it spreads, how it is being constantly modified in a process of further unconscious transformation, and how still later it becomes codified and institutionalized. The function of leadership can best be studied precisely at the centre of these struggles and conflicts. No genuine leadership can arise where customary and stereotyped solutions are the prevailing ones. Where this is the case, all action is controlled by the traditional authority of elected officials. Only in the presence of sudden change, necessitating entirely new responses, shall we see that new human type come to the fore which by virtue of its personality make-up will be able to create the new attitude destined to dominate the hour. (Behind Mr. Chamberlain's business-minded handling of affairs, we perceive the greater aggressiveness of Mr. Churchill, whose technique of the frontal attack is gaining more and more recognition.) The psychoanalyst may perhaps enlighten us in this context as to why certain pathological types are better able to find the new form of adjustment. Is this perhaps the case because the newly arising 'wartime society' is a 'sick' one in which 'sick' types are better adjusted—or is the pathological type, precisely because it never knew how to follow the normal path, in a better position to hit upon new and adequate solutions where the normal, tradition-bound type is bound to fail? This is precisely the point where an organic connection between the study of pathological types and that of the so-called normal ones can be established. Social processes of this kind and some others that are easy to distinguish, as well as the existence of groups one might describe as value-creating ones (intellectuals, journalists, priests, etc.), are responsible for changes such as the emergence of a wartime ego with its new norms. When the new evaluation is recognized as a public norm, this is not the result of a simple addition process, but an effect of social mechanisms which should be investigated just as carefully as are the ego mechanisms. And it is at this stage of the creation of dominant public norms that we observe a fresh struggle between the institutionalized norm and the living experience of the individual. Immediate experience will often refuse to recognize the norms as its own offspring that is still basically unchanged after having passed through the social medium.

To sum up: How does all this affect our methods of investigation?

Any research proposal is obviously subject to the limitations of the facilities available. But I shall completely disregard the limitations that will be probably placed upon our new departure (supposing that we can make a start at all). I shall talk as if we had unlimited facilities at our disposal. On the other hand, my suggestions will be very incomplete, because time does not permit us to mention all that should be included in a comprehensive research plan. At any rate, in going about the task of working out our investigation methods, we should not forget the following three or four principles:

(a) In our case, the principal task consists in relating the knowledge of psychic processes gained through depth psychology to major changes taking place in the outside world. Our final goal is to ascertain the mutual relationships between individual mechanisms and the social mechanisms impinging upon them.

(b) If we propose to create a model for dynamic research, we cannot be satisfied with the methods of purely descriptive field work or with observations made under artificially created conditions. We must seek to penetrate the dynamism active in group life.

(c) In addition to this, our new task involves the ascertainment of influences radiating from distant foci of society rather than from the family, the neighbourhood or the community.

(d) We must at all times confront and compare pathological forms of adjustment with normal ones, and study the function exercised by the former ones at the various stages of the social process.

Now a few concrete suggestions for the organization of research:

1. As regards the analysis of pathological cases, I should like to add a new suggestion to those made by Dr. Glover. It would not be difficult at all, it seems to me, to collect and co-ordinate all observations gained in private and clinical psychiatric practice concerning typical responses to the war, beginning with war fantasies and going all the way to war neuroses, etc.

2. Still remaining within the field of psychology proper operating with the technique of depth psychology, and still focusing upon individual cases rather than upon group phenomena, I

should like to call your attention to the method developed by Harold D. Lasswell in his book *Psychopathology and Politics*, a method he calls that of the 'prolonged interview'. This is something intermediary between full-fledged psychoanalysis and simple anamnesis. Its reliability, of course, is not to be compared with that of a long analysis, but it is less superficial than the usual type of interviewing done by journalists or anthropologists working in the field. It is a kind of short analysis, taking perhaps a few weeks, which enables an experienced analyst to reconstruct the inner life history of an individual primarily as to its principal stages, the fundamental system of his ideology and his values, and his reactions to the actual conflicts he has experienced in his life. Of course, only individuals who in their turn are deeply interested in psychology will volunteer for such interviews; but where this is the case, it is of the greatest importance that we gain some insight into the psychic state both of individuals we know to be representative personalities and of people who in their public behaviour at least seem to illustrate the reactions dominant in well-defined groups.

3. Also still within psychology proper, I would consider it very valuable to induce certain individuals to keep a war diary which on the one hand would give answers to specific questions relevant to some other lines of investigation, and on the other would contain notes recording free associations at the discretion of the diarist.

4. Passing now to techniques of research permitting a good organization of sociological material, I certainly would not discard group observations of the kind suggested by Dr. Glover. My position is rather that I would not restrict myself to them alone. In this respect, the happiest arrangement for psychiatrists or psychologists working with clinical material would be one enabling them to observe people connected with one and the same organization, such as e.g. the employees of one department store, or pupils of one school, or soldiers in one army unit. In such cases, one would obviously have to combine all methods, such as statistics, the questionnaire method, and various types of personality research.

5. I shall now come to the subject I have been discussing in some greater detail in the present lecture, that is, intra-group conflicts as units of investigation, and the most persistent following up of all the psychic and social factors which are active in these conflicts. I have mentioned the conflicts which the present situation touched off among pacifists and Communists; but I could just as well have pointed to the typical conflicts which arose in connection with evacuation problems. Every conflict of this kind would lay bare the dynamic reciprocal connection among psychic and social factors.

6. In studying influences radiating from distant foci of society, there are a few additional methods at our disposal. The first thing to do would be the writing of a war diary on which, if possible, a psychologist and a sociologist would collaborate. The main task of the authors would be to record the most important collective emotional currents in their growth and their development, in their flowing and ebbing. Posterity will easily reconstruct the more tangible outside events from the various sources, but we shall soon forget how long the first shock caused by the declaration of war lasted, when people returned to their normal occupations, when they stopped carrying their gas masks around, when intellectuals started discussions about peace aims, federation projects and human rights (probably to be interpreted in retrospect as the result of collective escape mechanisms). In any case, such a war diary, which would at least give a rough outline of the nature and duration of such fluctuations of collective moods, would provide an excellent background for the interpretation and co-ordination of individual data gathered either in psychiatric practice or in field research.

7. In concluding, I should like to state that it would be extremely urgent, not only for scientific purposes but also in order to help people effectively, to create a kind of clearing office for acute conflicts and difficulties. This clearing office not only would have to collect, classify, describe and diagnose the typical difficulties arising in connection with the adjustment to war conditions; it would also soon find out that wherever these typical difficulties arise, there also are individuals who invent models of a correct external and internal adjustment to the changed situation. The publication and circulation of such models would be that kind of assistance which a modern social security administration could provide. We must always keep in mind that in our modern large-scale society the individual cannot always be expected to find the correct adjustment to sudden changes all by himself. In the old, parochial world, even though changes took place very slowly, there were still some primitive methods in existence by which successful forms of psychic adaptation could be communicated to neighbours. It is only natural that in our modern world this has to be organized. I think that if we managed to combine our scientific yearning for knowledge for its own sake with a few such practical goals, we should find much greater support both in the public and in government.

PART FOUR

★

PLANNED SOCIETY AND THE PROBLEM
OF HUMAN PERSONALITY:
A SOCIOLOGICAL ANALYSIS

FIRST LECTURE[1]

The Age of Planning

THESE lectures have been called a sociological analysis. This means that the argument is neither that of the politician nor of the fieldworker. I shall avoid the purely political approach because, the problem being highly topical, such a treatment would lead us at the very beginning, instead of to an analysis of facts, to a quarrel and perhaps, I am afraid, to a regular fight, for which the lecture room is certainly not the proper place. Neither do I aim at a purely descriptive analysis of the existing totalitarian states as fieldworkers used to do, because others who have studied these societies on the spot have done it much better than I could do.

What I am trying to do is something in between the two. Based upon the facts available, it is an attempt at a theoretical analysis of the social forces underlying the formation of the new totalitarian states and of the factors reshaping men living under the changed conditions of a new system.

Now another preliminary remark, and even a personal one, is necessary. Although it is not my intention to speak as politician nor to propagate valuations, but rather to put into the foreground a technique of objective analysis, I do not think that questions concerning human affairs can wholly avoid being founded on attitudes of sympathy or antipathy which somehow influence our thought.

Even if we consciously avoid any kind of bias or propaganda in our analysis the vantage point from which we look at the object will be reflected in our presentation. Therefore it is only fair and should be made a rule that in our age of deep agitation every speaker should state his standpoint right at the beginning so as to help his audience to discount his partiality.

The vantage point from which I shall present the situation is to a certain extent that of a liberal, but of a liberal whose vested interests are not so much to be found in the economic world as in his being a member of a certain type of intelligentsia whose only capital is his learning and whose fundamental demands on life are freedom of thought and free development of personality.

[1] The four lectures in this section were delivered at Manchester College, Oxford, in 1938.

But this wing of the intelligentsia is liberal only so long as the future of culture and development of the personality is in question. As to the general transformations in society it is ready to see what is really happening in the world and it is not blind to the potential good in the movements of our age.

The longer we study present-day society the less can we avoid seeing that all the basic conditions of the age of liberalism are vanishing, or else transforming themselves into new ones, and that we are confronted with completely new configurations.

To begin with, there is a new kind of military technique which allows of a much greater concentration of power in the hands of the few than did the technique of any previous period. Whereas the armies of the eighteenth and nineteenth centuries were equipped with rifles and guns, modern armies use bombs, aeroplanes, gas, and mechanized army units. A man with a rifle at his disposal can only threaten a few people, but a man with bombs can threaten a thousand. This means that in our age the change in military technique for its part contributes a great deal to the chances of minority rule.

The same concentration has occurred in the field of government and administration. Telephone, telegraph, wireless, railways, motor-cars and, last but not least, the scientific management of any large-scale organization all facilitate centralized government and control. Just as we get a new understanding of the nature of feudalism if, instead of deducing it from 'the spirit of the age', we start rather from the fact that its decentralization was largely the consequence of the poor means of communication in large land areas; so the modern forms of political centralization depend to a very great extent on the growth and development of the means of communication and administration.

Similar concentration can also be observed in the means of forming public opinion. The mechanized mass production of ideas through press and wireless works in this direction. Add to this the possibility of controlling schools and the whole range of education from a single centre, and you will realize that the recent change from democratic government to totalitarian systems is due, here too, not so much to the changing ideas of man as to changes in social technique. And by social technique I understand all those means of influencing fundamental attitudes and opinion already mentioned.

The immediate consequence of this concentration in social technique is that where formerly occasional and private influence prevailed, now, gradually, public guidance has increasingly become the rule. Whereas formerly adjustment to immediate and narrow surroundings determined the character of man, now gradually the forces of the total structure of society condition the moulding of his essential features.

But the growth of new techniques in various fields is only one aspect of the factors making for the possibility of minority rule. The co-ordination (*Gleichschaltung*) of these techniques makes minority power much more formidable than the control of any single one of them.

If we consider, for example, education and the way in which a child may be conditioned in the same direction by the crèche, the kindergarten, the elementary school, the secondary school, and then by the university, by trade-school and adult education, we shall estimate the power of this co-ordinated training. But add to this interference or even complete management of leisure through sport, gymnastics and drill, the control of, and propaganda through literature, the cinema and the theatre, not to mention the press, daily and periodical—popular and scientific— and you will realize how the printed word and man's very recreations fall under the same control.

Even if people escape from these and meet their friends in small private gatherings, in pubs, restaurants or elsewhere, or if they succeed in forming sects and cliques, they have still to avoid the highly developed system of espionage and the intelligence service which watches not only overt behaviour, but seeks to ferret out the inmost unexpressed opinions as well.

On top of this there is also the possibility that the whole mechanism whereby people rise and fall in the social scale is controlled. Where formerly free competition, democratic selection or personal preference determined the social fate or the career of individuals, now there is the possibility that a central apparatus will design the place of everybody and decide the function and destiny of the individual.

The totalitarian state, where it exists, makes full use of this technique and apparatus to further co-ordination. And, unfortunately, to such a state co-ordination means a rigid conformity.

Conformity is desired, firstly, because it is simpler to govern people who are identically conditioned, and secondly, because those at the top are very often narrow-minded and primitive in their outlook, being frequently the products of the petty bourgeoisie, and primitivism is characterized by its intolerant treatment of deviations. Xenophobia, or hatred of the foreigner simply because he is different, is one of the oldest traits of social groups bounded by narrow surroundings, as are the peasants and the petty bourgeoisie.

But even if the leaders come from the ranks of the intellectuals, they reject the ideas of personality and individuality very often for merely dogmatic reasons, arguing that they belong to the age of liberalism which definitely belongs to the past.

In the description of the concentration of social technique I consciously referred to structural changes. This means: if the main reason of what happened in Germany, Italy, Russia and the other totalitarian countries is to be sought in the changed nature of social technique, it is only a question of time and opportunity for some group in the hitherto democratic countries to make use of it. In this connection, any catastrophe such as war, rapid depression, great inflation, growing unemployment, which requires extraordinary measures (that is, the concentration of the maximum power in the hands of some government), is bound to precipitate the process. This means that even before the outbreak of war the permanent tension brought about by the existing totalitarian states enforced in the democratic countries, very often, measures similar to those which in the totalitarian states came into force through revolution. It goes without saying that during a war in which the co-ordination of food industries and other supplies, and conscription, become necessary, the tendencies towards concentration will only increase.

But besides war and external pressure there is an inner reason which works in favour of planning: this is that in a mass society one cannot let things grow and find the right solution by continuous bargaining and occasional adjustment. As long as tasks have only to be solved on a small scale in a parochial world, slow experimentation is the right way of finding the solution. Where big institutions are to be adjusted to each other, some centralized prevision has to watch their operation or else their clash becomes catastrophic.

Against these factors which press upon the framework of democracies and *laisser-faire* from without and from within, there are naturally counteracting forces at work which we hope will be strong enough to prevent us from making the same mistakes which at present seem to be inseparably connected with the existing experiments.

In this connection I have in mind the longer tradition of democracy and liberalism in England and the United States of America; the greater difficulty of one party's becoming exclusive; the greater prosperity which usually dulls the edge of prevailing dogmatisms. Although they will not prevent the coming of an age of regulation, these factors together may contribute very much towards making the transformation slower and thus preparing the ground for a more considerate conception of planning.

Whether we like it or not, planning—though, I hope, not dictatorship—will come to the democratic countries of Europe and

America; therefore I consider it the great and urgent task of social science to classify the problems of planning and to think of means of guiding this process towards its optimum. The Church, for instance, preaches that it is wrong to kill; the State, that to do so may sometimes be a man's highest duty. The family teaches the idea of brotherly love, whereas society presents the same individual with situations to which egotism, if not hatred, is the only adequate response. Indeed, it is not wholly wrong to speak of our times as a 'neurotic age', neurosis being its characteristic illness, provoked by a series of institutionalized conflicts.

What we usually call free society and freedom reveals itself to the sociologist, therefore, essentially as a lack of co-ordination in its institutions. In this society the chief force which builds personality seems to be the necessity of continually making a choice between the different and contradictory tendencies presented by the uncoordinated institutions. In reality, freedom in unplanned societies is the possibility of escape; it is not a positive freedom but merely a negative one. Even so, it is still better than the society of dictators which is based upon complete coercion.

In contrast to this obvious practice of liberal society most of its theorists do not refrain from calling any kind of regulation and interference evil. They overlook the fact that the necessary social compulsion is effected by other powers, and they are spared sight of the catastrophe to which the complete abandonment of regulation, which they advocate, would necessarily lead.

The origin of this misinterpretation, which makes planning equivalent to occasional interference, is to be sought in an age in which an equilibrium of small self-adjusting units rightly seemed to be a healthy way of building up society. Indeed, in the first stages of liberal capitalism the competition between these small and therefore elastic units solved the problem of mutual adjustment most satisfactorily. Any occasional state interference in favour of some vested interest could only disturb this form of mutual adjustment. In the social sphere the best education for such pioneering types seemed to be the experience of life, which in sociological terms is nothing but acquiring the right behaviour in such a self-adjusting world.

But as soon as small elastic units give place to big economic corporations, isolated individuals to big associations such as the trade unions, and as soon as self-help is replaced by huge organizations like the social services (all too rigid to readjust themselves spontaneously) the alternative question is no longer: 'planning or *laisser-faire*?', but interference either with or without co-ordination or on the basis of a well-conceived plan. Thus the problem gradually comes to be: What is our exact conception of co-ordination?

Here another misinterpretation obscures the true meaning of planning. It is the bureaucratic and militaristic spirit of the totalitarian states which in practice unwittingly interprets co-ordination as being equal to conformity.

There is a simple reason why, in the long run, society on a large scale cannot survive if it fosters only conformity. It was Durkheim who first pointed out the social division of labour: that only very simple societies like those of the primitives can work on the basis of homogeneity and conformity. But the more complex the social division of labour becomes, the more it requires the differentiation of types. The integration and unity of a great society is not achieved through uniform behaviour but by way of the mutual complementing of functions.

In a highly industrialized society the various social groups depend on each other in many ways: the farmer, for instance, needs the industrial worker as a consumer and as a producer; the workman needs the management, and vice versa; whereas the management needs the assistance of the scientist and of the educationalist.

What is the meaning of this sociological concept of planning and co-ordination? Today I have to confine myself to its general characteristics, leaving it to the more empirical investigations of the next lectures to present details.

First, co-ordination need not necessarily mean 'goose-step' co-ordination. It is perfectly possible to co-ordinate for variety.

Second, co-ordination does not mean creating new facts by bureaucratic command, but the use of the indispensable spontaneous forces of society in fostering certain desirable aims. It means the harmonizing of all the spontaneous and vital forces of society by anticipating the ways in which they are likely to work and the continuous correlation of the necessary adjustments.

But there is a difference between whether I wish to replace the spontaneous forces by command, or whether I carefully arrange social stimuli so that they counterbalance each other.

Third, this concept of co-ordination does not involve the suppression of individuality but, rather, entails differentiation, providing the space where it may grow and the social stimuli which regularly foster it.

As soon as we present the task in this way, at once further questions arise:

1. Is it at all possible to influence and to foster the personality by social means? Is personality not something one has or one has not? 2. If it is possible, do we know anything about the social

forces and situations which favour differentiation and the growth of a well-marked self-centred personality?

As to the second, it will be the task of my lectures to prove by empirical instances that society in the course of its history worked with social forces and stimuli which fostered individualization, and as soon as some of these were suppressed the corresponding human type disappeared.

In this connection, too, we shall find a difference between planned and non-planned societies, in that formerly it was a matter of chance whether or not the social forces which fostered individualization were set free; and if some manipulation of these forces occasionally occurred, the stimulation was rather of a private nature and purely occasional.

In contrast to this, in the planned societies to come it gradually becomes necessary to acquire a detailed knowledge of the working of the forces making for individualization and to rearrange these social stimuli in such a way that they serve not only particular local needs but the central aims of a planned community.

Today I shall not begin by expounding the knowledge already collected by sociology concerning the social forces making for individualization. Such an exposition would be of no use at all so long as we continue to conceive of personality in terms of the liberal tradition.

This means that before any further discussion we must become aware of the fact that most of our ideas concerning the nature and function of personality start from assumptions which are not so much the result of a critical examination as the expression of unconscious wishes and ideals.

To go even further, it is one of the most interesting insights we have gained during the last decades that each age seems to build upon a set of concepts which to a certain extent are limited to that particular age because they comply with its unconscious strivings. Thus some of the basic ideals of our generation still seem to be linked with the philosophy of liberalism, and they become the more questioned the more we advance into an era of what might be termed New Collectivism.

Whereas the liberal age tended to over-emphasize the role of the individual in society, it seems to be the task of the new age to work out more thoroughly the social aspects of the same problems.

But it is also one of the intricacies of the historical process that the fundamental facts of a new age will be discerned only by those who are willing to learn from them and who are gradually disposing of those hypotheses of the declining age which act as prejudices and hamper the new approach to the facts in question.

As this first lecture unavoidably has to be devoted to clearing the ground, after this analysis of the sociological meaning of planning let me now turn to the sociological meaning of personality as contrasted with the liberal interpretation.

As I have said, there is nothing more intricate nor more exciting to the student of history than to watch how a new age gradually dismisses its old concepts, and how together with the changes in the social structure new axioms and hypotheses clear the ground for new types of experience. Psychology seems to be one of the disciplines in which the changing nature of the social structure is reflected first: a fact which is not altogether surprising if we recall to mind that the psychologist is himself also a member of society, and the psychological attitudes through which he approaches his fellow beings are always influenced by the contacts prevailing in his society.

Take the fact, for instance, that the older type of psychology was based upon 'introspective intuition' or 'pure description', whereas now measurement of attitudes and the close observation of 'overt behaviour' prevails. Does not this change correspond to the transition from small leading groups and their emphasis on the individual as they prevailed in the age of liberalism, to an organized mass society? In the former, people know each other very well and have time to interest themselves in each other; in the latter, the necessity for organizing great masses determines the nature of human contacts. The number of administrative and business contacts has increased, and the knowledge of average overt behaviour and standardized patterns has become of greater importance to society than the qualities and foibles of the members of a limited circle.

This being so, we may expect that further new trends in social life will also be reflected in modern psychology. Indeed, in contrast to the former liberal concept of the self, modern psychology is quite unconsciously working out a new sociological concept of the psyche which corresponds to the approach of planned mass-society. This does not mean that the new psychology denies the existence of personality, but merely that it detects aspects of it that had not been noticed before, and finds fresh explanations for its genesis.

1. The modern concept of the self is in many ways a gradual emancipation from the Greek idea of entelechy. In terms of the latter the soul is an unfolding entity and personality only achieves its own shape because it is inherent in it from the very outset. As compared with this rigid idea of pre-existence the evolutionary concept of the self (as it prevailed in the approach typical of the Age of Enlightenment and liberalism) is a significant step in the opposite direction. In the evolutionary idea, although unfolding

still rests upon the inherent growth of personality, environment comes more into its own since it acts at least as a releasing factor. Certain potentialities cannot be realized without certain environmental stimuli.

2. In this context the theory of predestination and that of innate qualities are only variations of the same theme. And the theological idea of predestination was not basically changed, when a later age dominated by the natural sciences turned the original metaphysical formulation of preformation into the idea of biological inheritance.

3. To complete this picture of the liberal view its emphasis on the *great man* must be added. It is only another and more heroic elaboration of the idea of the self-sufficiency of personality.

The theory of the great man as the real maker of history will mostly arise in societies which open up to the few possibilities of rapidly rising in the social scale. Accordingly, these types of society will be impressed by the rise of the so-called self-made man. Condottieri and great bankers of the Renaissance and the business barons of the liberal age always tend to interpret their life in heroic terms. In contrast to this, a trade-union leader, for instance, who rises in the social scale not as an individual but backed by a whole class, even if he reaches a very high position will still be conscious of the social forces which made that position. Typical statements made by people unconsciously dominated by the heroic concept are such as these:

'The fit person will make his way under any circumstances.'
'Personality cannot be made; it is innate.'

There are very few among us whose reasoning is not still dominated by the remnants of those thought patterns.

If we listen to these statements carefully, it becomes obvious that this heroic over-emphasis on the powers of the prominent man expresses the ideals of an age rather than its critically tested experiences. Concepts like that of the hero, the great individual, are symbols which express deep desires, stimuli for the pioneering types, and as such they are of the utmost practical importance, but they cannot be taken as sociological knowledge. The further development of the concept of personality consisted, therefore, in part in a modification of this over-emphasis on its independence and on the idea of complete predetermination.

A critical examination of attitudes dominant in the liberal age shows how the educated man of the passing epoch of liberalism had an inclination for introversion and contemplation, which made him often blind to environment. The price that type of thinker had to pay for the marvellous progress he made in the art of self-observation, as revealed in idealist philosophy, was his blindness to the details of the environment.

4. Once the habit of thinking in terms of predetermination was broken, it was only a consequent step in the same direction when in scientific psychology the attempt was made to redefine the instincts. Observed facts were revised, skilful experiments were arranged to prove that the former theory of preformed instincts was just part and parcel of the general idea of autonomous evolution from within. Much that was formerly considered as innate instinctive response was proved to be conditioned reflex (socially created habit). As a result, for the modern psychologist there are no longer ready-made instincts in man but only innate vague instinctual tendencies which receive shape and character by a continual conditioning through environment.

5. Another root of the doctrine of the self-contained character of soul and personality is to be found in the fact that the philosophy of the liberal era, as represented by idealism and romanticism, was a philosophy of introverted intellectual strata. Particularly in Germany, these had been excluded from practical political work, and had therefore never had a chance to combine self-observation with practical action and to follow up the ramifications of the interaction between the mind and its social environment. There are innumerable examples showing that when an entire social stratum is debarred from political action, and its dominant attitude becomes an introverted and contemplative one, passed on to the younger generation by birth and education, then this state of affairs remains unconscious and all influences received from the larger environment are either automatically ignored or devalued.

Hence it is no mere coincidence that the first radical breach with this introverted and introspective psychology occurred in American philosophy. Pragmatism, as developed by James and later by Dewey, and behaviourism which carried some aspects of this philosophy to extremes, represent a rupture with the platonizing tradition which had to a large extent dominated European academic life. It is no mere coincidence that this philosophy of the extravert originated in America, the land of the pioneers, where experimenting with a new world led to a kind of activism as the natural attitude towards life and a closed circle of intellectuals and academicians came into being only late and even then in a far less exclusive form than it had assumed on the Continent. Similarly it is no coincidence that a European counterpart of pragmatism developed in a non-academic ambiance, that is, in Marxism, which then had a certain stimulating effect upon academic thinking. The later evolution leading from Marxism to the sociology of knowledge also essentially contributed to questioning the introverted perspective from which the self appears exclusively as an entity wholly detached from social reality.

Pragmatism and behaviourism are in bad repute in Europe, in part because they are always completely misrepresented, but also because they are a disturbing challenge directed against deeply rooted introverted and contemplative attitudes which had been dominant in the academic philosophy of liberalism.

Certain aspects of these philosophies (pragmatism and behaviourism) no doubt suffer from exaggeration and extravagance; it is, however, an unproductive kind of criticism which focuses exclusively upon the excesses of a movement instead of taking over what is fruitful and new in it. In this sense, we consider a revision of the usual European judgment about pragmatism and behaviourism as an urgent necessity. If we adopt such an attitude and stress the positive elements of pragmatism, behaviourism, Marxism, and the sociology of knowledge, we may say that the achievement of these movements consisted in the fact that they were able to prove that the evolution of mental attitudes and even of knowledge does not occur in a vacuum but is strictly linked up with action. It is action which differentiates thought, it is external resistance and hindrance which makes us aware of the object and compels us to continual self-adjustment, it is resistance and conflict which really bring about the growth of personality. So step by step another sphere of alleged inner determination was replaced by the observation of the relevance of external contacts.

We can trace in detail the influence of this new attitude upon the study of the history of political ideas, and also of ideas in general. Something like a Copernican revolution took place when it was attempted to investigate the functioning and growth of Mind in its relatedness to the collective process and collective activity. Thus, functional anthropology achieved something new in the study of primitive peoples when it carefully traced back to their social context all those things which previously had been treated in abstract fashion, such as myths, customs, and forms of thought. This approach was very similar to that of the sociology of knowledge which tried to explain thinking on a more advanced evolutionary level in terms of the situation and practice of groups, classes, strata and so on. Here, too, the decisive novelty consists in the fact that ideas are no longer considered as mystical, transcendent entities which transform men and societies in and by themselves, but rather as parts of a continuous process of social adjustment to new conditions. Group adjustment in addition to individual adjustment provides the main key to the proper understanding of institutions, myths, attitudes and ideas. It is by grasping their ceaselessly changing function that we understand their history and penetrate more deeply into their meaning. Without insight into their function, ideas could be worshipped in religious rapture, or projected, as in Platonism, on to an imaginary plane of eternity, or visualized, as in neo-Platonism, in aesthetic contemplation. But they can come alive only if they are experienced and understood as ways and means serving the readjustment of the individual personality or of the group.

This grasp of the vital function is most difficult to achieve with thinking as our topic. We tend to identify ourselves too much with the contemporary stage of thinking to be able to admit that thinking with its conceptual apparatus is itself an organ, an instrument, that constantly remakes itself in order to fulfil the constantly changing task of adjustment to reality. We cannot reject this idea of the instrumentality of thought if we reflect upon its roots in biology and history: only those can oppose it who are unwilling to look at thinking 'from without', in its genesis and function within the environment, and confine themselves to a straight, direct, contemplative and non-functional reception of intellectual products.

The Structure of Personality in the Light of Modern Psychology

Our main problem in these lectures is to find out whether the recent drift of society towards planning will necessarily do harm to the development of personality. At first sight the growth of techniques of influencing human behaviour seems to increase the pressure put upon the individual. On the other hand, it is possible that a skilful use of more subtle techniques would give scope for more finesse in the art of social control; and provided that the groups using these techniques wished to conserve the individuality of their subjects, there would probably also be less danger to the formation of individual personalities. A primitive chieftain whose only method of control is a whip is more likely to damage the personality of his subjects than, for instance, a democratic society which works out a set of social rewards as incentives to the working man to produce spontaneous co-operation on his part.

This example reminds us that even past societies continuously exercised social control over their members, even though indirectly and unconsciously, and that the problem of the power of social influence upon personality formation is not really new, but has to be investigated anew in the present situation. The difference today is perhaps only that we shall gradually be able to speak about these influences not only in general terms but to specify them according to our growing knowledge of psychology and sociology, and that we shall assess the harm or profit that accrues from them by empirical methods. Whereas I shall devote my next lecture to problems of modern sociology which will enable us to see more clearly what impact the different social situations and processes may have upon the individual, this lecture will be devoted to the presentation of some of the results of the investigations of modern psychology concerning the nature of mind, especially with respect to its accessibility to environmental influences.

Thus, we shall first deal with the various kinds of channels through which environmental influences have to pass if they are to penetrate into the mind, and only then shall we try to describe more exactly the different environmental circumstances in terms of the specific traits they tend to create in our conscious and unconscious life.

If we succeed along these lines, we shall be able to speak not only in general terms of 'an influence of environment as such "upon" the mind as such', but we shall be able to point to environmental influences which penetrate in a definite way into definite spheres of our mental life. The main aim of this lecture is, therefore, to break us of the habit of speaking about the Mind in General, and to show that we can in fact distinguish different levels within the mind. Further, we shall try to show that on each of these different levels different kinds of environmental influences are at work. Of course, we shall not conceive of these levels as water-tight compartments—there is a continuous interaction between them; but in spite of that, this classification will help us to give a fairly adequate description of the processes in play, and to follow up the different environmental influences at work on each level. In my analysis I shall rely for the most part on psychoanalytical terminology. I do so for three reasons: firstly, because it is impossible to give all the different theories in a single lecture; secondly, because it can be shown that, as to these three levels which we shall distinguish, there is in fact far-reaching agreement among psychologists; and thirdly, because I think the psychoanalysts have gone farthest among psychologists in developing a detailed analysis of the processes at work in the mind.[1]

Let us then distinguish the following three levels of the mind:

1. There is first the lowest level where the drives and impulses originate. These drives and impulses are the dynamic elements in the mind, and are the ultimate initiators of all mental change and activity. The sum of these drives and impulses form what the psychoanalyst would call the *id* and which seems to me to be a part only of a broader realm which could be called the 'purely vital sphere' in man.

As we shall see later, we include in that *vital sphere* also:

(*a*) the unlearned *reflex reactions* of the body;

(*b*) the *involuntary reactions* to pleasurable and unpleasurable stimuli—which may be called *visceral or physiological behaviour*; and even those

(*c*) *automatic reactions, which were once learned*, but the memory of whose learning has lapsed.

In the *id* are the drives in their most crude form, awaiting the

---

[1] As to the presentation of the psychoanalytic theory I owe very much to an article by Dr. Bibring, 'Versuch einer allgemeinen Theorie der Heilung' (Part of a Symposium on Therapeutic Results) in *Internationale Zeitschrift für Psychoanalyse*, vol. 18, 1937. Cf. Erich Rothacker, *Die Schichten der Personlichkeit*, Leipzig, 1938.

moulding influence of the higher levels of the mind. No one has met a drive or instinct in its genuine form, and what we see of it is mostly the result of a more or less subtle process of elaboration, under pressure of environmental influences. Thus there is always an element of speculation in any description of the *id*. Nowadays, we are inclined to speak about instincts as open and vague tendencies towards some kind of satisfaction, rather than as highly specified drives with well-defined *a priori* purposes. Thus instead of 'instincts' we speak about open tendencies, since the concrete form they take will depend on environmental conditioning. In their genuine form, they are unconscious. The main thing that happens to them, apart from environmental conditioning, is their growth and development, so to speak, from within. The fundamental sexual drive, for instance, passes through different stages, anal, oral and genital, which correspond to the growth of the organism in which it functions. Environmental influence reflects itself mainly in certain pressures exerted on these drives from outside. Repression and release are exerted by the controlling agencies of the mind, but their ultimate source, the need for these repressions, is to be found in the demands of society—in its taboos and general social code of behaviour. As to their intensity and speed of response, the drives in their genuine form are largely determined by hereditary factors. These qualities, in their turn, depend directly, *inter alia*, on the glandular constitution of the individual, and on the quality and organization of the nerve cells and nervous pathways. Pre-natal influences and early childhood also decisively influence their functioning. Although it is the aim of the sociologist to emphasize as clearly as possible the significance of environmental influences, if he retains his sense of proportion he will never underrate the significance of the existence of this vital and hereditary sphere in the mind, and its biological foundations.

2. Above the vital sphere of fundamental drives which we have just described is the second level—that of the *ego* of the psychoanalysts. The *ego* is mainly a regulating agency. It has two functions. Firstly, it has to control the flow of emotions, to prevent the superfluous libidinous energy from coming into the foreground of consciousness; and, secondly, it has to test reality; that is to say, to test whether our ideas and imagery correspond to reality, and whether our action patterns cope with its demands. Although the ego is a controlling agency, it would be wrong to think that it is a rational thing only. The ego has, so to speak, two parts, one which is deeply immersed in the unconscious, and another which is conscious and rational. We can see the workings of that unconscious ego in our dreams, in which it still functions, although to a

lesser degree, as a censor of our wishes and emotions. What is fundamentally unconscious in the ego are the so-called mechanisms through which it operates. The task of these mechanisms is to mould, elaborate, and canalize the basic drives. They are responsible for the elaboration of our drives as they will function in our daily life, in our contact with the world. There are about seventeen of these mechanisms, whose task it is to adapt the drives to social life. They provide several alternatives, including repression and canalization of superfluous energy—that is to say, of energy which cannot be used in social life. Some of the better known of these mechanisms are: reaction-formation, projection, symbolization, and sublimation. Take, for instance, reaction-formation. This is prudery, very often of a militant kind, calculated to keep down a strong sexual impulse by giving us at the same time the opportunity of dealing with sexual matters in a roundabout way, which at least releases fantasies which otherwise would be too unhealthy to repress. Or there is the mechanism of introjection, through which aggressive energy, which naturally would take an outward flow, is turned against ourselves, and might develop in a kind of masochistic pleasure in self-punishment. Once this pathway is established in early childhood, it determines the later formation of the character. But all this happens, as we have said, in the darkness of the unconscious, and the unconscious part of the ego together with its controlling mechanisms works without our conscious participation. There is, however, another part of the ego, as we mentioned before. Its function is to elevate into the brightness of consciousness certain elements of the unconscious, and to subject them to rational scrutiny. The very nature of this part of the ego is rationality. It is the organizing function of the conscious ego which both brings about meaningful behaviour and is able to bear responsibility. It is obvious that we can speak about personality proper only on this level, even if we are careful not to underrate the importance of the vital sphere of the unconscious part of the mind. The ego is an active factor. Its initiative is decisive. Its control and influence is the guiding factor in mental life. Its awakening and strengthening is the ultimate aim of all education.

3. But by what kind of norms is the ego guided? From where does it take its standards? Here the Freudians introduce the concepts of the *super-ego* and the *ego-ideal*, which are a third and still higher level. The Freudians consider this third level as a part of the ego which has become an independent factor as a result of development and differentiation. The super-ego is a criticizing factor in us, a strictly negative judge of our deeds; while the ego-ideal is rather the image of ourselves in perfection against which

we measure our imperfections. The super-ego originates from a subconscious process by which we identify ourselves with, say, our father, setting up a parental image of perfection, and using it as a criterion for reference in the struggle of the ego with the impulses striving for satisfaction in their elemental form. Strange as it may seem, this super-ego again is not in the least a conscious part of ourselves, as the most important elements in it are formed in early childhood, and, as I said, reflect parental demands. Thus, it not only stabilizes infantile strivings in our mind but perpetuates ideals of former generations. By the very same mechanisms, namely, through which we have taken over these demands, through identification with our parents, the latter may have got them from their parents, so that they are mostly the reflection of a bygone age. Throughout life, the super-ego with its ego-ideal may take in new elements and may struggle to integrate the old ideas with the new ones; but only very seldom does that transformation occur in terms of a conscious selection. Consequently, if the ideals of the super-ego become too rigid, a time-lag develops between the changed conditions in our surroundings and the ideals of the bygone age, and the demands may become an impediment to reality-adjustment.

(a) There are, in the first place, unconscious influences at work on the unconscious spheres of the mind. As we have already seen, these unconscious parts of the mind are the drives themselves, or the unconscious part of the ego with its mechanisms. A direct influence on the drives themselves is hardly possible. They are mostly influenced indirectly through the unconscious or conscious parts of the ego. There is a continuous process of education of the drives, through these intermediaries. The unconscious part of the ego, for instance, is in continuous contact with influences coming from reality. Being an intermediary between the drives and environmental stimuli, it is the main agent of give and take between the world of the self and the world of environment. The most important influences upon the unconscious part of the ego occur as a result of trial and error processes. In them, the ego develops its power, and its mechanisms are set to work. As these processes of adjustment take place for the most part as unconscious responses, we cannot speak in any sense of conscious adaptation. In spite of this fact, there certainly exist correlations between typical social situations and typical ego responses, which have as yet not been sufficiently identified. Even the unconscious choice of the mechanisms must somehow depend on the circumstances of the environment. We do not yet know how society succeeds in inducing the ego in each particular case to use the appropriate mechanism—whether it be reaction-formation, sublimation, or mere repression—but it is a point of fact that different societies possess different techniques of social control, and thereby foster or hinder the development of certain psychological mechanisms. Victorian society, for instance, put a premium on reaction-formation—that militant prudery of which I spoke before. It would be worth while finding out how this came about. Indeed, it is the next task in the field of co-operation between psychoanalysis and sociology carefully to observe the way in which certain social mechanisms set in motion certain psychological mechanisms. But on this subject we shall have more to say at a later stage.

(b) Besides this influencing of the unconscious part of the ego, there is the unconscious influencing of the super-ego, where the operation of social influences becomes even more evident. The setting up of unconscious ideals and images, like that of the punishing but just Father, or the Good Samaritan, or the Gentleman, is the most obvious method of deeply impressing the mind without subjecting these ideals to rational criticism. As we can see, the unconscious influencing of the mind very often operates simultaneously on all its different levels according to the different opportunities for environmental conditioning.

It will be useful, therefore, before turning to the conscious influencing, to dwell just a little longer on the different forms and methods adopted by the unconscious social influences, as not every unconscious influence is of the same kind. Unconscious social influences occur in three ways:

(a) Firstly, through spontaneous unconscious adjustments to different situations. This is the method of trial and error we mentioned above, which mostly takes place on an unconscious level, although naturally at certain points it elevates itself to the level of conscious experimentation. But apart from conscious experiment, there is definitely a process continually going on, so to say on an organic level, where the body, with its activities, with the id and unconscious part of the ego, is carrying out adjustments to the environment without subjecting it to the criteria of rationality, without appealing to conscious judgment. This is the sphere where the smooth running-in of the living being into its own environment takes place, where that kind of organic balance between life conditions and internal adjustments is achieved that we call 'healthy'. These are the depths as yet unexplored, the concrete products of which could be studied in the mores and folk-ways of the different tribes, groups and classes where the nature of locality and of historical setting plays a great part. It is in this sphere of subconsciousness that the emigrant finds difficulties in adjusting himself to his new life. He will feel strange unless he is already beginning to share this unconscious patterning of life experience and those forms of adjustment which are peculiar to the new community.

(b) But it is not only through trial and error processes that this unconscious influencing occurs. There is another influence upon the mind which is not only unconscious, but also nearly mechanical. It is what we call the creation of conditioned reflexes and the making of habits. In them, contacts with the world are established in which our conscious decisions are not involved. Through them, automatic responses can be created, and, according to experiments made by behaviourists, just as these responses were originally built upon mechanical forms of conditioning, so they can equally well be de-conditioned (we can get rid of phobias and bad habits), and reconditioned. The idea of Habit Clinics is based upon the possibility of the unconscious conditioning or de-conditioning of certain spheres of the mind by clinical action. There is a very interesting discussion as to whether the findings of Pavlov, and of the behaviourists generally, are reconcilable with the hypotheses of the depth-psychologists, and of the psycho-analysts in particular. If the behaviourists were right, we should not need to penetrate the depths of the mind with the psycho-analyst. We could explain the most important forms of behaviour in terms of mechanical reactions. It cannot be doubted that there are such mechanical spheres in the mental and bodily organism which react like automata. But if I were to summarize the result of this discussion I should say that there were undoubtedly these automatic processes, but that they are embedded in an emotional setting, a disturbance of which will even prevent the automatism from functioning. Pavlov's dogs are good subjects for conditioning only if their general emotional state is in order.

(c) Apart from the unconscious trial and error process, and apart from mechanical conditioning, to which habit-making and drill belong, there is a third form of environmental influence—suggestion and hypnosis. Whatever their exact nature may be, it is definitely a fact that we can partly or wholly operate upon the mind through suggestion and hypnosis, which exclude its critical faculty. A great part of social guidance, as distinct from spontaneous trial and error and habit-making, is based upon these suggestive influences. There are certain social situations in which mass emotions are managed more easily and such suggestive influences are given a free rein.

Having dealt at some length with these unconscious influences, let us now turn to the impact of society on the conscious part of the mind, which means the conscious part of the ego. There is undoubtedly a considerable number of these as yet only very indistinctly observed influences. I wish to confine my discussion to four of them. Society influences the conscious part of the mind in four ways:

(a) through the method of intelligent adjustment on the part of the individual;

(b) through learning;

(c) through conscious education, to which belong re-education and post-education; and

(d) through psychoanalysis.

Here again, I think, the most natural and genuine form is the first one—intelligent adjustment. It is, so to say, a continuation of the process of trial and error, but this time in the light of conscious principles which, if systematically applied, may lead to totally new inventions in behaviour. The need for an intelligent rather than an unconscious adjustment becomes apparent when changed conditions render unconscious forms of adjustment useless. In these circumstances, the occasional flash of conscious and rational criticism and analysis of factors has to enter. A systematic elaboration of that rational and conscious technique in human affairs is the promise of a possible solution of the social and individual maladjustments which are a feature of our times. Only if we get into the habit, as we have done in our relationship to nature, of working out our psychological and social problems on the level of conscious self-criticism and rational analysis, can it be hoped that we shall cope with the new situation created by modern society. The technique of learning from our experiences in the light of conscious and rational thinking is the most gratifying way of dealing with the influences reaching our mind from the outside world.

If we make a distinction between intelligent adjustment and learning, it does perhaps involve a certain repetition of terms, since real learning is nothing but intelligent adjustment of our minds to nature and society. If nevertheless we speak about learning as if it were something different, it is because, in a highly developed civilization, we cannot try out everything concretely as a personal experience, and there is therefore a huge amount of collectively acquired knowledge in store, the incorporation and personal assimilation of which is a matter for a special technique. Although learning in its essential parts is rooted in the rational side of the ego, it would be wide of the mark to conceive of it as if it were purely intellectual activity, because all effective learning has to be linked up with the instinctive and emotional interests of the learner. Eliciting these interests, an operation often connected with the creation of social or spiritual rewards, is a part of that process of learning.

Thirdly, we must mention what we call conscious education.

Apart from the constant influencing of the different unconscious levels of the self as described, there is a conscious education at work, an education of the mind. When habits are formed, likes and dislikes conditioned, a certain facility in the use of experience and the trial and error process is gained. But we still have not got what could be called a complete education of the mind. The task of organizing these bits of acquired material and knowledge into an organic whole still remains. The simpler form of such an organization takes place through the super-ego and the ego-ideal which, as you will remember, may be completely unconscious. Even so, the function of the super-ego and ego-ideal is to work as an organizing agent in the world of personality formation. But our conscious education means more than this. It is based upon the creation of a conscience in which the system of principles which will be considered as the rules of conduct, the hierarchy of values by which we want to be guided, is subject to our conscious criticism. Conscious education is an arrangement of stimuli in such a way as to attain an individual responsible ego which is both able to discern good from bad, healthy from unhealthy influences, and to revise the values of its environment, and gradually to transform its behaviour appropriately.

If we make a distinction between conscious education and psychoanalysis, which is the last form of influencing the different levels of the self, it is because in psychoanalysis there has been discovered a technique by which we can operate with more or less success upon the different levels of the mind, and thereby bring about changes which would otherwise never, or only occasionally and haphazardly occur through the agency of the other processes we have described. Analysis is an operation by which the disturbed balance between the conscious and unconscious parts of the individual's mind is restored, and he is enabled once more to face the task of day-to-day adjustment to his surroundings. Its influence can for instance be directed on to the ego, in which case it may try to modify the operation of its mechanisms—to weaken or strengthen its control. It may try to work on the unconscious by bringing into consciousness dissociated material from the unconscious, which has to be re-assimilated in a healthy way. But it also operates on the level of the unconscious super-ego and ego-ideal, subjecting them to the conscious criticism of the ego. For instance, a cure very often consists in showing the patient that the unconsciously accepted parental ideal we have spoken about is too severe, and prevents him from making a sound adjustment to reality. In this case, a too abstract demand on the part of the super-ego is replaced through the analysis by sounder and more reasonable social norms. Promising as it may be in its future development, psychoanalysis is not yet so widespread as to be considered one of the established techniques by which modern society influences the psychology of the individual. It occasionally comes in as a remedial agency, but it is not an established everyday technique of influencing human behaviour.

Although my description has necessarily been a brief one, I have perhaps succeeded in showing that the moulding of the mind takes place on different planes, that mechanical conditioning is at least as important as adjustment through trial and error processes, and that the latter can be carried out with a greater or less degree of consciousness. We are mostly unaware of the wealth of forms in which unconscious and conscious influencing of the mind takes place, and how the points of attack of the environment upon the mind are dispersed. In what follows we shall not of course deal with all of them which might be called 'sociological'. There was a time when we were inclined to think that the formation of personality was mainly due to deliberate educational influences, of parent over child for instance, or of teacher over pupil, and so on. But as we have seen, these deliberate educational influences are only one set among the great many environmental influences which are at least equally important in the moulding of personality. One of the most decisive discoveries of our age is that social education is even more powerful than formal education, and that the educational value of a changing social context has hardly ever been adequately appreciated. When we speak of social education we mean the education which results from the fact that society through its established relationships, through its very texture, is continually moulding our personalities. If I were to say as shortly as possible what the meaning of social education is, I should say that we no longer think that the education of personality can emanate from a single focus, the classroom for instance, but that personality grows out of the social context and is to a large extent the result of social interaction. The most promising trend in education is the sociological approach which lays emphasis on the careful diagnosis of the social environment, and on a thorough elaboration of the influences at work on it. The making of a personality consists perhaps essentially in making responses to these influences at work in our environment, and sometimes the changing role of the person in the very same environment is more important for his future formation than any actual change in this environment itself. According to modern sociology, it is primarily through participation in different social groups and relationships that the character pattern develops. But these social relations are, as I said, no longer formulated in abstract terms. The great progress in sociology consists in the fact that all the various social relationships which were previously left unnoticed have now attracted the attention of the scientist, who is now able not only to identify each of them, but to diagnose their possible impact upon personality. I think even this sketchy description might have conveyed to you the impression that our earlier methods of influencing the mind or mobilizing its forces were in rather an infantile stage. We were mostly ignorant of what we were really doing and very often concentrated our attack on one level only, leaving it to chance whether the results thus achieved would be destroyed on another plane of the self. In our attempt to transform the individual in the direction desired we mostly failed because we satisfied ourselves with an influencing of the conscious parts of the ego. We thought, for example, that through preaching and enlightenment we should change the personality as a whole. Today we are becoming aware of the fact that enlightenment is only part of a total conditioning and reconditioning. It will remain inefficient unless the breaking up of old habits and the penetration into our super-ego transform the old emotional setting.

Psychology is on its way to detect the different entries into the mind. At the same time it tells us how to distinguish between different operational levels. Education (individual and social) is becoming a strategy and all the groups striving for influence are learning and will learn from it. The development of that strategy is neither good nor bad in itself, and like that of all techniques its value depends on the purpose for which it is used.

Having spoken so far of the different channels through which environmental influences have to pass, the next lectures will be devoted to the study of specific situations and social processes in their operation upon the mind, and we shall try to appreciate their impact on personality-formation.

Before the next lecture, it will be useful to say a word as to what we understand by personality. It is obvious that here, too, we can do no more than throw out a few hints, and we can offer no complete solution to the problem. But I hope they will suffice to save the discussion from becoming too vague. In order to make you appreciate the difficulty of defining personality, I only want to point out that one of the most recent writers on the subject, Allport, distinguished fifty meanings of the word in its current and scientific use! To us, in the first place, the term 'personality' will definitely mean uniqueness, or being different. If we put the question, whether planned society does not endanger the existence of personality, we surely first of all have in mind the idea of individualization; that is to say, we are afraid of too great a conformity which regulation may impose upon the individual. But it is obvious that this is only one aspect of the meaning of the term.

Even all the leaves of a tree are individualities, in the sense that none of them is exactly like all the rest or any other. Yet we surely would not be satisfied with a society which allowed great variety, but variety merely in a biological sense. The problem of personality formation can only be discussed in the sphere in which behaviour is being organized into conduct. Here we shall under-stand by 'personality' that kind of organization of the mind, specific to each individual, by which, through his mutual inter-action with the environment, he develops a pattern of inner organization which is unique in itself. It is this uniqueness on the level of personality formation which counts. This uniqueness expresses itself in the specific form of our organization of the materials of·experience, in a reorganization of our habit systems, in the development of new actions and work patterns, in the development of the capacity for taking the initiative and responsi-bility, and of having reflection and insight where others only muddle through. In this sense, it is a correct statement of Ander-son's, that personality is itself a form of adjustment; which means that you will only get individualization and individual personali-ties, where the social order itself needs the pioneering type—the type which is different—and creates it for itself by producing the scope for its development and bringing influences of a specific kind to bear on the minds of its members. In future lectures our task will therefore be to discover how former unregulated societies through their social processes further different elements of what we have just called a developed personality. Only if we know more about that shall we be able to ask ourselves whether a planned society, adequately organized, could provide us with social fields of opportunity which would really foster personalization. Our next task, therefore, will be to learn more about the nature of existing social processes and their impact upon personality formation.

The Impact of Social Processes on the Formation of Personality in the Light of Modern Sociology

PERHAPS one of the main reasons why present-day planned societies rely chiefly upon central regulations, ordering and command is that they have not as yet the knowledge of society and human behaviour which would enable them to use the spontaneous forces of society and to restrict interference to those fields where guidance and control are needed.

In the valuable book by Thomas and Znaniecki, *The Polish Peasant*, we find a very apt remark upon the origin of the magical attitude of primitive peoples. According to them, the magical attitude is an attempt at coercing nature in the same way as in decisive situations they coerced their fellow man. Thus the pattern of coercion penetrates even into the realm of nature. Even if we do not suppose that this is the only explanation of the origin of magic, it is certainly an important factor in its evolution.

This insight gives us the right approach to our problem, for the magical attitude was only given up when man learned another way of controlling nature, namely by finding the laws that regulate its behaviour. The same process of turning slowly from compulsion to understanding can be observed in education, save that there it meets with greater resistance and is as yet incomplete. Nevertheless it is a milestone on the road to progress in pedagogy whenever we find some means of replacing a command by getting a child to experiment with a situation and do the right thing spontaneously. It is better to show a child that he will hurt himself by playing with fire or a knife than simply to forbid him to do it.

So far we have only succeeded in effecting this replacement of command in relatively few fields, and this failure is closely linked up with our inability to control the social context in which adjustment occurs, and also with our lack of sociological knowledge which gives information about the main interrelations between human behaviour and situations. Never was the lack of a science of society more detrimental than in our age. For previous societies the knowledge of sociology would have been almost a luxury as they had not the necessary power to apply its results to the regulation of social processes. But today the opposite is true. Man often has the political power but not the knowledge which can prevent the misuse of that power. We can only replace the concept of a centralistic government based on command by a concept of planning based upon the use of the spontaneous forces of society if we have an insight into the nature of the very same social forces.

To this end I hope today to give a few examples of the significance of social factors in the formation of personality as they worked in the liberal, unregulated society, and I hope it will become evident how this knowledge might be extended if we were to devote as much energy to its study as has been devoted to the study of physical phenomena.

If you agreed with me in my first lecture, that planning in some form is inevitable and that we must make the best of it, and if you realize that in the long run an industrialized great society cannot do without individualization, and still more if you agree that the right form of planning does not entail conformity but rather uses spontaneous adjustment to controlled situations, then you will agree too that we have to direct our attention to that part of sociology which studies the social conditions of individualization.

In describing an historical epoch or society the social scientist should not be satisfied with accepting the object of his studies as a unique mystical entirety; instead it is necessary to investigate and analyse the various factors and situations and their interrelations which make up the broad and variegated canvas of that particular configuration. Only through this analytical approach shall we be able to visualize how the emergence and development of differentiated personality might be ensured in a planned society.

After the first lecture there is no need to refute such popular statements as 'the individual forms his own personality' and 'the Renaissance and the liberal age owe their great personalities to the lucky chance that a number of great men happened to ˙be born at the same time'. Even if one does not deny the importance of biological inheritance one can still assert that there must have been social situations and sets of factors which favoured the growth of these types. Only through an analytical approach, by breaking the mystical concept of the uniqueness of an age into a sum of smaller factors and situations, shall we be able to solve the riddle of what the nature of social configurations must be in a planned society so as to ensure the emergence and favourable development of differentiated personality.

My task is to replace such talk of ages of individualization by using the results of analytical and empirical observations to discover the relation between external situations and the growth of human personality. And although I am fully aware that our knowledge in this sphere is in its infancy I hope to convince you that there is much more accumulated experience than one usually expects and which simply needs survey and systematization.

In my account of these social factors and situations I shall start from the most obvious and simple forms of causation in order gradually to penetrate into the deeper levels of personality formation; so, in the course of this discussion, the concept of personality will be increasingly enriched. At the beginning individuality will only mean that the overt behaviour of a person is different from that of others.

One of the simplest external factors which produces differentiation of overt behaviour is isolation. In sociology we distinguish two kinds of isolation, of groups and of persons. Whenever a sub-group is separated from a larger one, as for example, after the settlement of migratory peoples in Europe when small sections of various tribes lived for centuries in secluded areas, then habits and ways of thought become different. Here the sociologist learned from the natural scientist. In nature too we are presented with the puzzle as to why we get different species from the same stock although the very same mechanism of adjustment is at work. The answer is that they have to adjust themselves to different surroundings.

The contrary of isolation is contact, and this usually leads to a diminution of differences. When hot and cold metals come into contact they tend to take on a common temperature. Just in the same way, people who meet many others tend, at least in those points on which contact is made, to adjust their behaviour, their attitudes, their views to one another. The process of give and take tends to produce a common atmosphere.

Another very obvious factor fostering individualization is division of labour, though it differentiates people into types rather than into individuals. The impact of professional differentiation on a person can sometimes be described with great exactness. It is very often possible clearly to enumerate the basic social factors and constellations prevailing in a trade or profession and to explain through them the typical professional attitudes and characteristics of individuals in professions. For instance, in his social monograph, *The Woman Who Waits*, Donovan describes the characteristic professional type of the waitress as 'markedly individualistic in her attitude to life and the state of her occupation as it exists today tends towards individualization. She does only what she has to do to earn her money and her only real interest is in the tip. In her work she does not often consider the house, the manager nor her fellow worker, but herself only, and she seldom hesitates to advance her own interests at the expense of others.'[1] Such a description does not mean that there are no unselfish and considerate waitresses, but simply that most of them are of this type. Perhaps this is the place to point out once and for all that the sociological statements made in these lectures merely aim at stating tendencies. Whereas the psychologist very often aims at predicting how a patient or an individual will develop, the sociologist attends to mass phenomena and formulates his predictions in terms of probabilities—if such and such conditions prevail, such and such psychological changes are likely to follow.

But not only overt behaviour in man can be influenced by regulated situations. There are well-defined circumstances which tend to incite or repress inner attitudes. Whether, for instance, people are capable of taking initiative or not may partly depend on their physical vitality or their gland system, but it is no less true that early conditioning plays a great role, and very often a planned social reconditioning might be successful.

Take, for instance, the experiments made by psychologists who observed children in the play room. One of the children in a given group took the initiative in 95 per cent of the cases whereas another in the same group did so only in 5 per cent of the cases. The old-fashioned psychologist would take this as a proof of inherited character differences in both of the children, whereas further experiments showed that if you put the child with 5 per cent initiative in a group in which he was not overwhelmed by a more successful type, he not only took the lead more often but he even improved his capacities by the greater number of opportunities and finally gave up his original shyness. Thus the organization of the group, i.e. whether it presents more or less opportunities of taking initiative to all the members, will react upon their characters. That character education can be planned by a skilful organization of the surroundings and methods can be shown by the example of the Montessori schools. A short anecdote I have seen quoted will illustrate what I mean:

'A Montessori teacher, told of a student who in her sixth semester did not yet know what she ought to study, said:

'"In a child who had gone through the Montessori system that would be impossible."'

The child in the Montessori school learns precisely and primarily this: to decide for himself, and to choose freely between possibilities which are given him.

The most suitable form of organization so far known making

[1] Frances Donovan, *The Woman Who Waits*, p. 128, Boston (Richard G. Badger, The Gorham Press), 1920.

for spontaneity in its members has been the democratic organization of small groups.

What people mostly tend to overlook is that democratization may take place in any field, not merely in the political one. A gang of workmen, a study group or an artistic group can all be organized on democratic lines. When it occurs in such small groups, democracy usually produces spontaneity and self-determination. But in a big state, a mass society, its healthy influence is largely checked. This is because democracy is only efficient if the individual feels that much depends on his peculiar and special decision and if others realize the importance of his contribution. But in a mass democracy the feeling that one is only a small and insignificant unit often discourages initiative. Thus small groups and minorities in a country are more likely to create individualized and fighting natures since they attribute great importance to single members, and, although they are at the same time part of a larger group, they are used to dissenting from the views of the majority. This leads me to another point. We usually attribute the freedom of thought to the freedom of the isolated individual. But to the sociologist it is in the long run not so much the freedom of the individual but the freedom of sects, cliques and other small groups which ensures free thought. The individual may achieve a good deal in certain fields and for a certain time, but it is the sect-like small group which really elaborates, propagates and defends new beliefs and the new experiments with life.

In modern times, with the decline of sects, the various and even more elastic group-forms in which we find the free-lance intelligentsia became the carriers of the new approach to life. To some the intelligentsia may seem an extravagance which in planned society could easily be replaced through some new status or rank like that of the clerics. But it is quite wrong to think that the fate of thought exclusively hinges upon the opportunities of education.

Thought is a social process, in which spontaneous experimentation of individuals and groups with varying situations in life, and the necessary integration of the will to action, plays a great role. The fate of the cognitive process on a large scale is based upon selection in which the struggle and the competition of groups decides upon the social efficiency of different ideas.[1] Mass society with its bureaucratic body is always too cumbersome and inelastic to take all the risks of adventures of thought which are needed in order to cope with changing reality. Once the intelligentsia as a group is exterminated or threatened mental dynamics

[1] Cf. 'Competition as an Intellectual Phenomenon', in K. Mannheim, *Essays on the Sociology of Knowledge*.

cannot keep pace with social dynamics. In this respect at least the Catholic Church as one of the great institutions which was first presented with the task of planning the social side of the cultural process shows its great social wisdom by allowing outsiders or partial outsiders to experiment on its periphery. When these outsiders are unsuccessful the Church disapproves, or even excommunicates them; but once they find successful forms of adjustment to changed surroundings their organizations are sometimes made fighting organizations in the Church itself. So it was with monastic orders and missionary groups like those of Cluny and the Jesuits, whose adventures of thought dealt not only with external situations but with the changing life of man, with the detection of new depths of the soul.

Some of this is also relevant to the study of the Soviet Union. For example the Webbs hinted at the fact that the Soviet system is not completely a dictatorship, for in many spheres of life, education and labour, there exist opportunities for stimulating spontaneity. The urge for self-determination is shifted from political struggle into the sphere of work. Even the humblest worker has opportunities of making suggestions for the improvement of the technique of production and management and the feeling of general experimentation kept incentive alive at the time when the Webbs observed them. However, this shifting of democratic chances into new realms does not compensate for one thing which will surely be detrimental to the further evolution of spontaneity, namely the suppression of quasi-sectarian organizations for free discussion, of an intelligentsia. Nor do their scientific experiments in the field of collective work, for instance where they try to find out in which social situation group work or individual work is more efficient, compensate for the integrating function of the intelligentsia. The bureaucratic mind and the mind of the scientist refines techniques of testing or surveys the fields of social reality, but cannot replace that kind of experience of life which grows out of immediate responses to changing situations. Here we have a case where it can be shown that planning, i.e. co-ordination rightly understood, cannot mean the ruthless carrying out of one principle. Although in a planned society it may be necessary to leave many functions which were formerly performed by competition to the scientist and the bureaucrat, one has to provide the scope in which free experimentation with the essential objectives of life is fostered. In the same way institutionalized channels have to be provided through which the new incentives produced by a kind of free-lance group (which is not handicapped by the burden of big organizations) can reach the planner. Unlike the demagogue, the sociologist is not compelled to think in terms of exclusive alternatives. To him only the right combination of institutions produces social systems which really work.

Any society needs some spheres where conformity is unavoidable but co-ordination, rightly understood, means that any sphere of enforced or spontaneous conformity has to be balanced by institutionalized freedom, such that in well-defined areas in life free experimentation with the fundamental issues is allowed. Otherwise society becomes so rigid that any essential improvement makes the destruction of the complete machinery necessary.

In order to illustrate what I have in mind when speaking about an institutionalized blending of conformity with freedom, let me mention an instance which was first described by Max Weber. According to his analysis, in classical India the main integrating force was ritual in which absolute conformity was observed and no deviation was allowed. Once one could rely upon its integrating power freedom was granted to any kind of thought or religious dogma. The sectarians could think whatever they wanted; even atheism was acknowledged. This has naturally only to be taken as a general pattern. Its application would mean a planning for freedom which differs from liberal freedom in so far as it is not left to chance where spontaneity has to set in but its scope (not its content) would be foreseen.

Thus we have seen how the most external things like isolation, division of labour, and the democratic organization of small groups affect personality. And although I do not think that the provision of opportunities for initiative is the only thing that builds up individuality, yet it goes a long way towards it.

A factor generally known as a social force making for spontaneity and to which many people almost exclusively attribute the individualizing power of the liberal age is free competition. Although this is generally acknowledged, few people could tell in terms of a more detailed analysis through which special mechanisms this initiative is brought about and under what conditions its forms vary. Sociologically speaking, free competition is a mechanism which compels the individual to adjust himself to his own peculiar situation and to take the initiative without waiting for command. This implies that the urge to self-adjustment is not completely innate; at least some social forces must be at work to get the urge trained and active, and even then it still depends upon the nature of these social forces whether the individual becomes used to individual adjustment or to collective group adjustment.

A reed blown by the wind moves differently around its axis if it stands by itself, or if it is part of a bunch: in the first case it is seeking for the best position in which it could stand as an individual; in the second as a part of a bunch. In the case of man, the optimum reaction is of a different kind if he is fighting for himself alone or for himself as a member of a group.

To both of these social mechanisms different types of mind correspond. If a man is brought up in a group in which forms of collective adjustments prevail, taboos are inculcated in the individual, everything in the world is explained in terms of a *Weltanschauung* which prevents him from reacting and thinking according to his own interest.

As long as this cohesion is secured there are in every society certain inhibited fields of the mind into which the individual's thought does not trespass. In an age of collectivism these taboos compelling the individual to self-denial may be of a magical or religious kind. In another more 'modern' form of collectivism it may be a belief in Communist or Fascist symbols which prevents him from doubting certain axioms.

Everything is quite different in such a community when free competition breaks through. At once it not only compels the individual to adapt himself to his own peculiar situation, but in the long run leads him to an increase of rational and calculating behaviour which can no longer acknowledge any inhibited fields. By adjusting himself to his individual situation he is increasingly brought into conflict with the formerly established taboos with collectively established definitions of the situation which he is obliged to abolish if he is to survive. Thus radical rationalism, scepticism, limitless calculation related to the peculiar interest of the individual are the unavoidable consequence and follow irresistibly. In my view, the age of Enlightenment from the Renaissance to liberalism is nothing but the mental product of the social mechanism of free competition and individual adjustment. Once free scope is given to this personal adjustment by giving certain people opportunity for full initiative and complete personal responsibility related exclusively to their own interest, then the inevitable consequence will be that they will continuously redefine all situations from the personal angle and thus acquire the habit of limitless rational analysis. Conversely, the abolition of free competition and the re-establishment of collective adjustment will largely limit the natural chances of enlightenment, and it is all the more necessary to compensate for this loss in rationalization by some other means, such as by creating fields where rational analysis is not only allowed but even fostered. Whereas it is the danger of competitive society that it tends to dissolve the ultimate soical bond of consensus, the danger of planned society is that it extends the necessary minimum of conformity to everything, and people lose the rational and critical power without which an industrial society cannot survive.

No one will deny that in Fascist states this inculcated credulity and enforced belief in the leader and in irrational arguments may lead to some catastrophe. In the long run I am not less sceptical about the fate of Communism if the exaggerated attitudes of belief and credulity are not limited to certain fields. It seems to be a rule of nature as well as of healthy social growth that the necessary variations should not be suppressed if organic adjustment to unexpected new conditions is to remain possible. Institutions are bound to decay which suppress all forms other than those which conform to their standards.

Real co-ordination means not so much the limitless extension of one principle but the provision of scope for the growth of the necessary attitudes.

As far as the Russians dealt with this problem in practice, they came to replace individual competition not so much by complete collectivism as by competition between groups. The latter has the advantage that it shifts competition from the individual to the group; thus it still excites ambition and increases initiative and efficiency, without loosening the social bond and without enhancing individual desires. The more individual chances they give and the more individual ambition they raise, the greater are the elements of dissent which may grow up, individual competition ceaselessly forming disruptive forces.

Another distinction that has to be made within the general concept of competition is between competition based on property and competition divorced from it. What the liberals did not understand and what the Russians in spite of many failures have proved by experiment is that competitiveness, acquisitiveness, and property sense are not in the least identical, but were rather an historical combination of attitudes united into one single complex in our society. Whereas it was often imagined that the competitive impulse worked only when strictly linked with acquisitiveness and property sense, Soviet experiments with society have shown that under certain circumstances competition works without being fostered by acquisitiveness and property sense. It is true that to a certain extent the Soviets were ultimately compelled to reintroduce the acquisitive spirit (although not the property sense); but the sociologist should not explain that political move by a rough-and-ready reference to 'eternal human nature', which allegedly could not forego property, but he must seek out those peculiar social conditions which made these changes necessary.

Never and nowhere should a sociologist's view and understanding of any social phenomenon be biased by his personal likes or dislikes; thus to him the Russian development is a test case, which he will not view as something that will either confirm or refute certain prejudices and general ideas *en bloc*, but rather as a great social experiment where every success and every failure should be carefully analysed from a comprehensive sociological point of view. This at least should be the attitude of those who realize that some sort of planning is bound to come everywhere, whether we like it or not, and ours should integrate into the new framework the Western tradition of freedom and democracy.

Now I come to discuss another problem: that of individualization as reflected in the fundamental wishes of man (and which to the economist is as important as that of working incentives), and that of the sociological determination of preferences and choice. It is one of the axioms of liberal economics that consumer's choice, being an ultimate and irreducible psychological factor, was necessarily the ultimate driving force of any successful economic system. But though consumer's choice may be a final element in a liberal system, it is not a final element in other economic systems, and is certainly not genuine from the point of view of a sociologist. I go so far as to risk the statement that to choose rather than to stick to values dictated by tradition and custom is a very exceptional attitude. The preference for choice is characteristic only of societies in transition or others in which a fundamental consensus is lacking, the varied choice of consumers being only one aspect of this lack of consensus.

Such a period of transition and lack of consensus is that between the dissolution of medieval society and the planned society which is now in the process of formation.

Man is presented with two possibilities: either he can enjoy a similar kipper for breakfast every day of the year according to the standards of his country, or else he can enjoy eating all conceivable breakfasts on different days. Again there are those who prefer to vary their neckties and those who are wedded to the same one.

Man is not born with a desire for variety, he can be conditioned in either way. There are social mechanisms which make for traditional conformity, and others which make for choice. Psychologically speaking, in one case our wishes or libidinous energies are directed to definite objects according to the traditions of our society, while in societies with great social mobility the libido is directed not so much towards a determined object as to the art of choosing. Thus in traditional societies the limitation of choice is considered as moral and beneficial, and in mobile ones we come to enjoy choosing for its own sake.

Under no conditions is the consumer's choice an insurmountable obstacle in the way of changing the liberal form of the capitalist order, because nothing can be reconditioned more easily by a planned society than the wish for a variety of goods.

The formation of wishes which will later lead to economic preferences is shaped first of all by the primary group, such as the family during childhood. If in childhood a person is so conditioned as to stick to certain traditional objects, the predilection for a certain kind of behaviour, a certain dress and certain foods will prevail. But when a child is spoiled, if for example he is given too many toys to play with, he will, even in after life, continuously seek for variety, and a craving for new sensations will determine his attitudes.

There are other factors, too, which affect the instability of wishes, among them, as I have pointed out, social mobility. People who travel much and live in different countries often get into the habit of desiring variety. Furthermore, in a competitive economy the rivalry between firms leads to a deliberate and continuous endeavour to implant new wishes among consumers and to promote a craving to surpass in quality and novelty the choice of one's neighbour.

This tendency is partly counteracted by the growth of large-scale industry, as this brings standardization in its train. This is enhanced by industrial propaganda and advertisement, which also in part lead to a standardization of taste. This process, which is present in late capitalism, reaches its peak in communistic planned societies where, in order to make planning easier, standardization is pushed still further without the slightest opposition from consumers who, as there is no competition, simply forget the desire for choice or even for better quality.

At least this is the impression one gets on reading André Gide's *Return from the Soviet Union*. According to him, and it is mentioned also by others, Soviet products are of very bad quality, but consumers do not complain about it. A craving for better quality and taste, he says, arises only if comparison and choice are permitted. But if no one dresses better than I, then I have no urge to get a better cut suit or one made of better material.

However it is not very easy to decide whether, in the case of the Soviet Union, it is rather the need to produce great quantities quickly which leads to the neglect of quality or simply the elimination of consumer's choice. In the latter case one could argue that in a planned society the improvement of taste and quality could be secured by leaving the selection of designs to competition among designers and other specialists.

Here again the guilds are an example of how the loss of incentive for improving the quality may be compensated in a planned society by some other means. The guilds introduced all kinds of competition on a non-economic basis in order to increase the sense for quality by forming boards composed of master craftsmen, committees who had to distribute prizes and to acknowledge masterpieces. This was so strong that it even became a method for judging literary production, as in the case of the *Meistersinger*.

In the cases so far analysed I have tried to show you how deeply the nature of overt behaviour and of prevailing attitudes is influenced by whether various forces making for individualization are at work or their opposites. Now I wish to present a case where the working of social forces is reflected in individualization on an even higher plane, on the level of introspective and self-regarding attitudes.

By introspective and self-regarding attitudes we usually understand attitudes which are not directed to the external world but towards the self, and the latter mean especially the ways in which we conceive of our personal worth or existence.

The field of self-evaluation was mostly regarded by philosophers and psychologists of the liberal age as an exclusive product of the individual mind attained through introspection. Contrary to the older theory, not only the becoming different in overt behaviour but also the awareness of our specific character and value proceed from the external to the internal; and it is mainly by this changing process of self-evaluation that society changes its members.

Self-evaluation may be based on different factors. In some societies it depends upon physical strength and power or fame or money. Originally, physical strength was probably most important. It can even be seen at work in animal societies. There it is primarily physical power, though sometimes some psychological superiority too, such as perseverance or courage and daring, which leads to the social acknowledgment of the leading animal. If we take the history of autobiography, there we can see the same sort of thing at work. This desire to see one's power reflected in the fear of others was the first impulse to the writing of a kind of autobiography. The feeling of strength and power and the desire to see one's power reflected in the fear of others is the first crude form of the individualization of the self-regarding attitudes which is found in despotic states only among the kings and nobles. Let us see how it looks at this early stage. I am going to quote a passage from the *Death Record of the Assyrian King Assurnasirpal*:

'I am the king. I am the Lord. I am the Sublime. I am the great, the strong, the famous. I am the Prince, the Noble, the War Lord. 'I am a Lion. . . . I am God's own appointed. I am the unconquerable weapon which lays the land of the enemies in ruins. I captured them alive and stuck them on poles. I covered the mountains like wool with their blood. From many of them I tore off the skin and covered the walls with it. I built a pillar of still living bodies and another of heads. And in the middle I hung their heads on vines.

'I prepared a colossal picture of my royal personage and inscribed my might and sublimity upon it. My face radiates on the ruins, in the service of my fury I find my satisfaction.'

This self-glorification which cannot be contradicted rests upon a false interpretation of the source of power. The king or despot attributes to his personal virtues and prowess what is really the result of centuries of power accumulation. He fails to see that it is not he who is almighty, but his position. The social position produces the despot and not the other way round.

Democracy is based on the existence of many individuals of equal power, so that the despotic strivings of each are checked by the others. When this is the case an attitude of humility and modesty will cloak the desire for self-assertion. When we say 'Your humble servant' to one another, frustrated despot calls to frustrated despot.

On the whole the social origin of self-esteem was a kind of introjection of external prestige. People first acknowledge one's superiority according to the nature of changing society which puts a premium on different types, then individuals themselves get hold of their social acknowledgment and unconsciously organize around it their personality traits.

Self-esteem varies with the social structure. When a society needs the individualized heroic personality, as for example in the Homeric age in Greece, or among the Germanic tribes when they were fighting the Roman Empire, it is heroism and initiative which are socially admired and which set the standard of self-appraisal. If landed property is the basis of aristocracy and family prestige is dependent upon land ownership, then there is an identification with the soil wholly unknown to the élites of mobile property, to whom it is money and property in general which give prestige and not any particular form of it. Again, in literary circles it is fame and acknowledgment which make for prestige, and there it is the uniqueness of personality which is conceived of as a specific value.

Thus self-evaluation is a fulcrum by which one can centrally influence personality traits and their integration. While even unplanned societies were, more or less consciously, busy in influencing these external sources of self-evaluation, in planned societies this can be done much more easily, as all the key positions and the objectives upon which self-evaluation depends are controlled by the planners. It is, however, not enough merely to change the standards of self-respect, and the behaviourists are right in saying that if petty habits are not changed one by one, then it is impossible to change the personality simply from the centre. Nevertheless if the two processes proceed together and the self aids in the integration of external forces, then the transformation is far more easy and more successful.

This internal source of readjustment was adequately taken into account by the liberal theory, but that theory failed because it rushed too quickly to the centre of the self and omitted the more external, elementary, almost mechanical factors in the formation of character. This neglect of detailed observation of these lower and external but integral forces was a stultifying handicap.

Finally, there is an even more complex stage in the formation of self-regarding attitudes which, though one might not expect it, can also be traced to certain social conditions. However much self-esteem might primarily develop from without, there comes a point where it is no longer derived from the social mask of prestige based on physical prowess, money or fame, but rather from purely internal qualities.

This occurs when the introverted type plays off the values of the inner self against the external sources of prestige, when the ultimate source of valuations is shifted from the external social sphere into the uniqueness of one's inner character. About this process of internalization of values I shall have to say a few words in my next lecture.

Today, I wish to confine the remaining remarks to one single phase in this evolution, when not only the uniqueness of the personality but the uniqueness of one's life history becomes realized.

To us it is common sense to think in terms of life history, to interpret our characters as the outcome of the peculiar experiences we had in the past. If we look at history we suddenly realize that a concept of life history was not in the least self-evident, but that it had to be worked out by a few pioneering individuals in a peculiar historical situation from the very beginning.

Historical research brought home to us the knowledge that it was the achievement of the Stoics first to work out the concept of inner life history. They were the founders of a new kind of autobiography, of an autobiography in which the individual reaches the stage of understanding of the self not so much by referring to the framework of some external events as by recalling earlier experiences in the context of his inner life history.

In the light of this approach no one is either too humble or too poor for his soul not to have had its own experiences and triumphs which are even more important than great empires. The historical origins of this individualized concept of the inner self are to be found in the history of the late Roman Empire. The writing of autobiographies in the sense of an inner life history is initiated by the Stoics and reaches its peak in St. Augustine.

Faced with this very subtle form of individualization of the inner self one would expect no social external causes to be responsible for it. But the present stage of research enables us to hint at those social changes in the world which very likely are the ultimate sources of this type of transformation of the self. The Stoics are an early type of highly individualized intelligentsia who after the breakdown of the empire are left without the external frame of reference of the polity.

As long as the communal spirit prevailed among the citizens of classical antiquity, the frame of reference of the world and of personal life was the sacred polity. As soon as the idea of the polity disappeared, it seemed as if the scaffolding of life were withdrawn. The unrest which followed was only partly due to external disturbances; internally it was caused by the vanishing of a centre to which one can relate experiences. The unrest did not cease until, by a process of internalization, a new ultimate source of values was slowly worked out. This new source of values was the concept of an internal life and an internal life history. One might imagine that if during the next decades after the world war chaos were to follow, with the downfall of national states and the dissolution of the Empire, and with the collapse of hopes in Communism and Fascism, the few intellectuals surviving in some hidden nooks would in the same way think again exclusively in terms of such extremely individualistic concepts. Having followed up the implications of the sociological concept of the self I have tried to show how in non-planned societies isolation, division of labour, competition, democratization, etc., react not only upon the overt behaviour but on the initiative, wishes, preferences and choice of man, and even upon the self as it is reflected on the level of self-regarding attitudes, in self-esteem and in the concept of the uniqueness of the self.

I hope to have at least conveyed to you the idea that by a careful research in this field one could open up some new avenues to a better understanding of the making of man in changing society. In my next lecture I shall try to answer two questions: (1) How far could planned society make use of such sociological insights into the nature of social forces and situations making for individualization, if planning were not to mean to the planners planning for conformity. (2) Secondly, we must at least touch upon the question of where the limitations of both the sociological concept of the self and of planning based upon it become apparent.

FOURTH LECTURE

Limits of the Sociological Approach to Personality and the Emergence of the New Democratic Idea of Planning

THE task of the last lecture was to convince you that even in unplanned societies a conditioning of behaviour is going on perpetually. Individualization on different levels takes place in different societies and under different social conditions. Not only can external traits be induced or modified by adequately changed surroundings, not only is there a well-defined mechanism which furthers or prevents the growth of spontaneity and favours or suppresses the rise of an individual viewpoint, but even such complex phenomena as man's self-evaluation and the estimation of his own life history as something unique can be correlated with definite social situations. Thus on the level of self-awareness and of self-regarding attitudes too there is external social conditioning, and social authorities therefore are able to foster or hinder their formation.

We have always to remember that guidance of the formation of personality can take place not only in the form of command and repression but also through arranging the environment in a certain way, particularly the social environment. The thorough analysis of the social environment, the breaking up of its totality into factors, is the new method which will bridge this gap in our knowledge and lead to a scientific control of man by man.

In the first half of my lecture today I have to say a few words more about the social factors making for the introjection of experiences and for the widespread emergence of the introverted type.

To the psychologist of individuality introversion and extraversion appear merely to depend either on the inherited constitution or on the structure of personality acquired during childhood. And indeed we need not deny that with certain individuals factors either inherited or acquired in early childhood may be so strong as to block the influences of adult life.

The experience of the psychologist treating more or less neurotic types tends to confirm a belief in the unchangeability of the human type once formed. But the historian and sociologist must not let this invalidate his knowledge and experience, which tends rather to show that human nature in general is more elastic than the psychologist expects it to be.

Thus it was observed that during revolutionary periods or during a general boom, when formerly passive groups are suddenly presented with opportunities for action, a general spirit of enterprise prevails; whereas in counter-revolutionary periods or in phases of economic depression when these chances disappear, a spirit of introversion and quietism may follow. Such a period of general extraversion was, for instance, that of the French Revolution; whereas in the atmosphere of the reaction after the Napoleonic wars in Germany, for instance, a romanticist introversion followed. By studying the life-history of representative personalities at different periods we can often see how their character traits and attitudes vary according to changes in the social structure. The individual concerned tends to experience these transformations in terms of some catharsis or redemption by which he condemns his former life as too worldly or too passive, as the case may be.

We mostly connect the ideal of a highly individualized personality with his having a differentiated inner life. But this is to confuse individualization with introversion. Individualization merely means acquiring a richer pattern of attitudes towards either the external world or towards the self: and this process may be connected both with introversion and with extraversion. Thus we get the extraverted individualized type like Napoleon or the introverted individualized type like St. Augustine—or even mixed types. The distinction is important because, as we have seen, quite different social forces are at work in making for general introversion or extraversion.

Usually man's overt behaviour is affected first; then he becomes aware of this difference and consciously cultivates it. Finally, there is a period in which the differentiation penetrates the deepest layer of his personality.

Modern sociology does not like to speak in terms of stages because we cannot foresee in which sequence the external historical and social situations may follow each other and we have therefore carefully to watch sequences in the transformation of personality in strict correlation to the changing surroundings.

Nevertheless, since in this lecture our aim is to raise problems rather than to solve them, it will do no harm if we state, in a somewhat over-simplified manner, that in our own civilization the main historic trend was from an external individualization to an internalized one, as can be shown in the change of the meaning of words such as 'noble' or 'villain', which once signified external social rank but have now come to indicate internal character traits.

I think what happened to the word 'noble' happened also to other phenomena; and the internalization of values is only a symptom of the general trend towards internalization of former external qualities. For example, 'sin' formerly meant external pollution, contact with tabooed objects, after which ceremonial purification or cleansing was necessary. Later, by introjection, sin became internal pollution and the soul was cleansed by spiritual expiation.

As I said before, there are many complex factors and situations which are responsible for these changes, especially for the process of internalization of values and for the spread of the introverted personality. But let me deal at least with one social factor in detail which to me seems to be an extremely important one in discussing the origins of introversion in our culture.

A close connection can be observed between the growth of cities and mysticism in the late Middle Ages. The growth of lay orders and sects is a symptom of individualization combined with introversion. I think the sociological factor responsible for this is primarily the new conditions of city life and the democratizing process which suddenly changes the sources of self-evaluation.

As to the changing conditions brought about by the growth of cities, the increase of handicrafts and commerce created a great deal of leisure and with it opportunities for individual solitude. The original forms of a communal spending of leisure, although at first very elaborate in the guilds, gradually declined.

With the growth of cities the number of business contacts lacking in intimacy increases, anonymity prevails and the individual no longer feels sheltered in public. He therefore seeks privacy either by withdrawing into his family circle or into individual solitude. ,

To these changes in the external surroundings correspond changes in the mental setting which exercise a profound influence upon the individual. Among these mental changes none was as important as the change in the sources of self-evaluation just alluded to. Let us examine for the moment these changing sources of self-evaluation in the light of their impact upon the growth of introversion.

If we first look at societies in the heroic age, e.g. of the Homeric type, or the Germanic tribes where continuous warfare prevails, the self-esteem of the hero tends to be based on his visible behaviour or even on his physical appearance. The hero is not an introverted type, not merely because he continuously expresses his emotion in external action but also because his self-respect rests on such external facts as his strength and his deeds. These qualities, which are most highly esteemed by the group, will be those upon which the individual too will base his self-evaluation.

In a society based on rank, such as feudalism, and even in cities as long as the mentality of rich burghers is dominant, the final source of prestige in many classes is still found mainly in the outside world. The social status of the feudal lord is primarily based upon land, and that of the rich burgher upon wealth and family extraction. If we look at the portraits of rich burghers, we feel that their self-evaluation almost resides in their attire, that they are conscious that everyone knows them and their descent. We feel that as long as society is primarily ordered by rank, everybody, even the handicraftsman and the peasant, lives on borrowed prestige, i.e. on the prestige of his rank. He feels safe and secure because his status, even if it is relatively low, is well defined, known to everybody, and there is no need to fight for it. But if the son of such a man were to come to a large city in which anonymity was a characteristic feature and where he could no longer rely upon other people's knowledge of his family and social status, then a feeling of great uncertainty and insecurity would arise. This sudden disappearance of the external basis of self-evaluation would lead him to seek to restore his psychological equilibrium by some other means.

This is what happens even today to all who come to large towns from places where status and position are well defined, as for example on the family estate or in some small village. It is very likely with many of them that among the younger generation of such immigrants the source of self-evaluation will shift to the inner personality as a kind of compensation. In Europe this transformation occurs in a succession of waves from the introversion characteristic of the early sects and the mystical currents in the new lay orders of the cities to the more secularized Romantic revival of the early nineteenth century.

In a thorough, even statistical, analysis of the social origins of the early romantic intelligentsia in Britain and Germany, the German scholar Schöffler observed how they were recruited mainly from amongst the younger sons of pastors and ministers who, on coming to the towns, became an intellectual proletariat. In this situation they projected their own insecurity feeling on to the world, working out a *Weltanschauung* along the lines of old religious patterns of introversion but using them no longer in connection with their former dogmatic religious frame of reference.

These appear to me some of the social and psychological origins of the new self-evaluation, of withdrawal from the world, of acute self-analysis, and of a belief that differentiated sentiment and internal values are what make personality important. The insecurity of the isolated person in the process of the dissolution of a society based on rank, combined with the anonymity in cities, compels groups of individuals to replace the lost outward guarantee of their self-esteem by playing off inner worth against external prestige.

But this is only the first half of the story, and the social dynamics of modern society could not be understood without realizing how important these introverted personalities became for the transformation of the external world.

These individuals who experienced insecurity in a changing world on a deeper level than the rest were driven into an increasingly painful state of introversion and self-analysis. In such situations, when the individual cannot bear the torments of the self, frantic rushes into social reality may easily follow.[1] This is the reason why in Western society since the time of the sects these introverted types have very often become reformers in various fields, and these hidden experiences of the soul are the ultimate sources of utopian strivings.

There is another form of individualization too which although similar to the first has to be analysed if one wants to understand the dynamics of modern capitalist mass societies. This is the modern phenomenon of privacy, especially the privacy of inner life.

I think the correct definition of privacy was given by Max Geiger when he called it a walling off of a sphere in one's inner self from contact with the outer world, a withdrawal of a set of values from public control. The consequence of this elimination of public control is that it prevents the ironing out of peculiarities through contact with others. The inner core of the secluded self differentiates itself and sets itself against the public norm and the stereotypes which work in society. Such a process of becoming private in our inner life may be partial or total. The life of most of the monastic orders aims at complete privacy, whereas the ideal of the lay mystics and lay brotherhoods was to link up the privacy of the soul with the surface attitudes operating in ordinary life.

That the nature of the social setting is important in the creation or prevention of privacy becomes evident if it is remembered how village life makes it difficult to maintain such privacy. In a world of mutual assistance there is always an opportunity for the neighbour

[1] H. Lasswell, *World Politics and Personal Insecurity*, p. 80, New York and London (Whittlesey House, McGraw-Hill), 1935.

to see what is cooking in the pot, and although in the village there may be types who desire privacy, there is no strict division between what is private and what is public and no acknowledged right to privacy.

Similarly, in early city life the guilds still tended to control the whole life of their members and their attitudes of all kinds. It was principally the Reformation which gave shape and ideological legitimation to this growing wish for privacy and the individualization of the core of our self. From that time our conscience was immediately responsible to God alone and free from the control of any earthly power. Once established, these inner attitudes, though sanctioned first by religion, play an important role in secularized society too, and they form the nucleus for the liberal concept of personality, blending as it does external political freedom with freedom of conscience.

This right to introversion and privacy is one of the strongest guarantees of a reorganization of society. As long as these spheres of privacy and internalization are not wholly cut off from the social order and are not separated by institutional barriers from the world in one way or other, the distance gained through seclusion will react in a healthy way upon the transformation of the worldly order.

This was quite different in the Far East where introverted saints were almost wholly concerned with passivity and endurance. The psychoanalyst Robert Wälder distinguishes two ways of adjustment of the world. One he calls autoplastic (that is, we change ourselves rather than the world), and the other, alloplastic (that is, we prefer to change the world rather than ourselves). We may say, in terms of this distinction, that the prevailing attitude in Europe was alloplastic, always ready to change the world, whereas in Eastern society autoplastic attitudes prevailed.

If we ask how the Soviet Union has dealt with these phenomena, we get the impression that the introverted types have been almost eliminated. A member of a Kolkhoz spends all his time with his comrades both in his work and in his leisure. His room is nothing but a sleeping cabin. The worker's interests are invested in the club and its life, and in the parks of Rest and Culture. This preparation for an all-absorbing community life which will kill the possibility of individualization even on the level of private attitudes is found particularly in the socialization of the child. In this annihilation of private life not only are many attractive nuances and shades of the European tradition lost but society is deprived of its deepest psychological driving forces.

For to withdraw into the areas of privacy is something like pioneering into a new province of the soul. What the solitary man finds there for himself becomes at the next stage a new experiment for the rest of the community. How else could Nietzsche find in his solitary house in the Engadine and in the solitary experiences of his illness a new diagnosis of modern life and the new patterns for its productive harnessing? At that period when the new Germany built up its imperialist structure under Bismarck and the new industrial leaders in a temporary phase of prosperity displayed the neurotic self-assertiveness of the extraverted get-rich-quick mentality, Nietzsche unlocked the entrance to the unconscious, forecast the modern analysis of the mind and gave the first expression to the re-evaluation of the century to come.

Society needed this outsider in order to understand its own deepest potentialities. But what of a society which not only forbids such a type to influence others but prevents its very emergence through its social mechanism? We cannot avoid asking: 'Does prevention of privacy and introversion belong to the very essence of planned society or is it merely a Russian misinterpretation?'

This leads me to the main question with which I want to deal, namely, whether everything that is now happening in the Soviet Union, not to say Germany and Italy, represents the ultimate possibilities of planning and can be taken over without further analysis as an answer to the theoretical problem of planning as such.

The question is, which among the shortcomings of the Soviet system as it exists today are due simply to the extremely bad conditions that were inherited from the old regime, and which are inherent in the nature of the system itself? Which among its achievements are due to the original *élan* of the first revolutionary generation only with its faith in utopian visions, and which to Communism? And which of the deteriorations are due to the Stalinist brand of bureaucracy? How can we disentangle which shortcomings and advantages belong to planned society and which do not? This can only be done through a theoretical analysis which breaks up huge social complexes into their constituent factors and tries to observe to which of these social factors various mental traits belong. Only new institutions which by themselves stimulate the necessary new incentives and modes of behaviour can be considered as creations of the new system as such.

In this connection we must not forget that the pioneer types of the first generation in the Soviet Union were not the products of the new system, but the highly individualized social representatives of an older society which, even if it did not want them, yet left them with some possibility of evolving along their own lines. Such miracles of achievement as the Bolsheviks performed at the beginning of their regime are typical accomplishments of confident pioneering groups in general. But if we are concerned with the problem of individuality, we want to know what will happen in the long run when this generation dies out, as the tendency of most of the institutions they erect is to check the growth of individualized types.

Another point that must be borne in mind is that in the U.S.S.R. a general experimentation is still going on. The necessity for this in a period when the central bureaucracy has not yet sufficient knowledge to manage this immense country is in itself something which offers a chance for the growth of individualized personalities in factories, in the schools, and on the collective farms. This chance will perhaps gradually vanish, when the main patterns of administration, education, etc., have been crystallized, and then the tendency towards stereotypes and inertia may become much greater. People who are not trained in sociological analysis tend to believe that it is only the suppression of free thought which is making for the prevailing uniformity, and thus they are hopeful that such an intellectual freedom may be later admitted.

But it is not only the suppression of free thought which hinders individualization; even more important in the annihilation of individuality are all the other social factors and their co-ordinated operation. Whilst Tsarist Russia with its absolutism could not suppress the growth of very marked individualist thinkers and politicians simply because it could not reach into all the nooks and crannies of society, a dictatorship in a planned society is much more detrimental to the growth of individualization than any earlier form of tyranny and absolutism.

One could argue, however, that in Russia this phase is due in part to the need to turn ignorant peasants into skilled workers in a very short time, which necessitates mass education and re-education rather than the creation of differentiated types. One might suggest that the original dogmatism is only characteristic of the period when the whole system is still insecure and the leaders imagine it is necessary to watch all deviations. But even here it is a very dangerous thing to transfer expectations concerning typical trends in a liberal society from a liberal into a planned society. Marxist dialecticians are wont to stress that the sociological laws of evolution of the liberal era are no longer applicable to the socialist phase. Still, one is justified in asking whether certain positive potentialities of the liberal era will not be lost at that stage. It may be true only of non-planned societies that such things as dogmatism disappear in the course of time or that the tendency towards conformity gives place to an inner differentiation. Only where free adjustment continually produces a free transformation can one count on trends which automatically rule out dogmatism. It is the paradox of planned society that there are far greater possibilities of correcting mistakes at the beginning than there are later, when the outlines are definitely set up. In planned societies much more depends on the insights and original concepts and even dogmatism of the élites than in one which is more or less growing without interference and planning.

But if planned society is lacking in that elasticity which in liberal societies makes for spontaneous adjustment, it is all the more necessary to free the way for a new type of thinking which is anxious of its own accord to get hold of those corrections which in liberal societies are produced by a free integration of counter-acting tendencies; it is the more important to create institutions which on a higher plane provide some sort of substitute for the elasticity of unregulated society.

Whenever in the past in some partial field some rational organization had to replace the rules of spontaneous adjustment (as for instance when small shops developed into department stores) the organizer had to think on behalf of the whole and had to transform the principles of struggle of all against all into controlled competition between departments in favour of the whole system. He had to build into the social machinery safety valves where formerly free interplay was the natural thing. In the same way, when the whole economic and social fabric of a country is united in a plan, the plan should not only provide those regulations which guarantee conformity, but should also provide areas of activity that must remain free and that will make for individualization.

Thus two problems have to be answered:

1. Is it possible that a new kind of thinking will grow up which realises its own limitations and anticipates the justified arguments of its opponents?

2. Is it conceivable that freedom and the growth of personality are not the result of *laisser-faire* but are planned in a new sense of the term?

As to the first question, it is quite conceivable that the new situation produces a new type of thinking, just as it can be shown that in history the new forms of thought always answered the unspoken demands of changing society. In order to make more concrete what I mean by a new type of thinking which itself realizes its limits and makes use of the correct arguments of its adversary, let me turn to the analysis of the controversy between the liberal and the sociological concept of the self.

In my previous lectures, I first argued against a purely idealistic, liberal concept of personality which as a result of extreme internationalization treats it as a symbol rather than as a concept based on observation of facts. Against this introverted concept, I have tried to emphasize all the facts and possibilities which present themselves to those who devote their whole attention to a closer analysis of the interdependence of the ego and the environment and lay due stress on the potentialities of the latter.

However, the more we follow up the new possibilities of influencing the growth of the self by shaping the environment, the less can· we deny that in its turn the new externalization and analytic dismemberment tends to neglect certain elements whose complete omission may be as dangerous as the neglect of the environment. This perhaps brings us back to a certain extent to that concept of personality which underlies liberal thought. Nevertheless I do not think that the liberal argument emerges out of this discussion in the same form as before meeting the challenge of the sociological.approach to the study of personality.

I want to mention at least two of those danger spots in the sociological concept of the self which have to be realized by the planner himself if he wants to rise above a partisan view.

1. The limitless manipulation of the environment means the limitless manipulation of the self and does not improve but kills the personality centre.

2. The transfer of the methods of the natural sciences in the sense of mechanical patterns into the field of society is possible as long as partial management is attempted, but a new approach is needed if total management becomes necessary.

As to the first point, we have seen that the original idea of the sociological concept of the self was inspired by the wish to rebuild man through a regulation of his surroundings. We have seen how this idea in its growth first got hold of the immediate surroundings like the home, the school, the workshop. Later, we said, it developed into the control of regional units and at last it expanded so as to control the total area of a country, using the new social technique to regulate everything from a centre, from the new key positions of society.

Besides these methods of conditioning the self on different levels of its existence by various social factors, another expansion of the sociological concept of environment can be observed which is even more fundamental than this territorial expansion of the regulated environment. As the last lecture showed, elements previously considered inherent in the personality itself are treated as part of the general environment as they come increasingly under external control. Thus what is considered the general environment is constantly enlarged by the shifting of formerly subjective factors into a position in which they can be handled objectively. One of the main discoveries of modern psychology and sociology has been to find that elements formerly thought to belong exclusively to the personality really belong to the environment. At first, 'environment' meant to the theorists of *milieu* only the geographical and artificial background—mountains, houses, and climatic conditions. Later, the significance of the social environment, of social relations prevailing in a group, was. detected; e.g. how the nature of authority, family organization, economic adjustment, react on the personality. And finally, the importance of the symbolic environment, of language, meaning, norms, beliefs, etc., was discovered and seen to be a part of the total environment.

Once we reach this stage it is difficult to decide whether in managing values, for instance, we manage surroundings or the self. If a society consciously determines and not only suggests its values, economic preferences, the appreciation of extraversion and introversion, what is left to the individual? Whereas to the nineteenth century an interference with values would have meant an interference with personality, to us the management of values is becoming as natural as the management of business relations. And if this guidance of values is said to be a management of surroundings, what then should we call the management of self-valuation, which is the next step in the process? Is self-valuation something which belongs to the environment and not to the self, like any other object? What is left to the subject in such a situation is merely to accept, refuse, or integrate these induced experiences.

But as we have seen, even this acceptance, refusal, or integration can be regulated, or at least strongly influenced, by propagandizing particular models of ideals of conduct like the 'gentleman' or the socialist 'hero'. Here we reach the uttermost limit of the attack on the self which may ultimately lead to its complete evaporation. To be sure, we cannot forbid the scientist to shift former subjective elements into the position of environmental facts for scientific purposes. But we can safely assert that with each new application of his theories concerning the power of the environment on the self there is a danger of killing spontaneity and of destroying opportunities for choice, decision, and self-control. The conclusion may be that the whole population will live on the psychological dole and dope they get from the state and will forget to act on their own.

The mistake of the liberal was to become too introverted, not to realize the importance of the environment, and to attribute instead all the creative forces to the subject. As I have said, liberals were in many ways environment-blind, perhaps because their knowledge and ability to guide the environment was too small. But if the liberal tended to be environment-blind, socialists and fascists tend to become subject-blind.

In a liberal society all these interferences are not so detrimental because the possibility of escaping is still present and correspondingly the self in the last resort can accept or refuse; it has scope for acting like a subject, not only like a reacting mechanism.

This leads me to the second fallacy in the uncritical application of scientific patterns to the regulation of society. The discussion of this point is necessary, since planned society will have to rely upon science, but then it is all the more necessary to become conscious of all the limitations of the value of the special pattern it uses. All the examples I mentioned were based upon the mechanical pattern of conditioning which was first observed in physics.

The main limitation of the sociological concept of planning is that it tends to confound control over physical realities with that over human beings. Control over physical objects relies upon the idea of mechanical causation, which means that to a well-determined cause corresponds a well-determined effect. But even in biology complete determination does not prevail; according to their nature organisms have a range of possible reactions to a given stimulus. Their answer to stimuli is not determinate reaction but possible response. This greater variability in the range of possible responses applies even more to man, both individually and in groups. The early conditioning or history of an individual may lead one man to answer aggression by flight and another by active reaction. Or, another example, a people who through many centuries have worked out a tradition of self-control and slow evolutionary adjustment may, for quite a long time, resist deteriorating social conditions more passionately than a people whose tradition is one of anarchy, individualism, and revolt.

The scientific pattern of social conditioning distorts human reality very often in so far as it fails to reckon with these individual deviations which come chiefly from a special individual or group history. That social regulation nevertheless approximately reaches its goal is due to the fact that it does not need to take into account all the adequate reactions of all the members of a community, but only of a majority or a statistical average, and that it does not attempt in any given situation to affect the whole personality. This is the reason why the sociological observations concerning correlations cannot be applied with certainty to a single individual but yet work fairly well with great masses.

And there is another reason why mechanical conditioning of a certain type of reaction may be successful without always taking into account the organic structure of the specific individual in question.

It is because, as modern biology shows, there are partial systems in man which react mechanically and can therefore for a while be isolated from the whole personality system. This is the case especially with fully automatized habits.

Behaviourism seems to owe its results to focusing upon the most elementary factors in psychic life, or to these isolated mechanical habit systems; and it can manage to interpret very many changes in the human psyche with the help of an almost mechanical pattern either because it refers to such isolated systems or because in its general theory it is satisfied with a relative simplification. Psychoanalysis also tends in the same direction of simplification, even if on a higher level. Nobody can reject the idea of such a simplifying procedure which at the beginning leaves aside the more complex levels of the self. One cannot oppose it as long as one agrees that science needs simplification for the sake of a first approach to reality and that the general control of the fundamental movements in society needs nothing more than this. This is the reason why sociology, behaviourism, Marxism, Freudism have always been in the right when they have opposed the over-subtle concepts of historians and individualists who try to deal with the differences before having worked out the basic similarities. These latter fill in the fine points of the portrait of society without having drawn the outlines.

In my analysis of the basic correlations I have tried to show that by a method of gradually refined observations one can penetrate a certain way even into the core of the self and grasp interrelations between variations in the environment and in the deeper personality. But, in spite of the great possibilities which lie in the further development of sociology and psychology and the co-operation between them, there is nevertheless a great danger in using their results and concepts indiscriminately. If we use sociological and psychological knowledge for the better understanding of historical societies, then it is beneficial; but it becomes dangerous if we try to plan society on such a basis.

What is the difference between these two uses? In the first place, psychology and sociology have not to create life by their knowledge but to extract principles for the purposes of cognition. But if planning follows scientific simplifications too dogmatically, it will force round pegs into square holes. In liberal society partial interference through single institutions, even if it is built upon mechanical correlations, leaves outlets for those deviations which it has overlooked. It leaves room for adjustment in the case of those human tendencies which are overlooked by the generalizing, mechanistic approach, because they are far removed from the statistical norm.

As soon as the co-ordination of all the existing regulations is attempted, the possibility for the social atoms to escape is reduced to its minimum, self-adjustment is almost excluded, and the sum of co-ordinated mechanical regulations tends to replace the hidden organic unity of the whole. It is as if the doctor were to use his fragmentary knowledge of physics, chemistry, anatomy and biology to replace the original forces in nature rather than—as he actually does—let nature cure the illness.

If we follow up this line of argument, we almost come to the point of giving up the idea of planning. But if anything is clear, it is that there is no way back to an unplanned society any longer. Our occasional interferences have increased in number so much that without guidance the sum of regulations on a large scale must lead to a terrific clash. Total regulation on the other hand leads to a deadening mechanization of man and society. There is only one way left: the acceptance of planning but in a new sense.

At the end of these lectures I cannot do more than lay down some of the general principles of a new sort of planning. I envisage a type of planning which will not appeal to the bureaucrat or the soldier, since it is not a mere series of orders and interferences, but rather a continuous watch on the key-positions of society and the attempt to avoid maladjustments which might lead to catastrophe.

I. The first rule to be laid down in this connection is that it is the greatest wisdom of the planner not to interfere where there is no necessity for it, i.e. where the spontaneous forces do not endanger basic trends which we regard as indispensable.

II. Another axiom of social planning ought to be that wherever command can be replaced by spontaneity it shall be so replaced. All commands are merely substitutes for spontaneous action where we cannot be sure that people will react in the appropriate way to planned situations.

III. Thus the contrast with liberal society is planned society and not dictatorship (although in critical situations, mainly in periods of transition, it may be sometimes unavoidable to use this).

The essence of planning is control over those functional achievements which formerly grew up spontaneously and worked together without being consciously correlated. In planned society their mutual adjustment will not be left to chance but will be guaranteed through consciously planned institutions. That this can be achieved can be proved by the fact that we have a series of cases in history when formerly spontaneous and uncontrolled social achievements were later institutionalized and co-ordinated as parts of a whole through human regulations.

Take parliament, which in many ways is nothing but the institutionalization of a process which without it is pure struggle. As has been correctly said, parliamentarism is counting people's heads instead of cutting them off. Parliamentarism, like democracy in general, transforms destructive opposition into creative criticism.

IV. I am naturally too realistic in my outlook to believe that a society can be kept going without being based upon a certain amount of conformity. The next task therefore is very carefully to study the different means by which traditional societies and modern mass societies have brought conformity about. From the almost mechanical conditioning during early childhood through the teaching of emotionalized ideals and symbols, through co-ordinated, planned surroundings, teamwork and games, and later even through intelligent propaganda, some of the fundamentals of a new common life have to be induced without necessarily being always based upon rational argument. Man is not pure intel-lect, but the intellect has its proper place in his personal life and in the life of the community; and the question is not how to avoid the use of conscious conditioning of habits and emotions but how to limit it to that basic sphere without which consensus, co-operation, is impossible.

V. But once this minimum of conformity concerning fair play, decency, community spirit, sense of justice, incentive for work, and the necessarily greater conformity in the wants of the consumer is guaranteed, the social scope has to be provided for individualiza-tion and freedom.

What these lectures mainly aim at is to convey the idea that in the near future freedom and individualization cannot be achieved by *laisser-faire* but only by planning for freedom, that is, by carefully providing scope for free development and indivi-dualization on the different levels of the self, and correlating the social factors which favour it.

I refer again to a historical example which has to do with the Catholic Church. Not for the reason that I agree with its contents, but because the Church in the Middle Ages and the guilds are so far the best historical examples of an attempt to plan the subjec-tive side of human affairs. With reference to our problem the Church interests us because, although it aimed at a kind of totalitarian planning, it was nevertheless anxious to provide cer-tain forms of individualization and was even able to evolve institutions which quite successfully produced them. I have already mentioned monastic life, which was consciously producing those elements of individualization which I called introversion and privacy. Seclusion from the world, controlled surroundings and strictly observed programmes for the activities of the day have produced a certain type of mentality. Not only were the imme-diate surroundings planned but also the functions of whole orders. The idea of the orders was to provide a nucleus within the life of the Church in which those primary emotional elements and inner attitudes towards the self and the world which were considered to be the essence of religion could be preserved through the ages. They knew that this could only be achieved through social isolation, through preventing contact with what they called 'the world', and by leaving the non-monastic clergy to carry out the adjustments which the changing world made necessary. Indeed from the beginning of the Cluniac movement through the centuries these orders were not simply obedient servants but very often a strong opposition to a historical transformation and deterioration of the Church and a source of regeneration.

No one will understand me as proposing some Catholic formula or as being in agreement with this type of individualization, but the life of the Church as the bearer of a long tradition in social planning will provide the student with some sort of example of achievements and failures in an attempt to plan the scope for the growth of the most subtle elements of human personality.

Once such a possibility is realized, it can be modified according to new demands, and we may hope that so far as planning has to come it may find some such palliative for the detrimental tendencies inherent in it.

What I have attempted to do in these lectures is to show that such an important and difficult question as that of the interdependence between individualization and social factors can be discussed on the basis of a rational analysis in which the main concern is to observe relationships and not merely to express likes and dislikes.

You may ask me whether correct knowledge will induce people to act in the right way. Indeed knowledge itself gives no guarantee that it will be used in practice. But it is the precondition for productive control.

When man turns to the task of remaking himself through managing his total environment, the conscious or unconscious notions he may have about human personality, the self, planning and co-ordination become of extreme importance.

The possibilities of planning are great, but the dangers are greater. We cannot avoid seeing that planning will come, and is already upon us. At this time it is all the more necessary to make up our minds about the kind of planning we want. It must be not the deadening interference of a bureaucratic regulation of all and everything but a sociological guidance of inherent forces from the key position of society.

To say one more word about the moral side of the question. The new society has to be based upon a new synthesis between the self-assertive forces of liberal society and the over-estimated possibilities of some kind of complete altruism. A synthesis which I have never found more exactly expressed than in a saying of the old Jewish sage Hillel:

'If I am not for myself, who will be for me?
If I am only for myself—then what am I for?'

Index

The International Library of
Sociology
and Social Reconstruction

Edited by W. J. H. SPROTT
Founded by KARL MANNHEIM

ROUTLEDGE & KEGAN PAUL
BROADWAY HOUSE, CARTER LANE, LONDON, E.C.4

CONTENTS

PRINTED IN GREAT BRITAIN BY HEADLEY BROTHERS LTD
109 KINGSWAY LONDON WC2 AND ASHFORD KENT

GENERAL SOCIOLOGY

Brown, Robert. Explanation in Social Science. *208 pp. 1963. (2nd Impression 1964.) 25s.*

Gibson, Quentin. The Logic of Social Enquiry. *240 pp. 1960. (3rd Impression 1968.) 24s.*

Homans, George C. Sentiments and Activities: Essays in Social Science. *336 pp. 1962. 32s.*

Isajiw, Wsevelod W. Causation and Functionalism in Sociology. *165 pp. 1968. 25s.*

Johnson, Harry M. Sociology: a Systematic Introduction. *Foreword by Robert K. Merton. 710 pp. 1961. (5th Impression 1968.) 42s.*

Mannheim, Karl. Essays on Sociology and Social Psychology. *Edited by Paul Kecskemeti. With Editorial Note by Adolph Lowe. 344 pp. 1953. (2nd Impression 1966.) 32s.*

Systematic Sociology: An Introduction to the Study of Society. *Edited by J. S. Erös and Professor W. A. C. Stewart. 220 pp. 1957. (3rd Impression 1967.) 24s.*

Martindale, Don. The Nature and Types of Sociological Theory. *292 pp. 1961. (3rd Impression 1967.) 35s.*

Maus, Heinz. A Short History of Sociology. *234 pp. 1962. (2nd Impression 1965.) 28s.*

Myrdal, Gunnar. Value in Social Theory: A Collection of Essays on Methodology. *Edited by Paul Streeten. 332 pp. 1958. (3rd Impression 1968.) 35s.*

Ogburn, William F., and Nimkoff, Meyer F. A Handbook of Sociology. *Preface by Karl Mannheim. 656 pp. 46 figures. 35 tables. 5th edition (revised) 1964. 45s.*

Parsons, Talcott, and Smelser, Neil J. Economy and Society: A Study in the Integration of Economic and Social Theory. *362 pp. 1956. (4th Impression 1967.) 35s.*

Rex, John. Key Problems of Sociological Theory. *220 pp. 1961. (4th Impression 1968.) 25s.*

Stark, Werner. The Fundamental Forms of Social Thought. *280 pp. 1962. 32s.*

FOREIGN CLASSICS OF SOCIOLOGY

Durkheim, Emile. Suicide. A Study in Sociology. *Edited and with an Introduction by George Simpson. 404 pp. 1952. (4th Impression 1968.) 35s.*

Professional Ethics and Civic Morals. *Translated by Cornelia Brookfield. 288 pp. 1957. 30s.*

Gerth, H. H., and Mills, C. Wright. From Max Weber: Essays in Sociology. *502 pp. 1948. (6th Impression 1967.) 35s.*

Tönnies, Ferdinand. Community and Association. *(Gemeinschaft und Gesellschaft.) Translated and Supplemented by Charles P. Loomis. Foreword by Pitirim A. Sorokin. 334 pp. 1955. 28s.*

SOCIAL STRUCTURE

Andreski, Stanislav. Military Organization and Society. *Foreword by Professor A. R. Radcliffe-Brown. 226 pp. 1 folder. 1954. Revised Edition 1968. 35s.*

Cole, G. D. H. Studies in Class Structure. *220 pp. 1955. (3rd Impression 1964.) 21s. Paper 10s. 6d.*

Coontz, Sydney H. Population Theories and the Economic Interpretation. *202 pp. 1957. (3rd Impression 1968.) 28s.*

Coser, Lewis. The Functions of Social Conflict. *204 pp. 1956. (3rd Impression 1968.) 25s.*

Dickie-Clark, H. F. Marginal Situation: A Sociological Study of a Coloured Group. *240 pp. 11 tables. 1966. 40s.*

Glass, D. V. (Ed.). Social Mobility in Britain. *Contributions by J. Berent, T. Bottomore, R. C. Chambers, J. Floud, D. V. Glass, J. R. Hall, H. T. Himmelweit, R. K. Kelsall, F. M. Martin, C. A. Moser, R. Mukherjee, and W. Ziegel. 420 pp. 1954. (4th Impression 1967.) 45s.*

Jones, Garth N. Planned Organizational Change: An Exploratory Study Using an Empirical Approach. *About 268 pp. 1969. 40s.*

Kelsall, R. K. Higher Civil Servants in Britain: From 1870 to the Present Day. *268 pp. 31 tables. 1955. (2nd Impression 1966.) 25s.*

König, René. The Community. *232 pp. Illustrated. 1968. 35s.*

Lawton, Denis. Social Class, Language and Education. *192 pp. 1968. (2nd Impression 1968.) 25s.*

McLeish, John. The Theory of Social Change: Four Views Considered. *About 128 pp. 1969. 21s.*

Marsh, David C. The Changing Social Structure in England and Wales, 1871-1961. *1958. 272 pp. 2nd edition (revised) 1966. (2nd Impression 1967.) 35s.*

Mouzelis, Nicos. Organization and Bureaucracy. An Analysis of Modern Theories. *240 pp. 1967. (2nd Impression 1968.) 28s.*

Ossowski, Stanisław. Class Structure in the Social Consciousness. *210 pp. 1963. (2nd Impression 1967.) 25s.*

SOCIOLOGY AND POLITICS

Barbu, Zevedei. Democracy and Dictatorship: Their Psychology and Patterns of Life. *300 pp. 1956. 28s.*

Crick, Bernard. The American Science of Politics: Its Origins and Conditions. *284 pp. 1959. 32s.*

Hertz, Frederick. Nationality in History and Politics: A Psychology and Sociology of National Sentiment and Nationalism. *432 pp. 1944. (5th Impression 1966.) 42s.*

Kornhauser, William. The Politics of Mass Society. *272 pp. 20 tables. 1960. (3rd Impression 1968.) 28s.*

Laidler, Harry W. History of Socialism. Social-Economic Movements: An Historical and Comparative Survey of Socialism, Communism, Co-operation, Utopianism; and other Systems of Reform and Reconstruction. *New edition. 992 pp. 1968. 90s.*

Lasswell, Harold D. Analysis of Political Behaviour. An Empirical Approach. *324 pp. 1947. (4th Impression 1966.) 35s.*

Mannheim, Karl. Freedom, Power and Democratic Planning. *Edited by Hans Gerth and Ernest K. Bramstedt. 424 pp. 1951. (3rd Impression 1968.) 42s.*

Mansur, Fatma. Process of Independence. *Foreword by A. H. Hanson. 208 pp. 1962. 25s.*

Martin, David A. Pacificism: an Historical and Sociological Study. *262 pp. 1965. 30s.*

Myrdal, Gunnar. The Political Element in the Development of Economic Theory. *Translated from the German by Paul Streeten. 282 pp. 1953. (4th Impression 1965.) 25s.*

Polanyi, Michael. F.R.S. The Logic of Liberty: Reflections and Rejoinders. *228 pp. 1951. 18s.*

Verney, Douglas V. The Analysis of Political Systems. *264 pp. 1959. (3rd Impression 1966.) 28s.*

Wootton, Graham. The Politics of Influence: British Ex-Servicemen, Cabinet Decisions and Cultural Changes, 1917 to 1957. *316 pp. 1963. 30s.*
Workers, Unions and the State. *188 pp. 1966. (2nd Impression 1967.) 25s.*

FOREIGN AFFAIRS: THEIR SOCIAL, POLITICAL AND ECONOMIC FOUNDATIONS

Baer, Gabriel. Population and Society in the Arab East. *Translated by Hanna Szöke. 288 pp. 10 maps. 1964. 40s.*

Bonné, Alfred. State and Economics in the Middle East: A Society in Transition. *482 pp. 2nd (revised) edition 1955. (2nd Impression 1960.) 40s.*
Studies in Economic Development: with special reference to Conditions in the Under-developed Areas of Western Asia and India. *322 pp. 84 tables. 2nd edition 1960. 32s.*

Mayer, J. P. Political Thought in France from the Revolution to the Fifth Republic. *164 pp. 3rd edition (revised) 1961. 16s.*

CRIMINOLOGY

Ancel, Marc. Social Defence: A Modern Approach to Criminal Problems. *Foreword by Leon Radzinowicz. 240 pp. 1965. 32s.*

Cloward, Richard A., and Ohlin, Lloyd E. Delinquency and Opportunity: A Theory of Delinquent Gangs. *248 pp. 1961. 25s.*

Downes, David M. The Delinquent Solution. A Study in Subcultural Theory. *296 pp. 1966. 42s.*

Dunlop, A. B., and **McCabe, S.** Young Men in Detention Centres. *192 pp. 1965. 28s.*

Friedländer, Kate. The Psycho-Analytical Approach to Juvenile Delinquency: Theory, Case Studies, Treatment. *320 pp. 1947. (6th Impression 1967). 40s.*

Glueck, Sheldon and **Eleanor.** Family Environment and Delinquency. *With the statistical assistance of Rose W. Kneznek. 340 pp. 1962. (2nd Impression 1966.) 40s.*

Mannheim, Hermann. Comparative Criminology: a Text Book. *Two volumes. 442 pp. and 380 pp. 1965. (2nd Impression with corrections 1966.) 42s. a volume.*

Morris, Terence. The Criminal Area: A Study in Social Ecology. *Foreword by Hermann Mannheim. 232 pp. 25 tables. 4 maps. 1957. (2nd Impression 1966.) 28s.*

Morris, Terence and **Pauline,** assisted by **Barbara Barer.** Pentonville: A Sociological Study of an English Prison. *416 pp. 16 plates. 1963. 50s.*

Spencer, John C. Crime and the Services. *Foreword by Hermann Mannheim. 336 pp. 1954. 28s.*

Trasler, Gordon. The Explanation of Criminality. *144 pp. 1962. (2nd Impression 1967.) 20s.*

SOCIAL PSYCHOLOGY

Barbu, Zevedei. Problems of Historical Psychology. *248 pp. 1960. 25s.*

Blackburn, Julian. Psychology and the Social Pattern. *184 pp. 1945. (7th Impression 1964.) 16s.*

Fleming, C. M. Adolescence: Its Social Psychology: With an Introduction to recent findings from the fields of Anthropology, Physiology, Medicine, Psychometrics and Sociometry. *288 pp. 2nd edition (revised) 1963. (3rd Impression 1967.) 25s. Paper 12s. 6d.*

The Social Psychology of Education: An Introduction and Guide to Its Study. *136 pp. 2nd edition (revised) 1959. (4th Impression 1967.) 14s. Paper 7s. 6d.*

Homans, George C. The Human Group. *Foreword by Bernard DeVoto. Introduction by Robert K. Merton. 526 pp. 1951. (7th Impression 1968.) 35s.*

Social Behaviour: its Elementary Forms. *416 pp. 1961. (3rd Impression 1968.) 35s.*

Klein, Josephine. The Study of Groups. *226 pp. 31 figures. 5 tables. 1956. (5th Impression 1967.) 21s. Paper 9s. 6d.*

Linton, Ralph. The Cultural Background of Personality. *132 pp. 1947. (7th Impression 1968.) 18s.*

Mayo, Elton. The Social Problems of an Industrial Civilization. With an appendix on the Political Problem. *180 pp. 1949. (5th Impression 1966.) 25s.*

Ottaway, A. K. C. Learning Through Group Experience. *176 pp. 1966. (2nd Impression 1968.) 25s.*

Ridder, J. C. de. The Personality of the Urban African in South Africa. A Thematic Apperception Test Study. *196 pp. 12 plates. 1961. 25s.*

Rose, Arnold M. (Ed.). Human Behaviour and Social Processes: an Interactionist Approach. *Contributions by Arnold M. Rose, Ralph H. Turner, Anselm Strauss, Everett C. Hughes, E. Franklin Frazier, Howard S. Becker, et al. 696 pp. 1962. (2nd Impression 1968.) 70s.*

Smelser, Neil J. Theory of Collective Behaviour. *448 pp. 1962. (2nd Impression 1967.) 45s.*

Stephenson, Geoffrey M. The Development of Conscience. *128 pp. 1966. 25s.*

Young, Kimball. Handbook of Social Psychology. *658 pp. 16 figures. 10 tables. 2nd edition (revised) 1957. (3rd Impression 1963.) 40s.*

SOCIOLOGY OF THE FAMILY

Banks, J. A. Prosperity and Parenthood: A study of Family Planning among The Victorian Middle Classes. *262 pp. 1954. (3rd Impression 1968.) 28s.*

Bell, Colin R. Middle Class Families: Social and Geographical Mobility. *224 pp. 1969. 35s.*

Burton, Lindy. Vulnerable Children. *272 pp. 1968. 35s.*

Gavron, Hannah. The Captive Wife: Conflicts of Housebound Mothers. *190 pp. 1966. (2nd Impression 1966.) 25s.*

Klein, Josephine. Samples from English Cultures. *1965. (2nd Impression 1967.)*
  1. Three Preliminary Studies and Aspects of Adult Life in England. *447 pp. 50s.*
  2. Child-Rearing Practices and Index. *247 pp. 35s.*

Klein, Viola. Britain's Married Women Workers. *180 pp. 1965. (2nd Impression 1968.) 28s.*

McWhinnie, Alexina M. Adopted Children. How They Grow Up. *304 pp. 1967. (2nd Impression 1968.) 42s.*

Myrdal, Alva and **Klein, Viola.** Women's Two Roles: Home and Work. *238 pp. 27 tables. 1956. Revised Edition 1967. 30s. Paper 15s.*

Parsons, Talcott and **Bales, Robert F.** Family: Socialization and Interaction Process. *In collaboration with James Olds, Morris Zelditch and Philip E. Slater. 456 pp. 50 figures and tables. 1956. (3rd Impression 1968.) 45s.*

Schücking, L. L. The Puritan Family. *Translated from the German by Brian Battershaw. 212 pp. 1969. About 42s.*

THE SOCIAL SERVICES

Forder, R. A. (Ed.). Penelope Hall's Social Services of Modern England. *288 pp. 1969. 35s.*

George, Victor. Social Security: Beveridge and After. *258 pp. 1968. 35s.*

Goetschius, George W. Working with Community Groups. *256 pp. 1969. 35s.*

Goetschius, George W. and **Tash, Joan.** Working with Unattached Youth. *416 pp. 1967.* (*2nd Impression 1968.*) *40s.*

Hall, M. P., and **Howes, I. V.** The Church in Social Work. A Study of Moral Welfare Work undertaken by the Church of England. *320 pp. 1965. 35s.*

Heywood, Jean S. Children in Care: the Development of the Service for the Deprived Child. *264 pp. 2nd edition (revised) 1965.* (*2nd Impression 1966.*) *32s.*

An Introduction to Teaching Casework Skills. *190 pp. 1964. 28s.*

Jones, Kathleen. Lunacy, Law and Conscience, 1744-1845: the Social History of the Care of the Insane. *268 pp. 1955. 25s.*

Mental Health and Social Policy, 1845-1959. *264 pp. 1960.* (*2nd Impression 1967.*) *32s.*

Jones, Kathleen and **Sidebotham, Roy.** Mental Hospitals at Work. *220 pp. 1962. 30s.*

Kastell, Jean. Casework in Child Care. *Foreword by M. Brooke Willis. 320 pp. 1962. 35s.*

Morris, Pauline. Put Away: A Sociological Study of Institutions for the Mentally Retarded. *Approx. 288 pp. 1969. About 50s.*

Nokes, P. L. The Professional Task in Welfare Practice. *152 pp. 1967. 28s.*

Rooff, Madeline. Voluntary Societies and Social Policy. *350 pp. 15 tables. 1957. 35s.*

Timms, Noel. Psychiatric Social Work in Great Britain (1939-1962). *280 pp. 1964. 32s.*

Social Casework: Principles and Practice. *256 pp. 1964.* (*2nd Impression 1966.*) *25s. Paper 15s.*

Trasler, Gordon. In Place of Parents: A Study in Foster Care. *272 pp. 1960.* (*2nd Impression 1966.*) *30s.*

Young, A. F., and **Ashton, E. T.** British Social Work in the Nineteenth Century. *288 pp. 1956.* (*2nd Impression 1963.*) *28s.*

Young, A. F. Social Services in British Industry. *272 pp. 1968. 40s.*

SOCIOLOGY OF EDUCATION

Banks, Olive. Parity and Prestige in English Secondary Education: a Study in Educational Sociology. *272 pp. 1955.* (*2nd Impression 1963.*) *32s.*

Bentwich, Joseph. Education in Israel. *224 pp. 8 pp. plates. 1965. 24s.*

Blyth, W. A. L. English Primary Education. A Sociological Description. *1965. Revised edition 1967.*

1. Schools. *232 pp. 30s. Paper 12s. 6d.*
2. Background. *168 pp. 25s. Paper 10s. 6d.*

Collier, K. G. The Social Purposes of Education: Personal and Social Values in Education. *268 pp. 1959. (3rd Impression 1965.) 21s.*

Dale, R. R., and **Griffith, S.** Down Stream: Failure in the Grammar School. *108 pp. 1965. 20s.*

Dore, R. P. Education in Tokugawa Japan. *356 pp. 9 pp. plates. 1965. 35s.*

Edmonds, E. L. The School Inspector. *Foreword by Sir William Alexander. 214 pp. 1962. 28s.*

Evans, K. M. Sociometry and Education. *158 pp. 1962. (2nd Impression 1966.) 18s.*

Foster, P. J. Education and Social Change in Ghana. *336 pp. 3 maps. 1965. (2nd Impression 1967.) 36s.*

Fraser, W. R. Education and Society in Modern France. *150 pp. 1963. (2nd Impression 1968.) 25s.*

Hans, Nicholas. New Trends in Education in the Eighteenth Century. *278 pp. 19 tables. 1951. (2nd Impression 1966.) 30s.*
Comparative Education: A Study of Educational Factors and Traditions. *360 pp. 3rd (revised) edition 1958. (4th Impression 1967.) 25s. Paper 12s. 6d.*

Hargreaves, David. Social Relations in a Secondary School. *240 pp. 1967. (2nd Impression 1968.) 32s.*

Holmes, Brian. Problems in Education. A Comparative Approach. *336 pp. 1965. (2nd Impression 1967.) 32s.*

Mannheim, Karl and **Stewart, W. A. C.** An Introduction to the Sociology of Education. *206 pp. 1962. (2nd Impression 1965.) 21s.*

Morris, Raymond N. The Sixth Form and College Entrance. *231 pp. 1969. 40s.*

Musgrove, F. Youth and the Social Order. *176 pp. 1964. (2nd Impression 1968.) 25s. Paper 12s.*

Ortega y Gasset, José. Mission of the University. *Translated with an Introduction by Howard Lee Nostrand. 86 pp. 1946. (3rd Impression 1963.) 15s.*

Ottaway, A. K. C. Education and Society: An Introduction to the Sociology of Education. *With an Introduction by W. O. Lester Smith. 212 pp. Second edition (revised). 1962. (5th Impression 1968.) 18s. Paper 10s. 6d.*

Peers, Robert. Adult Education: A Comparative Study. *398 pp. 2nd edition 1959. (2nd Impression 1966.) 42s.*

Pritchard, D. G. Education and the Handicapped: 1760 to 1960. *258 pp. 1963. (2nd Impression 1966.) 35s.*

Richardson, Helen. Adolescent Girls in Approved Schools. *Approx. 360 pp. 1969. About 42s.*

Simon, Brian and **Joan** (Eds.). Educational Psychology in the U.S.S.R. *Introduction by Brian and Joan Simon. Translation by Joan Simon. Papers by D. N. Bogoiavlenski and N. A. Menchinskaia, D. B. Elkonin, E. A. Fleshner, Z. I. Kalmykova, G. S. Kostiuk, V. A. Krutetski, A. N. Leontiev, A. R. Luria, E. A. Milerian, R. G. Natadze, B. M. Teplov, L. S. Vygotski, L. V. Zankov. 296 pp. 1963. 40s.*

SOCIOLOGY OF CULTURE

Eppel, E. M., and **M.** Adolescents and Morality: A Study of some Moral Values and Dilemmas of Working Adolescents in the Context of a changing Climate of Opinion. *Foreword by W. J. H. Sprott. 268 pp. 39 tables. 1966. 30s.*

Fromm, Erich. The Fear of Freedom. *286 pp. 1942. (8th Impression 1960.) 25s. Paper 10s.*

The Sane Society. *400 pp. 1956. (4th Impression 1968.) 28s. Paper 14s.*

Mannheim, Karl. Diagnosis of Our Time: Wartime Essays of a Sociologist. *208 pp. 1943. (8th Impression 1966.) 21s.*

Essays on the Sociology of Culture. *Edited by Ernst Mannheim in co-operation with Paul Kecskemeti. Editorial Note by Adolph Lowe. 280 pp. 1956. (3rd Impression 1967.) 28s.*

Weber, Alfred. Farewell to European History: or The Conquest of Nihilism. *Translated from the German by R. F. C. Hull. 224 pp. 1947. 18s.*

SOCIOLOGY OF RELIGION

Argyle, Michael. Religious Behaviour. *224 pp. 8 figures. 41 tables. 1958. (4th Impression 1968.) 25s.*

Nelson, G. K. Spiritualism and Society. *313 pp. 1969. 42s.*

Stark, Werner. The Sociology of Religion. A Study of Christendom.
Volume I. Established Religion. *248 pp. 1966. 35s.*
Volume II. Sectarian Religion. *368 pp. 1967. 40s.*
Volume III. The Universal Church. *464 pp. 1967. 45s.*

Watt, W. Montgomery. Islam and the Integration of Society. *320 pp. 1961. (3rd Impression 1966.) 35s.*

SOCIOLOGY OF ART AND LITERATURE

Beljame, Alexandre. Men of Letters and the English Public in the Eighteenth Century: 1660-1744, Dryden, Addison, Pope. *Edited with an Introduction and Notes by Bonamy Dobrée. Translated by E. O. Lorimer. 532 pp. 1948. 32s.*

Misch, Georg. A History of Autobiography in Antiquity. *Translated by E. W. Dickes. 2 Volumes. Vol. 1, 364 pp., Vol. 2, 372 pp. 1950. 45s. the set.*

Schücking, L. L. The Sociology of Literary Taste. *112 pp. 2nd (revised) edition 1966. 18s.*

Silbermann, Alphons. The Sociology of Music. *Translated from the German by Corbet Stewart. 222 pp. 1963. 32s.*

SOCIOLOGY OF KNOWLEDGE

Mannheim, Karl. Essays on the Sociology of Knowledge. *Edited by Paul Kecskemeti. Editorial note by Adolph Lowe. 352 pp. 1952. (4th Impression 1967.) 35s.*

Stark, W. America: Ideal and Reality. The United States of 1776 in Contemporary Philosophy. *136 pp. 1947. 12s.*

The Sociology of Knowledge: An Essay in Aid of a Deeper Understanding of the History of Ideas. *384 pp. 1958. (3rd Impression 1967.) 36s.*

Montesquieu: Pioneer of the Sociology of Knowledge. *244 pp. 1960. 25s.*

URBAN SOCIOLOGY

Anderson, Nels. The Urban Community: A World Perspective. *532 pp. 1960. 35s.*

Ashworth, William. The Genesis of Modern British Town Planning: A Study in Economic and Social History of the Nineteenth and Twentieth Centuries. *288 pp. 1954. (3rd Impression 1968.) 32s.*

Bracey, Howard. Neighbours: On New Estates and Subdivisions in England and U.S.A. *220 pp. 1964. 28s.*

Cullingworth, J. B. Housing Needs and Planning Policy: A Restatement of the Problems of Housing Need and "Overspill" in England and Wales. *232 pp. 44 tables. 8 maps. 1960. (2nd Impression 1966.) 28s.*

Dickinson, Robert E. City and Region: A Geographical Interpretation. *608 pp. 125 figures. 1964. (5th Impression 1967.) 60s.*

The West European City: A Geographical Interpretation. *600 pp. 129 maps. 29 plates. 2nd edition 1962. (3rd Impression 1968.) 55s.*

The City Region in Western Europe. *320 pp. Maps. 1967. 30s. Paper 14s.*

Jackson, Brian. Working Class Community: Some General Notions raised by a Series of Studies in Northern England. *192 pp. 1968. (2nd Impression 1968.) 25s.*

Jennings, Hilda. Societies in the Making: a Study of Development and Redevelopment within a County Borough. *Foreword by D. A. Clark. 286 pp. 1962. (2nd Impression 1967.) 32s.*

Kerr, Madeline. The People of Ship Street. *240 pp. 1958. 28s.*

Mann, P. H. An Approach to Urban Sociology. *240 pp. 1965. (2nd Impression 1968.) 30s.*

Morris, R. N., and **Mogey, J.** The Sociology of Housing. Studies at Berinsfield. *232 pp. 4 pp. plates. 1965. 42s.*

Rosser, C., and **Harris, C.** The Family and Social Change. A Study of Family and Kinship in a South Wales Town. *352 pp. 8 maps. 1965. (2nd Impression 1968.) 45s.*

RURAL SOCIOLOGY

Chambers, R. J. H. Settlement Schemes in Africa: A Selective Study. *Approx. 268 pp. 1969. About 50s.*

Haswell, M. R. The Economics of Development in Village India. *120 pp. 1967. 21s.*

Littlejohn, James. Westrigg: the Sociology of a Cheviot Parish. *172 pp. 5 figures. 1963. 25s.*

Williams, W. M. The Country Craftsman: A Study of Some Rural Crafts and the Rural Industries Organization in England. *248 pp. 9 figures. 1958. 25s. (Dartington Hall Studies in Rural Sociology.)*

The Sociology of an English Village: Gosforth. *272 pp. 12 figures. 13 tables. 1956. (3rd Impression 1964.) 25s.*

SOCIOLOGY OF MIGRATION

Humphreys, Alexander J. New Dubliners: Urbanization and the Irish Family. *Foreword by George C. Homans. 304 pp. 1966. 40s.*

SOCIOLOGY OF INDUSTRY AND DISTRIBUTION

Anderson, Nels. Work and Leisure. *280 pp. 1961. 28s.*

Blau, Peter M., and **Scott, W. Richard.** Formal Organizations: a Comparative approach. *Introduction and Additional Bibliography by J. H. Smith. 326 pp. 1963. (4th Impression 1969.) 35s. Paper 15s.*

Eldridge, J. E. T. Industrial Disputes. Essays in the Sociology of Industrial Relations. *288 pp. 1968. 40s.*

Hollowell, Peter G. The Lorry Driver. *272 pp. 1968. 42s.*

Jefferys, Margot, with the assistance of Winifred Moss. Mobility in the Labour Market: Employment Changes in Battersea and Dagenham. *Preface by Barbara Wootton. 186 pp. 51 tables. 1954. 15s.*

Levy, A. B. Private Corporations and Their Control. *Two Volumes. Vol. 1, 464 pp., Vol. 2, 432 pp. 1950. 80s. the set.*

Liepmann, Kate. Apprenticeship: An Enquiry into its Adequacy under Modern Conditions. *Foreword by H. D. Dickinson. 232 pp. 6 tables. 1960. (2nd Impression 1960.) 23s.*

Millerson, Geoffrey. The Qualifying Associations: a Study in Professionalization. *320 pp. 1964. 42s.*

Smelser, Neil J. Social Change in the Industrial Revolution: An Application of Theory to the Lancashire Cotton Industry, 1770-1840. *468 pp. 12 figures. 14 tables. 1959. (2nd Impression 1960.) 50s.*

Williams, Gertrude. Recruitment to Skilled Trades. *240 pp. 1957. 23s.*

Young, A. F. Industrial Injuries Insurance: an Examination of British Policy. *192 pp. 1964. 30s.*

ANTHROPOLOGY

Ammar, Hamed. Growing up in an Egyptian Village: Silwa, Province of Aswan. *336 pp. 1954. (2nd Impression 1966.) 35s.*

Crook, David and **Isabel.** Revolution in a Chinese Village: Ten Mile Inn. *230 pp. 8 plates. 1 map. 1959. (2nd Impression 1968.) 21s.*

The First Years of Yangyi Commune. *302 pp. 12 plates. 1966. 42s.*

Dickie-Clark, H. F. The Marginal Situation. A Sociological Study of a Coloured Group. *236 pp. 1966. 40s.*

Dube, S. C. Indian Village. *Foreword by Morris Edward Opler. 276 pp. 4 plates. 1955. (5th Impression 1965.) 25s.*

India's Changing Villages: Human Factors in Community Development. *260 pp. 8 plates. 1 map. 1958. (3rd Impression 1963.) 25s.*

Firth, Raymond. Malay Fishermen. Their Peasant Economy. *420 pp. 17 pp. plates. 2nd edition revised and enlarged 1966. (2nd Impression 1968.) 55s.*

Gulliver, P. H. The Family Herds. A Study of two Pastoral Tribes in East Africa, The Jie and Turkana. *304 pp. 4 plates. 19 figures. 1955. (2nd Impression with new preface and bibliography 1966.) 35s.*

Social Control in an African Society: a Study of the Arusha, Agricultural Masai of Northern Tanganyika. *320 pp. 8 plates. 10 figures. 1963. (2nd Impression 1968.) 42s.*

Ishwaran, K. Shivapur. A South Indian Village. *216 pp. 1968. 35s.*

Tradition and Economy in Village India: An Interactionist Approach. *Foreword by Conrad Arensburg. 176 pp. 1966. (2nd Impression 1968.) 25s.*

Jarvie, Ian C. The Revolution in Anthropology. *268 pp. 1964. (2nd Impression 1967.) 40s.*

Jarvie, Ian C. and **Agassi, Joseph.** Hong Kong. A Society in Transition. *396 pp. Illustrated with plates and maps. 1968. 56s.*

Little, Kenneth L. Mende of Sierra Leone. *308 pp. and folder. 1951. Revised edition 1967. 63s.*

Lowie, Professor Robert H. Social Organization. *494 pp. 1950. (4th Impression 1966.) 50s.*

Mayer, Adrian C. Caste and Kinship in Central India: A Village and its Region. *328 pp. 16 plates. 15 figures. 16 tables. 1960. (2nd Impression 1965.) 35s.*

Peasants in the Pacific: A Study of Fiji Indian Rural Society. *232 pp. 16 plates. 10 figures. 14 tables. 1961. 35s.*

Smith, Raymond T. The Negro Family in British Guiana: Family Structure and Social Status in the Villages. *With a Foreword by Meyer Fortes. 314 pp. 8 plates. 1 figure. 4 maps. 1956. (2nd Impression 1965.) 35s.*

DOCUMENTARY

Meek, Dorothea L. (Ed.). Soviet Youth: Some Achievements and Problems. *Excerpts from the Soviet Press, translated by the editor. 280 pp. 1957. 28s.*

Schlesinger, Rudolf (Ed.). Changing Attitudes in Soviet Russia.

2. The Nationalities Problem and Soviet Administration. Selected Readings on the Development of Soviet Nationalities Policies. *Introduced by the editor. Translated by W. W. Gottlieb. 324 pp. 1956. 30s.*

Reports of the Institute of Community Studies

(*Demy 8vo.*)

Cartwright, Ann. Human Relations and Hospital Care. *272 pp. 1964. 30s.*

Patients and their Doctors. A Study of General Practice. *304 pp. 1967. 40s.*

Jackson, Brian. Streaming: an Education System in Miniature. *168 pp. 1964. (2nd Impression 1966.) 21s. Paper 10s.*

Jackson, Brian and **Marsden, Dennis.** Education and the Working Class: Some General Themes raised by a Study of 88 Working-class Children in a Northern Industrial City. *268 pp. 2 folders. 1962. (4th Impression 1968.) 32s.*

Marris, Peter. Widows and their Families. *Foreword by Dr. John Bowlby. 184 pp. 18 tables. Statistical Summary. 1958. 18s.*
Family and Social Change in an African City. A Study of Rehousing in Lagos. *196 pp. 1 map. 4 plates. 53 tables. 1961. (2nd Impression 1966.) 30s.*
The Experience of Higher Education. *232 pp. 27 tables. 1964. 25s.*

Marris, Peter and **Rein, Martin.** Dilemmas of Social Reform. Poverty and Community Action in the United States. *256 pp. 1967. 35s.*

Mills, Enid. Living with Mental Illness: a Study in East London. *Foreword by Morris Carstairs. 196 pp. 1962. 28s.*

Runciman, W. G. Relative Deprivation and Social Justice. A Study of Attitudes to Social Inequality in Twentieth Century England. *352 pp. 1966. (2nd Impression 1967.) 40s.*

Townsend, Peter. The Family Life of Old People: An Inquiry in East London. *Foreword by J. H. Sheldon. 300 pp. 3 figures. 63 tables. 1957. (3rd Impression 1967.) 30s.*

Willmott, Peter. Adolescent Boys in East London. *230 pp. 1966. 30s.*
The Evolution of a Community: a study of Dagenham after forty years. *168 pp. 2 maps. 1963. 21s.*

Willmott, Peter and **Young, Michael.** Family and Class in a London Suburb. *202 pp. 47 tables. 1960. (4th Impression 1968.) 25s.*

Young, Michael. Innovation and Research in Education. *192 pp. 1965. 25s. Paper 12s. 6d.*

Young, Michael and **McGeeney, Patrick.** Learning Begins at Home. A Study of a Junior School and its Parents. *About 128 pp. 1968. 21s. Paper 14s.*

Young, Michael and **Willmott, Peter.** Family and Kinship in East London. *Foreword by Richard M. Titmuss. 252 pp. 39 tables. 1957. (3rd Impression 1965.) 28s.*

The British Journal of Sociology. *Edited by Terence P. Morris. Vol. 1, No. 1, March 1950 and Quarterly. Roy. 8vo., £3 annually, 15s. a number, post free. (Vols. 1-18, £8 each. Individual parts £2 10s.*

All prices are net and subject to alteration without notice

1268 H.B.